Organizational Behavior

Core Concepts

Angelo Kinicki

McGraw-Hill Irwin

Boston   Burr Ridge, IL   Dubuque, IA   Madison, WI   New York   San Francisco   St. Louis
Bangkok   Bogotá   Caracas   Kuala Lumpur   Lisbon   London   Madrid   Mexico City
Milan   Montreal   New Delhi   Santiago   Seoul   Singapore   Sydney   Taipei   Toronto

ORGANIZATIONAL BEHAVIOR: CORE CONCEPTS

Published by McGraw-Hill/Irwin, a business unit of The McGraw-Hill Companies, Inc., 1221 Avenue of the Americas, New York, NY, 10020. Copyright © 2008 by The McGraw-Hill Companies, Inc. All rights reserved. No part of this publication may be reproduced or distributed in any form or by any means, or stored in a database or retrieval system, without the prior written consent of The McGraw-Hill Companies, Inc., including, but not limited to, in any network or other electronic storage or transmission, or broadcast for distance learning.

Some ancillaries, including electronic and print components, may not be available to customers outside the United States.

This book is printed on acid-free paper.

2 3 4 5 6 7 8 9 0 DOC/DOC 0 9

ISBN 978-0-07-353029-1

MHID 0-07-353029-8

Editorial director: *Brent Gordon*
Executive editor: *John Weimeister*
Editorial assistant: *Heather Darr*
Associate marketing manager: *Margaret A.Beamer*
Media producer: *Greg Bates*
Project manager: *Dana M. Pauley*
Senior production supervisor: *Carol A. Bielski*
Lead designer: *Matthew Baldwin*
Senior media project manager: *Susan Lombardi*
Typeface: *10/12 Times New Roman*
Compositor: *International Typesetting and Composition*
Printer: *R. R. Donnelley*

Library of Congress Cataloging-in-Publication Data

Kinicki, Angelo.
    Organizational behavior : core concepts / Angelo Kinicki.
      p. cm.
    Includes index.
    ISBN-13: 978-0-07-353029-1 (alk. paper)
    ISBN-13: 0-07-353029-8 (alk. paper)
    1. Organizational behavior. I. Title.
HD58.7.K5264 2008
302.3'5--dc22   2007014896

To all students, the future leaders and stewards of our planet.

About the Author

Angelo Kinicki is a Professor of Management and Dean's Council of 100 Distinguished Scholar at the W. P. Carey School of Business at Arizona State University. He also was awarded the Weatherup/Overby Chair in Leadership in 2005. He has held his current position since 1982 when he received his doctorate in organizational behavior from Kent State University.

Angelo is recognized for both his teaching and research. As a teacher, Angelo has been the recipient of several awards, including the John W Teets Outstanding Graduate Teacher Award (2004–2005), Graduate Teaching Excellence Award (1998–1999), Continuing Education Teaching Excellence Award (1991–1992), and Undergraduate Teaching Excellence Award (1987–1988). He also was selected into *Who's Who of American Colleges and Universities* and *Beta Gamma Sigma*. Angelo is an active researcher. He has published more than 80 articles in a variety of leading academic and professional journals and has coauthored seven college textbooks (17 counting revisions). His textbooks have been used by hundreds of universities around the world. Angelo's experience as a researcher also resulted in his selection to serve on the editorial review boards for the *Academy of Management Journal,* the *Journal of Vocational Behavior,* and the *Journal of Management.* He received the All-Time Best Reviewer Award from the *Academy of Management Journal* for the period of 1996–1999.

Angelo also is an active international consultant who works with top management teams to create organizational change aimed at increasing organizational effectiveness and profitability. He has worked with many *Fortune* 500 firms as well as numerous entrepreneurial organizations in diverse industries. His expertise includes facilitating strategic/operational planning sessions, diagnosing the causes of organizational and work-unit problems, implementing performance management systems, designing and implementing performance appraisal systems, developing and administering surveys to assess employee attitudes, and leading management/executive education programs. He developed a 360-degree leadership feedback instrument called the Performance Management Leadership Survey (PMLS) that is used by companies throughout the United States and Europe.

One of Angelo's strengths is his ability to teach students at all levels within a university. He uses an interactive environment to enhance undergraduates' understanding about management and organizational behavior. He focuses MBAs on applying management concepts to solve complex problems; PhD students learn the art and science of conducting scholarly research.

Angelo and his wife, Joyce, have enjoyed living in the beautiful Arizona desert for 25 years but are natives of Cleveland, Ohio. They enjoy traveling, golfing, and hiking.

Preface

In my many years of teaching organizational behavior and management to undergraduate and graduate students in various countries, I never had a student say, "I want a longer, more expensive textbook with more chapters." I got the message! Indeed there is a desire for shorter and less expensive textbooks in today's fast-paced world where overload and time demands are a way of life. Within the field of organizational behavior (OB), so-called "essentials" texts have attempted to satisfy this need. Too often, however, brevity has been achieved at the expense of up-to-date research and examples, and artful layout. I believe that "brief" does not have to mean outdated and boring.

EXPERIENCE DRIVES THE CHOICE OF CORE CONCEPTS

The first edition of *Organizational Behavior: Core Concepts*—a concepts book for an introductory course in Organization Behavior—was written with the following quest in mind: "Create a short, up-to-date, practical, user-friendly, interesting, and engaging introduction to the field of organizational behavior." Accomplishing this objective required me to be very selective in determining what OB concepts to include in the text. Content decisions are based on my many years of teaching and writing about organizational behavior. For example, I have received multiple teaching awards and have authored or coauthored over 17 textbooks. I select and cover topics that I believe are essential to helping students gain an understanding about individual, group, and organizational behavior. Further, this book contains lean and efficient coverage of topics recommended by the accreditation organizations AACSB International and ACBSP.

FLEXIBILITY AND DEPTH SUPERSEDE PEDAGOGY

Given that I wanted to produce a short 14 chapter book, I wrestled with the trade-off between providing content coverage of core concepts and pedagogical enhancements such as cases or exercises to illustrate or apply these concepts. I decided to focus more on content than pedagogy in order to allow instructors the flexibility to incorporate their own cases and supplementary materials into their courses. Other than starting out each chapter with a set of learning objectives, there are no cases or exercises included in the text. This decision allowed me to cover the maximum amount of material within 14 chapters.

ONLINE TOOLS FACILITATE LEARNING AND AN INTERACTIVE CLASSROOM

You have asked for ways to tie resources to specific chapters, so I did it! This first edition contains a specially designed boxed feature that is inserted where chapter content is augmented by one of 38 Test Your Knowledge quizzes, 20 self-assessments, 23 group exercises, and 15 Hot Seat DVD segments. The quizzes provide a great way for students to assess their understanding of the book's content, and the self-assessments' rich feedback enables students to achieve a personal link with the content being considered.

To supplement the use of these online materials, you can use the *Group and Video Resource Manual,* authored by Amanda Johnson and me. The manual was compiled to help you create a livelier and stimulating classroom environment. It contains in-class group and individual exercises as well as notes on how to use the self-assessments, group exercises, and Hot Seat programs that have been flagged in the boxed feature contained in the book.

A SOLID BASE OF FRESH AND RELEVANT MATERIAL

Wise grocery shoppers gauge the freshness of essential purchases such as bread and milk by checking the "sell by" dates. So, too, OB textbooks need to be checked for freshness to ensure the reader's time is well spent on up-to-date and relevant theory, research, and practical examples. By my count, you will find over 190 chapter endnotes dated 2006, indicating a thorough and current textbook. Cutting-edge topics discussed in the first edition include e-business implications for OB, human and social capital, positive organizational behavior, managing diversity, proactive personality, emotions, emotional intelligence, emotional labor, organizational justice, virtual teams, knowledge management, impact of information technology on OB, cross-cultural conflict, workplace incivility, impression management, full-range model of leadership, Level 5 leadership, shared leadership, and learning organizations, just to name a few.

USE OF META-ANALYSIS TO SUMMARIZE RESEARCH

My goal of producing a short book did not enable me to review all of the relevant research regarding OB concepts. I therefore used meta-analytic studies whenever possible to summarize the state of knowledge about a specific OB concept. A meta-analysis is a statistical pooling technique that permits researchers to draw general conclusions about certain variables from many different studies. It typically encompasses a vast number of studies and individual participants, often reaching the thousands. Meta-analyses are instructive because they focus on general patterns of research evidence, not fragmented bits and pieces or isolated studies. Their use also enabled me to summarize research in a much shorter fashion, thereby enabling me to cover more content about organizational behavior.

GRATEFUL APPRECIATION

I could not have completed this product without the help of a great number of others. Karen Hill, development director from Elm Street Publishing, was instrumental in my finishing the first edition. She was a joy to work with and never missed a deadline. My sincere thanks and gratitude go to my executive editor John Weimeister, and his first-rate team at McGraw-Hill/Irwin. Key contributors include Meg Beamer, Marketing Manager; Dana Pauley, Project Manager; Heather Darr, Editorial Coordinator; Carol Bielski, Lead Production Supervisor; Matt Baldwin, Lead Designer; and Susan Lombardi, Senior Media Project Manager. We would also like to thank Mindy West of Northern Arizona University for her work on the Instructor's Manual, Eileen Hogan of Kutztown University for her work on creating the test bank, Amit Shah of Frostburg State University for his work on the Online Quizzes, and Brad Cox of Midlands Technical College for developing the PowerPoint presentation slides.

Finally, I would like to thank my wife, Joyce. She has supported me through the completion of many books and I could have not finished this one without her love, support, and understanding.

I hope you enjoy reading and applying the book. Best wishes for success and happiness!

Angelo

Brief Contents

Contents

Chapter One

Organizational Behavior: Why People Matter to Organizations

Don't need the part on ethics yet.

Learning Objectives

After reading the material in this chapter, you should be able to:

- Explain the importance of people skills to management success.
- Summarize principles for making ethical decisions.
- Describe how the role of managers is affected by global business and the changing workplace.
- Define *organizational behavior*, and identify disciplines that contribute to OB.
- Discuss how OB has been shaped by total quality management, the contingency approach, appreciation of human and social capital, and positive psychology.
- Define *e-business*, and specify ways the Internet is affecting the management of people at work.

How important are people to organizational success? Take a quick look at some of the most successful organizations, and you'll find out. Where would Southwest Airlines be if its staff—from pilots to flight attendants to counter personnel—didn't all pitch in wherever they are needed to satisfy customers and operate efficiently? Southwest has consistently remained in the black in an industry filled with red ink. Or what about Apple Computer's amazing comeback with its iPod music and video players? Under the leadership of Steve Jobs, its creative staff turned out innovative designs that made the iPod a market leader—and added significantly to the company's bottom line.

These and other successes demonstrate that people *do* matter in today's organizations. Stanford's Jeffrey Pfeffer reviewed research from the United States and Germany showing that people-centered practices (for example, hiring carefully and giving employees decision-making power) are strongly associated with higher profits and lower employee turnover.[1] Yet many organizations act counter to their declarations that people are their most important asset, choosing instead to boost short-term

1

profit at the expense of job security and employee development. Such organizations view people as a cost, not as an asset. Only 12% of organizations, according to Pfeffer, have the systematic approaches and persistence to qualify as true people-centered organizations, which gives them a competitive advantage.

An 88% shortfall in the quest for people-centered organizations represents a tragic loss to society and to the global economy. In contrast, *Fortune* magazine's annual list of "The 100 Best Companies to Work For" shows what is being done at organizations that put people first. Leaders include Genentech, the San Francisco biotech firm ranked as the best place to work in 2005. At Genentech only 5% of employees choose to leave the company each year, and 95% of workers own shares of the company's stock.[2] Importantly, a recent study found that companies making *Fortune*'s 100 Best list tend to outperform the competition.[3] This book is written to increase the number of people-centered managers and organizations around the world. In this chapter, we discuss the manager's job, define organizational behavior and examine its evolution, and explore new directions for the field.

MANAGERS GET RESULTS WITH AND THROUGH OTHERS

Management
Process of working with and through others to achieve organizational objectives efficiently and ethically.

Managers touch our lives in many ways. Schools, hospitals, government agencies, and large and small businesses all require systematic management. **Management** is the process of working with and through others to achieve organizational objectives in an efficient and ethical manner. The manager's role is constantly evolving. Today's successful managers are no longer the "I've got everything under control" order-givers of yesteryear. Instead, they creatively envision and actively sell bold new directions in an ethical and sensitive manner. Effective managers are team players empowered by the willing and active support of others in spite of conflicting self-interests. Henry Mintzberg, a respected management scholar, observed that managers determine "whether our social institutions serve us well or whether they squander our talents and resources."[4]

A Skills Profile for Managers

Observational studies by Mintzberg and others have found the typical manager's day to be a fragmented collection of brief episodes.[5] Interruptions are commonplace, while large blocks of time for planning and reflective thinking are rare. A study of four top-level managers found that they spent 63% of their time on activities lasting less than nine minutes each and only 5% on activities lasting more than an hour.[6]

Many attempts have been made to paint a realistic picture of what managers do during these hectic days.[7] A stream of research over the past 25 years by Clark Wilson and others has given us a practical and statistically validated profile of managerial skills.[8] Wilson's managerial skills profile focuses on 11 observable categories of managerial behavior:[9]

1. *Clarifies goals and objectives* for everyone involved.
2: *Encourages participation*, upward communication, and suggestions.
3. *Plans and organizes* for an orderly work flow.

SELF-ASSESSMENT
Assessing Your Ethical Decision-Making Skills

Go online at [www.mhhe.com/obcore] to discover how well you make ethical decisions. Once you have completed the assessment, consider the following questions:

- Has ethics played an important role in your decision making in the past?
- Why might ethics be important to your business decisions?
- In what areas do you want to improve your ethical decision-making skills?

4. Has *technical and administrative expertise* to answer organization-related questions.
5. *Facilitates work* through team building, training, coaching, and support.
6. *Provides feedback* honestly and constructively.
7. *Keeps things moving* by relying on schedules, deadlines, and helpful reminders.
8. *Controls details* without being overbearing.
9. Applies reasonable *pressure for goal accomplishment*.
10. *Empowers and delegates* key duties to others while maintaining goal clarity and commitment.
11. *Recognizes good performance* with rewards and positive reinforcement.

Notice that management is primarily about dealing effectively with *people*. The 11 skills constitute a cycle of goal creation, commitment, feedback, reward, and accomplishment, with human interaction at every turn.

Importance of Ethical Behavior

Ethics
Study of moral issues and choices.

Besides acting skillfully, managers and their employees need to behave ethically. **Ethics** involves the study of moral issues and choices. It is concerned with right versus wrong, good versus bad, and the many shades of gray in supposedly black-and-white issues. Moral implications spring from virtually every decision, both on and off the job. Because managers set the ethical tone in the workplace, they are continually challenged to have imagination and the courage to do the right thing.

A Model of Ethical Behavior

Ethical and unethical conduct is the product of a complex combination of influences, modeled in Figure 1–1.[10] At the center of this model is the individual decision maker, who has a unique combination of personality characteristics, values, experiences, and moral principles. The individual also has role expectations, which are shaped by influences inside and outside the organization. Finally, the individual's behavior may be affected by neutralizing or enhancing factors related to the characteristics of the organization's top management.

Whatever a person's individual skills in making ethical decisions, internal organizational influences on ethical behavior also play a role. These influences include corporate codes of conduct and organizational culture (discussed in Chapter 12). Ethical behavior is

FIGURE 1–1 **A Model of Ethical Behavior in the Workplace**

Source: Based in part on A J Daboub, A M A Rasheed, R L Priem, and D A Gray, "Top Management Team Characteristics and Corporate Illegal Activity," *Academy of Management Review,* January 1995, pp 138–70.

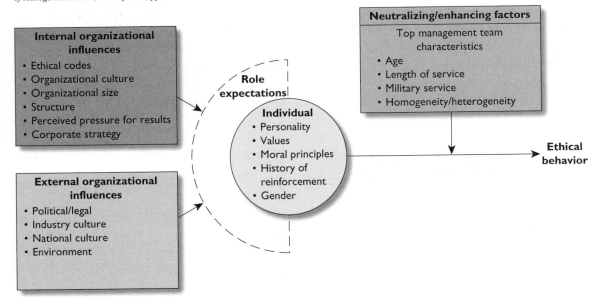

more likely in organizations that express ethical values in a written code of conduct and in the kinds of behavior rewarded by the culture. Rudder Finn, a public relations agency, does this by holding ethics committee meetings, chaired by the chief executive officer, to openly discuss actual ethical problems faced by staffers.[11] In addition, organizational size may affect ethics. A number of studies have determined that unethical behavior is more common in large companies. Managers also have been found to behave more unethically in organizations that are decentralized, perhaps because managers want to "look good" to top management. Similarly, many studies have found that middle- and lower-level managers tend to behave more unethically if they perceive they are under pressure to deliver results. So, reward systems can influence the choice of ethical behavior.

External influences on ethics are the political/legal system, industry culture, societal culture, and environment in which the organization operates. Despite a recent rash of ethical abuses by top managers in corporations such as Enron and Tyco, the United States has traditionally placed stronger demands on its political/legal system to ensure that corporations behave ethically. Other nations do not emphasize such legal oversight. Research has also uncovered a tendency for firms in certain industries to commit more illegal acts than companies do overall, perhaps because the shared norms, values, and beliefs in some industries predispose managers to act unethically. Societal cultures also affect ethical behavior by shaping the values of the people in an organization. In a study of managers from 10 nations, the managers rated whether certain behaviors—for example, concealing one's errors, divulging personal information, and accepting gifts in exchange for preferential treatment—are ethical.

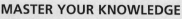

MASTER YOUR KNOWLEDGE
Ethics

Increase your knowledge of how to apply ethics by completing the online quiz at [www.mhhe.com/obcore].

- What moral principles did you apply to arrive at your decisions in these exercises?
- Did you have to make trade-offs in order to arrive at your decisions? If so, which principles did you consider most important?

Managers' ratings differed significantly depending on their nationality.[12] Other aspects of the external environment that influence ethical behavior include industry profitability and the value placed on generosity.

Finally, in their search for the causes of ethical behavior, researchers have uncovered several neutralizing or enhancing factors in the relationship between internal and external influencers and ethical behavior. All these factors center around the characteristics of an organization's top management team—the CEO and his or her direct reports. The relationship between ethical influencers and ethical behavior is weaker in an organization where the top managers are older and have spent more years with the organization, suggesting that more experienced leaders are less likely to permit unethical behavior. Further, the influencers are less likely to lead to unethical behavior when more top managers have military experience and when the top management team is heterogeneous (that is, diverse in terms of gender, age, race, religion, and so on).

Making Ethical Decisions

Ethical decision making frequently involves trade-offs. For example, what benefits shareholders (at least in the short term) may not be in employees' best interests. One way to make ethical decisions is to begin by asking whether a proposed action is legal and to eliminate any options that are illegal.[13] The next step is to consider the impact of the alternative on shareholder value. If the alternative maximizes shareholder value, then weigh its effect on all stakeholders—customers, employees, the community, the environment, and suppliers—and verify that it does no harm that outweighs the shareholder benefits. If the alternative does not maximize shareholder value, then ask whether it would be ethical *not* to take the action, considering the impact on all stakeholders. If the alternative does not maximize shareholder value but must be done anyway to treat others ethically, then the organization should take the action but also disclose its effect on shareholders.

Another way to arrive at ethical decisions is to apply general moral principles. Management consultant Kent Hodgson identifies seven principles he deems timeless and relevant: the dignity of human life, autonomy, honesty, loyalty, fairness, humaneness, and the common good.[14] According to Hodgson, there are no absolute ethical answers; the goal should be to rely on moral principles so that decisions are principled, appropriate, and defensible.

The Global Context: Cultural Differences

Organizations today operate in a global economy, and managing them is as much about patterns of thinking and behavior as it is about trade agreements, goods and services, and

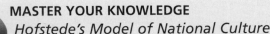

MASTER YOUR KNOWLEDGE
Hofstede's Model of National Culture

Increase your knowledge of societal culture by completing the online quiz at [www.mhhe.com/obcore].

- How easily could you identify cultural patterns in the organizations that were described in the exercise?
- In which of those cultures would you feel most at home? Choose one of the organizations described, and identify the cultural characteristics that you would find most challenging there. How would you adapt to those characteristics if you worked in that organization?

Societal cultures
Socially derived, taken-for-granted assumptions about how to think and act.

currency exchange rates. People in different parts of the world grow up learning different **societal cultures**—that is, socially derived, taken-for-granted assumptions about how to think, act, perceive, and feel.[15] Culture can be difficult to understand because it operates on many layers, from the external products like works of art, down through family customs, to deeply held but unstated values.

Whether in culturally diverse U.S. companies or in international firms, managers need to consider how management theory applies to their particular employees. Dutch researcher Geert Hofstede compared IBM employees in more than 50 countries and found significant cultural differences that would affect their workplace values and behavior.[16] However, it is important to keep in mind that cultural patterns are only *tendencies* and do not describe every individual within a culture.

Another important effort to identify societal cultures and their impact on organizational behavior is Project GLOBE (Global Leadership and Organizational Behavior Effectiveness), the brainchild of Robert J House.[17] During the first two phases of the GLOBE project, the international team of researchers developed a list of nine basic cultural dimensions:

1. *Power distance.* How unequal the distribution of power should be in organizations and society.
2. *Uncertainty avoidance.* How much people should rely on social norms and rules to avoid uncertainty and limit unpredictability.
3. *Societal collectivism.* How much to reward loyalty to the social unit, rather than pursuit of individual goals.
4. *In-group collectivism.* How much to have pride in and loyalty toward one's family or organization.
5. *Gender egalitarianism.* How much to minimize gender discrimination and role inequalities.
6. *Assertiveness.* How confrontational and dominant to be in social relationships.
7. *Future orientation.* How much to delay gratification by planning and saving for the future.
8. *Performance orientation.* How much to reward improvement and excellence.
9. *Humane orientation.* How much society should encourage and reward people for being kind, fair, friendly, and generous.[18]

TABLE 1–1   Evolution of the 21st-Century Manager

	Past Managers	Future Managers
Primary role	Order giver, privileged elite, manipulator, controller	Facilitator, team member, teacher, advocate, sponsor, coach, partner
Learning and knowledge	Periodic learning, narrow specialist	Continuous life-long learning, generalist with multiple specialties
Compensation criteria	Time, effort, rank	Skills, results
Cultural orientation	Monocultural, monolingual	Multicultural, multilingual
Primary source of influence	Formal authority	Knowledge (technical and interpersonal)
View of people	Potential problem	Primary resource
Primary communication pattern	Vertical	Multidirectional
Decision-making style	Limited input for individual decisions	Broad-based input for joint decisions
Ethical considerations	Afterthought	Forethought
Nature of interpersonal relationships	Competitive (win–lose)	Cooperative (win–win)
Handling of power and key information	Hoard and restrict access	Share and broaden access
Approach to change	Resist	Facilitate

In the United States, for example, managers score high on assertiveness and performance orientation. Swiss managers score high on uncertainty avoidance and future orientation, and managers in Singapore score high on social collectivism, future orientation, and performance orientation. Future chapters will apply these cultural differences to the ways people behave in organizations.

Twenty-first-Century Managers

Organizational behavior (OB)
Interdisciplinary field dedicated to better understanding and managing people at work.

Today's workplace is undergoing immense and permanent changes.[19] Organizations have been "reengineered" for greater speed, efficiency, and flexibility.[20] Teams are pushing aside the individual as the primary building block of organizations.[21] Command-and-control management is giving way to participative management and empowerment.[22] Ego-centered leaders are being replaced by customer-centered leaders. Employees increasingly are viewed as internal customers. All this creates a mandate for a new kind of manager in the 21st century.[23] Table 1–1 contrasts the characteristics of past and future managers. As the balance of this book will demonstrate, the managerial shift in Table 1–1 is not just a good idea, it is an absolute necessity in the new workplace.

ROOTS OF ORGANIZATIONAL BEHAVIOR AS A DISCIPLINE

Organizational behavior (OB) is an interdisciplinary field dedicated to better understanding and managing people at work. By definition, organizational behavior is both research- and application-oriented. It carries out three basic levels of analysis: individual, group, and organizational.

Organizational behavior is an academic designation. With the exception of teaching/research positions, OB is not an everyday job category such as accounting, marketing, or finance. Students of OB typically do not get jobs in organizational behavior per se, but the lessons it teaches apply to all an organization's functions. So, OB is a *horizontal* discipline that cuts across virtually every job category, business function, and professional specialty. Those who plan to make a living in a large or small, public or private organization need to study organizational behavior, whether or not they will be managers.

Disciplines of Organizational Behavior

OB draws upon a diverse array of disciplines. The largest share of contributions comes from *psychology,* which seeks to explain individual behavior and influences on individual behavior, including human perceptions, self-concept, personality, and emotions (see Chapters 2 and 3), as well as the ways that rewards shape behavior (Chapter 5). Other important fields are *sociology* and *social psychology,* which examine how groups influence individuals and how individuals fill group roles. These fields have contributed especially to such topics as motivation (Chapters 4 and 5), group processes (Chapter 6), conflict (Chapter 8), communication (Chapter 9), and human responses to change (Chapter 14). Sociology is particularly important for the study of organizational structures (Chapter 13). *Anthropology,* which studies the characteristics of different societies, sheds additional light on the differences among employees' cultures (Chapter 2) and the culture that the organization itself develops (Chapter 12).

Many OB topics draw on a wide variety of fields. For example, the way people arrive at decisions (see Chapter 7) is a subject of interest to the branches of behavioral science just described. *Ethicists* and *economists* also weigh in with insights related to decision making. The field of *decision theory* applies these lessons and *statistical* methods to explain and predict decision-making behavior. Also, *information technology* provides innovations that can improve decision making when used appropriately. Likewise, the topics of power and influence (Chapter 10) and of leadership (Chapter 11) draw on the behavioral sciences, as well as the study of *management* and *political science.*

Other fields whose research has been applied to particular areas of organizational behavior include organization theory, general systems theory, vocational counseling, human stress management, psychometrics, and ergonomics. Engineering, too, contributes to OB-related topics such as productivity and work design. This rich heritage has spawned many competing perspectives and theories about human work behavior. In fact, one researcher has identified 73 established OB theories.[24]

Historical Roots: The Human Relations Movement

A unique combination of factors during the 1930s fostered the human relations movement. First, following the legalization of union–management collective bargaining in the United States in 1935, management began looking for new ways of dealing with employees. Second, behavioral scientists conducting on-the-job research started calling for more attention to the "human" factor. Managers who had lost the battle to keep unions out of their factories heeded the call for better human relations and improved working conditions.

One study, conducted at Western Electric's Chicago-area Hawthorne plant, was a prime stimulus for the human relations movement. Ironically, many of the Hawthorne findings have turned out to be more myth than fact. Researchers observed that employees worked harder following almost any intervention, and they concluded that this indicated a positive effect of supportive supervision. But interviews conducted decades later with three subjects of the Hawthorne studies and reanalysis of the original data with modern statistical techniques do not support these initial conclusions. Instead, money, fear of unemployment during the Great Depression, managerial discipline, and high-quality raw materials—not supportive supervision—turned out to be responsible for high output in the relay assembly test room experiments.[25] Nonetheless, the human relations movement gathered momentum through the 1950s, as academics and managers alike made stirring claims about the powerful effect that individual needs, supportive supervision, and group dynamics apparently have on job performance.

Essential to the human relations movement were the writings of Elton Mayo and Mary Parker Follett. In his 1933 classic, *The Human Problems of an Industrial Civilization,* Mayo, who headed the Harvard researchers at Hawthorne, advised managers to attend to employees' emotional needs. Follett was a true pioneer, not only as a female management consultant in the male-dominated industrial world of the 1920s but also as a writer who saw employees as complex bundles of attitudes, beliefs, and needs. Follett was way ahead of her time in telling managers to motivate job performance instead of merely demanding it, a "pull" rather than "push" strategy. She also built a logical bridge between political democracy and a cooperative spirit in the workplace.[26]

In 1960, Douglas McGregor wrote *The Human Side of Enterprise,* which has become an important philosophical base for the modern view of people at work.[27] Drawing upon his experience as a management consultant, McGregor formulated two sharply contrasting sets of assumptions about human nature (see Table 1–2). His Theory X assumptions are pessimistic, negative, and, according to McGregor's interpretation, typical of how managers traditionally perceived employees. To help managers break with this negative tradition, McGregor formulated his **Theory Y,** a modern and positive set of assumptions about people. McGregor believed managers can accomplish more through others by viewing them as self-energized, committed, responsible, and creative beings.

A survey of 10,227 employees from many industries across the United States challenges managers to do a better job of acting on McGregor's Theory Y assumptions. From the

Theory Y

McGregor's modern and positive assumptions about employees being responsible and creative.

TABLE 1–2
McGregor's Theory X and Theory Y

Source: Adapted from D McGregor, *The Human Side of Enterprise* (New York: McGraw-Hill, 1960), Ch 4.

Outdated (Theory X) Assumptions about People at Work	Modern (Theory Y) Assumptions about People at Work
1. Most people dislike work; they avoid it when they can.	1. Work is a natural activity, like play or rest.
2. Most people must be coerced and threatened with punishment before they will work. People require close direction when they are working.	2. People are capable of self-direction and self-control if they are committed to objectives.
3. Most people actually prefer to be directed. They tend to avoid responsibility and exhibit little ambition. They are interested only in security.	3. People generally become committed to organizational objectives if they are rewarded for doing so.
	4. The typical employee can learn to accept and seek responsibility.
	5. The typical member of the general population has imagination, ingenuity, and creativity.

employees' perspective, Theory X management practices are the major barrier to productivity improvement and employee well-being. Overwhelmingly, workers preferred Theory Y practices, including "the conditions for collaboration, commitment, and creativity research has demonstrated as necessary for both productivity and health," although employers tended not to provide such conditions.[28]

Unsophisticated behavioral research methods caused the human relationists to embrace some naive and misleading conclusions. For example, human relationists believed in the axiom, "A satisfied employee is a hardworking employee." Subsequent research, discussed later in this book, shows the satisfaction–performance linkage to be more complex than originally thought. But despite its shortcomings, the human relations movement opened the door to more progressive thinking about human nature. Rather than continuing to view employees as passive economic beings, managers began to see them as active social beings and took steps to create more humane work environments.

Total Quality Management

During the 1980s, concern that North American companies were losing market share to higher-quality products from Japanese electronics and automobile companies led to a full-fledged movement promoting quality improvement. Thanks to the concept of *total quality management (TQM),* the quality of much that Americans buy today is significantly better than in the past. The underlying principles of TQM are more important than ever, given the growth of business on the Internet and the overall service economy. According to one writer, a commitment to "zero defects" no longer differentiates companies, because this standard has become widespread, along with a commitment to more responsive customer service.[29] In a survey of 1,797 managers from 36 countries, customer service and quality ranked as the top two concerns.[30] TQM principles have profound practical implications for managing people today.[31]

Total quality management
An organizational culture dedicated to training, continuous improvement, and customer satisfaction.

According to experts on the subject, **total quality management** is an approach to management in which "the organization's culture is defined by and supports the constant attainment of customer satisfaction through an integrated system of tools, techniques, and training" aimed at continuously improving organizational processes to deliver high-quality products and services.[32] Whereas there are many ways to improve quality, with TQM these efforts are continuous, customer-centered, and employee-driven.[33] TQM must be employee-driven because continuous improvements in good/service quality require the active learning and participation of *every* employee. Thus, in successful quality improvement programs, TQM principles are embedded in the organization's culture.

The Deming Legacy

TQM is firmly established today, thanks largely to the pioneering work of W Edwards Deming.[34] Ironically, the mathematician credited with Japan's post–World War II quality revolution rarely talked in terms of quality. He instead preferred to discuss "good management" during the hard-hitting seminars he delivered until his death at age 93 in 1993.[35] Although Deming's passion was the statistical measurement and reduction of variations in industrial processes, he had much to say about how employees should be treated. Regarding the human side of quality improvement, Deming called for the following:

- Formal training in statistical process control techniques and teamwork.
- Helpful leadership, rather than order giving and punishment.
- Elimination of fear so employees will feel free to ask questions.
- Emphasis on continuous process improvements rather than on numerical quotas.
- Teamwork.
- Elimination of barriers to good workmanship.[36]

One of Deming's most enduring lessons for managers is his 85–15 rule.[37] Specifically, when things go wrong, there is roughly an 85% chance the *system* (including management, machinery, and rules) is at fault. Only about 15% of the time is the individual employee at fault. Unfortunately, as Deming observed, the typical manager spends most of his or her time wrongly blaming and punishing individuals for system failures. Uncovering system failures requires statistical analysis.

Principles of TQM

TQM programs vary in language and scope but have four common principles:

1. Do it right the first time to eliminate costly rework.
2. Listen to and learn from customers and employees.
3. Make continuous improvement an everyday matter.
4. Build teamwork, trust, and mutual respect.[38]

As with the human relations movement, people are considered the key factor in organizational success.

TQM's advocates have made a valuable contribution to the field of OB by providing a *practical* context for managing people. When people are managed according to TQM principles, everyone is more likely to get desirable employment opportunities and high-quality goods and services. As you will see many times in later chapters, this book is anchored to Deming's philosophy and TQM principles.

Contingency Approach to Management

Contingency approach
Using management tools and techniques in a situationally appropriate manner; avoiding the one-best-way mentality.

Scholars have wrestled for many years with the problem of how best to apply the diverse and growing collection of management tools and techniques. Their answer is the contingency approach. The **contingency approach** calls for using management concepts and techniques in a situationally appropriate manner, instead of trying to rely on "one best way."

The contingency approach encourages managers to view organizational behavior within a situational context. According to this modern perspective, evolving situations, not hard-and-fast rules, determine the appropriateness of various management techniques.[39] For example, contingency researchers have determined that there is no single best style of leadership (see Chapter 14). Organizational behavior specialists embrace the contingency approach

HOT SEAT VIDEO
Project Management: Steering the Committee

because it helps them realistically relate individuals, groups, and organizations. Moreover, the contingency approach sends a clear message to managers in today's global economy: Carefully read the situation, and then apply lessons learned from published research studies, observation of role models, self-study and training, and personal experience in situationally appropriate ways.

NEW DIRECTIONS IN OB

The field of OB is a dynamic work in progress. It is being redirected and reshaped by forces inside and outside the discipline, including new concepts, models, and technology. Three general new directions for OB are human and social capital, positive organizational behavior, and a place in the Internet revolution.

The Age of Human and Social Capital

Management is a lot like juggling. Everything is constantly in motion, with several things up in the air at any given time. Managers juggle human, financial, material, informational, and technological resources, each of them vital to success in some way. But jugglers remind us that some objects are rubber and some are glass. Dropped rubber objects bounce; dropped glass objects break. As more and more managers have realized, we cannot afford to drop the people factor. Rather, managers must take care in handling both its facets, shown in Figure 1–2: individual human capital and social capital.

Human Capital

According to a team of management authors, organizations in today's fast-moving, high-stakes business environment are coming to appreciate the importance of human capital.[40]

Human capital is the productive potential of an individual's knowledge and actions.[41] The left side of Figure 1–2 lists dimensions of human capital. In this intentionally broad definition, the operative word is *potential*. When you are hungry, money in your pocket is good because it has the potential to buy a meal. Likewise, a present or future employee with the right combination of knowledge, skills, and motivation to excel represents human capital with the potential to give the organization a competitive advantage. For computer chip maker Intel, future success depends on innovative engineering. Making world-class engineers takes years of math and science studies. Not wanting to leave the future supply of engineers to chance, Intel annually spends millions of dollars to fund education at all levels. The company encourages youngsters to study math and science and sponsors science competitions with generous scholarships for the winners.[42] Additionally, Intel encourages its employees to volunteer at local schools by giving the schools $200 for every 20 hours contributed.[43] Will all of the students end up working for Intel? No, but the point is much bigger—namely, to build the *world's* human capital.

Human capital
The productive potential of one's knowledge and actions.

FIGURE 1–2
Dimensions of
Human and
Social Capital

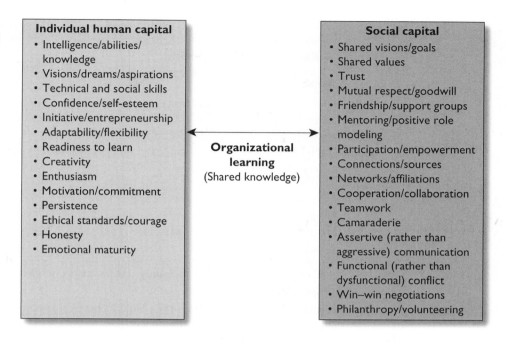

Individual human capital
- Intelligence/abilities/
  knowledge
- Visions/dreams/aspirations
- Technical and social skills
- Confidence/self-esteem
- Initiative/entrepreneurship
- Adaptability/flexibility
- Readiness to learn
- Creativity
- Enthusiasm
- Motivation/commitment
- Persistence
- Ethical standards/courage
- Honesty
- Emotional maturity

↔ **Organizational
learning**
(Shared knowledge)

Social capital
- Shared visions/goals
- Shared values
- Trust
- Mutual respect/goodwill
- Friendship/support groups
- Mentoring/positive role
  modeling
- Participation/empowerment
- Connections/sources
- Networks/affiliations
- Cooperation/collaboration
- Teamwork
- Camaraderie
- Assertive (rather than
  aggressive) communication
- Functional (rather than
  dysfunctional) conflict
- Win–win negotiations
- Philanthropy/volunteering

Social Capital

Social capital
The productive
potential of
strong, trusting,
and cooperative
relationships.

In contrast to human capital's focus on the individual, **social capital** is productive potential resulting from strong relationships, goodwill, trust, and cooperative effort.[44] It thus
emphasizes relationships, and again the word *potential* is key. The right side of Figure 1–2
lists dimensions of social capital. Relationships do matter. In a recent general survey, 77%
of the women and 63% of the men rated "Good relationship with boss" extremely important. Other factors—including good equipment, resources, easy commute, and flexible
hours—received lower ratings.[45]

Building Human and Social Capital

Making the leap from concept to practice within this broad domain appears to be a daunt-
ing task. But new examples are available every January in *Fortune* magazine's annual list
of "The 100 Best Companies to Work For." The brief comments about the 100 selected
companies are interesting and inspiring—as well as a great resource for job hunters. These
model companies are good at building human and/or social capital. Edward Jones in
St. Louis builds human capital by spending 2.5% of its payroll on training and by operating a mentoring program in which new hires work with veterans for a year. American
Express builds social capital by allowing workers to rotate to a different job or different
country after working 12 to 24 months in one position.[46]

In addition, businesses tend to focus on and succeed at the things they measure and
reward. Measuring successful development of human and social capital is therefore important.
Researchers have defined five measures of human capital outcomes: *leadership/managerial
practices* such as delivering performance feedback and instilling confidence; *workforce
optimization* through guiding and sustaining the use of people's talents on the job; *learning*

capacity, which refers to the organization's overall ability to learn and improve; *knowledge accessibility,* meaning the ease of sharing ideas and knowledge; and *talent engagement,* or the ability to retain and engage the best talent.[47]

Another area to watch is the *social entrepreneurship* movement, which challenges students and businesspeople to create businesses with a dual bottom line. Laura D'Andrea Tyson, dean of London Business School, defines a social entrepreneur as someone who is "driven by a social mission, a desire to find innovative ways to solve problems that are not being or cannot be addressed by either the market or the public sector."[48] Of the organization's two "bottom lines," one measures financial performance, and the other the company's success in meeting these social goals, be they solutions to illiteracy or to environmental degradation.

Relative to the field of OB, many of the ideas discussed in this book relate directly or indirectly to building human and social capital. Examples include managing diversity, self-efficacy, self-management, emotional intelligence, goal setting, positive reinforcement, group problem-solving, group development, building trust, teamwork, managing conflict, communicating, empowerment, leadership, and organizational learning.

Positive Organizational Behavior

As mentioned earlier, OB draws heavily on the field of psychology. So, major shifts and trends in psychology eventually ripple through to OB. One such shift being felt in OB is the positive psychology movement. This exciting new direction promises to broaden OB's scope and practical relevance.

The Positive Psychology Movement

During the last half of the 20th century, the field of psychology took a distinctly negative turn. Theory and research became preoccupied with mental and behavioral pathologies—in other words, what is *wrong* with people. Following the traditional medical model, most researchers and practicing psychologists devoted their attention to diagnosing people's ailments and trying to make them better. At the turn of the 21st century, bits and pieces of an alternative perspective advocated by pioneering psychologists such as Abraham Maslow and Carl Rogers were pulled together under the label of *positive psychology.* This approach recommended focusing on human strengths and potential as a way to possibly prevent mental and behavioral problems and improve the general quality of life. A pair of positive psychologists described positive psychology as operating at three levels:[49]

1. *Subjective level.* "Well-being, contentment, and satisfaction (in the past); hope and optimism (for the future); and flow and happiness (in the present)."
2. *Individual level.* "The capacity for love and vocation, courage, interpersonal skill, aesthetic sensibility, perseverance, forgiveness, originality, future mindedness, spirituality, high talent, and wisdom."
3. *Group level.* "The civic virtues and the institutions that move individuals toward better citizenship: responsibility, nurturance, altruism, civility, moderation, tolerance, and work ethic."

This is an extremely broad agenda for understanding and improving the human condition. However, we foresee a productive marriage between the concepts of human and social capital and the positive psychology movement, as it evolves into positive organizational behavior.[50]

What Is Positive Organizational Behavior?

Positive organizational behavior (POB)

The study and improvement of employees' positive attributes and capabilities.

OB scholar Fred Luthans defines **positive organizational behavior (POB)** as "the study and application of positively oriented human resource strengths and psychological capacities that can be measured, developed, and effectively managed for performance improvement in today's workplace."[51] His emphasis on study and measurement (meaning a coherent body of theory and research evidence) clearly sets POB apart from the quick-and-easy self-improvement books commonly found on best-seller lists. Also, POB focuses positive psychology more narrowly on the workplace. To identify five key dimensions of POB, Luthans uses the acronym CHOSE:[52]

1. *Confidence/self-efficacy.* One's belief (confidence) in being able to successfully execute a specific task in a given context (see Chapter 3).
2. *Hope.* Setting goals, figuring out how to achieve them, and being self-motivated to accomplish them—a combination of willpower and "waypower" (see Chapters 3 and 4).
3. *Optimism.* Expectation of positive outcomes or attribution of positive causes that is emotional and linked to happiness, perseverance, and success (see Chapters 2, 3, 4, and 14).
4. *Subjective well-being.* Positive understanding and evaluation of one's life; satisfaction with one's life (see Chapters 2, 3, and 4).
5. *Emotional intelligence.* Capacity for recognizing and managing one's own and others' emotions—self-awareness, self-motivation, empathy, and social skills (see Chapters 3, 6, 8, 9, 10, and 11).

Progressive managers already know the value of a positive workplace atmosphere. At Plante & Moran, a Southfield, Michigan, accounting firm, a stated goal is to have a "jerk-free" workplace. And in Mountain View, California, Intuit's employees, who develop financial software, "are legendary for their Friday afternoon socials, summer cookouts, and beach parties at the end of tax season."[53]

The Internet Revolution and OB

The Internet revolution has moved at a dizzying pace. In just a few years, dot-coms exploded onto the scene with promises of making everything for sale cheap on the Internet. Although many of those start-ups crashed, the Internet is here to stay as a valuable business tool. And as with any new technology, the business challenge is to figure out how *people* can use that technology to meet the organization's goals.

E-Business: Much More than E-Commerce

E-business

Running the *entire* business via the Internet.

Experts on the subject draw an important distinction between *e-commerce* (buying and selling goods and services over the Internet) and **e-business,** using the Internet to facilitate every aspect of running a business.[54] Says one industry observer: "The Internet is a tool that dramatically lowers the cost of communication. That means it can radically alter any industry or activity that depends heavily on the flow of information."[55] Relevant information includes everything from customer needs and product design specifications to prices, schedules, finances, employee performance data, and corporate strategy. Intel, discussed earlier as a champion of human capital, has taken this broad view of the Internet to heart. The computer-chip giant is striving to become what it calls an e-corporation, one that relies primarily on the Internet not only to buy and sell things but also to facilitate all business functions, exchange knowledge among its employees, and build partnerships with outsiders. E-business has significant implications for managing people at work because it eventually will seep into every corner of life both on and off the job.

E-Business Implications for OB

The following list is intended to open doors and explore the possibilities for OB, not serve as a final analysis. It also is a preview of later discussions in this book.

- *E-management.* Twenty-first-century managers, profiled earlier in Table 1–1, are needed in the fast-paced Internet age. They are able to create, motivate, and lead teams of far-flung specialists linked by e-mail and project-management software and by fax and phone. Networking skills, applied both inside and outside the organization, are essential today.
- *E-leadership.* In e-business, leadership involves electronically mediated interactions in combination with the traditional face-to-face variety. Therefore, experts say e-leadership raises several major issues for modern management:
  - Leaders and followers have more access to information and each other, and this is changing the nature and content of their interactions.
  - Leadership is migrating to lower organizational levels and out through the boundaries of the organization to customers and suppliers.
  - Leadership creates and exists in networks that go across traditional organizational and community boundaries.
  - Followers know more at earlier points in the decision-making process, and this can affect the credibility and influence of leaders.
  - Unethical leaders with limited resources can now mislead or harm a much broader audience of potential followers.
  - The amount of time and contact that even the most senior leaders can have with their followers has increased, although the contact is not in the traditional face-to-face mode.[56]

  In the age of e-leadership, it is more important than ever to make wise hiring and job assignment decisions, nurture productive relationships, and build trust.
- *E-communication.* E-mail has become one of the most used and abused forms of organizational communication. Today's managers need to be masters of concise, powerful e-mail and voice mail messages. Communicating via the World Wide Web is fast and efficient for those who know how to fully exploit it. Consider the experience of Pietro Senna, a buyer for Nestlé. To get the best prices and quality, Nestlé's hazelnut buyers would visit processing plants in Italy and Turkey, but Senna saved many buyers the trip. After he visited some Turkish processing plants, he posted his report online, where 73 other buyers could learn from his experience.[57] E-mail and other online communication also are useful for employees who telecommute from home or report in from remote locations. Their managers face unique motivational and performance measurement problems. For their part, telecommuters must strike a productive balance between independence and feelings of isolation.
- *Goal setting and feedback.* Abundant research evidence supports the coupling of clear and challenging goals with timely and constructive feedback for keeping employees headed in the right direction. Thanks to Web-based software programs such as

eWorkbench, managers can efficiently create, align, and track their employees' goals.[58]

- *Organizational structure.* The Internet and modern telecommunications technology have given rise to "virtual teams" and "virtual organizations."[59] Time zones, facilities, and location no longer are hard constraints on accomplishing tasks. Got a great product idea but don't have the time to build a factory? No problem. Just connect with someone via the Internet who can get the job done. This virtual workplace, with less face-to-face interaction, requires managers and employees who are flexible and adaptable and not bound by slow and rigid bureaucratic structures and methods.

- *Job design.* The work itself is a powerful motivator for many employees today, especially those in information technology. A New Economy study by Harvard's Rosabeth Moss Kanter led her to conclude, "The 'stickiest' work settings (the ones people leave less frequently and more reluctantly) involve opportunity and empowerment. Cutting-edge work with the best tools for the best customers is important in the present because it promises even greater responsibility and rewards in the future."[60] Boring, unchallenging, and dead-end jobs will repel rather than attract top talent in the Internet age.

- *Decision making.* The flow of information in the workplace does move faster and faster in the Internet age. Just ask the typical overloaded manager. In a survey asking 479 managers about their previous three years, 77% reported making more decisions, but 43% said they had less time to make decisions.[61] Adding to the pressure, databases linked to the Internet give today's decision makers unprecedented amounts of data—both relevant and irrelevant. The trick is to be energized and selective, not overwhelmed. A clear sense of purpose is necessary when sifting for useful information. Moreover, decision makers cannot ignore the trend away from command-and-control tactics and toward employee empowerment and participation. In short, there is more "we" than "me" for Internet-age decision makers.

- *Knowledge management.* Of growing importance today are e-training, e-learning, and distance learning via the Internet.[62] In fact, a recent survey of almost 300 organizations found that they are expanding e-learning opportunities, with over half of respondents saying they offer e-learning to the majority of their employees.[63] At Hewlett-Packard, employees in almost 60 countries can log on to the company's online learning portal, which makes training efficient as well as widely available.[64] Brandon Hall, a Sunnyvale, California, training specialist, recommends a contingency approach, combining e-learning with face-to-face learning.[65]

- *Speed, conflict, and stress.* The name of the popular Internet-age magazine *Fast Company* captures the nature of the present business environment. Unfortunately, conflict and stress are unavoidable by-products of strategic and operational speed. The good news, as you will learn in later chapters, is that conflict and stress can be managed.

- *Change and resistance to change.* As Old Economy companies race to become e-corporations, employees are being asked to digest huge doses of change in every aspect of their work lives. Inevitable conflict and resistance to change will need to be skillfully managed.

- *Ethics.* Internet-centered organizations are littered with ethical landmines needing to be addressed humanely and responsibly. Among the ethical issues are around-the-clock work binges, offshoring of jobs to India and elsewhere, exaggerated promises about rewards, electronic monitoring, questionable antiunion tactics, repetitive-motion injuries from excessive keyboarding, unfair treatment of part-timers, and privacy issues.[66]

Overall, the problems, challenges, and opportunities embodied in the Internet revolution are immense. Skillful management is needed, and the field of organizational behavior can provide well-conceived and carefully tested guidance.

Part One

Managing Individuals in Organizations

Chapter **Two**

Perception and Diversity: Why Viewpoints Differ

Learning Objectives

After reading the material in this chapter, you should be able to:

- Describe *perception* in terms of the social information processing model.
- Give examples of how social perception affects organizational behavior.
- Explain how individuals formulate causal attributions.
- Discuss why diversity is important in today's organizations.
- Summarize organizational practices for managing diversity.

As a quick glance at the news will tell you, people are fascinated by the lives of celebrities. We can't seem to get enough photos and updates of the beautiful people, such as Jennifer Lopez, Matthew McConaughey, Jennifer Anniston, and Sean Combs. We love or hate them based on what we see and read about them, what we interpret their actions to mean, what their roles in movies or on television portray, and what our friends' and family's opinions are. We may even adopt similar hairstyles or wardrobes, in the hope that some of their glamour and style will change other people's perceptions of us. In short, appearances and the beliefs associated with them are important, and we strive to modify our images to affect others' perceptions of us.

Whenever we receive information from newspapers, magazines, television, radio, family, and friends, we use memories to interpret that information, and our interpretations influence how we respond to and interact with others. We human beings constantly strive to make sense of our surroundings. The resulting knowledge influences our behavior and helps us navigate through life. Think of meeting someone for the first time. Your attention is drawn to the individual's physical appearance, actions, and reactions to what you say and do. From what you observe, you arrive at conclusions about the person. A similar process of perception, interpretation, and response also applies to many work situations. That process made job hunting more difficult for Lisa Bromiley Meier after she lost her job with Enron, a corporation that almost collapsed after a scandal exposed financial misdeeds at high levels. Meier told a *BusinessWeek* reporter that one prospective employer after another asked her, "Were you corrupt, or were you stupid?" because they believed that someone from the company must have had a chance to know about the scandalous behavior. Meier, who was not actually accused of any misdeeds, eventually managed to find an employer without those perceptions and became chief financial officer for Flotek Industries.[1] As Meier's experience demonstrates, it is far better for managers to understand how individuals perceive situations. That understanding should include ways to prevent misunderstandings that can arise when the workforce is diverse (composed of men and women of different cultures, ages, educational background, and so on).

A SOCIAL INFORMATION PROCESSING MODEL OF PERCEPTION

Perception
Process of interpreting one's environment.

We interpret and understand our surroundings through the cognitive process of **perception.** The perception process allows us to recognize objects, people, and written words. Since OB focuses on people, we are particularly interested in *social* perception, or the cognitive process by which we interpret and understand people. Social perception involves information processing through the four-stage sequence shown in Figure 2–1. In the first three stages—selective attention/comprehension, encoding and simplification, and storage and retention—the individual observes social information and stores it in memory. In the final stage, retrieval and response, the individual turns these mental representations into judgments and decisions. For example, if you were thinking of taking a course in personal finance, with three sections taught by different professors using different types of instruction and testing procedures, you would arrive at a preference through the steps of social information processing.

FIGURE 2–1   **Social Perception: A Social Information Processing Model**

Source: R Kreitner and A Kinicki, *Organizational Behavior* (7th ed) (Burr Ridge, IL: McGraw-Hill), p 207.

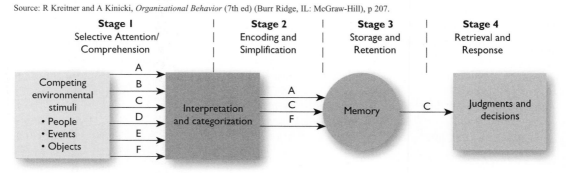

STAGE 1: SELECTIVE ATTENTION/COMPREHENSION

Attention
Being consciously aware of something or someone.

People are constantly bombarded by physical and social stimuli in the environment. Lacking the mental capacity to fully comprehend all of this information, people selectively perceive subsets of environmental stimuli. This is a matter of **attention**—the process of becoming consciously aware of something or someone. Attention can be focused on information either from the environment or from memory. If you sometimes find yourself thinking about totally unrelated events or people while reading a textbook, your attention is focused on your memory.

Research has shown that people tend to pay attention to salient stimuli. Something is *salient* when it stands out from its context. For example, a 250-pound man would be salient in a women's aerobics class but not at a meeting of the National Football League Players' Association. Needs and goals also dictate which stimuli are salient. When a driver's gas gauge is on empty, an Exxon or Shell sign is more salient than a McDonald's or Burger King sign. Moreover, people tend to pay more attention to negative than positive information—a negativity bias.[2] This bias helps explain the gawking that slows traffic to a crawl following a car accident. In the example of choosing a personal finance professor, you gather information from classmates and other sources (stimuli A through F in Figure 2–1). You are concerned about the method of instruction (stimulus A), testing procedures (stimulus C), and past grade distributions (stimulus F), so you pay attention to these three salient pieces of information and progress to the second stage of information processing.

STAGE 2: ENCODING AND SIMPLIFICATION

Cognitive categories
Mental depositories for storing information.

Schema
Mental picture of an event or object.

Stereotype
Beliefs about the characteristics of a group.

Observed information is not stored in memory in its original form. Encoding is required; raw information is interpreted or translated into mental representations. To accomplish this, perceivers assign pieces of information to **cognitive categories,** putting together equivalent objects, such as people, automobile accidents, or college courses.[3] The perceiver will interpret people, events, and objects by comparing their characteristics with information contained in schemata. A **schema** represents a person's mental picture or summary of a particular event or type of stimulus.[4]

To organize and simplify social information during encoding, people use stereotypes.[5] A **stereotype** is "an individual's set of beliefs about the characteristics or attributes of a group."[6] Stereotypes are not always negative. For example, the belief that engineers are good at math is part of a stereotype. But stereotypes may or may not be accurate. Engineers may in fact be better at math than the general population. In general, stereotypic characteristics are used to differentiate a particular group of people from other groups.

GROUP EXERCISE
Win, Lose, or Schema

Unfortunately, stereotypes can lead to poor decisions; create barriers for women, older individuals, people of color, and people with disabilities; and undermine loyalty and job satisfaction. For example, a study of 427 members of the National Association of Black Accountants revealed that 59% believed they had received biased performance evaluations because of their race, and 63% felt no obligation to remain with their current employer.[7] It thus is not surprising that the turnover rate for African-American executives is 40% higher than for their white counterparts.[8] Furthermore, in a sample of 238 males and females of different ethnicity and color, women of color reported being harassed more often than male and female whites and males of color.[9]

Stereotyping is a four-step process. It begins by categorizing people into groups according to various criteria, such as gender, age, race, and occupation. Next, we infer that all people within a particular category possess the same traits or characteristics (e.g., all women are nurturing, all professors are absentminded). Then we form expectations of others and interpret their behavior according to our stereotypes. Finally, stereotypes are maintained by overestimating the frequency of stereotypic behaviors exhibited by others, incorrectly explaining expected and unexpected behaviors, and differentiating minority individuals from oneself.[10] Although these steps are self-reinforcing, there are ways to break the chain of stereotyping. Research shows that the use of stereotypes is influenced by the amount and type of information available to an individual and his or her motivation to accurately process information.[11] People are less apt to use stereotypes to judge others when they encounter salient information that is highly inconsistent with a stereotype. For instance, you are unlikely to assign stereotypic "professor" traits to a new professor if he or she rides a Harley-Davidson, wears leather pants to class, and has a pierced nose. People also are less likely to rely on stereotypes when they are motivated to avoid using them. Accurate information processing requires mental effort, and stereotyping is generally viewed as a less strenuous strategy of information processing.

With or without stereotypes, we use the encoding process to interpret and evaluate our environment. This process can result in differing interpretations and evaluations of the same person or event. Table 2–1 describes five common perceptual errors that influence our judgments about others. These perceptual errors often distort the evaluation of job applicants and of employee performance, so managers need to guard against them when hiring applicants, evaluating performance, and in many other practical situations. In the example of personal finance professors, you compare the information to which you paid attention with other details contained in schemata. This leads you to form an impression and evaluation of what it would be like to take a course from each professor. In Figure 2–1, the relevant information contained on paths A, C, and F is passed along to the third stage of information processing.

GROUP EXERCISE
Do Stereotypes Unconsciously Influence the Perception Process?

MASTER YOUR KNOWLEDGE
Potential Errors in the Rating Process

Increase your knowledge of perception basics by completing the online quiz at
[www.mhhe.com/obcore].

- Have you ever received a performance appraisal at work or a grade or other
  assessment at school where you thought the rater made errors in perceiving your
  performance? If so, describe the situation. If not, explain what aspects of those
  appraisal processes have kept them accurate.
- Besides appraising employee performance and selecting job applicants, name
  one or two other situations in the workplace where accurate perception would
  be important.

STAGE 3: STORAGE AND RETENTION

The third stage of the perception process involves storage of information in long-term
memory. Long-term memory is like an apartment complex consisting of separate units connected to one another. Although different people live in each apartment, they sometimes
interact. In addition, a large apartment complex contains different wings. Similarly, long-term
memory consists of separate but related categories, which are connected so that the different

TABLE 2–1   Common Perceptual Errors

Perceptual Error	Description	Example
Halo	A rater forms an overall impression about an object and then uses that impression to bias ratings about the object.	Rating a professor high on the teaching dimensions of ability to motivate students, knowledge, and communication because we like him or her.
Leniency	A personal characteristic that leads an individual to consistently evaluate other people or objects in an extremely positive fashion.	Rating a professor high on all dimensions of performance regardless of his or her actual performance. The rater who hates to say negative things about others.
Central tendency	The tendency to avoid all extreme judgments and rate people and objects as average or neutral.	Rating a professor average on all dimensions of performance regardless of his or her actual performance.
Recency effects	The tendency to remember recent information. If the recent information is negative, the person or object is evaluated negatively.	Although a professor has given good lectures for 12 to 15 weeks, he or she is evaluated negatively because lectures over the last 3 weeks were done poorly.
Contrast effects	The tendency to evaluate people or objects by comparing them with characteristics of recently observed people or objects.	Rating a good professor as average because you compared his or her performance with three of the best professors you have ever had in college. You are currently taking courses from the three excellent professors.

types of information pass among these categories. In addition, long-term memory is made up of three compartments:[12]

1. *Event memory.* This compartment is composed of categories containing information about specific and general events. These memories describe appropriate sequences of events in well-known situations, such as going to a restaurant, job interview, or food store.[13]
2. *Semantic memory.* This compartment includes memories referring to general knowledge about the world, so it functions as a mental dictionary of concepts. Each concept contains a definition (e.g., a good leader) and associated traits (outgoing), emotional states (happy), physical characteristics (tall), and behaviors (works hard). Just as there are schemata for general events, concepts in semantic memory are stored as schemata. Given our discussion of societal culture in Chapter 1, it should come as no surprise that there are cultural differences in the type of information stored in semantic memory.
3. *Person memory.* Categories within this compartment contain information about a single individual (your supervisor) or groups of people (managers).

In the example of choosing a personal finance professor, your schemata of the professors are stored in these three compartments of long-term memory. These schemata are available for immediate comparison and/or retrieval.

STAGE 4: RETRIEVAL AND RESPONSE

People retrieve information from memory when they make judgments and decisions. Our ultimate judgments and decisions may be based on the process of drawing on, interpreting, and integrating categorical information stored in long-term memory. Or we can retrieve a summary judgment that was already made.[14] On registration day, when you choose which professor to take for personal finance, you can retrieve from memory your schemata-based impressions of the three professors, selecting one who meets salient criteria from the earlier stages, such as testing procedures (line C in Figure 2–1). You also might choose your preferred professor by simply recalling the decision you made two weeks ago.

Monochronic time
Preference for doing one thing at a time because time is limited, precisely segmented, and schedule driven.

Polychronic time
Preference for doing more than one thing at a time because time is flexible and multidimensional.

Cultural Influences: Perceptions of Time

Especially in stages 2 and 3, the process of perception is influenced by the perceiver's culture. Cultures shape the way we categorize and interpret what we observe. For example, time is more than the objective measurement of hours and minutes; it is perceived differently by different cultures. In North American and northern European cultures, people tend to think of time as linear—marching forward relentlessly, never to be wasted.[15] This perception of time, called **monochronic time,** considers time to be limited and precisely segmented, so value is placed on schedules and on accomplishing one task after another. As a result, Americans are taught to show up 10 minutes early for appointments. But in other parts of the world, including Latin America and the Middle East, the perception is of **polychronic time,** which sees time as having a cyclical nature with many dimensions, allowing for multiple activities. People in polychronic cultures view time as flexible, fluid, and multidimensional.

Imagine, then, a typical New Yorker waiting 45 minutes to meet with a Latin American official to discuss a business matter.[16] When he is finally admitted to the official's office, he finds the person meeting with several others at the same time. To the New Yorker, whose view of time is monochronic, the schema for business meetings includes being prompt and focusing entirely on the matter at hand. The current situation seems disrespectful, and the official may seem to be rude or incompetent. However, if the businessman is aware of different cultural perceptions of time, he is prepared for this situation.

Monochronic and polychronic time are relative rather than absolute concepts. Generally, the more tasks a person tends to do at once, the more polychronic that person is.[17] With modern technology, many businesspeople today engage in behavior that appears to reflect a polychronic view; they try to talk on the phone, reply to e-mail, and print a report all at the same time. Unfortunately, evidence suggests that this behavior is not as efficient as hoped and can be very stressful.[18]

Managerial Implications

Social cognition is the window through which we all observe, interpret, and prepare our responses to people and events. So, perception influences a wide variety of managerial activities, including hiring, performance appraisal, leadership, communication, and other forms of influence.

Interviewers make hiring decisions based on their impression of how an applicant fits the perceived requirements of a job. Inaccurate impressions in either direction produce poor hiring decisions. In addition, interviewers with racist or sexist schemata can undermine the accuracy and legality of hiring decisions. Those invalid schemata need to be confronted and improved through coaching and training to avoid poor hiring decisions. For example, a study of male and female managers of financial institutions revealed that their hiring decisions were biased by the physical attractiveness of applicants. Managers tended to hire more attractive men and women over less attractive applicants with equal qualifications.[19] Another study demonstrated that interviewer training can reduce the use of invalid schemata. Training improved interviewers' ability to obtain high-quality, job-related information and to stay focused on the interview task. Trained interviewers provided more balanced judgments about applicants than did untrained interviewers.[20]

Employee performance appraisals also suffer when schemata about what constitutes good versus poor performance are faulty. Consequently, before the review period begins, managers need to accurately identify the behavioral characteristics and results that indicate good performance and then use those characteristics as the actual measures for evaluating employee performance. One way to avoid bias and inaccuracy is to use objective, rather than subjective, measures of performance as much as possible. Also, memory for specific instances of employee performance deteriorates over time, so managers need a mechanism for accurately recalling employee behavior, such as taking periodic notes. Research indicates that individuals can be trained to be more accurate raters of performance.[21]

Perceptual errors can occur in the opposite direction, too. Employees' evaluations of leader effectiveness are influenced strongly by their schemata of good and poor leaders. A leader will have a difficult time influencing employees when he or she exhibits behaviors contained in employees' schemata of poor leaders. A team of researchers investigated the behaviors contained in our schemata of good and poor leaders. Good leaders were perceived as those who assigned specific tasks to group members, told others they had done well, set specific goals for the group, let other group members make decisions, tried to get the group to work as a team, and maintained definite standards of performance. In contrast, poor leaders were perceived to be those who told others they had performed poorly, insisted on having their own way, acted without explaining themselves, expressed worry over the group members' suggestions, frequently changed plans, and let the details of the task become overwhelming.[22]

Managers also must remember that social perception is a screening process that can distort communication, both coming and going. Because people interpret oral and written communications by using schemata developed through experiences, your own ability to influence others is affected by information contained in others' schemata regarding age, gender, ethnicity, appearance, speech, mannerisms, personality, and other personal characteristics. For example, when someone is trying to sell them on an idea, people usually have a negative perception if the person trying to persuade them fails to defend the idea, replies with standard answers, argues rather than listens, or begs and pleads.[23] Avoiding these behaviors can help you achieve greater acceptance of your ideas or opinions.

CAUSAL ATTRIBUTIONS

Causal attributions
Suspected or inferred causes of behavior.

When you notice drivers passing you, parents out with their children, or actions of other students, do you arrive at conclusions about their behavior? Rightly or wrongly, we constantly formulate cause-and-effect explanations for our own and others' behavior—for example, "Joe drinks too much because he has no willpower; but I need a couple of drinks after work because I'm under a lot of pressure." **Causal attributions** are suspected or inferred causes of behavior. The premise that people attempt to infer causes for observed behavior is the basis for attribution theory. Even though our causal attributions tend to be self-serving and are often invalid, it is important to understand how we formulate attributions, because they profoundly affect organizational behavior. Consider a supervisor's attributions about an employee's poor performance. If the supervisor attributes the problem to a lack of effort, the supervisor might reprimand that individual, but if the supervisor attributes the poor performance to a lack of ability, the supervisor would more likely request training.

Kelley's Model of Attribution

Internal factors
Personal characteristics that cause behavior.

Current models of attribution are based on the pioneering work of Fritz Heider, the founder of attribution theory. Heider proposed that behavior can be attributed either to **internal factors** within a person (such as ability) or to **external factors** within the environment (such as a difficult task). Building on Heider's work, Harold Kelley attempted to pinpoint major antecedents of internal and external attributions. Kelley hypothesized that people make causal attributions after gathering information about three dimensions of behavior:[24]

External factors
Environmental characteristics that cause behavior.

1. *Consensus* involves a comparison of an individual's behavior with that of his or her peers. Consensus is high when one acts like the rest of the group and low when one acts differently. For instance, if all assembly-line workers are completing about the same number of components each day, consensus is high; if output varies, consensus is low.

2. *Distinctiveness* is a comparison of a person's behavior on one task with his or her behavior on other tasks. High distinctiveness means the individual has performed the task in a significantly different manner than he or she has performed other tasks. Low distinctiveness means stable performance or quality from one task to another. If a supervisor gives detailed, objective performance feedback but supplies vague directions when giving assignments, distinctiveness is high.

3. *Consistency* measures whether the individual's performance on a given task is the same over time. High consistency implies the same level of performance for a certain task, time after time. Unstable performance of a given task over time would mean low consistency. Suppose an employee is consistently helpful to customers. If the employee begins to be irritable and unhelpful with customers on some days, consistency declines.

In summary, consensus relates to other *people,* distinctiveness relates to other *tasks,* and consistency relates to *time.*

These dimensions vary independently, thus forming various combinations and leading to differing attributions. Kelley hypothesized that people attribute behavior to *external* causes (environmental factors) when they perceive high consensus, high distinctiveness, and low consistency. *Internal* attributions (to personal factors) tend to be made when observed behavior is characterized by low consensus, low distinctiveness, and high consistency. Suppose all employees are performing poorly (high consensus), but on only one of several tasks (high distinctiveness) and only during one time period (low consistency). In that situation, a supervisor will probably attribute an employee's poor performance to an external source such as peer pressure or an overly difficult task. In contrast, if only the individual in question is performing poorly (low consensus), and the inferior performance is found across several tasks (low distinctiveness) and over time (high consistency), the supervisor is likely to attribute the poor performance to the employee's personal characteristics, such as laziness or lack of intelligence (an internal attribution). Many studies support this predicted pattern of attributions.[25]

Attributional Tendencies

Researchers have uncovered two attributional tendencies that distort people's interpretation of observed behavior:

Fundamental attribution bias
Ignoring environmental factors that affect behavior.

1. The **fundamental attribution bias** is the tendency to attribute another person's behavior to his or her personal characteristics, as opposed to situational factors. This bias causes perceivers to ignore important environmental forces that often significantly affect behavior. In a study of employees of a large utility company, supervisors tended to make more internal attributions about worker accidents than did the workers; that is, they blamed the workers. However, other research shows that people from Westernized cultures tend to exhibit the fundamental attribution bias more than individuals from East Asia.[26]

Self-serving bias
Taking more personal responsibility for success than failure.

2. The **self-serving bias** is the tendency to take more personal responsibility for success than for failure. The self-serving bias suggests employees will attribute their success to internal factors (high ability or hard work) and their failures to uncontrollable external factors (tough job, bad luck, unproductive coworkers, or an unsympathetic boss). A high-profile example is Ken Lay, former CEO of Enron Corporation, during his trial for deceiving investors about his company's financial difficulties. During his testimony,

Lay blamed *The Wall Street Journal* for conducting a "witch hunt" against his company, blamed his chief financial officer for misleading him, and blamed a category of investors called short sellers, who purchase options to sell stock later at a lower price, for in effect betting that the company would do worse than expected.[27] Lay's testimony did not, however, prevent the jury from convicting him. (He died before he could be sentenced, so the conviction was later voided.)

Attribution models can explain how managers handle poorly performing employees. One study revealed that managers gave employees more immediate, frequent, and negative feedback when they attributed their performance to low effort. This reaction was even more pronounced when the manager's success depended on an employee's performance. A second study indicated that managers tended to transfer employees whose poor performance was attributed to a lack of ability. These same managers also decided not to take immediate action when poor performance was attributed to external factors beyond an individual's control.[28]

The preceding findings have several important implications for managers. First, managers tend to disproportionately attribute behavior to *internal* causes.[29] As a result, they may prepare inaccurate performance evaluations, reducing employee motivation when employees perceive they have been blamed because of factors beyond their control. In addition, because managers' responses to employee performance vary according to their attributions, attributional biases may lead to inappropriate managerial actions, including promotions, transfers, and layoffs. This, too, can dampen motivation and performance. The solution is to provide managers with training sessions at which basic attributional processes are explained and managers are taught to detect and avoid attributional biases. Finally, an employee's attributions for his or her own performance dramatically affect subsequent motivation, performance, and personal attitudes such as self-esteem. For instance, when people attribute their failure to a lack of ability, they tend to give up, develop lower expectations for future success, and experience decreased self-esteem. When they attribute success to internal factors such as ability and effort, employees are more likely to display high performance and job satisfaction.[30]

Fortunately, attributional realignment can improve both motivation and performance. The goal of attributional realignment is to shift attributions of failure away from ability and toward external attributions such as low effort or lack of resources. Since taking over as head coach of the Arizona Cardinals NFL football team, which won 4 games and lost 12 in 2003, Dennis Green has been trying to use attributional realignment to motivate his players. Green's message to his players is "that they are good, that they're [just] not playing good."[31] Based on past research, this shift in players' attributions for their losses from a lack of ability to a lack of effort should pave the way for improved motivation and performance.

DEFINING AND MANAGING DIVERSITY

Diversity
The host of individual differences that make people different from and similar to each other.

Perceptions and attributions are even more significant and complex in today's diverse workplace. **Diversity** represents the multitude of individual differences and similarities that exist among people.[32] This definition underscores a key issue about managing diversity: There are many different dimensions or components of diversity, so diversity pertains to everybody. It is not an issue of age, race, or gender. It is not an issue of being heterosexual, gay, or lesbian or of being Catholic, Jewish, Protestant, or Muslim. Diversity also

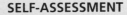

does not pit white males against all other groups of people. Diversity pertains to the host of individual differences that make all of us unique and different from others.

You might appreciate human diversity by making an analogy to seashells on a beach; like those shells, people come in a variety of shapes, sizes, and colors. This variety represents the essence of diversity. To help distinguish the important ways in which people differ, Lee Gardenswartz and Anita Rowe, a team of diversity experts, identified four layers of diversity (see Figure 2–2). Taken together, these layers define your personal identity and influence how each of us sees the world.[33] The innermost layer is personality (see Chapter 3), because it represents a stable set of characteristics that is responsible for a person's identity. The next layer consists of a set of internal dimensions—the "primary dimensions" of diversity,[34] which are mostly outside our control but strongly influence our attitudes and our expectations and assumptions about others, thus influencing our behavior. The third layer consists of external dimensions, over which individuals have some control, including income, religion, personal habits, educational background, and work experience. These dimensions also exert a significant influence on our perceptions, behavior, and attitudes. Following the terrorist attacks of September 11, 2001, many Americans noted that the attackers all identified themselves as Muslims, and some Americans reacted with suspicion or even animosity toward all Muslims and people of Middle Eastern descent. Ford Motor Company conducted a series of Islam 101 training sessions in Dearborn, Michigan, aimed at creating a positive work climate and fostering positive relations with its community of Dearborn, home to one of the largest Arab-American and Middle Eastern communities in the United States.[35] The final, outermost layer of diversity includes organizational dimensions, such as an individual's job title, work content, work group, and management status.

Affirmative Action and Managing Diversity

Affirmative action
Voluntary and involuntary efforts to achieve equality of opportunity for everyone.

Effectively managing diversity requires organizations to adopt a new way of thinking about differences among people. Rather than pitting one group against another, managing diversity entails recognition of the unique contribution every employee can make. Many people associate diversity management with affirmative action, but the two are, in fact, quite different.

Affirmative action represents "voluntary and mandatory efforts undertaken by federal, state, and local governments; private employers; and schools to combat discrimination and to promote equal opportunity in education and employment for all."[36] Affirmative action is proactive, aimed at eliminating discrimination and creating equal opportunity. According to a

FIGURE 2–2
The Four Layers of Diversity

Source: From L Gardenswartz and A Rowe, *Diverse Teams at Work: Capitalizing on the Power of Diversity*, 1994, 2003, p 33. Published by the Society for Human Resource Management. Reprinted with permission.

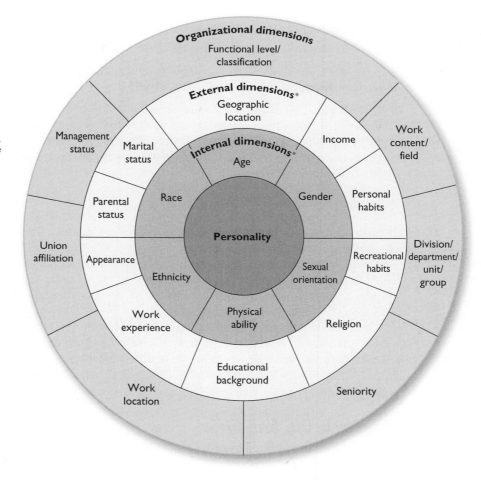

*Internal dimensions and external dimensions are adapted from Loden and Rosener, *Workforce America!* (Homewood, IL: Business One Irwin, 1991).

variety of Equal Employment Opportunity laws, it is illegal to discriminate on the basis of race, color, religion, gender, national origin, age, religious affiliation, and physical abilities. Quotas, however, are illegal (unless imposed by a judge as a remedy for past discrimination), and affirmative action does not legitimize quotas. Also, under no circumstances does affirmative action require companies to hire unqualified people.

Although affirmative action created tremendous opportunities for women and minorities, it does not foster the type of thinking that is needed to effectively manage diversity.[37] Many people perceive affirmative action as involving preferential hiring and treatment based on group membership. Affirmative-action plans are more successful when employees view them as fair and equitable.[38] The programs were even found to hurt the women and minorities expected to benefit from them. Research demonstrated that women and minorities felt stigmatized, because others assumed they had been hired on the basis of

MASTER YOUR KNOWLEDGE

Comparing Affirmative Action, Valuing Diversity, and Managing Diversity

Increase your knowledge of diversity basics by completing the online quiz at [www.mhhe.com/obcore].

- Consider your school and the organizations where you have worked. Based on the descriptions in this exercise, would you say that each of these organizations used affirmative action? Valued diversity? Managed diversity?
- Would management have to *value* diversity in order to *manage* diversity effectively? Why or why not?

Managing diversity
Creating organizational changes that enable all people to perform up to their maximum potential.

affirmative action and were therefore unqualified or incompetent. They experienced less job satisfaction and more stress than employees supposedly selected on the basis of merit.[39]

In contrast to affirmative action, **managing diversity** enables all the organization's people to perform up to their maximum potential by changing the organization's culture and infrastructure. Ann Morrison, a diversity expert, conducted a study of 16 organizations that successfully managed diversity. Her results uncovered three key strategies for success: education (preparing "nontraditional" managers for greater responsibility while helping "traditional" managers work with diverse people), enforcement (rules, policies, and consequences), and exposure to people of different backgrounds and personal characteristics.[40] In summary, consultants and academics believe that organizations should strive to manage diversity rather than only valuing it or simply using affirmative action.

Diversity in the Workforce

In the United States today, four demographic trends are creating an increasingly diverse workforce. Women continue to enter the workforce in greater numbers, people of color (non-Caucasian) represent a growing share of the labor force, workers' educational attainment is failing to meet occupational requirements, and the workforce is aging.

Women in the Workforce

According to forecasts by the U.S. Bureau of Labor Statistics, slightly more than half of the new entrants into the workforce between 2000 and 2010 will be women.[41] At the same time, women will represent about 45% of the departures from the workforce (mainly retirees). As a result, women's share of the workforce is expected to grow from 46% in 1996 to about 48% by 2010.

Glass ceiling
Invisible barrier blocking women and minorities from top management positions.

In spite of their growing numbers, women continue to encounter the **glass ceiling**—an invisible barrier that separates women and minorities from advancing into top management positions. It can be particularly demotivating because employees can see coveted top-management positions but are unable to obtain them. A variety of statistics support the existence of a glass ceiling. In the 500 largest publicly traded companies known as the *Fortune* 500, only 10 of the CEOs were female as of 2006, and less than 16% of the corporate officers were female.[42] Also, as of 2004, women were still underpaid relative to men, receiving on average 80% of men's earnings.[43] Even when women are paid the same as men, they

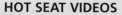

HOT SEAT VIDEOS
Office Romance: Groping for Answers

Diversity: Mediating Morality

Personal Disclosure: Confession Coincidence

Diversity in Hiring: Candidate Conundrum

may suffer in other areas of job opportunities. In a study of 69 male and female executives from a large multinational financial services corporation, no differences were found in base salary or bonuses, but the women received fewer stock options than the male executives (even after controlling for level of education, performance, and job function) and reported less satisfaction with future career opportunities.[44] A follow-up study of 13,503 female managers and 17,493 male managers from the same organization demonstrated that women at higher levels in the managerial hierarchy received fewer promotions than males at comparable positions.[45]

How can women overcome the glass ceiling? A team of researchers attempted to answer this question by surveying 461 executive women who held titles of vice president or higher in *Fortune* 1000 companies. Respondents evaluated the extent to which they used 13 different career strategies to break through the glass ceiling. Findings indicated that four strategies were critical for breaking the glass ceiling: consistently exceeding performance expectations, developing a style with which male managers are comfortable, seeking out difficult or challenging assignments, and having influential mentors.[46]

People of Color in the Workforce

People of color in the United States are projected to add 39.4% of the new entrants in the workforce from 2000 to 2010.[47] Hispanics are predicted to account for the largest share of this increase (17.9%). The Hispanic population also continues to grow faster than other ethnic or racial groups, and Hispanics surpassed the African-American population in 2000. The Census Bureau projects that people of color will represent about half of the population by 2050.[48]

Unfortunately, four additional trends suggest that people of color are experiencing their own glass ceiling. First, people of color are advancing even less in the managerial and professional ranks than women. For example, African-Americans and Hispanics held 11.3% and 10.9%, respectively, of all managerial and professional jobs in 2001; women held 46.6% of these positions. Second, the number of race-based charges of discrimination that were deemed to show reasonable cause by the U.S. Equal Employment Opportunity Commission increased from 294 in 1995 to 2,397 in 2001, declining only to 1,161 in 2005. Companies paid a total of $76.5 million to resolve these claims outside of litigation in 2005.[49] Third, people of color tend to earn less than whites. Median household income in 2002 was $30,032 for African-Americans, $33,946 for Hispanics, and $47,194 for whites. Interestingly, Asians and Pacific Islanders had the highest median income, at $54,910.[50] Finally, a number of studies show that people of color experience more perceived discrimination than whites.[51]

Educational Attainment and Occupational Requirements

Underemployment
The result of taking a job that requires less education, training, or skills than possessed by a worker.

Approximately 27% of the labor force has a college degree.[52] Unfortunately, many of these people are working in jobs for which they are overqualified. This creates **underemployment,** meaning people's jobs require less than employees' full potential as determined by their formal education, training, or skills. Underemployment is associated with higher arrest rates and the likelihood of becoming an unmarried parent for young adults. It also is negatively correlated with job satisfaction, work commitment, job involvement, internal work motivation, life satisfaction, and psychological well-being. Underemployment also is related to higher absenteeism and turnover.[53] However, research reveals that over time, a college graduate's income ranges from 50% to 100% higher than that obtained by a high school graduate.[54] It pays to graduate from college!

At the same time that modern jobs require more skills and pay better, educational attainment produces another important mismatch. The national high-school dropout rate is approximately 16%, and more than 20% of the adult U.S. population read at or below a fifth-grade level, which is below the level needed to earn a living wage. In addition, more than 40 million Americans age 16 and older are illiterate, meaning they cannot read, write, and solve problems well enough to function at work and in society.[55] These statistics are worrisome because 70% of on-the-job reading materials are written for ninth-grade to college levels.

The Aging Workforce

America's population and workforce are getting older. Between 1995 and 2020, the number of individuals in the United States over age 65 will increase by 60%, the 45- to 64-year-old population by 34%, and those between ages 18 and 44 by only 4%.[56] Life expectancy is increasing as well. The number of people living into their 80s is increasing rapidly. The United States is not the only country with an aging population. Japan, Eastern Europe, and the former Soviet republics, for example, are expected to encounter significant economic and political challenges due to an aging population.

Impact of Diversity on Organizations

Highly skilled women and people of color will be in great demand. For example, the University of North Carolina Health Care System at Chapel Hill, North Carolina, reaches a larger pool of recruits and builds its ability to serve Spanish-speaking patients by actively seeking Hispanic workers. The system printed Spanish information on its application forms and hired translators to assist with orientation of new employees.[57] Also, to attract and retain the best workers, companies need to adopt policies and programs that meet the needs of women and people of color. Programs such as day care, elder care, flexible work schedules, and benefits such as paternity leaves, less rigid relocation policies, and mentoring programs are likely to become more popular.

To meet the problem of underemployment among college graduates, which threatens to erode job satisfaction and work motivation, some organizations are taking fresh approaches to job redesign (see Chapter 4). On-the-job remedial skills and literacy training will be necessary to help the growing number of dropouts and illiterate workers cope with job demands. The influx of workers whose first language is something other than English is likely to require more companies to offer foreign language training. The need for foreign language training can be a life-or-death matter in the health-care industry. Deborah Lance, director of professional development for Erlanger Health System in the Southeast, in Chattanooga, Tennessee, explains, "We need to be able to communicate with all our patients and families, and foreign language education is one way to help us meet that need."[58]

For organizations that must adapt to an aging workforce, there are two general recommendations. The first involves many employees' need to deal with personal issues associated with elder care for aging parents; failing to help these employees can drive up an employer's costs as employees are distracted and need time off. For example, MetLife estimates that a lack of elder care costs organizations at least $11 billion a year in lost productivity and increased absenteeism, workday interruptions, and turnover.[59] Second, employers need to make a concerted effort to keep their older workers engaged and committed and their skills current. Ways to accomplish this objective include giving experienced workers challenging and meaningful work assignments, autonomy, access to training (including training in new technology), frequent recognition, opportunities to serve as mentors, high-quality supervision, and a stimulating work environment.[60]

ORGANIZATIONAL PRACTICES THAT EFFECTIVELY MANAGE DIVERSITY

Many organizations throughout the United States are unsure of what it takes to manage diversity effectively, considering the sensitive and potentially volatile nature of the subject. But despite the barriers to managing diversity, there are several ways of managing organizational diversity initiatives.

Barriers and Challenges

When organizations try to implement diversity initiatives, they encounter a variety of barriers.[61] Some of these involve perceptions and attitudes. Inaccurate stereotypes and prejudice manifest themselves in the belief that differences are weaknesses, so hiring a diverse workforce will require sacrificing competence and quality. Similarly, *ethnocentrism* is the feeling that one's cultural rules and norms are superior or more appropriate than the rules and norms of another culture. Also, effectively managing diversity entails significant organizational and personal change, but people resist change for many reasons (see Chapter 14).

The organization may contribute to other barriers. Poor career planning, for example, limits opportunities for diverse employees to get the type of work assignments that qualify them for senior management positions. Some work environments are unsupportive and hostile, so diverse employees are excluded from social events and the friendly camaraderie that takes place in most offices. Some employees believe that managing diversity is a smoke screen for reverse discrimination. This belief leads to very strong resistance because people feel that one person's gain is another's loss. If management does not treat diversity as a top priority, subtle resistance may show up in the form of complaints and negative attitudes. Employees may object to time, energy, and resources devoted to diversity that could have been spent doing "real work." This reaction can especially be true when reward systems do not measure progress on diversity-related goals.

In some cases, employees face challenges because they need more social support than employees who have enjoyed the benefits of a traditional business network. Diverse employees may lack political savvy. In other words, they may not get promoted because they do not know how to "play the game" of getting along and getting ahead in an organization. Research reveals that women and people of color are often excluded from organizational networks.[62] A challenge that tends to hit women especially hard is balancing career and family needs. Women still assume the majority of the responsibilities associated with raising children, and when they do, it is harder for them to work evenings and weekends or to take frequent trips.

Diversity Initiatives

Ann Morrison conducted a landmark study of the diversity practices used by 16 organizations that successfully managed diversity. Her results uncovered 52 different practices, 20 of which were used by the majority of the companies sampled. She classified the 52 practices into three main types: accountability, development, and recruitment practices.[63]

Accountability practices
Focus on treating diverse employees fairly.

Accountability practices relate to managers' responsibility to treat diverse employees fairly. Companies predominantly accomplish this objective by creating administrative procedures aimed at integrating diverse employees into the management ranks. In addition, work and family policies focus on creating an environment that fosters employee commitment and productivity. At Progress Energy, an energy company that serves the Carolinas and Florida, the chairman and CEO leads the company's diversity council and holds every manager accountable for achieving goals related to diversity perceptions and practices. The company also follows up on the results of annual employee surveys.[64]

Development practices
Focus on preparing diverse employees for greater responsibility and advancement.

Development practices are a relatively new way to manage diversity; they focus on preparing diverse employees for greater responsibility and advancement. These activities are needed because most nontraditional employees have not been exposed to the type of activities and job assignments that develop effective leadership and social networks. The most frequently used developmental practices include diversity training programs, networks and support groups, and mentoring programs. Home mortgage agency Fannie Mae has 14 Employee Networking Groups for a variety of employee segments, including African-Americans, Hispanics, Native Americans, Catholics, Christians, Muslims, older workers, gays, lesbians, and veterans. "The groups serve as social and networking hubs, and they foster workplace communication about diversity issues among all employees, including senior managers."[65]

Recruitment practices
Attempts to attract qualified, diverse employees at all levels.

Recruitment practices focus on attracting job applicants who are willing to accept challenging work assignments. This focus is critical because accomplishing increasingly difficult and responsible work assignments teaches the leadership skills needed for advancement. Common recruitment practices are targeted recruitment of nonmanagers and managers aimed at identifying and recruiting women and people of color.

Chapter **Three**

Individual Differences: What Makes Employees Unique

Learning Objectives

After reading the material in this chapter, you should be able to:

- Explain how a person's self-esteem, self-efficacy, and self-monitoring affect the person's self-concept and behavior.
- Describe how people change their behavior through self-management.
- Identify important personality dimensions and their relationship to job performance.
- Define the individual differences of locus of control, attitudes, and intelligence.
- Summarize the role of emotions and emotional intelligence in the workplace.

How do star athletes come through in the clutch? We watch breathlessly as Tiger Woods sinks an impossible putt or Michelle Kwan lands effortlessly after a triple jump on the ice rink. We shake our heads and wonder what they have that the rest of us don't—a good coach? lots of practice? luck? Aside from innate physical abilities, something inside these athletes just seems to prime them for success. They have a strong belief in themselves and their ability to succeed despite tremendous odds. As we'll see in this chapter, a person's expectations, self-concept, and attitudes do affect his or her performance, not only on the playing field but also in the workplace.

Differences among individuals give today's organizations a rich and interesting human texture, but they also complicate the manager's role. Especially among workers holding complex jobs, individual performance differences are dramatic.[1] In addition, workforce diversity (discussed in Chapter 2) compels managers to view individual differences in a fresh new way. Rather than limiting diversity, as in the past, today's managers need to understand and accommodate employee diversity and individual differences.[2] They also need to understand themselves in relation to others in the organization. As Terri Kelly, chief executive of W L Gore & Associates, observed,

"Leaders have to be very self-aware. They have to understand their flaws, their own behavior, and the impact they have on others."[3] This chapter explores several important dimensions of individual differences: self-concept and self-management, personality, attitudes, mental abilities, and emotions.

FROM SELF-CONCEPT TO SELF-MANAGEMENT

Self-concept
Person's self-perception as a physical, social, spiritual being.

Cognitions
A person's knowledge, opinions, or beliefs.

Self is the core of one's conscious existence. As modeled in Figure 3–1, the awareness of one's self, along with one's personality (how you appear to others), is related to key forms of self-expression. Awareness of self is referred to as one's self-concept. Sociologist Viktor Gecas defines **self-concept** as "the concept the individual has of himself as a physical, social, and spiritual or moral being."[4] In other words, because you have a self-concept, you recognize yourself as a distinct human being. A self-concept would be impossible without the capacity to think—that is, to have **cognitions,** meaning "any knowledge, opinion, or belief about the environment, about oneself, or about one's behavior."[5] Among many different types of cognitions, those involving anticipation, planning, goal setting, evaluating, and setting personal standards are particularly relevant to OB. Cognitively based topics in this book include social perception (discussed in the previous chapter), behavioral self-management, modern motivation theories, and decision-making styles.

Ideas of self and self-concept vary from one historical era to another, from one socio-economic group to another, and from culture to culture.[6] How well one detects and adjusts to different cultural notions of self can spell the difference between success and failure in international dealings. For example, Japanese–U.S. communication and understanding often are hindered by different degrees of self-disclosure. With a comparatively large public self, Americans pride themselves in being open, honest, candid, and to the point. The Japanese, who culturally discourage self-disclosure, typically view Americans as blunt, prying, and insensitive to formalities. For their part, Americans tend to see Japanese as distant,

FIGURE 3–1
An OB Model for Studying Individual Differences

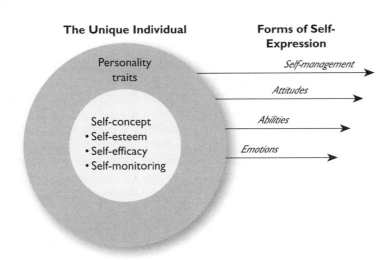

The Unique Individual

Personality traits

Self-concept
• Self-esteem
• Self-efficacy
• Self-monitoring

Forms of Self-Expression

Self-management

Attitudes

Abilities

Emotions

cold, and evasive.[7] One culture is not right and the other wrong. They are just different, and a key difference involves culturally rooted conceptions of self and self-disclosure.

Self-Esteem

Self-esteem
One's overall self-evaluation.

A person's **self-esteem** is the person's belief about his or her self-worth based on an overall self-evaluation.[8] To measure self-esteem, behavioral scientists ask survey respondents to indicate their agreement or disagreement with numerous positive and negative statements. On one general self-esteem survey, the positive statements include "I feel I am a person of worth, the equal of other people," and a negative item is "I feel I do not have much to be proud of."[9] Those who agree with the positive statements and disagree with the negative statements have high self-esteem. They see themselves as worthwhile, capable, and acceptable. People with low self-esteem view themselves in negative terms. They do not feel good about themselves and are hampered by self-doubts.[10]

Self-esteem has been called a uniquely Western concept. How well does it cross cultures? A survey of 13,118 students from 31 countries found a moderate positive correlation between self-esteem and life satisfaction. The relationship was stronger in individualistic cultures (e.g., the United States, Canada, New Zealand, the Netherlands) than in collectivist cultures (e.g., Korea, Kenya, Japan). The researchers concluded that individualistic cultures socialize people to focus more on themselves, while people in collectivist cultures "are socialized to fit into the community and to do their duty," so their satisfaction in life depends less on how they feel about themselves.[11] Global managers need to remember to deemphasize self-esteem when doing business in collectivist ("we") cultures, as opposed to emphasizing it in individualistic ("me") cultures.[12]

In general, self-esteem can be improved through conscious choices: deciding to be fully engaged in life, taking responsibility but avoiding excessive self-criticism.[13] More detailed answers come from research. In one study, youth-league baseball coaches who were trained in supportive teaching techniques had a positive effect on the self-esteem of young boys. A control group of untrained coaches had no such positive effect.[14] Another study considered the way people think of themselves and concluded that self-esteem increased more when people thought of "*desirable* characteristics *possessed* rather than of undesirable characteristics" they lack.[15] Yet another comprehensive study threw cold water on the popular view that high self-esteem leads to better performance. Although high performers had higher self-esteem, the researchers concluded, "Long overdue scientific scrutiny points out the foolishness of supposing that people's opinion of themselves can be the *cause* of achievement. Rather, high-esteem is the *result* of good performance."[16]

Self-Efficacy

Self-efficacy
Belief in one's ability to do a task.

Have you noticed how those who are confident about their ability tend to succeed, while those who are preoccupied with failure tend to fail? At the heart of this performance mismatch is a specific dimension of self-esteem called **self-efficacy**—a person's belief about his or her chances of successfully accomplishing a specific task. According to one OB writer, "Self-efficacy arises from the gradual acquisition of complex cognitive, social, linguistic, and/or physical skills through experience."[17]

Helpful nudges in the right direction from parents, role models, and mentors are central to the development of high self-efficacy. Consider, for example, the impact on Tiger Woods of his father, former U.S. Army Green Beret Earl Woods. While the son was learning the game, the father stood by, challenging him verbally just before each swing. The elder Woods told a reporter, "He would look at me with the most evil look, but he wasn't permitted to say anything," until one day, "I did all my tricks, and he looked at me and smiled." The father was trying to develop "mental toughness," and the day his son could smile during the experience, the father felt sure he had fully developed his self-efficacy as a golfer.[18]

The relationship between self-efficacy and performance is cyclical. Efficacy → performance cycles can spiral upward toward success or downward toward failure.[19] Researchers have documented a strong link between high self-efficacy expectations and success in widely varied physical and mental tasks, anxiety reduction, addiction control, pain tolerance, illness recovery, and avoidance of seasickness in naval cadets.[20] Conversely, those with low self-efficacy expectations tend to have low success rates. Chronically low self-efficacy is associated with a condition called **learned helplessness,** the severely debilitating belief that one has no control over one's environment.[21]

Learned helplessness
Debilitating lack of faith in one's ability to control the situation.

Mechanisms of Self-Efficacy

Although self-efficacy sounds like some sort of mental magic, it operates in a very straightforward manner. The basic model of self-efficacy displayed in Figure 3–2 draws on the work

FIGURE 3–2   **Self-Efficacy Beliefs Pave the Way for Success or Failure**

Sources: Adapted from discussion in A Bandura, "Regulation of Cognitive Processes through Perceived Self-Efficacy," *Developmental Psychology,* September 1989, pp 729–35; and R Wood and A Bandura, "Social Cognitive Theory of Organizational Management," *Academy of Management Review,* July 1989, pp 361–84.

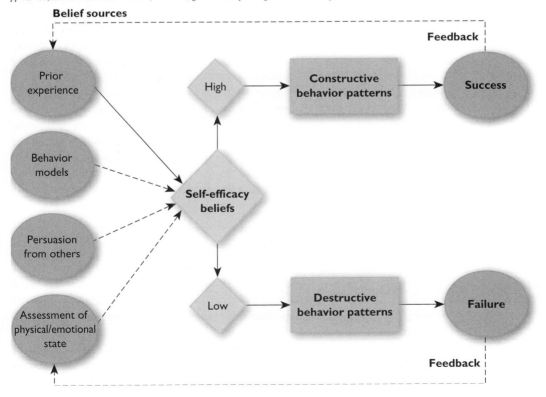

of Stanford psychologist Albert Bandura.[22] To explore this model, imagine you have been told to prepare and deliver a 10-minute talk to an OB class of 50 students on the workings of this same self-efficacy model. Your self-efficacy calculation would involve cognitive appraisal of the interaction between your perceived capability and situational opportunities and obstacles.

As you begin preparing for your presentation, the four sources of self-efficacy beliefs come into play. The most potent source, according to Bandura, is experience.[23] Past success in public speaking would boost your self-efficacy, and bad experiences with delivering speeches would foster low self-efficacy. Other sources of self-efficacy beliefs are behavior models, persuasion from others, and assessment of one's physical and emotional state. In terms of your classroom presentation, you would be influenced by the success or failure of your classmates in delivering similar talks, classmates' assurances that you will do a good job, and such physical and emotional factors as a case of laryngitis or a bout of stage fright. Your resulting cognitive evaluation of the situation would yield a self-efficacy belief, ranging from high to low expectations of success. These self-efficacy beliefs are not merely boastful statements based on bravado; they are deep convictions supported by experience.

The individual acts out these high or low self-efficacy beliefs through behavior patterns. People with a high expectation of success tend to actively select the best opportunities, manage the situation, set goals, prepare thoroughly, persevere, solve problems creatively, learn from setbacks, visualize success, and limit stress. People with a low expectation of success are more likely to be passive, avoiding difficult tasks, developing low standards, focusing on their shortcomings, putting forth little effort, becoming discouraged by setbacks, making excuses for setbacks and failure, worrying, and feeling stressed and depressed. Thus, if you have high self-efficacy about giving your 10-minute speech, you will work harder, more creatively, and longer than will your classmates with low self-efficacy. The results take shape from the efforts. People program themselves for success or failure by enacting their self-efficacy expectations. Then the positive or negative results become feedback: personal experience that influences future self-efficacy beliefs. Bob Schmonsees, a software entrepreneur whose legs became paralyzed in a skiing accident, is an inspiring example of the success pathway. In response to his major physical setback, Schmonsees "discovered a formula for his different world: Figure out the new rules for any activity, then take as many small steps as necessary to master those rules. After learning the physics of a tennis swing on wheels and the geometry of playing a second bounce (standard rules), he became the world's top wheelchair player over age 40."[24]

Managerial Implications

On-the-job research evidence encourages managers to nurture self-efficacy in themselves and in others. A meta-analysis—a statistical pooling technique that allows general conclusions to be drawn from many different studies—encompassing 21,616 subjects found a significant positive correlation between self-efficacy and job performance.[25] Self-efficacy requires constructive action in the following management areas:

- *Recruiting/selection/job assignments.* Interview questions can probe job applicants' general self-efficacy to determine orientation and training needs but not for hiring decisions. Pencil-and-paper tests for self-efficacy are not in an advanced stage of development and validation. Also, discrimination may be a concern, because studies have detected below-average self-esteem and self-efficacy among women and protected minorities.[26]

- *Job design.* Complex, challenging, and autonomous jobs tend to enhance perceived self-efficacy.[27] Boring, tedious jobs generally do the opposite.
- *Training and development.* Employees' self-efficacy expectations for key tasks can be improved through guided experiences, mentoring, and role modeling.[28]
- *Self-management.* Systematic self-management training involves enhancement of self-efficacy expectations.[29]
- *Goal setting and quality improvement.* Goal difficulty needs to match the individual's perceived level of self-efficacy.[30] As self-efficacy and performance improve, standards can be raised.
- *Creativity.* Supportive managerial actions can enhance the strong linkage between self-efficacy beliefs and workplace creativity.[31]
- *Coaching.* Those with low self-efficacy and employees victimized by learned helplessness need lots of constructive pointers and positive feedback.[32]
- *Leadership.* Leadership talent surfaces when top management gives managers with high self-efficacy a chance to prove themselves under pressure.
- *Rewards.* Small successes need to be rewarded as stepping-stones to a stronger self-image and greater achievements.

Self-Monitoring

Self-monitoring
Observing one's own behavior and adapting it to the situation.

Imagine you are rushing to an important meeting when a co-worker pulls you aside and starts to discuss a personal problem. You want to break off the conversation, so you glance at your watch. He keeps talking. You say, "I'm late for a big meeting." He continues. You turn and start to walk away. The person keeps talking as if he never received any of your signals that the conversation was over. Besides being an all-too-common and irritating situation, this encounter highlights a significant and measurable individual difference in self-expression behavior, called *self-monitoring*. **Self-monitoring** is the extent to which a person observes his or her own self-expressive behavior and adapts it to the demands of the situation.[33] Persons who are high self-monitors tend to regulate how they present themselves to others; they respond to "social and interpersonal cues" about what behavior is appropriate to the situation. In contrast, individuals who are low self-monitors seem to lack that ability or motivation and instead express themselves in behaviors that "functionally reflect their own enduring and momentary inner states, including their attitudes, traits, and feelings."[34]

In organizational life, both high and low self-monitors are subject to criticism. High self-monitors are sometimes called "chameleons" because they readily adapt how they present themselves to their surroundings. Low self-monitors often are criticized for seeming to dwell on their own planet and being insensitive to others. Within an OB context, self-monitoring is like any other individual difference—not a matter of right or wrong or good versus bad, but instead a source of diversity that managers need to understand. In addition, self-monitoring is not an either–or proposition but a matter of degree—a matter of being relatively high or low in terms of related patterns of self-expression.

According to field research, high self-monitoring is correlated with career success. Among 139 MBA graduates tracked for five years, high self-monitors enjoyed more internal and external promotions than did their classmates who were low self-monitors.[35]

In another study of 147 managers and professionals, high self-monitors had a better record of acquiring a mentor (someone to act as a personal career coach and professional sponsor).[36] These results mesh well with an earlier study that found managerial success (in terms of speed of promotions) was tied to political savvy (knowing how to socialize, network, and engage in organizational politics).[37]

This evidence and practical experience suggest some recommendations. Individuals should become more consciously aware of their self-image and the way it affects others. Those who are *high self-monitors* should take care not to overdo this behavior, or they could be perceived as insincere, dishonest, phony, and untrustworthy. Those who are *low self-monitors* should try to be a bit more accommodating while remaining true to their basic beliefs. In particular, don't wear out your welcome when communicating. Practice reading and adjusting to nonverbal cues in various public situations. If your conversation partner is bored or distracted, stop—because he or she is not really listening.

Self-Management: A Social Learning Model

Albert Bandura, the Stanford psychologist introduced earlier, extended his self-efficacy concept into a comprehensive model of human learning. According to Bandura's *social learning theory,* an individual acquires new behavior through the interplay of cognitive processes with environmental cues and consequences.[38] When you consciously control this learning process yourself, you are engaging in self-management. Bandura explains, "By arranging environmental inducements, generating cognitive supports, and producing consequences for their own actions, people are able to exercise some measure of control over their own behavior."[39] In other words, to the extent that you can control your environment and your cognitive representations of it, you are the master of your own behavior. The model in Figure 3–3 is derived from social learning theory. The two-headed arrows reflect

FIGURE 3–3
A Social Learning Model of Self-Management

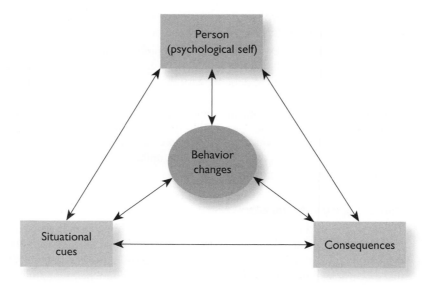

dynamic interaction among all factors in the model. The four major components of this self-management model require a closer look, beginning with the focal point: *behavior change,* shown in the center.[40]

An Agenda for Self-Improvement

In today's fast-paced Internet age, corporate hand-holding is a thing of the past when it comes to career management. Our age of *career self-management* challenges you to do a better job of setting personal goals, having clear priorities, being well-organized, skillfully managing your time, and developing a self-learning program.[41] Stephen R Covey, in his best-selling books *The 7 Habits of Highly Effective People* and *The 8th Habit,* has given managers a helpful agenda for improving themselves:[42]

1. Be proactive. Choose goals, and take responsibility for achieving them.
2. Begin with the end in mind; be goal-oriented.
3. Put first things first. Set priorities including work and personal goals, present and future.
4. Think win/win. Look for mutually beneficial solutions.
5. Seek first to understand, then to be understood. Listen carefully.
6. Synergize. Generate teamwork, and value people's differences.
7. Sharpen the saw. Renew yourself mentally, spiritually, socially/emotionally, and physically.
8. Find your voice by seeking fulfillment, acting passionately, and making a significant contribution—then help others do the same.

The first step for applying the social learning model in Figure 3–3 is to pick one or more of the eight habits that are personal trouble spots and translate them into specific behaviors. For example, "think win/win" might remind a conflict-prone manager to practice cooperative teamwork behaviors with co-workers. Habit number five might prompt another manager to stop interrupting during conversations.

Managing Situational Cues

Trying to give up a habit such as smoking is difficult. Many people (friends who smoke) and situations (after dinner, when under stress at work, or when relaxing) serve as subtle yet powerful cues telling the individual to light up. Success requires rearranging situational cues so that they trigger a different behavior. Several techniques are helpful for managing these cues:

- *Reminders and attention focusers* keep people thinking about what they want to do. Many students and managers cue themselves about deadlines and appointments by sticking Post-it notes all over their work areas, refrigerators, and dashboards.

- *Self-observation data,* when compared against a goal or standard, can be a potent cue. Those who keep a weight chart near their bathroom scale will attest to the value of this tactic.

- Successful self-management calls for *avoiding negative cues* while *seeking positive cues.* Managers in Northwestern Mutual Life Insurance Company's new-business department devote Wednesdays solely to processing new insurance policies. To avoid negative cues (distractions from the main task), the department refuses incoming calls on Wednesdays, enabling it to prepare 23% more policies than it does on the other days of the week.[43]

- Challenging yet attainable *personal goals* are important for effective self-management. Personal finance expert Jean Chatzky says research has found a much greater incidence of happiness among people who have at least started achieving goals than among those who have not set goals for themselves or begun to achieve them.[44] Goals are both a target and a measuring stick of progress.

- Finally, a *self-contract* is an "if-then" agreement with oneself. For example, if you can define all the key terms in this chapter, treat yourself to something special.

Arranging Cognitive Supports

Referring to the *person* portion of the self-management model (Figure 3–3), cognitive supports are ways of thinking about oneself to promote the desired behavior changes. These cues are psychological, as opposed to environmental, but they prompt appropriate behavior in the same manner. Three cognitive supports are symbolic coding, rehearsal, and self-talk.

Symbolic coding refers to the social learning theory's perspective that the human brain stores information in visual and verbal codes, which are helpful for remembering information. A sales manager who wants to remember Woodman, the name of a promising new client, could visualize a picture of a man chopping down a huge tree. People also rely on acronyms—a type of verbal code—to recall names, rules for behavior, and other information. An acronym that is often heard in managerial circles is the KISS principle, standing for "Keep It Simple, Stupid."

Mental *rehearsal* of challenging tasks also can increase a person's chances of success. In contrast to daydreaming, it involves a systematic visualization of how to proceed. Consultant Judith Schuster explains, "A daydream typically has gaps in it—we jump immediately to where we want to wind up. In visualization, we use building blocks and, step-by-step, construct the result we want."[45]

This sort of visualization has been recommended for use in managerial planning.[46] Mental rehearsal, used by many successful athletes, also operates in the job-finding seminars that have become popular on college campuses today, which typically involve mental and actual rehearsal of tough job interviews. Such manufactured experiences can build confidence and self-efficacy for real-world success.[47]

Self-talk
Evaluating thoughts about oneself.

According to an expert on the subject, "**Self-talk** is the set of evaluating thoughts that you give yourself about facts and events that happen to you."[48] Personal experience tells us that negative self-talk tends to pave the way for failure, while positive self-talk often facilitates success. Replacing negative self-talk ("I'll never get a raise") with positive self-talk ("I deserve a raise, and I'm going to get it") is fundamental to better self-management. One business writer offers this example to salespeople: "If you don't like cold calling, . . . think of how good you'll feel when you're finished, knowing you have a whole list of new selling opportunities."[49]

Administering Consequences

The completion of self-contracts and other personal achievements calls for a reward, giving you a good feeling that makes you want to try again. That kind of reward, described in Chapter 5 as *reinforcement,* depends on three criteria:

1. The individual must have control over the consequences.
2. The individual must reward him- or herself only for meeting the conditions of success. Failure to meet the performance requirement must lead to self-denial.
3. The individual needs performance standards that establish the quantity and quality of target behavior required for receiving the reward.[50]

Of course, rewarding oneself is not simple, or people wouldn't keep ruining their diets and breaking their New Year's resolutions. One complication is that, along with the planned long-term consequences of a goal, there can be short-term rewards for *not* meeting the goal—for example, the immediate pleasure of an ice-cream sundae versus the longer-term reward of looking great at the beach. So, experts advise that individuals need to be creative and "weave a powerful web of cues, cognitive supports, and internal and external consequences to win the tug-of-war with status-quo payoffs."[51] Also, rewards tend to be more effective than punishments, the negative side of consequences. Individuals can further reward themselves by seeking encouragement from supportive friends, co-workers, and relatives.

PERSONALITY DYNAMICS

Personality
Stable physical and mental characteristics responsible for a person's identity.

Individuals have their own way of thinking and acting, their own unique style or personality. **Personality** is the combination of stable physical and mental characteristics that give an individual his or her identity. These characteristics or traits—including how one looks, thinks, acts, and feels—are the product of interacting genetic and environmental influences.[52]

The Big Five Personality Dimensions

Long and confusing lists of personality dimensions have been distilled in recent years to the Big Five: extraversion, agreeableness, conscientiousness, emotional stability, and openness to experience, described in Table 3–1.[53] Standardized personality tests determine how positively or negatively a person scores on each of the Big Five. A negative score indicates the opposite dimension, so a person scoring negatively on extraversion would be considered introverted, prone to shy and withdrawn behavior.[54] A negative score on emotional stability would signal a person who is nervous, tense, angry, and worried. A person's scores on the Big Five reveal a unique personality profile.

Questions have been raised about how well personality models such as the Big Five apply to different cultures. Is the Big Five model ethnocentric? So far, the evidence from

TABLE 3–1 The Big Five Personality Dimensions

Source: Adapted from M R Barrick and M K Mount, "Autonomy as a Moderator of the Relationships between the Big Five Personality Dimensions and Job Performance," *Journal of Applied Psychology,* February 1993, pp 111–18.

Personality Dimension	Characteristics of a Person Scoring Positively on the Dimension
1. Extraversion	Outgoing, talkative, sociable, assertive
2. Agreeableness	Trusting, good-natured, cooperative, softhearted
3. Conscientiousness	Dependable, responsible, achievement oriented, persistent
4. Emotional stability	Relaxed, secure, unworried
5. Openness to experience	Intellectual, imaginative, curious, broad-minded

cross-cultural research suggests that it is not. The Big Five personality structure held up very well in a study of women and men from Russia, Canada, Hong Kong, Poland, Germany, and Finland.[55] However, this does *not* mean there is a global personality profile. A recent study of 27,965 adults from 36 different cultures showed geographic clustering of the Big Five dimensions. For example, the European and American cultures studied showed greater levels of extraversion and openness to experience than the Asian and African cultures. The European and American subjects as a group had lower scores in agreeableness.[56]

Personality and Job Performance

Applying personality theory to organizational behavior, researchers have looked for a connection between the Big Five personality dimensions and job performance. If some Big Five personality dimensions are related to good job performance, that information would be helpful for selecting, training, and appraising employees. According to an analysis of 117 studies involving 23,994 subjects from many professions, *conscientiousness* had the strongest positive correlation with job performance and training performance.[57]

Extraversion also was associated with success for managers and salespeople. Across all professions, extraversion was a stronger predictor of job performance than agreeableness. The researchers concluded, "It appears that being courteous, trusting, straightforward, and softhearted has a smaller impact on job performance than being talkative, active, and assertive."[58] Not surprisingly, in a recent study, a strong link between conscientiousness and performance was found among those who had polished social skills.[59] As an added bonus for extraverts, a recent positive-psychology study led to the conclusion that people who merely "act extraverted" can "get a happiness boost."[60]

The Proactive Personality

Proactive personality
Action-oriented person who shows initiative and perseveres to change things.

Building on the idea that someone who scores high on conscientiousness is probably a good worker, Thomas S Bateman and J Michael Crant formulated the concept of the proactive personality. They characterize the **proactive personality** as "someone who is relatively unconstrained by situational forces and who effects environmental change. Proactive people identify opportunities and act on them, show initiative, take action, and persevere until meaningful change occurs."[61] In short, people with proactive personalities are hardwired to change the status quo. In a review of relevant studies, Crant found the proactive personality to be positively associated with individual, team, and organizational success.[62]

Successful entrepreneurs exemplify the proactive personality in their willingness to tackle the creative and hard work of starting a business. For example, when Jeff Gallino and Cliff LaCoursiere worked at a telecommunications equipment company called ThinkEngine Networks, customers frequently asked them if ThinkEngine would provide them with a way to sort and analyze the content of calls they had recorded. Gallino and LaCoursiere proposed this idea to the company, but management was unenthusiastic. The two men responded by developing their own business plan and the software to do the job. Thanks to their perseverance, their product, named CallMiner, is now used in business call centers and government agencies.[63] For their own business or an employer, individuals with proactive personalities truly are valuable *human capital,* a concept discussed in Chapter 1.

No "Ideal" Employee

Although the Big Five personality dimensions of conscientiousness and extraversion and the proactive personality are generally desirable in the workplace, they are not panaceas. Given the complexity of today's work environments, the diversity of today's workforce, and recent research evidence,[64] the search for an ideal employee personality profile is futile. Just as one shoe does not fit all people, one personality profile does not fit all job situations. Good management involves taking the time to get to know each employee's *unique combination* of personality traits, abilities, and potential and then creating a productive and satisfying person-job fit.

Locus of Control: Self or Environment?

Individuals vary in terms of how much personal responsibility they take for their behavior and its consequences. To explain these differences, Julian Rotter, a personality researcher, identified a dimension of personality he labeled *locus of control*. He proposed that people tend to attribute the causes of their behavior primarily to either themselves or environmental factors.[65] This personality trait produces distinctly different behavior patterns.

Internal locus of control

Attributing outcomes to one's own actions.

People who believe they control the events and consequences that affect their lives are said to possess an **internal locus of control.** This kind of person tends to attribute positive outcomes, such as getting a passing grade on an exam, to her or his own abilities. Similarly, an "internal" tends to blame negative events, such as failing an exam, on personal shortcomings—not studying hard enough, perhaps. Many entrepreneurs eventually succeed because their *internal* locus of control helps them overcome setbacks and disappointments. They see themselves as masters of their own fate, not as simply lucky.

External locus of control

Attributing outcomes to circumstances beyond one's control.

On the other side of this personality dimension are those who believe their performance is the product of circumstances beyond their immediate control. These individuals, said to possess an **external locus of control,** tend to attribute outcomes to environmental causes, such as luck or fate. Unlike someone with an internal locus of control, an "external" would attribute passing an exam to something external (an easy test or a good day) and attribute a failing grade to an unfair test or problems at home.

Researchers have found important behavioral differences between internals and externals. Internals display greater work motivation and have stronger expectations that effort leads to performance. Internals exhibit higher performance on tasks involving learning or problem solving, when performance leads to valued rewards. Also, there is a stronger relationship between job satisfaction and performance for internals than for externals, and

SELF-ASSESSMENT
Assessing Your Empathy Skills

Go online at [www.mhhe.com/obcore] to explore your ability to empathize with other people in your daily actions. Empathy is an important skill in today's team-work environment.

- Based on the assessment of your strengths, opportunities, and weaknesses, how do you compare with your classmates?
- How can you improve your weaknesses?

internals obtain higher salaries and greater salary increases than externals. Externals tend to be more anxious than internals.[66]

Since internals tend to believe they control the work environment through their behavior, they try to exert control over the work setting by influencing work procedures, working conditions, task assignments, or relationships with peers and supervisors. As a result, internals may resist a manager's attempts to closely supervise their work, so management may want to place internals in jobs requiring high initiative and low compliance. Externals might be more amenable to highly structured jobs requiring greater compliance. Direct participation also can bolster externals' attitudes and performance. In a field study of 85 computer system users in various organizations, externals who had been significantly involved in designing their organization's computer information system had more favorable attitudes toward the system than their external-locus co-workers who had not participated.[67]

Locus of control also has implications for reward systems. Given that internals have a greater belief that their effort leads to performance, internals likely would prefer and respond more productively to incentives such as merit pay or sales commissions.[68]

Attitudes

Hardly a day goes by without the popular media reporting the results of another attitude survey. What do we think about candidate X, the war on drugs, or the environment? In the workplace, managers also conduct attitude surveys to monitor job and pay satisfaction. All this attention to attitudes is based on the assumption that attitudes somehow influence behavior, whether it involves voting for someone, working hard, or quitting a job.

Attitude
Learned predisposition toward a given object.

An **attitude** is "a learned predisposition to respond in a consistently favorable or unfavorable manner with respect to a given object."[69] Attitudes affect behavior at a different level than do values. Whereas values represent global beliefs that influence behavior across *all* situations, attitudes relate only to behavior directed toward *specific* objects, persons, or situations. Values and attitudes generally are in harmony, but not always. For instance, a manager who strongly values helpful behavior may have a negative attitude toward helping an unethical coworker.

How stable are attitudes? In a landmark study, researchers found the *job* attitudes of 5,000 middle-aged male employees to be very stable over a five-year period. Positive job attitudes remained positive; negative ones remained negative. Even those who changed jobs or occupations tended to maintain their prior job attitudes.[70] But according to more recent research, that study, because it sampled only middle-aged subjects, may have overstated the stability of attitudes. When researchers asked what happens to attitudes over the entire span of adulthood, they found that *general* attitudes were more susceptible to change during early and late adulthood than during middle adulthood. In middle age, attitudes were relatively stable because of greater personal certainty, a perceived abundance of knowledge, and a need for strong attitudes. Thus, elderly people, along with young adults, can and do change their general attitudes because they are more open and less self-assured.[71]

Intelligence and Cognitive Abilities

Intelligence
Capacity for constructive thinking, reasoning, problem solving.

Although experts do not agree on a specific definition, **intelligence** represents an individual's capacity for constructive thinking, reasoning, and problem solving.[72] Intelligence once was believed to be an innate capacity, passed genetically from one generation to the next. But research has shown that intelligence (like personality) is a function of environmental influences.[73] More recently, organic factors have been added to the formula as mounting evidence linked alcohol and drug abuse by pregnant women with intellectual development problems in their children.[74]

Researchers have produced interesting findings about abilities and intelligence. A unique five-year study documented people's tendency to "gravitate into jobs commensurate with their abilities."[75] This prompts a vision of the labor market acting as a giant sorting machine, with employees tumbling into various ability bins. Meanwhile, average intelligence among those in developed countries has steadily and significantly risen over the last 70 years. Why? At an American Psychological Association conference, experts speculated the credit might go to "some combination of better schooling, improved socioeconomic status, healthier nutrition, and a more technologically complex society."[76]

Human intelligence has been studied mainly through the empirical approach. By examining the relationships between measures of mental abilities and behavior, researchers have statistically isolated major components of intelligence. Using this procedure, pioneering psychologist Charles Spearman proposed in 1927 that all cognitive performance is determined by two types of abilities: a general mental ability needed for *all* cognitive tasks and abilities unique to the task at hand. For example, an individual's ability to complete crossword puzzles is a function of his or her broad mental abilities as well as the specific ability to perceive patterns in partially completed words.

According to a recent comprehensive research review, standard intelligence (IQ) tests do a good job of predicting both academic achievement and job performance.[77] This contradicts the popular notion that different cognitive abilities are needed for school and work. Plainly stated, "smarts" are "smarts."

ORGANIZATIONAL BEHAVIOR GETS EMOTIONAL

In the ideal world of management theory, employees pursue organizational goals logically and rationally. Emotional behavior seldom is factored into the equation. Yet day-to-day organizational life shows how prevalent and powerful emotions can be. Anger and jealousy, both potent emotions, often push aside logic and rationality in the workplace. Managers use fear and other emotions to motivate and intimidate. Consider Selina Y Lo, the head of marketing at Alteon WebSystems in San Jose, California, who is reportedly known as a tough manager with a quick temper. An Alteon software engineer, John Taylor, told a *BusinessWeek* reporter about a meeting at which Lo "sprang up yelling from her chair, banged her fist on the table, and shoved a finger in his face after Taylor said he couldn't add a feature she had asked for."[78] Lo won through intimidation. A combination of curiosity and fear is said to drive Barry Diller, one of the media world's legendary dealmakers. Says Diller: "I and my friends succeeded because we were scared to death of failing."[79] These corporate leaders would not have achieved what they have without the ability to be logical and rational decision makers *and* be emotionally charged. Too much emotion, however, could have spelled career and organizational disaster.

Positive and Negative Emotions

Emotions
Complex human reactions to personal achievements and setbacks that may be felt and displayed.

Richard S Lazarus, an authority on the subject, defines **emotions** as "complex, patterned, organismic reactions to how we think we are doing in our lifelong efforts to survive and flourish and to achieve what we wish for ourselves."[80] The word *organismic* is appropriate because emotions involve the whole person—biological, psychological, and social. Importantly, psychologists distinguish between *felt* and *displayed* emotions.[81] For example, you might feel angry (felt emotion) at a rude co-worker but refrain from making a nasty remark in return (displayed emotion). Emotions play roles in both causing and adapting to stress and its associated biological and psychological problems. The destructive effect of emotional behavior on social relationships is all too obvious.

Lazarus's definition of emotions centers on a person's goals. So his distinction between positive and negative emotions is goal oriented. Some emotions—anger, fright or anxiety, guilt or shame, sadness, envy or jealousy, and disgust—are triggered by frustration and failure when pursuing one's goals. Lazarus calls these *negative* emotions because they are goal incongruent—that is, inconsistent with goals. For example, you are likely to experience negative emotions if you fail the final exam in a required course, which is incongruent with your goal of graduating on time. In contrast, *positive* emotions—happiness or joy, pride, love or affection, and relief—are congruent (consistent) with an important lifetime goal. You probably experience positive emotions whenever you pass a final exam with an A.

Moods Are Contagious

Have you ever had someone's bad mood sour your mood? That person could have been a parent, supervisor, co-worker, friend, or someone serving you in a store or restaurant. Researchers call this effect *emotional contagion*. Like catching a cold, we can catch another person's good or bad mood or displayed emotions. According to a recent study of 131 bank tellers and 220 exit interviews with their customers, tellers who expressed positive emotions tended to have more satisfied customers.[82] Two field studies of nurses and accountants found a strong link between the work group's collective mood and the individual's mood.[83] Both foul moods and good moods turned out to be contagious. Perhaps more managers should follow the lead of Lorin Maazel, director of the New York Philharmonic Orchestra: "I have learned to come to rehearsal fresh, energetic, projecting enthusiasm and go-go-go. It's got to be irresistible. If I don't think I'm up to it, I take a cold shower. That's my job—to energize people. . . . Music making without emotion and passion is nothing."[84]

Emotional Labor

Although they lacked a catchy label or a body of sophisticated research, generations of managers have known about the power of emotional contagion in the marketplace. They tell their employees, "Smile! Look happy for the customers." But what if some employees are having a rotten day? What if they have to mask their true feelings and emotions? Researchers have begun studying the dynamics of what they call *emotional labor.* So far, their research suggests that emotional labor can be taxing because of the effort required to identify and suppress emotions that are negative or inappropriate to the situation.[85] People become exhausted unless they have a healthy outlet for those emotions.

A pair of laboratory studies of U.S. college students found no gender difference in *felt* emotions. But the women were more emotionally *expressive* than the men.[86] This stream of research on emotional labor has major practical implications for productivity and job satisfaction, as well as for workplace anger, aggression, and violence. Clearly, managers need to be attuned to (and responsive to) the emotional states and needs of their people. This requires emotional intelligence.

TABLE 3–2   **Developing Emotional Intelligence**

Source: Reprinted by permission of Harvard Business School Press. D Goleman, R Boyatzis, and A McKee, *Primal Leadership: Realizing the Power of Emotional Intelligence* (Boston: Harvard Business School Press, 2002), p 39. Copyright © 2002 by Daniel Goleman; all rights reserved.

Personal Competence		Social Competence	
Self-Awareness		**Social Awareness**	
Emotional self-awareness	Reading one's own emotions and recognizing their impact; using "gut sense" to guide decisions	Empathy	Sensing others' emotions, understanding their perspective, and taking active interest in their concerns
Accurate self-assessment	Knowing one's strengths and limits	Organizational awareness	Reading the currents, decision networks, and politics at the organizational level
Self-confidence	A sound sense of one's self-worth and capabilities	Service	Recognizing and meeting follower, client, or customer needs
Self-Management		**Relationship Management**	
Emotional self-control	Keeping disruptive emotions and impulses under control	Inspirational leadership	Guiding and motivating with a compelling vision
Transparency	Displaying honesty and integrity; trustworthiness	Influence	Wielding a range of tactics for persuasion
Adaptability	Flexibility in adapting to changing situations or overcoming obstacles	Developing others	Bolstering others' abilities through feedback and guidance
Achievement	The drive to improve performance to meet inner standards of excellence	Change catalyst	Initiating, managing, and leading in a new direction
Initiative	Readiness to act and seize opportunities	Conflict management	Resolving disagreements
Optimism	Seeing the upside in events	Building bonds	Cultivating and maintaining a web of relationships
		Teamwork and collaboration	Cooperation and team building

Emotional Intelligence

In 1995, Daniel Goleman, a psychologist turned journalist, created a stir in education and management circles with the publication of his book *Emotional Intelligence,* which brought an obscure topic among positive psychologists into the mainstream. According to Goleman, traditional models of intelligence (IQ) are too narrow, failing to consider interpersonal competence. Goleman's broader agenda includes "abilities such as being able to motivate oneself and persist in the face of frustrations; to control impulse and delay gratification; to regulate one's moods and keep distress from swamping the ability to think; to empathize and to hope."[87] Thus, **emotional intelligence** is the ability to manage oneself and one's relationships in mature and constructive ways. It has four key components: self-awareness, self-management, social awareness, and relationship management.[88] The first two constitute *personal competence;* the second two feed into *social competence* (see Table 3–2). These emotional intelligence skills need to be well polished in today's pressure-packed workplaces.

Emotional intelligence
Ability to manage oneself and interact with others in mature and constructive ways.

Self-assessment instruments that supposedly measure emotional intelligence have appeared in the popular management literature, featuring questions such as "I believe I can stay on top of tough situations,"[89] and "I am able to admit my own mistakes."[90] However, recent research casts doubt on the reliability and validity of such instruments.[91] Even Goleman concedes, "It's very tough to measure our own emotional intelligence, because most of us don't have a very clear sense of how we come across to other people."[92] Honest feedback from others is necessary. Still, the area of emotional intelligence is useful because, unlike IQ, social problem solving and the ability to control one's emotions can be taught and learned. But scores on emotional intelligence tests should *not* be used for making hiring and promotion decisions until valid measuring tools are developed.

Chapter **Four**

Motivation in Theory: What Makes Employees Try Harder

Learning Objectives

After reading the material in this chapter, you should be able to:

- Describe how individuals may be motivated by their needs.
- Discuss how individuals may be motivated by their perceptions of equity and justice.
- Summarize how people's motivation can be influenced by their attitudes toward outcomes and their belief they can influence outcomes.
- Explain how goal setting motivates individuals.
- Review ways to design jobs so as to influence employee motivation.

What makes people want to excel or to do their very best at completing tasks? How is it that some people can delay gratifying their needs while working long and hard to accomplish a goal such as obtaining a medical degree or starting a company? Part of the answer is related to an individual's level of motivation. Motivation is the fuel that drives sustained effort at accomplishing goal-driven behavior. Because of the link between motivation and performance, organizations want to know more about what keeps their employees motivated and satisfied. To help you understand how you can motivate yourself and others, this chapter provides an overview of the key motivation theories.

Motivating employees to do their best is one of managers' most difficult and important duties, especially in today's organizations, which are focused on accomplishing more with fewer but empowered workers. In terms of organizational behavior, **motivation** represents "those psychological processes that cause the arousal, direction, and persistence of voluntary actions that are goal directed."[1] To explain these psychological processes, researchers have proposed two categories of motivation theories: **Content theories of motivation** identify internal factors such as instincts,

Motivation
Psychological processes that arouse and direct goal-directed behavior.

Content theories of motivation
Identify internal factors influencing motivation.

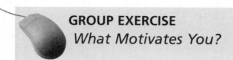

needs, satisfaction, and job characteristics that energize employee motivation. **Process theories of motivation** explain the process by which internal factors and cognitions influence a person's motivation.[2] This chapter describes both sets of theories, identifies ways to design jobs that motivate employees, and concludes with recommendations for applying the theories.

CONTENT THEORIES OF MOTIVATION

Process theories of motivation
Identify the process by which internal factors and cognitions influence motivation.

Most content theories of motivation revolve around the notion that motivation is influenced by an employee's **needs**—physiological or psychological deficiencies that arouse behavior. Needs can be strong or weak and are influenced by environmental factors, so they vary over time and place. Need theories of motivation indicate that unmet needs motivate people to satisfy these needs, but satisfied needs do not motivate.

Maslow's Need Hierarchy Theory

Needs
Physiological or psychological deficiencies that arouse behavior.

In 1943 psychologist Abraham Maslow published his now-famous **need hierarchy theory** of motivation. Although the theory was based on his clinical observation of a few neurotic individuals, it has subsequently been used to explain the entire spectrum of human behavior. Maslow proposed that motivation is a function of five basic needs:

Need hierarchy theory
Five basic needs—physiological, safety, love, esteem, and self-actualization—influence behavior.

1. *Physiological.* Having enough food, air, and water to survive.
2. *Safety.* Being safe from physical and psychological harm.
3. *Love.* Giving and receiving love, including affection and belonging.
4. *Esteem.* Reputation, prestige, and recognition from others, as well as self-confidence and strength.
5. *Self-actualization.* Self-fulfillment; becoming the best that one is capable of becoming.

Maslow arranged these needs in the hierarchy shown in Figure 4–1 to signify that human needs emerge in a predictable stair-step fashion. Accordingly, when one's physiological needs are relatively satisfied, one's safety needs emerge, and so on up the need hierarchy, one step at a time. Satisfying a need activates the next-higher need, continuing until the need for self-actualization is activated.[3]

Although research does not clearly support this theory, an important implication is that a satisfied need may lose its motivational potential. So managers should motivate employees by devising programs or practices aimed at satisfying emerging or unmet needs. IndyMac Bank applies this idea by using results from employee surveys to explore reasons for employee turnover. The organization then developed programs aimed at satisfying employees' needs, even targeting employees according to their functions in the bank, tenure on the job, and performance ranking.[4]

FIGURE 4–1
Maslow's Need
Hierarchy

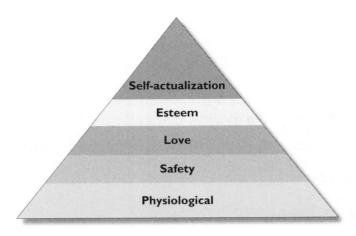

(handwritten note: same just kind of condensed)

Alderfer's ERG Theory

Clayton Alderfer developed an alternative theory of human needs in the late 1960s. Alderfer's theory differs from Maslow's in three major respects. First, behavior is explained by a smaller set of core needs:

- *Existence needs.* Desire for physiological and materialistic well-being.
- *Relatedness needs.* Desire to have meaningful relationships with significant others.
- *Growth needs.* Desire to grow as a human and use one's abilities to their fullest.

ERG theory
Three basic needs—existence, relatedness, and growth—influence behavior.

The first letters of these needs (*E, R, G*) give the name to the **ERG theory.** The second difference from Maslow's theory is that the ERG theory does not assume needs are related in a hierarchy but that more than one need may be activated at a time. Finally, ERG theory says frustration of higher-order needs can influence the desire for lower-order needs.[5] For example, if employees are dissatisfied with the quality of relationships with their colleagues, they may demand higher pay or better benefits (existence needs). Research has provided mixed support for some of the theory's key propositions.[6]

ERG theory has managerial implications. First, employees may be motivated to pursue lower-level needs when they are frustrated with a higher-order need. Also, ERG theory is consistent with the finding that individual and cultural differences influence our need states.[7] People are motivated by different needs at different times, so managers should customize reward and recognition programs to meet varying needs. Marc Albin, CEO of a California staffing firm, approaches the problem directly by sending newly hired employees an e-mail at the end of their orientation asking how they prefer to be recognized for accomplishments—for their cheerful attitude, quality or quantity of their work, or their individual or team achievements. So far, Albin reports, "No one has ever said, 'Just recognize me for anything I do well.'"[8]

McClelland's Need Theory

David McClelland, a well-known psychologist, has been studying the relationship between needs and behavior since the late 1940s. He is most recognized for his research on the need for achievement, but he also investigated the needs for affiliation and power.

Need for achievement
Desire to accomplish something difficult.

Need for affiliation
Desire to spend time in social relationships and activities.

Need for power
Desire to influence, coach, teach, or encourage others to achieve.

The **need for achievement** encompasses the desire to excel, overcome obstacles, accomplish difficult tasks, and manipulate or organize objects, human beings, or ideas independently and rapidly.[9] Achievement-oriented people prefer to work on moderately difficult tasks, prefer situations in which success depends on their own efforts, and desire more feedback on their successes and failures than do people who score low on this need. Entrepreneurs have tended to score high on need for achievement.[10]

People with a high **need for affiliation** prefer to spend more time maintaining social relationships, are apt to join groups, and want to be loved. Individuals high in this need are not the most effective managers or leaders because they have a hard time making difficult decisions without worrying about being disliked.[11]

The **need for power** reflects an individual's desire to influence, teach, coach, or encourage others to achieve. People with a high need for power like to work, and they care about discipline and self-respect. This need has a positive and a negative side (see Chapter 10 on influence, power, and politics). The negative face of power has an "If I win, you lose" mentality. The positive orientation to power focuses on accomplishing group goals and helping employees feel competent. Because effective managers positively influence others, McClelland says top managers should have a high need for power coupled with a low need for affiliation, and he doubts that individuals with high achievement motivation are the best candidates for top management. Several studies support those propositions.[12]

Adults can be trained to increase their achievement motivation, so organizations should consider giving employees achievement training.[13] In addition, achievement, affiliation, and power needs can be considered during the selection process, for better placement. For example, a study found that people with a high need for achievement were more attracted to companies with a pay-for-performance environment than were those with a low achievement motivation.[14] Finally, managers should create challenging assignments or goals because the need for achievement is positively correlated with goal commitment, which influences performance.[15] Adding autonomy and employee empowerment to the mix lets managers capitalize on the characteristics of high achievers.

Herzberg's Motivator-Hygiene Theory

Motivators
Job characteristics associated with job satisfaction.

Hygiene factors
Job characteristics associated with job dissatisfaction.

Frederick Herzberg's theory of motivation is based on a landmark study in which he interviewed 203 accountants and engineers to identify the factors responsible for job satisfaction and dissatisfaction.[16] Herzberg found distinct clusters of factors associated with job satisfaction and dissatisfaction. Job satisfaction was more often associated with achievement, recognition, characteristics of the work, responsibility, and advancement—all related to the *content* of the task. Herzberg labeled these factors **motivators** because each was related to strong effort and good performance. He hypothesized that motivators cause a person to move from a state of no satisfaction to satisfaction, so managers can motivate individuals by incorporating motivators into their jobs.[17]

Herzberg found job *dissatisfaction* to be associated mainly with factors in the work *context* or environment. Specifically, employees expressing job dissatisfaction mentioned company policy and administration, technical supervision, salary, interpersonal relations with their supervisor, and working conditions. Herzberg labeled this cluster of factors **hygiene factors** and proposed that they are not motivational. At best, an individual experiences no job dissatisfaction when he or she has no grievances about hygiene factors. But when poor hygiene factors lead to job dissatisfaction, employees like Katrina Gill—who earned $9.32 an hour to carry out the grueling, even dangerous work of caring for occasionally violent nursing home patients—tend to quit.[18]

In Herzberg's motivator-hygiene theory, satisfaction and dissatisfaction are not opposites. Instead, the opposite of job satisfaction is considered "no job satisfaction," and the opposite of dissatisfaction is "no dissatisfaction."[19] In other words, there is a continuum from dissatisfaction to satisfaction, with a zero midpoint at which both are absent. Conceivably, an employee with good supervision, pay, and working conditions but a tedious and unchallenging task offering little chance of advancement would be at this midpoint, lacking both satisfaction and dissatisfaction.

Herzberg's theory has generated much research and controversy.[20] Research does not support the two-factor aspect of his theory or the proposition that hygiene factors are unrelated to job satisfaction. For example, in a recent national survey of 600 employees, the five most important job satisfaction factors were benefits, compensation/pay, feeling safe in the work environment, job security, and flexibility to balance work/life issues.[21] However, Herzberg correctly concluded that people are motivated when their needs for achievement, recognition, stimulating work, and advancement are satisfied.

PROCESS THEORIES OF MOTIVATION

In contrast to the preceding theories, which look for internal factors influencing motivation, the process theories go a step further by identifying the process through which various internal factors influence motivation. These models also are cognitive, meaning they are based on the premise that motivation is a function of individuals' perceptions, thoughts, and beliefs.

Equity Theory

Equity theory
Holds that motivation is a function of fairness in social exchanges.

Psychologist J Stacy Adams's **equity theory** is a model of motivation that explains how people strive for fairness and justice in social exchanges or give-and-take relationships. It explains how an individual's motivation to behave in a certain way is fueled by feelings of inequity or a lack of justice. Adams pioneered application of the equity principle to the workplace, saying employees perceive equity and inequity in terms of the individual–organization exchange relationship. This exchange involves two primary components, *inputs* and *outcomes*. An employee's inputs, for which he or she expects a just return, include education/training, skills, creativity, seniority, age, personality traits, effort expended, and personal appearance. On the outcome side of the exchange, the organization provides pay, bonuses, fringe benefits, and so on.

Negative and Positive Inequity

On the job, feelings of inequity arise from a person's evaluation of whether he or she receives adequate rewards to compensate for the inputs contributed. People perform these evaluations by comparing the perceived fairness of their employment exchange with that of relevant others. This comparative process, which is based on an equity norm, was found across countries.[22] People tend to compare themselves with other individuals with whom they have close interpersonal relationships (for example, friends) or with similar others, such as persons who perform the same job or have the same gender or education level, and not with persons who are dissimilar.[23]

FIGURE 4–2   Negative and Positive Inequity

A. An Equitable Situation

B. Negative Inequity

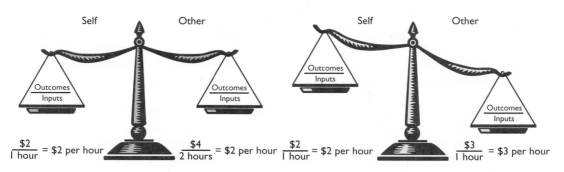

C. Positive Inequity

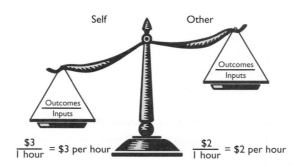

Negative inequity
Comparison in which another person receives greater outcomes for similar inputs.

Positive inequity
Comparison in which another person receives lesser outcomes for similar inputs.

Equity sensitivity
An individual's tolerance for negative and positive equity.

Three possible equity relationships, illustrated with examples in Figure 4–2, are equity, negative inequity, and positive inequity. Assume the two people whose equity relationships are shown in Figure 4–2 have equivalent backgrounds (equal education, seniority, and so forth) and perform identical tasks. Equity exists for an individual when his or her ratio of perceived outcomes to inputs equals the ratio of outcomes to inputs for a relevant co-worker (example A in the figure). Because equity is assessed by comparing *ratios* of outcomes to inputs, greater rewards will not necessarily be interpreted as inequity. Equity may exist if the other person's greater outcomes are due to his or her greater inputs. However, if the comparison person enjoys greater outcomes for similar inputs, **negative inequity** will be perceived (example B). Conversely, if a person has a greater outcome-to-input ratio than the relevant co-worker, as in example C, the person will experience **positive inequity.**

Dynamics of Perceived Inequity

People have varying sensitivities to perceived equity. **Equity sensitivity** reflects an individual's "different preferences for, tolerances for, and reactions to the level of equity associated with any given situation."[24] People's equity sensitivity places them along a continuum. At one extreme are *benevolents,* who have a high tolerance for negative inequity and are altruistic in that they prefer their own outcome/input ratio to be lower than ratios for comparison others. At the other extreme are *entitleds,* who have no tolerance for negative inequity and even expect to obtain greater output/input ratios than comparison others. In between are *sensitives,* who adhere to a strict norm of reciprocity and are quickly motivated to resolve both negative and positive inequity.[25]

People change equity ratios by attempting to alter their outcomes or adjust their inputs. To resolve negative inequity, an employee might ask for a raise or promotion (raising outputs) or exert less effort (reducing inputs). In resolving positive inequity, few individuals have gone as far as Susan Lyne, who led Martha Stewart Living Omnimedia through the difficult years when the company's founder was in prison. After the company made a successful comeback, Lyne received a cash bonus of $625,000. She asked the board of directors to give $200,000 of that amount to a bonus pool for employees, noting that they had shared the burden of the turnaround, earning smaller bonuses during harder times.[26] Besides restoring equity behaviorally, a person can alter equity ratios cognitively by distorting perceptions of the outcomes and inputs. For example, the employee experiencing negative inequity might conclude that the better-paid co-worker actually has more experience or works harder.

Organizational Justice

Distributive justice
The perceived fairness of how resources and rewards are distributed.

Procedural justice
The perceived fairness of the process and procedures used to make allocation decisions.

Interactional justice
Extent to which people feel fairly treated when procedures are implemented.

Beginning in the late 1970s, researchers began to expand the role of equity theory in explaining employee attitudes and behavior, investigating what became known as *organizational justice.* Organizational justice—the extent to which people perceive they are treated fairly at work—may be distributive, procedural, and interactional.[27] **Distributive justice** reflects the perceived fairness of how resources and rewards are distributed or allocated. **Procedural justice** is the perceived fairness of the process and procedures used to make allocation decisions. Research shows that organizations enhance positive perceptions of distributive and procedural justice by giving employees a voice in decisions that affect them—in other words, when the employees can present relevant information about the decision to others. **Interactional justice** relates to the "quality of the interpersonal treatment people receive when procedures are implemented."[28] It does not pertain to the outcomes or procedures of making a decision but instead to the extent to which people feel they are treated fairly when decisions are implemented. For managers, this requires communicating truthfully and treating employees with courtesy and respect.

In two recent meta-analyses of more than 190 studies of organizational justice, job performance was positively associated with both distributive and procedural justice; the latter had a stronger effect.[29] In addition, all three components of justice were positively correlated with positive employee work attitudes such as job satisfaction. Finally, justice perceptions were negatively related to negative emotions.[30] These results reinforce the management philosophy of Joe Lee, CEO of Darden Restaurants: "At the core of my thoughts [about management] is to operate with integrity and fairness. Treat people fairly and give them an environment that they can work in and trust. If you do that, you then can take care of your business objectives and your employee's needs and everybody can win."[31]

Practical Lessons from Equity Theory

Among its practical implications, equity theory offers yet another explanation of how beliefs and attitudes affect job performance. It suggests that managing job behavior requires an understanding of employees' cognitive processes. If a person's ideas of fairness and justice have been offended, he or she will be powerfully motivated to correct the situation. Managers can monitor equity and justice perceptions through informal conversations, interviews, and attitude surveys. Researchers have developed and validated many surveys that can be used for this purpose. In addition, research reveals that people are just as concerned with fairness in group settings as they are with their own personal interests.[32]

Managers should take note of employees' perceptions of what is fair and equitable. No matter how fair management thinks the organization's policies, procedures, and rewards system are, each employee's *perception* of their equity is what counts. According to a survey called the 2000 Global Employee Relationship Report, 25% of the employees surveyed perceived that their employer treated employees unfairly.[33] Managers can increase their odds of being in the favored 75% by basing hiring and promotion decisions on merit-based, job-related information and by explaining their decisions.

Managers should let employees participate in decisions about important work outcomes, because employees experience procedural justice when they have a voice in decisions.[34] For example, employees who can actively participate in their performance appraisals were more satisfied with their appraisals and resulting outcomes.[35] Employees also should have a chance to appeal decisions that affect their welfare. Being able to appeal a decision fosters perceptions of distributive and procedural justice.

Finally, managers need to pay attention to the organization's climate for justice, which was found to significantly influence employees' organizational commitment and job satisfaction.[36] A climate of justice can influence the type of customer service provided by employees. In turn, this level of service influences customers' perceptions of "fair service" and their subsequent loyalty and satisfaction.[37]

Expectancy Theory

Expectancy theory
Holds that people are motivated to behave in ways that produce valued outcomes.

According to **expectancy theory,** people are motivated to behave in ways that produce desired combinations of expected outcomes. Expectancy theory can be used to predict motivation and behavior in situations requiring a choice of alternatives. For instance, it can predict whether a person will quit or stay on the job, will exert substantial or minimal effort, and will major in management, finance, psychology, or communication.

Victor Vroom formulated a mathematical model of expectancy in 1964.[38] Motivation, according to Vroom, boils down to the decision of how much effort to exert in a specific task situation. This choice is based on a two-stage sequence of expectations: first, that a certain level of effort will produce the intended performance goal, and second, that accomplishing the performance goal will lead to various outcomes. Individuals also are motivated to the extent they value the outcomes to be received.

Expectancy

Expectancy
Belief that effort leads to a specific level of performance.

An **expectancy,** in Vroom's terminology, represents an individual's belief that a particular degree of effort will be followed by a particular level of performance. In other words, it is an effort → performance expectation. Expectancies take the form of subjective probabilities, statistics that range from 0 (no chance) to 1 (certainty). If you have never studied accounting, your expectancy for successfully preparing a corporation's financial statements is probably at or near 0. If you have been reading books for years, your expectancy for being able to read this text is probably at or near 1. Influences on an employee's expectancy perceptions include self-esteem, self-efficacy, previous success at the task, help received from a supervisor and other employees, information necessary to complete the task, and suitable materials and equipment.[39]

Instrumentality

Instrumentality
A performance → outcome perception.

An **instrumentality** is a performance → outcome perception. It represents a person's belief that a particular outcome is contingent on accomplishing a specific level of performance. Thus, performance is instrumental when it leads to something else—for example, passing exams is instrumental to graduating from college.

Instrumentalities range from −1.0 to +1.0. An instrumentality of +1.0 indicates that attainment of a particular outcome is totally dependent on task performance. If a supervisor says, "Take the rest of the day off when you finish that report," the time off depends on completing the report. An instrumentality of 0 indicates there is no relationship between performance and outcome. At most companies, high performance has no relationship to the number of vacation days granted. An instrumentality of −1.0 means the outcome will not result from high performance or will result from failure to perform. Entertaining co-workers in the hallway for hours will probably not result in a promotion; in fact, it may make the supervisor less inclined to promote the amateur comedian.

Valence

Valence
The value of a reward or outcome.

As Vroom used the term, **valence** refers to the positive or negative value people place on outcomes. Valence mirrors our personal preferences.[40] Most employees have a positive valence for receiving additional money and a negative valence for layoffs. In Vroom's expectancy model, *outcomes* are different consequences that are contingent on performance, such as pay or recognition. An outcome's valence depends on an individual's needs and can be measured with scales ranging from a negative value to a positive value. For example, a scale measuring an individual's valence toward more recognition ranges from −2 (very undesirable) to 0 (neutral) to +2 (very desirable).

Expectancy Theory in Action

Vroom's expectancy model can be used to analyze real-life motivation programs. Consider the performance problem faced by Federal Express Corp. According to the company's chief executive, Frederick W Smith, delays were occurring when airplanes landed, and efforts to control performance were ineffective. Managers determined that the workers had an incentive to earn more hourly pay by working slowly. The solution was to establish standards for what employees must accomplish on their shift, after which they could leave with full pay. Smith said, "In the space of about 45 days, the place was way ahead of schedule. And I don't even think it was a conscious thing on [the employees'] part."[41] Vroom's model explains the change in terms of two valued outcomes: guaranteed pay plus the opportunity to leave early. The motivation to exert high effort exceeded the motivation to exert low effort. Apparently, the workers had high effort → performance expectancies and positive performance → outcome instrumentalities, and the valence for the outcomes was positive.

Many researchers have tested expectancy theory. A meta-analysis of 77 studies indicated that expectancy theory significantly predicted performance, effort, intentions, preferences, and choice.[42] In a summary of 16 studies, expectancy theory correctly predicted occupational or organizational choice 63.4% of the time—significantly better than chance predictions.[43] Nonetheless, expectancy theory has been criticized for being difficult to test, and the measures used to assess expectancy, instrumentality, and valence have questionable validity.[44]

In the final analysis, however, expectancy theory has important practical implications. Managers should determine what outcomes employees value, set and reward achievable performance standards, link desired outcomes to targeted performance levels, and monitor the reward system for inequities. They also can use training, coaching, and encouragement to help employees accomplish their goals. Organizations should reward people for desired performance, use a flexible reward system, communicate pay decisions, design challenging jobs, build teamwork with group rewards, reward managers for applying the theory's principles, and use questionnaires or interviews to monitor employee motivation.

Motivation through Goal Setting

Whatever the nature of their achievements, successful people tend to be goal-oriented. As a process model of motivation, goal-setting theory explains how the simple behavior of setting goals activates a powerful motivational process that leads to sustained high performance. This section explores the theory and research pertaining to goal setting, and Chapter 5 focuses on the practical application of goal setting.

Goal
What an individual is trying to accomplish.

Edwin Locke, an authority on goal setting, and his colleagues define a **goal** as "what an individual is trying to accomplish; it is the object or aim of an action."[45] The motivational effect of performance goals and goal-based reward plans has long been recognized. At the turn of the last century, Frederick Taylor attempted to scientifically establish how much work of a specified quality an individual should be assigned each day. More recently, goal setting has been promoted through the technique of *management by objectives (MBO)*, described in the next chapter.

How Goal Setting Works

At Wyeth, a maker of prescription drugs, the number of new drug compounds developed each year increased after the company started setting goals for how many compounds each scientist in its research and development group must produce.[46] Despite such examples and abundant goal-setting research and practice, goal-setting theories are scarce. But an instructive model formulated by Locke and his associates suggests that goal setting has four motivational mechanisms:

1. *Goals direct attention.* Goals direct a person's attention and effort toward relevant activities and away from activities that are irrelevant to achieving the goal.
2. *Goals regulate effort.* Besides influencing perception, goals influence actions. Generally, the level of effort expended is in proportion to the goal's difficulty.
3. *Goals increase persistence.* Here, persistence represents the effort expended on a task over an extended time period—a 100-meter run takes effort, and a marathon requires persistence as well. Persistent people see obstacles as challenges to overcome, not as reasons for failing. A difficult but important goal reminds the individual to persist.
4. *Goals foster the development and application of task strategies and action plans.* A person with a goal must figure out how to arrive at that goal. Goals encourage people to develop action plans specifying what they will do to achieve the goals.

Applications of Goal-Setting Research

The research into goal setting consistently supports its use as a motivational technique. Setting performance goals increases individual, group, and organizational performance. The effect crosses cultural and geographic lines; positive effects of goal setting have been found beyond the United States in Australia, Canada, the Caribbean, England, West Germany, and Japan.

Goal difficulty
The amount of effort required to meet a goal.

One important application involves **goal difficulty,** or the amount of effort required to meet a goal. Performance is higher when goals are difficult. In a meta-analysis spanning 4,000 people in 65 studies, goal difficulty was positively related to performance.[47]

Goal specificity
Quantifiability of a goal.

Another important factor is **goal specificity**—the quantifiability of a goal. For simple tasks, goals that are specific as well as difficult lead to higher performance. According to a meta-analysis of 125 studies, the association of specificity and performance was weaker for complex tasks.[48]

Feedback enhances the effect of specific, difficult goals. It lets people know whether they are headed toward their goals or off course. Combining goals with feedback provides information needed to adjust direction, effort, and strategies for goal accomplishment.[49]

Goals can be effective whether they are assigned, participative, or self-set.[50] In other words, managers can set goals for their employees, ask employees to participate in setting them with the manager, or let employees set their own goals. Managers should use a contingency approach, picking a method that seems best suited for the particular employee and situation.

Goal commitment
Amount of commitment to achieving a goal.

The outcome of goal setting is influenced by **goal commitment,** the extent to which an individual is personally committed to achieving a goal. Persistence tends to be greater with stronger goal commitment. Researchers believe difficult goals lead to higher performance only when employees are committed to the goals. When employees lack goal commitment, difficulty may actually reduce performance. A meta-analysis of 21 studies supported these predictions.[51] People also are more likely to commit to difficult goals when they have high self-efficacy about accomplishing their goals.[52]

MOTIVATING EMPLOYEES THROUGH JOB DESIGN

Job design
Changing the content and/or process of a specific job to increase job satisfaction and performance.

A manager may suspect that motivational problems stem from the type of work an employee performs or characteristics of the work environment. The solution may involve **job design** (also known as *job redesign*): "any set of activities that involve the alteration of specific jobs or interdependent systems of jobs with the intent of improving the quality of employee job experience and their on-the-job productivity."[53] A team of researchers integrated the methods of job design into an interdisciplinary framework containing four major approaches: mechanistic, motivational, biological, and perceptual-motor.[54] Each of these emphasizes different outcomes.[55]

Mechanistic Approach

The mechanistic approach draws from research in industrial engineering and scientific management and is most heavily influenced by the work of Frederick Taylor. Taylor, a mechanical engineer, developed the principles of scientific management while working at steel companies in Pennsylvania. He observed little cooperation between management and workers and saw that employees were underachieving by restricting their output. Taylor's interest in scientific management grew from his desire to improve this situation.

Scientific management
Using research and experimentation to find the most efficient way to perform a job.

Scientific management is "that kind of management which conducts a business or affairs by *standards* established by facts or truths gained through *systematic* observation, experiment, or reasoning."[56] Taylor's approach used research and experimentation to determine the most efficient way to perform jobs. The application of scientific management involves five steps:[57]

1. Use time and motion studies to develop standard methods for performing jobs.
2. Carefully select employees with the appropriate abilities.
3. Train workers to use the standard methods and procedures.
4. Support workers and reduce interruptions.
5. Provide incentives to reinforce performance.

Because jobs designed according to these principles are highly specialized and standardized, this approach targets efficiency, flexibility, and employee productivity.

Designing jobs according to the principles of scientific management has both positive and negative consequences. Employee efficiency and productivity increase. However, simplified, repetitive jobs also lead to job dissatisfaction, poor mental health, higher levels of stress, and low sense of accomplishment and personal growth.[58]

Motivational Approaches

The motivational approaches to job design seek to improve employees' affective and attitudinal reactions such as job satisfaction and intrinsic motivation, as well as behavioral outcomes such as absenteeism, turnover, and performance.[59] Approaches include job enlargement, job enrichment, job rotation, and the job characteristics model.

Job enlargement
Putting more variety into a job.

Job enlargement involves putting more variety into a worker's job by combining specialized tasks of comparable difficulty. Some call this *horizontally loading* the job. This technique was first used in the late 1940s in response to complaints about tedious and overspecialized jobs. Researchers recommend using job enlargement along with other motivational methods; used alone, it does not have a significant and lasting positive effect on job performance.[60]

Job rotation
Moving employees from one specialized job to another.

Job rotation adds variety to work by moving employees from one specialized job to another. Employees are trained and assigned to perform two or more jobs on a rotating basis. The goal is to stimulate interest and motivation while giving employees a broader perspective of the organization. Organizations also may benefit from increased worker flexibility and easier scheduling because employees are cross-trained to perform different jobs. General Electric has used job rotation for entry-level human resource (HR) employees, including rotations into functions outside HR. The job rotation appeals to candidates and improves HR employees' ability to work with employees in GE's business operations.[61] However, positive experiences at GE and other companies do not provide enough information to draw conclusions about job rotation programs because they have not been adequately researched.

Job enrichment
Building achievement, recognition, stimulating work, responsibility, and advancement into a job.

Job enrichment entails modifying a job to give employees an opportunity to experience achievement, recognition, stimulating work, responsibility, and advancement. Thus, it is the practical application of Herzberg's motivator-hygiene theory. The desired characteristics are incorporated into the job through *vertical loading,* which means employees take on responsibilities normally handled by their supervisors.

Two OB researchers, J Richard Hackman and Greg Oldham, played a central role in developing the job characteristics approach by studying how work can be structured so that employees are intrinsically motivated. **Intrinsic motivation** occurs when a person is "turned on to one's work because of the positive internal feelings that are generated by doing well, rather than being dependent on external factors (such as incentive pay or compliments from the boss) for the motivation to work effectively."[62] These positive feelings power a self-perpetuating cycle of motivation. As shown in Figure 4–3, intrinsic work motivation depends on three psychological states, which are fostered by the presence of five core job characteristics. This approach promotes high intrinsic motivation by designing jobs to have the core job characteristics. Employees experience their work as more meaningful if their job requires a variety of skills, involves all the tasks for completing a whole or identifiable piece of work, and affects other people. People feel a sense of responsibility when their job gives them independence and discretion over how to carry out their tasks. And they recognize the results of their work if they receive feedback about how well they are doing the job.

Hackman and Oldham recognized that not everyone wants a job containing high amounts of the core job characteristics. In their model, *moderators* are attributes that affect individual

Intrinsic motivation
Motivation caused by positive internal feelings.

FIGURE 4–3 **The Job Characteristics Model**

Source: From J R Hackman and G R Oldham, *Work Redesign,* 1st Edition. Copyright © 1980. Adapted by permission of Pearson Education, Inc., Upper Saddle River, NJ.

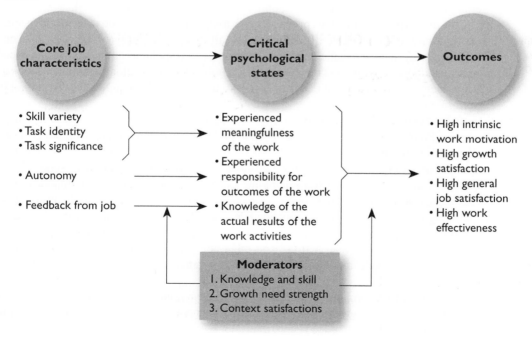

responses to job enrichments. So, how well the model applies to an individual depends on his or her knowledge and skill, the strength of his or her need for growth and development, and the person's satisfaction with the context, such as satisfaction with pay or co-workers. To apply this model, a manager diagnoses the work environment to see whether performance problems may be related to job characteristics. If so, the manager determines whether job design is likely to work with the particular employees; it is most likely to work in a participative environment where employees have the necessary knowledge and skills and have at least average job satisfaction. Finally, using employee input, the manager may redesign the job to offer more of the core job characteristics.

Research overwhelmingly demonstrates a moderately strong relationship between job characteristics and satisfaction.[63] Principal Financial Group gave employees more autonomy by allowing them to make choices about their work schedules; a majority of them have chosen to use flexible hours, and one-fifth selected compressed workweeks. Many spend part of the week working from home.[64] This effort is supported by research linking autonomy to higher job performance.[65] But job redesign appears to reduce the quantity of output as often as it has a positive effect. Caution is advised to be sure the changes are appropriate for the situation. In one study, job redesign worked better in less complex organizations (small plants or companies).[66] Furthermore, making jobs more complex can result in poorer performance and greater stress when the organization is not fully staffed.[67] In terms of quality of performance, however, a comparison of results from 21 experimental studies determined that job redesign resulted in a median increase of 28% in performance quality.[68] Also, two meta-analyses support the use of the job characteristics model to reduce absenteeism and turnover.[69] At Petaluma-based Athleta Corp., a sports apparel firm, employee turnover fell after the company gave employees more autonomy over their schedules.[70]

BIOLOGICAL AND PERCEPTUAL-MOTOR APPROACHES

The biological approach to job design is based on research from biomechanics, work physiology, and ergonomics. It focuses on designing the work environment to reduce employees' physical strain, fatigue, and health complaints.[71] This approach redesigns jobs to eliminate or reduce the amount of repetitive motions from a worker's job. Intel, for example, customizes its employees' workstations to suit their height, chair preferences, mouse arrangement, and right- or left-handedness.[72]

The perceptual-motor approach is derived from research that examines human factors engineering, perceptual and cognitive skills, and information processing. This approach to job design emphasizes the reliability of work outcomes by examining error rates, accidents, and workers' feedback about facilities and equipment.[73]

The frequency of using the biological and perceptual-motor approaches to job design is increasing in light of the number of workers who experience injuries related to overexertion or repetitive motion. Such injuries are among the musculoskeletal disorders blamed for causing the longest absences from work and are among the leading causes of absenteeism. The median time lost to repetitive-motion disorders in 2005 was 23 days.[74] The Occupational Safety and Health Administration (OSHA) has issued guidelines regarding ergonomics in some industries.

PUTTING MOTIVATIONAL THEORIES TO WORK

Designing and implementing motivational programs is not easy. An organization's dynamics interfere with applying motivation theories in their "pure" form. According to management scholar Terence Mitchell, these dynamics may include "the kinds of jobs or people present, the technology, [and] the presence of a union," and the role of these factors has not been systematically identified.[75]

For introducing or changing a motivational program, the first issue is to distinguish motivation from performance. Motivation is only one of the influences on performance, along with appropriate equipment, clear goals, political behavior and conflict, supervisory support, and nature of the work flow. In evaluating performance, managers must consider these elements of the work context as well as employee motivation. Managers also should use training and coaching to ensure that employees have the ability and job knowledge required for high performance.[76] Clear feedback helps employees accurately measure their performance against their goals (see Chapter 5).

Managers should take into account individual differences (discussed in Chapters 2 and 3), which influence motivation and motivated behavior. For example, Pat Summitt, head coach of Tennessee's successful women's basketball team, told a reporter, "I love what I do . . . One thing that motivates me is the competition. It's greater than it's ever been. So is the desire to help this program stay at the top."[77] Summitt has such strong internal needs that she needs no external sources of motivation. For other employees, managers have to nurture self-esteem, self-efficacy, positive emotions, and need for achievement.

*some
competition
some self esteem.*

Chapter **Five**

Motivation in Practice: How to Bring Out the Best in People

Learning Objectives

After reading the material in this chapter, you should be able to:

- Explain how goals contribute to performance management.
- Describe how feedback can provide information for improved performance.
- Define types of rewards, and summarize their relationship to performance.
- Describe how the effects and consequences of behaviors can influence future behaviors.

How much effort will you expend to succeed in this course on organizational behavior? If completing it is part of achieving goals that are important to you, such as earning a degree that will help you pursue a career in management, you probably are trying harder than if you had enrolled in the course only because you need the credits. As you pursue your goals by taking courses, you receive feedback from your instructors—formally in grade reports and perhaps informally in conversations outside the classroom. Goal-oriented students use that feedback to figure out where they need to improve their efforts.

Similarly, in the business world, goals and feedback can motivate employees to focus their efforts in productive directions. Organizations use these tools because their overall success depends on the job performance of individual employees. Job performance is influenced by cultural and individual differences, perception, and motivation—the topics of preceding chapters. Of these, managers can directly control motivation through goal setting and feedback. Many organizations think their managers give employees the support they need for improving their job performance, but research contradicts this rosy view. A consulting firm's ongoing study of more than 500 managers since 1993 found that just 1% of the managers give their employees the basic information and rewards they need to meet their goals and improve their

FIGURE 5–1 Improving Individual Job Performance: A Continuous Process

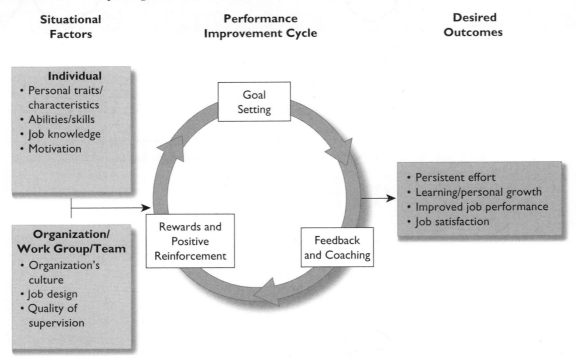

performance.[1] Typically, employees get performance-related information in annual appraisals, which they find largely unsatisfying.[2]

Performance management
Continuous cycle of improving job performance with goal setting, feedback and coaching, and rewards and positive reinforcement.

A better alternative to the yearly review is well-planned **performance management,** an organizationwide system for improving performance by setting, monitoring, and evaluating goals; providing feedback and coaching; and rewarding employees on a continuous basis.[3] As Figure 5–1 illustrates, these activities take place in an environment designed to enable performance improvement. Given the situation—the characteristics of individual employees and the groups in which they work—ongoing performance management seeks the desired outcomes of persistent effort, learning and growth, improved job performance, and increased job satisfaction. Understanding OB principles, particularly the key activities of goal setting, feedback, and positive reinforcement, can assist performance management efforts.

GOAL SETTING

According to a recent survey of managers, 46% said their project teams are not given specific, attainable goals. Not surprisingly, only one-third of those managers indicated that their teams complete their work on time and within budget.[4] Yet methods exist for setting and communicating the major types of goals an organization needs to accomplish.

Types of Goals

Performance outcome goal
Targets a specific end result.

Goals can define either the job to be done (the outcome) or the employee's ability to get the job done (a needed skill). A **performance outcome goal** targets a specific result. A **learning goal,** in contrast, defines the particular skills, knowledge, and abilities the employee will acquire. As managers attempt to motivate their employees to try harder, they typically overemphasize performance outcome goals. But when employees lack the necessary skills, knowledge, or abilities, they become frustrated rather than motivated by their goals. To use a sports analogy, if you wanted to improve your golf score (performance outcome), you might need to work on mastering your swing (learning goal).[5] Employees with goals related to sales, customer service, and new technology may first have to achieve learning goals such as mastering new software or defining customers' needs.

→ Need learning goals to accomplish the other

Learning goal
Encourages learning, creativity, and skill development.

Management by Objectives

Management by objectives (MBO)
Management system incorporating participation in decision making, goal setting, and feedback.

The idea of motivating employees through goals and goal-based reward plans has been around for a long time. More than a century ago, Frederick Taylor tried to establish scientifically how much work an individual should be assigned each day, with bonuses to be based on accomplishment of the standards. More recently, goal setting has been promoted in the form of **management by objectives (MBO),** a management system that incorporates employee participation in decision making, goal setting, and objective feedback.[6]

Studies of MBO programs have linked this method to improvements in productivity and job satisfaction.[7] In one meta-analysis (research comparing multiple studies) looking at MBO outcomes, productivity improved in 68 out of 70 organizations. The amount of improvement was far greater when top management's commitment to MBO was high. In another meta-analysis, employees' job satisfaction was significantly related to top management's commitment to MBO. These impressive results are tempered by reports of ethical problems stemming from extreme pressure for results. In other words, ethics and employee morale can be undermined by a strict focus on the bottom line.

Goal-Setting Process

A complete goal-setting program involves three steps: setting goals, promoting commitment to the goals, and providing support and feedback. Deficiencies in one step cannot make up for strength in the other two. All three steps need to be implemented in a systematic fashion. How well each person does this depends in part on that person's unique characteristics.

Step 1: Set Goals

During the first step—setting goals—input can come from several sources. Time and motion studies provide information about what employees can physically accomplish. Goals also may be based on the average past performance of job holders. Employees and their manager may negotiate goals together in a give and take. Also, benchmarking can show desirable performance levels achieved by other organizations (external benchmarking) or other units, departments, or divisions within the organization (internal benchmarking). In addition, goal setters should consult the organization's overall strategy. Employees' individual goals should support, not undermine, the strategic goals.

A useful way to remember the characteristics of effective goals is to think of goals that are SMART—an acronym for specific, measurable, attainable, results oriented, and time bound:

SELF-ASSESSMENT
Assessing How Personality Type Impacts Your Goal-Setting Skills

Go online at [www.mhhe.com/obcore] to discover how your personality type affects your goal-setting skills.

- According to this assessment, what are your primary motive, needs, and wants? Do they describe you accurately?
- According to this assessment, what are the strengths and weaknesses of this personality type for setting goals?
- What aspect of setting goals are you most interested in improving?

- *Specific* goals are stated in precise, not vague, terms. A supervisor's goal to provide each employee with 20 hours of technical training is more specific than deciding to send as many employees as possible to training classes. When possible, keep goals specific by stating them in terms of numbers.
- *Measurable* goals apply some kind of measurement method or device to ensure that the goals have been met. Measurement should consider the quality as well as the quantity of output.
- *Attainable* goals are realistic as well as challenging. If people believe their goals are impossible, they will be frustrated.
- *Results-oriented* goals focus on the desired outcomes in support of the organization's vision. Words that define a results-oriented goal include *complete, acquire, produce, increase,* and *decrease.* In contrast, the words *develop, conduct, implement,* and *monitor* describe activities rather than achievements.
- *Time-bound* goals name a target date for completion.

When a goal involves complex tasks, it requires an action plan specifying the activities to be used to achieve the goal. Employees with complex goals should be trained in problem-solving techniques and involved in developing their action plans.

A set of goals may cover one or more employees performing a particular job. Because of individual differences (see Chapter 3), different goals may be necessary even for employees holding the same job. Relevant individual differences include traits such as conscientiousness, as well as differences in goal orientation. Some individuals are more oriented to learning goals; others are more inclined to performance goals, in terms of either looking good or avoiding problems.[8] Although some studies showed that persons with a learning orientation set higher goals, exerted more effort, engaged in more performance planning, and achieved higher performance, other research has demonstrated a more complex series of relationships.[9] However, we can conclude that a person's goal orientation influences the way he or she goes about pursuing those goals, so individual differences do matter when setting goals.

Step 2: Promote Goal Commitment

Besides knowing what is expected of them, employees need to be committed to achieving their goals. Employees are more motivated to pursue goals they view as reasonable, obtainable, and fair. To achieve goal commitment, managers should explain why the organization is implementing a goal-setting program, present the corporate goals, and explain how the employee's goals support them. Once they can see the big picture, employees should establish their own goals and action plans, including some stretch goals that are challenging but not impossible.[10] Thus, managers must know how to conduct participative goal-setting sessions, and employees must know how to develop action plans. Managers should never use goals to threaten employees but should ensure that employees have needed resources to control and achieve goals. Finally, managers can strengthen goal commitment by offering monetary and other rewards for accomplishing goals.[11]

Step 3: Provide Support and Feedback

To accomplish their goals, employees need support and resources, including the abilities and information needed to reach goals. Sometimes training is necessary to reach difficult goals. Managers also should pay attention to employees' perceptions of effort → performance expectancies, self-efficacy, and valence of rewards. Finally, as we discuss next, employees need timely, specific feedback on how they are doing.[12]

FEEDBACK

Feedback
Objective information about performance.

Following a difficult exam, many students want to know how they and their peers did. Why? When students know how their work measures up to grading and competitive standards, they can adjust their study habits to reach their goals. Likewise, managers in well-run organizations follow up on goal setting with a feedback program that provides a rational basis for adjustment and improvement. In this context, **feedback** is objective information about individual or collective performance.

Numerous surveys indicate that employees want more feedback than they receive. For example, in a recent survey, 43% of employees said they don't get enough guidance to help them perform their jobs better.[13] Typically, managers should be giving more feedback, and the need for more good feedback is most acute at higher levels of the organization.[14]

One problem is using feedback that is subjective: Statements such as "You're doing a poor job" or "We really appreciate your hard work" lack specific information about what the employee is doing well or inadequately. More helpful feedback is objective; it describes behaviors, gives examples, and cites data about results, such as units sold or scrapped, days absent, dollars saved, and customers satisfied. This kind of feedback tells more about a person's behavior and results than about the person's general traits. Objective feedback can come through a variety of channels, including managers' recollection of incidents and regular postings of sales, defects, or output posted on company bulletin boards.[15] This type of information is important to use when preparing formal performance appraisals, as well as in frequent informal feedback. In addition, employees improve their performance more when feedback is part of a comprehensive process of mentoring or coaching (see Chapter 12).[16]

Functions of Feedback

Feedback serves two functions: *instructional* and *motivational*. Feedback instructs employees by clarifying roles or teaching new behavior. When a supervisor advises an accounting

MASTER YOUR KNOWLEDGE
Appraisal Methods

Increase your knowledge of feedback content by completing the online quiz at [www.mhhe.com/obcore].

- Based on the examples from this exercise, do you think it would be easiest to gather and report feedback on traits, behaviors, or results?
- Which kinds of feedback do you think the employees would have found most helpful? Which kinds would have produced the most emotional response?
- Which types of feedback would you expect to lead to the best performance in the future?

assistant that a particular entry is a capital item rather than an expense, the feedback is instructional. Feedback is motivational when it serves as or promises a reward.[17] Feedback is itself a reward when it makes the recipient feel good—for example, when the boss praises your perseverance in front of the divisional vice president. Promising a reward might include saying, "We met this quarter's goal" when employees know the group earns a bonus each quarter that it reaches its goal. Feedback is most motivational when *specific* challenging goals are paired with *specific* feedback about results.[18]

Recipients of Feedback

The effectiveness of feedback depends not only on the content of the feedback but also on the people who are receiving it. As a result, feedback itself is not automatically effective. In a meta-analysis, feedback had a generally positive impact on performance, but in more than 38% of the incidents, performance declined.[19] Subjective feedback is easily contaminated by situational factors. For example, researchers at Stanford University tested feedback on the content (subjective feedback) and writing mechanics (objective feedback) of written essays, noting the race of the individuals giving and receiving the feedback. White students gave African-American students *less* critical *subjective* feedback than they gave white students. But this bias disappeared with objective feedback.[20] Yet, even with objective feedback, managers must understand how feedback recipients interact with their environment.[21]

Characteristics of the Recipient

Personality characteristics such as self-esteem and self-efficacy (see Chapter 3) can influence one's readiness for feedback.[22] Those having low self-esteem and low self-efficacy tend not to actively seek feedback that would confirm those problems. Needs and goals also influence openness to feedback. In a study of psychology students, those who scored high on need for achievement responded more favorably to feedback than did their peers with low need for achievement.[23] At a large public utility, 331 employees sought feedback on issues that were important or situations that were uncertain. Long-tenured employees sought feedback less than employees who were relatively new to their jobs.[24] Also, high self-monitors, those chameleonlike people discussed in Chapter 3, are more open to feedback

[handwritten margin note: sometimes feedback makes people do less well]

because it helps them adapt their behavior to the situation. Thus, they are better at initiating relationships with mentors, who typically provide feedback.[25]

Everyday experience tells us that people don't always sincerely want performance feedback, even when they ask. A restaurant server who asks, "How was everything?" while presenting the bill may not be seeking a detailed response. The general contingency approach to management would require different strategies for giving feedback depending on employees' desire for it.

Perception of Feedback

The way people perceive feedback is related to whether it is positive (praise) or negative (criticism). Generally, people tend to perceive and recall positive feedback more accurately than negative feedback.[26] Destructive criticism tends to cause conflict and reduce motivation.[27] Still, negative feedback can improve motivation. In one study, people who were told they were below average on a creativity test subsequently outperformed those who were led to believe their results were above average. The subjects apparently took the negative feedback as a challenge to set and pursue higher goals, while the positive feedback gave no incentive to do better.[28] Nonetheless, negative feedback needs to be administered carefully to avoid creating insecurity and defensiveness. Negative feedback also can damage self-efficacy.[29]

Cognitive Evaluation of Feedback

Upon receiving feedback, people cognitively evaluate factors such as its accuracy, the credibility of the source, the fairness of the system (e.g., performance appraisal system), their performance-reward expectancies, and the reasonableness of the standards. Any feedback that fails to clear one or more of these cognitive hurdles will be rejected or downplayed.

How people weigh these factors depends largely on personal experiences. You would probably discount feedback from someone who often exaggerates or who struggled with the same task you just completed successfully. Also, recipients of feedback perceive it as more accurate when they actively participate in the feedback session.[30] In addition, personal credibility of the manager is essential. If managers have proven to be untrustworthy and failed to establish credibility, improving job performance through feedback is difficult.[31] However, they can enhance their credibility by developing expertise and creating a climate of trust.[32]

Fairness also is important. Feedback from a source who apparently shows favoritism or relies on unreasonable behavior standards would be suspect.[33] Instead, employees want feedback they can apply. It should describe matters that are relevant to the employee's job and under the employee's control, and it should be clear and timely so that employees can make changes.[34] Also, to be effective, feedback must foster high effort → performance expectancies and performance → reward instrumentalities. Feedback that creates doubt that an employee will ever be able to master a task is unlikely to motivate.

Nontraditional Feedback: Upward and 360 Degrees

Traditional top-down feedback programs have given way to some interesting variations recently, including upward feedback and 360-degree feedback. Not only do these newer approaches change the direction of feedback, but they also often include multiple sources: from supervisors, subordinates, peers, and even customers.

Upward Feedback

Upward feedback
Employees evaluate their boss.

In some organizations, subordinates provide feedback on a manager's style and performance; this practice is called **upward feedback.** Usually, upward feedback is anonymous. At Dell Inc., employees rate their bosses every six months in "Tell Dell" surveys, and these ratings influence managers' bonuses and promotions.[35]

Managers often resist upward feedback programs because they believe this method erodes their authority.[36] Critics also say anonymous upward feedback can become a mere personality contest or, worse, be manipulated by managers' promises or threats. However, research finds practical value in upward feedback that is anonymous and combined with other sources of performance feedback.[37] Because of the concerns, upward feedback is most useful for management development, rather than for decisions about promotions and pay.

360-Degree Feedback

360-degree feedback
Comparison of anonymous feedback from one's superior, subordinates, and peers with self-perceptions.

The concept of **360-degree feedback** involves letting individuals compare their own perceived performance with behaviorally specific (and usually anonymous) performance information from their manager, subordinates, and peers. Even outsiders may be involved in what is sometimes called *full-circle feedback*.[38] Under certain conditions, 360-degree feedback can be very effective. Based on a meta-analysis of 360-degree feedback studies, researchers found that performance was most likely to improve when "feedback indicates that change is necessary, recipients have a positive feedback orientation, perceive a need to change their behavior, react positively to the feedback, believe change is feasible, set appropriate goals to regulate their behavior, and take actions that lead to skill and performance improvement."[39] Our recommendation is to use 360-degree feedback with anonymity and primarily to support management development, rather than pay and promotion decisions.

ORGANIZATIONAL REWARD SYSTEMS

Rewards are an ever-present and controversial feature of organizational life. Some employees see their jobs primarily as the source of a paycheck, but others derive pleasure from their work or co-workers. In fact, 55% of American workers responding to a recent survey said they would keep working even if they won $10 million in a lottery.[40] Hence, the subject of organizational rewards includes but goes far beyond money.

Reward Systems

Extrinsic rewards
Financial, material, or social rewards from the environment.

Intrinsic rewards
Self-granted, psychic rewards.

As modeled in Figure 5–2, a reward system has three important components: types of rewards, distribution criteria, and desired outcomes. Rewards may take the form of money and material rewards, social rewards, or psychic rewards. Financial/material and social rewards qualify as **extrinsic rewards,** meaning they come from the environment, not the job itself. An employee who works to obtain extrinsic rewards, such as a bonus or praise, is said to be extrinsically motivated. **Intrinsic rewards** come from the job itself; they are psychic rewards, the good feeling of a job well done or a customer well served. A person who enjoys the feeling of competence or self-determination in doing a job is being intrinsically motivated. The relative importance of extrinsic and intrinsic rewards is a matter of culture and personal tastes. Circumstances may heighten the importance of a job and, thus, the intensity of the intrinsic rewards. In New Orleans after Hurricane Katrina, BellSouth

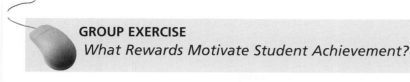

worker Nancy Talbot Shebsta said, "Providing phone service to people isn't just a business for us. It's a real point of pride."[41]

In setting criteria for distributing rewards, organizations have several options. They can base rewards on the results of performance, such as the quality of a service or the quantity produced. They also can link rewards to performance-related actions and behaviors, such as teamwork, cooperation, risk taking, or creativity. Or they can use nonperformance criteria—that is, following customary practices or contractual requirements for rewarding tenure, level in the organization, or other measures.[42] In organizations today, the trend is toward performance criteria.

An organization's reward system is intended to achieve certain outcomes with regard to employees. A good reward system attracts talented people, motivates them, and develops their skills. In return, employees feel satisfied and are more likely to stay with the organization. At Worthington Industries, an Ohio steel-processing firm, rewards such as a generous health insurance plan and profit-sharing checks equaling 40% to 70% of base pay help the company achieve low employee turnover and an abundance of job applicants.[43]

Intrinsic Rewards

Although intrinsic rewards are, by definition, self-granted, managers can do much to create situations in which those rewards occur and are motivating.[44] Applying the job characteristics model of job design (see Chapter 4), the concept of empowerment (see Chapter 10), and cognitive evaluation theory (which says people must satisfy their needs for autonomy and competence for a task to be intrinsically motivating),[45] Kenneth Thomas developed

FIGURE 5–2
A General Model of Organizational Reward Systems

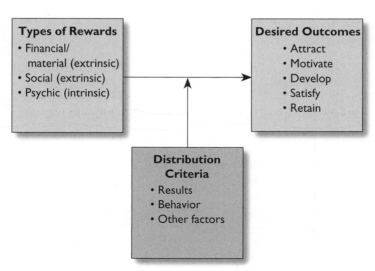

Types of Rewards	Desired Outcomes
• Financial/ material (extrinsic)	• Attract
• Social (extrinsic)	• Motivate
• Psychic (intrinsic)	• Develop
	• Satisfy
	• Retain

Distribution Criteria
• Results
• Behavior
• Other factors

a motivational model that says managers can establish the right conditions for intrinsic motivation by using four building blocks:[46]

1. *Leading for meaningfulness.* To make work meaningful, managers inspire their employees and model the behaviors they desire. Managers can do this by helping employees identify their work-related passions and by creating an organizational vision with which employees can connect.

2. *Leading for choice.* Managers offer choice by empowering employees and delegating meaningful tasks. Such a system requires a degree of trust in employees, allowing them room to try ideas, even if mistakes are inevitable. At Merck & Co., senior vice president Judy Lewent has her employees run staff meetings, which lets her observe and develop their leadership skills.[47]

3. *Leading for competence.* Managers lead for competence by supporting and coaching their employees. They make sure employees have the knowledge they need to perform their jobs successfully, providing any necessary training and mentoring. Employees also can learn from tackling difficult assignments. Recognition and feedback encourage them as they learn.

4. *Leading for progress.* To lead for progress, managers monitor and reward employees. Performance measures indicate areas where an employee is improving. Access to customers shows employees the impact of their efforts. Celebrations and recognition of milestones also serve as rewards and a way to measure progress.

Extrinsic Rewards

Organizations invest huge amounts of time and money to provide salaries, benefits, bonuses, prizes, and other forms of compensation, but these extrinsic rewards often fail to have the desired impact. There are many reasons why extrinsic rewards fail to motivate, including too much emphasis on money, a sense of entitlement, failure to link rewards to individual wants and needs, and use of one-shot rewards when long-term commitment is needed.[48] In some cases, employees become so focused on receiving a particular reward that they actually behave in undesirable ways. At a pizza delivery company, rewards for on-time deliveries motivated delivery personnel to drive recklessly. A detailed discussion of compensation practices is beyond the scope of this text, but two methods that have become popular as ways to reward desirable behavior are pay for performance and team-based pay.

Pay for Performance

Pay for performance
Monetary incentives tied to one's results or accomplishments.

Compensation systems linking at least some portion of employees' paychecks directly to their results or accomplishments are called **pay for performance,** also known as *incentive pay* or *variable pay.* By one measure, 8 out of 10 U.S. companies use some form of variable pay.[49] The objective is to give employees an incentive to work harder or smarter, with the incentive pay being in addition to basic wages and salaries. The basic wage is thought to induce the employee to show up on time and do the minimum to get by, while pay for performance motivates employees to excel.[50]

These plans may include merit pay, bonuses, and profit sharing. The most basic form of pay for performance is the traditional piece-rate plan, paying the employee a specified amount of money for each unit of work. Ohio-based Longaberger uses a piece-rate system when it pays its artisans a fixed amount for each handcrafted wooden basket they weave.[51]

Another longstanding type of pay for performance is the sales commission, in which salespeople receive a predetermined percentage or dollar amount for each sale they complete. Yet, in today's service economy, management often has to go beyond traditional pay schemes to emphasize product and service quality, interdependence, and teamwork.[52]

Despite the logic that people will try harder in order to earn more, pay for performance is not always a clear success. In one study, incentive pay had a *negative* effect on the performance of managers from financially distressed companies.[53] A meta-analysis of 39 studies found only a modest positive correlation between financial incentives and performance quantity, and no impact on performance quality.[54] Similarly, the large executive bonuses paid out in good years are linked only weakly to subsequent improvement in corporate profitability.[55] In a recent study by Hewitt Associates, a leading human resources consulting firm, variable pay was associated with positive outcomes in companies that enjoyed strong revenue growth but not in weaker companies. Hewitt's Paul Schafer says this difference occurs because successful companies "provide the appropriate amount of administrative, communication and monetary support."[56]

The findings from the Hewitt study suggest that motivation from pay for performance depends at least partly on how well such programs are managed. The following guidelines are associated with success:[57]

- Make pay for performance an integral part of the organization's strategy.
- Determine incentives based on objective performance measures.
- Have employees participate in setting and revising the pay formulas.
- Encourage two-way communication so problems can be detected early.
- Build pay-for-performance plans around systems in which employees offer suggestions or participate in quality improvement.
- Reward teamwork and cooperation.
- Actively sell the plan to supervisors and middle managers.
- If there is an annual bonus, pay it in a lump sum, so its impact will be greatest.
- To be motivating, incentive pay should come in significant amounts.

Team-Based Pay

Team-based pay
Linking pay to teamwork behavior and/or team results.

Another effort to make pay more motivating is to use **team-based pay,** or incentive compensation that rewards individuals for teamwork, rewards teams for collective results, or both. In rewarding some combination of individual *behavior* and team *results,* team-based pay implies that team success requires team players.

Research into team-based pay has not been encouraging thus far. A comprehensive review of studies that examined team-based rewards in the workplace found only "limited and inconclusive" support for this approach.[58] The biggest barrier to effective team-based pay is cultural, especially in individualistic cultures such as the United States, Canada, Norway, and Australia.[59] Individual competition for pay and pay raises has long been the norm in the United States. Entrenched grading schemes in schools and colleges, focusing on individual competition, are a preview of the traditional American workplace.[60] So, team-based pay conflicts with the cultural tradition of putting the individual above the group. Indeed, a poll of U.S. employees found little support for team-based rewards.[61] A related problem is a general lack of teamwork skills, such as communicating, conflict handling, and negotiating.

The state of the art in team-based pay is primitive today. Given the many different kinds of teams (see Chapter 6), there is certainly no single best approach. However, anecdotal evidence from the general management literature and case studies suggests some recommendations.[62] First, managers should prepare employees for team-based systems, providing training in teamwork skills such as communication and conflict resolution. Second, the organization should also be sure teams are established and running smoothly before team-based pay is introduced. Third, the pay plan should blend individual rewards with team incentives. Fourth, rewards should be linked first to behaviors, such as cooperation and group problem solving, and only later to results. Finally, when pay is linked to results, employees must be able to see a clear connection between their own work and the team results.

POSITIVE REINFORCEMENT

Feedback and extrinsic reward programs are often ineffective because they are administered haphazardly. For example, a young programmer stops e-mailing creative ideas to his boss because she never responds. Or a promotion goes to the office politician, rather than to co-workers who are more skilled, and they gossip about the injustice rather than try for the next promotion. Managers who want to achieve better discipline and motivate employees can find help from the field of behavior modification.

Law of effect
Behavior with favorable consequences is repeated; behavior with unfavorable consequences disappears.

During the early 1900s, Edward L Thorndike, using laboratory research in which cats discovered they could escape from a box by operating a lever, formulated his **law of effect,** which says behavior with favorable consequences tends to be repeated, while behavior with unfavorable consequences tends to disappear.[63] This finding was a dramatic departure from the then-prevailing notion that behavior is the product of inborn instincts.

Respondent behavior
Skinner's term for unlearned stimulus–response reflexes.

B F Skinner refined Thorndike's conclusion in his theory of *behaviorism,* which deals strictly with observable behavior, rather than with inner states such as needs, drives, attitudes, and thought processes.[64] In his 1938 classic, *The Behavior of Organisms,* Skinner distinguished between two types of behavior: respondent and operant behavior.[65] **Respondent behavior** comprises unlearned reflexes, or stimulus–response (S–R) connections, thought to describe a very small proportion of adult human behavior. Examples include shedding tears while peeling onions and reflexively withdrawing one's hand from a hot stove.[66] **Operant behavior** is behavior that organisms learn when they "operate on" the environment to produce desired consequences. Some call this the response–stimulus (R–S) model. Years of controlled experiments with pigeons helped Skinner develop a sophisticated technology of behavior control, or operant conditioning. For example, he taught pigeons how to pace figure-eights by reinforcing the underweight (and thus hungry) birds with food whenever they closely approximated target behaviors. Skinner's work spawned the field of behavior modification and has significant implications for OB because the vast majority of organizational behavior falls into the category of operant behavior.[67]

Operant behavior
Skinner's term for learned, consequence-shaped behavior.

Contingent Consequences

If you don't go to work, you'll be fired. If you give silly answers to the questions on the test, you'll get a zero. These consequences are *contingent,* meaning there is a systematic

FIGURE 5–3
Contingent Consequences in Operant Conditioning

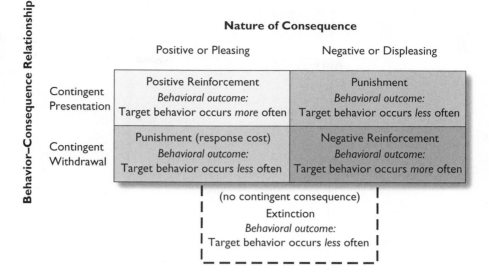

Nature of Consequence

Positive or Pleasing   Negative or Displeasing

Behavior–Consequence Relationship

	Positive or Pleasing	Negative or Displeasing
Contingent Presentation	Positive Reinforcement *Behavioral outcome:* Target behavior occurs *more* often	Punishment *Behavioral outcome:* Target behavior occurs *less* often
Contingent Withdrawal	Punishment (response cost) *Behavioral outcome:* Target behavior occurs *less* often	Negative Reinforcement *Behavioral outcome:* Target behavior occurs *more* often

(no contingent consequence)
Extinction
Behavioral outcome:
Target behavior occurs *less* often

Positive reinforcement
Making behavior occur more often by contingently presenting something positive.

Negative reinforcement
Making behavior occur more often by contingently withdrawing something negative.

Punishment
Making behavior occur less often by contingently presenting something negative or withdrawing something positive.

Extinction
Making behavior occur less often by ignoring or not reinforcing it.

if-then linkage between the target behavior (going to work, answering test questions) and the consequence (job tenure, test grade). According to Skinner's operant theory, contingent consequences—or the absence of such consequences—control behavior in the ways shown in Figure 5–3:

• **Positive reinforcement** is the process of strengthening a behavior by contingently presenting something pleasing. (Importantly, a behavior is strengthened when it increases in frequency and weakened when it decreases in frequency.) An engineer who works overtime because of praise and recognition from the boss is responding to positive reinforcement.[68]

• **Negative reinforcement** is the process of strengthening a behavior by contingently withdrawing something displeasing. An army sergeant who stops yelling when a recruit jumps out of bed has negatively reinforced that particular behavior. The term *negative reinforcement* is often confused with punishment, but the two strategies have opposite effects on behavior. Negative reinforcement strengthens (reinforces) a behavior because it provides relief from an unpleasant situation.

• **Punishment** is the process of weakening behavior through either the contingent presentation of something displeasing or the contingent withdrawal of something positive. A manager assigning a tardy employee to a dirty job exemplifies the first type of punishment. Docking a tardy employee's pay is an example of the second type of punishment, called *response cost punishment.* Salespeople who must make up any cash register shortages out of their own pockets are being managed through response cost punishment. Ethical questions can and should be raised about this type of on-the-job punishment.[69]

• **Extinction** is the weakening of a behavior by ignoring it or making sure it is not reinforced. Ending a relationship with a vendor (or with a boyfriend or girlfriend) by refusing to answer phone calls and e-mail would be an extinction strategy. A behavior without occasional reinforcement eventually dies. Thus, although extinction is very different from punishment, both weaken a behavior.

MASTER YOUR KNOWLEDGE
Reinforcing Performance

Increase your knowledge of reinforcement theory by completing the online quiz at [www.mhhe.com/obcore].

- Think of a situation at work or school where you appreciate something a co-worker, classmate, or professor has been doing. How can you apply these methods to encourage that behavior to continue?
- Think of a situation where you dislike the behavior of a co-worker, classmate, or professor. How can you apply these methods to discourage that behavior in the future?
- Are your ideas for these two situations practical? Are they ethical?

Schedules of Reinforcement

Along with the type of contingent consequences, the timing of those consequences is an important—and sometimes more important—determinant of future behavior. Based on years of laboratory experiments in highly controlled environments, Skinner and his colleagues discovered distinct patterns of responding for various schedules of reinforcement.[70]

Types of Schedules

Continuous reinforcement
Reinforcing every instance of a behavior.

As indicated in Table 5–1, **continuous reinforcement (CRF)** is a schedule in which every instance of a target behavior is reinforced. For instance, if your computer is operating properly, you are reinforced by its booting up every time you turn it on. But as with any CRF schedule of reinforcement, the behavior of pressing the On button will undergo rapid extinction if the computer breaks and won't start up.

Intermittent reinforcement
Reinforcing some but not all instances of behavior.

Intermittent reinforcement involves reinforcement of some, but not all, instances of a target behavior. It may follow a *ratio* schedule, in which the reinforcement is contingent on the number of responses emitted. Or it may follow an *interval* schedule, in which the reinforcement is tied to the passage of time. Four types of intermittent reinforcement are possible:

1. *Fixed ratio.* Reinforcement after a fixed number of responses (for example, piece-rate pay or bonuses tied to the number of units sold).
2. *Variable ratio.* Reinforcement after a varying or random number of responses (praise offered occasionally, not every time the employee delivers excellent service but whenever the supervisor happens to observe it or hears about it from a customer).
3. *Fixed interval.* Reinforcement following the first response after a specific period of time has elapsed (regular pay, such as a weekly paycheck or quarterly bonus).
4. *Variable interval.* Reinforcement following the first response after varying or random periods of time (outings or awards delivered when the supervisor feels the work group needs encouragement or appreciation).

Choice of Schedule

The reinforcement schedule can influence behavior more powerfully than the magnitude of reinforcement. Although this proposition grew out of experiments with pigeons, subsequent

TABLE 5–1   **Schedules of Reinforcement**

Source: Based on F Luthans and R Kreitner, *Organizational Behavior Modification and Beyond: An Operant and Social Learning Approach* (Glenview, IL: Scott, Foresman, 1985), p 58.

Schedule	Description	Probable Effects on Responding
Continuous	Reinforcement after every response	Steady high rate of performance as long as continuous reinforcement continues
		Early satiation possible with high frequency of reinforcement
		Rapid weakening of behavior if reinforcement ends
Intermittent	Reinforcement after some responses	High frequencies of response
		Early satiation avoided with low frequency of reinforcement
Fixed ratio	Reinforcement after a fixed number of responses	High rate of response
		Vigorous, steady response
Variable ratio	Reinforcement after a varying or random number of responses	High rate of response
		Vigorous, steady response, resistant to extinction
Fixed interval	Reinforcement following the first response after a specific period of time	Uneven response pattern, varying from slow, unenergetic response immediately after reinforcement to fast, vigorous response immediately before reinforcement
Variable interval	Reinforcement following the first response after varying or random periods of time	High rate of response
		Vigorous, steady response, resistant to extinction

on-the-job research confirmed it. For example, at a lumber company, researchers tried offering two different reinforcement schedules to a group of 12 unionized beaver trappers responsible for keeping beavers from eating newly planted tree seedlings. One group of trappers earned $7 per hour plus $1 for each beaver caught (continuous reinforcement); the other trappers earned $7 per hour plus a one-in-four chance—based on rolling dice—of receiving $4 for each beaver trapped (a variable ratio schedule). In the long run, the pay under both schemes was the same, but the trappers paid under the variable ratio schedule were 58% more productive.[71]

Generally, variable ratio and variable interval schedules of reinforcement produce the strongest behavior that is most resistant to extinction. As gamblers will attest, variable schedules hold the promise of reinforcement after the next target response. Organizations without at least some variable reinforcement are less likely to prompt the dedication commonly associated with a casino visitor seated at a slot machine. More often, however, organizations rely on continuous reinforcement schemes such as hourly wages, monthly salaries, and annual performance appraisals—even though continuous reinforcement is the weakest schedule.

Shaping
Reinforcing closer and closer approximations to a target behavior.

Behavior Shaping

Have you ever wondered how trainers at aquarium parks manage to get bottle-nosed dolphins to do flips or killer whales to carry people on their backs? The training method is a learning process called **shaping,** or the process of reinforcing closer and closer approximations of a target behavior. Two-ton killer whales have a big appetite and find buckets of fish very reinforcing. A trainer who wants to ride a killer whale uses fish to reinforce behaviors that will eventually lead to riding the whale. The killer whale is contingently reinforced with a few fish for coming near the trainer, then for being touched, then for putting its nose in a harness, then for being straddled, and eventually for swimming with the trainer on its back. In effect, the trainer systematically raises the behavioral requirement for reinforcement.[72]

Shaping works with people, too, especially in training and quality programs involving continuous improvement. Praise, recognition, and instructive and credible feedback cost managers little more than moments of their time. Yet when used in conjunction with learning goals and a behavior-shaping program, these consequences can efficiently foster significant improvements in job performance. Successful behavior shaping requires reducing a complex target behavior to easily learned steps and then faithfully (and patiently) reinforcing any improvement. Several years ago, Continental Airlines shaped behavior with a cash bonus program in which employees received $65 each month the company earned a top-five ranking in on-time arrivals. After employees improved the company's on-time performance from one of the worst in the industry to one of the best, Continental raised the target and began paying the bonus only when the company received at least a top-three ranking. Sweetening the pot, it pays $100 each month the airline finishes in first place.[73]

Some guidelines can help managers shape job behavior effectively.[74] Managers should keep in mind that behavior changes gradually. They should communicate exactly what is expected and give specific, immediate feedback on performance. Reinforcements should be valued by employees and delivered as quickly as possible. Continuous reinforcement will help establish the behavior, and then a variable reinforcement schedule will help maintain the change. Managers should never stop reinforcing the desired behavior, and they should make all rewards contingent on performance.

Part

Managing Groups and Making Decisions in Organizations

ups and Teamwork: How Groups Work and How to Lead Them

Learning Objectives

After reading the material in this chapter, you should be able to:

- Describe stages of group development.
- Contrast roles and norms, and give four reasons why norms are enforced in organizations.
- Explain how a work group becomes a team, and identify five teamwork competencies.
- Summarize how managers can build trust.
- Describe self-managed teams and virtual teams.
- Identify symptoms of groupthink and social loafing and the ways to guard against them.

"She's really a team player." "There is no 'I' in team." "He took one for the team." We are surrounded daily with comments about the importance of teams—in sports, in school, in business. Often the highest compliment someone can receive is to be called a team player. To function effectively, today's organizations and their employees need to understand how teams form, how they differ, and what processes they use to accomplish their goals.

Daily experience and research show that social skills are essential for individual and organizational success. In an ongoing study by the Center for Creative Leadership involving diverse samplings from Belgium, France, Germany, Italy, the United Kingdom, the United States, and Spain, researchers determined that executives' careers tended to become derailed, with little chance for advancement, because of four stumbling blocks: (1) problems with interpersonal relationships; (2) failure to meet business objectives; (3) failure to build and lead a team; and (4) inability to change or adapt during a transition.[1] The first and third career stumbling blocks involve interpersonal

forming → storming → norming → performing

skills—the ability to get along and work effectively with others. Managers with interpersonal problems—which encompassed two-thirds of the derailed European managers and one-third of the derailed U.S. executives—typically were described as manipulative and insensitive.[2] With so many managers lacking skills in an environment that calls for successful teamwork, it is important to take a closer look at how teams form and function. This chapter shifts the focus from individual behavior to collective behavior by exploring groups and teams, including the topics of group development, trust, self-managed teams, virtual teams, and groupthink.

FUNDAMENTALS OF GROUP BEHAVIOR

Group
Two or more freely interacting people with shared norms and goals and a common identity.

Sociologists define a **group** as two or more freely interacting individuals who share collective norms and goals and have a common identity.[3] According to organizational psychologist Edgar Schein, a group therefore differs from a crowd, which lacks interaction and a sense of common identity, and from an organization (such as a corporation or labor union), which may be too large and complex for all its members to interact with or even be aware of one another.[4] However, these organizations generally contain groups, such as work teams, committees, and social cliques.

Formal and Informal Groups

Formal group
Formed by the organization.

Informal group
Formed by friends.

Individuals join groups, or are assigned to groups, to accomplish various purposes. If a group is formed by a manager to help the organization accomplish its goals, then it qualifies as a **formal group.** Formal groups typically wear such labels as work group, team, committee, or task force. An **informal group** exists when the members' overriding purpose of getting together is friendship.[5] Formal and informal groups often overlap, such as when a team of corporate auditors heads for the tennis courts after work. A recent survey of 1,385 office workers in the United States found 71% had attended important events with co-workers, such as weddings and funerals.[6] Some managers firmly believe personal friendship fosters productive teamwork on the job, while others view workplace "bull sessions" as a serious threat to productivity. Both situations are common, so managers have to strike a workable balance, based on the maturity and goals of the people involved.

Formal groups fulfill two basic functions: *organizational* and *individual,* described in Table 6–1.[7] Complex combinations of these functions occur in formal groups at any given time. For example, when Mazda's new American employees spent a month working in Japan before the opening of the firm's Flat Rock, Michigan, plant, they became enthusiastic, even accepting unfamiliar practices such as doing calisthenics before work.[8] Mazda pursued the organizational functions it wanted—interdependent teamwork, creativity, coordination, problem solving, and training. The American workers benefited from the individual functions of formal groups, including affiliation with new friends, enhanced self-esteem, exposure to the Japanese social reality, and reduction of anxieties about working for a foreign-owned company. In short, Mazda created a workable blend of organizational and individual group functions by training its newly hired American employees in Japan.

TABLE 6–1   **Formal Groups Fulfill Organizational and Individual Functions**

Source: Adapted from E H Schein, *Organizational Psychology,* 3rd ed (Englewood Cliffs, NJ: Prentice-Hall, 1980), pp 149–51.

Organizational Functions	Individual Functions
1. Accomplish complex, interdependent tasks that are beyond the capabilities of individuals.	1. Satisfy the individual's need for affiliation.
2. Generate new or creative ideas and solutions.	2. Develop, enhance, and confirm the individual's self-esteem and sense of identity.
3. Coordinate interdepartmental efforts.	3. Give individuals an opportunity to test and share their perceptions of social reality.
4. Provide a problem-solving mechanism for complex problems requiring varied information and assessments.	4. Reduce the individual's anxieties and feelings of insecurity and powerlessness.
5. Implement complex decisions.	5. Provide a problem-solving mechanism for personal and interpersonal problems.
6. Socialize and train newcomers.	

Group Development

Groups and teams in the workplace go through a maturation process, such as one would find in a life cycle. While theorists generally agree that group development is a process with identifiable stages, they disagree about the exact number, sequence, length, and nature of those stages.[9] An oft-cited model is the one proposed in 1965 by educational psychologist Bruce W Tuckman. Shown in Figure 6–1, Tuckman's model includes four stages of his original model plus a fifth stage (adjourning) added by Tuckman and a doctoral student in 1977:[10]

   1. *Forming.* During this "ice-breaking" stage, group members tend to be uncertain and anxious about their roles and the group's leadership and goals. Mutual trust is low as group members hold back to see who takes charge and how. Mistakes may be more common— and are dangerous for some groups, such as surgical teams and airline cockpit crews.

FIGURE 6–1
Tuckman's
Five-Stage
Theory
of Group
Development

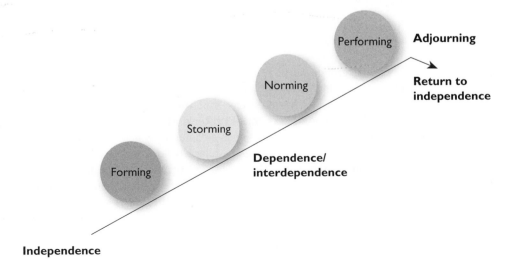

GROUP EXERCISE
Identifying Task and Maintenance Roles within Groups

(Data from the National Transportation Safety Board indicate that almost three-fourths of serious mistakes by commercial airline pilots occur on their crew's first day together.)[11] If the formal leader, such as the supervisor, does not assert his or her authority, an emergent leader will eventually step in to fulfill the group's need for leadership and direction. Leaders typically mistake this honeymoon period as a mandate for permanent control, but later problems may force a leadership change.

2. *Storming.* This second stage is a time of testing during which individuals test the leader's policies and assumptions as they try to determine how they fit into the power structure.[12] Subgroups take shape, and subtle forms of rebellion, such as procrastination, occur. Many groups stall in this stage because power politics erupts into open rebellion.

3. *Norming.* Groups that make it through stage 2 generally do so because a respected member, other than the leader, challenges the group to resolve its power struggles so it can accomplish something. Questions about authority and power are resolved through unemotional, matter-of-fact group discussion. Members experience a feeling of team spirit because they believe they have found their proper roles. The principal by-product of this stage is **group cohesiveness,** the "we feeling" that binds members of a group together.[13]

4. *Performing.* Activity during this vital stage is focused on solving task problems. As members of a mature group, contributors get their work done without hampering others. A climate of open communication, strong cooperation, and lots of helping behavior exist. Conflicts and job boundary disputes are handled constructively and efficiently. Cohesiveness and personal commitment to group goals help the group achieve more than could any one individual acting alone.

5. *Adjourning.* At this stage, the work is done; it is time to move on to other things. Having worked so hard to get along and get something done, many members feel a sense of loss. The return to independence can be eased by rituals celebrating "the end" and "new beginnings." Parties, award ceremonies, graduations, or mock funerals can provide the needed punctuation at the end of a significant group project. By emphasizing valuable lessons learned in group dynamics, leaders prepare everyone for future group and team efforts.

As individuals join and participate in a group moving through these stages, they give up a measure of their independence.[14] The various stages are not necessarily of the same duration or intensity. For instance, the storming stage may be practically nonexistent or painfully long, depending on the goal clarity and the commitment and maturity of the members.

Somewhat akin to Maslow's need hierarchy theory (see Chapter 4), Tuckman's theory has been repeated and taught so often and for so long that many have come to view it as documented fact. However, Tuckman himself cautioned that his model was derived more from group therapy sessions than from natural-life groups. Despite this important caution, many in the OB field like Tuckman's five-stage model of group development because of its easy-to-remember labels and commonsense appeal.

Group cohesiveness
A "we feeling" binding group members together.

TABLE 6–2   Task and Maintenance Roles

Source: Adapted from discussion in K D Benne and P Sheats, "Functional Roles of Group Members," *Journal of Social Issues*, Spring 1948, pp 41–49.

Task Roles	Description
Initiator	Suggests new goals or ideas.
Information seeker/giver	Clarifies key issues.
Opinion seeker/giver	Clarifies pertinent values.
Elaborator	Promotes greater understanding through examples or exploration of implications.
Coordinator	Pulls together ideas and suggestions.
Orienter	Keeps group headed toward its stated goal(s).
Evaluator	Tests group's accomplishments with various criteria such as logic and practicality.
Energizer	Prods group to move along or to accomplish more.
Procedural technician	Performs routine duties (e.g., handing out materials or rearranging seats).
Recorder	Performs a "group memory" function by documenting discussion and outcomes.

Maintenance Roles	Description
Encourager	Fosters group solidarity by accepting and praising various points of view.
Harmonizer	Mediates conflict through reconciliation or humor.
Compromiser	Helps resolve conflict by meeting others "half way."
Gatekeeper	Encourages all group members to participate.
Standard setter	Evaluates the quality of group processes.
Commentator	Records and comments on group processes/dynamics.
Follower	Serves as a passive audience.

Group Member Roles

Four centuries have passed since William Shakespeare had his character Jaques speak the following memorable lines in Act II of *As You Like It:* "All the world's a stage, And all the men and women merely players; They have their exits and their entrances; And one man in his time plays many parts." This intriguing notion of all people as actors in a universal play was not lost on 20th-century sociologists who developed a complex theory of human interaction based on roles. An OB scholar defines **roles** as "sets of behaviors that persons expect of occupants of a position."[15]

Roles
Expected behaviors for a given position.

For a work group to accomplish anything, its members must perform a combination of task and maintenance roles, identified in Table 6–2.[16] **Task roles** enable the work group to define, clarify, and pursue a common purpose. Meanwhile, **maintenance roles** foster supportive and constructive interpersonal relationships. In short, task roles keep the group *on track* while maintenance roles keep the group *together*. A project team member is performing a task function when he or she says at an update meeting, "What is the real issue here? We don't seem to be getting anywhere." Another individual who says, "Let's hear from those who oppose this plan," is performing a maintenance function. Importantly, each of the various task and maintenance roles may be played in varying combinations and sequences by the group's leader or any of its members.

Task roles
Task-oriented group behavior.

Maintenance roles
Relationship-building group behavior.

Managers and group leaders who wish to ensure proper group development can use a list of roles such as the one in Table 6–2 as a checklist. If some roles are not always performed when needed, the formal leader may take them on or assign them to other members. The task roles of initiator, orienter, and energizer are especially important because

they are *goal-directed* roles. Research studies on group goal setting confirm the motivational power of challenging goals. As with individual goal setting (see Chapters 4 and 5), difficult but achievable goals are associated with better group results.[17] Also in line with individual goal-setting theory and research, group goals are more effective if group members clearly understand them and are both individually and collectively committed to achieving them. Initiators, orienters, and energizers can be very helpful in this regard.

In an international or multicultural context, managers need to be sensitive to cultural differences regarding the relative importance of task and maintenance roles. In Japan, for example, cultural tradition calls for more emphasis on maintenance roles, especially the roles of harmonizer and compromiser. Arguing is discourteous, so people with differing views prefer to work out a solution in private. Not only do they avoid pushing their viewpoints with arguments and logic, but they also "do not hesitate to shift their beliefs if doing so will preserve smooth interpersonal relations."[18]

Norms

Norm
Shared attitudes, opinions, feelings, or actions that guide social behavior.

Ostracism
Rejection by other group members.

More broadly than roles, norms govern group behavior. According to a respected team of management consultants, a **norm** "is an attitude, opinion, feeling, or action—shared by two or more people—that guides their behavior."[19] Whereas roles involve behavioral expectations for specific positions, norms help all group members determine right from wrong and good from bad. Although norms are typically unwritten and seldom discussed openly, they have a powerful influence on group and organizational behavior.[20] Group members positively reinforce those who adhere to current norms with friendship and acceptance. Nonconformists experience criticism and even **ostracism**, or rejection by group members. Anyone who has experienced the "silent treatment" from a group of friends knows what a potent social weapon ostracism can be.[21]

Experts say norms evolve in an informal manner as the group or organization determines what it takes to be effective. Norms generally develop in various combinations of the following four ways:

- *Explicit statements by supervisors or co-workers*. For instance, a group leader might explicitly set norms about not drinking alcohol at lunch.
- *Critical events in the group's history*. At times a critical event in the group's history establishes an important precedent. For example, if a key recruit has decided to work elsewhere

because a group member said too many negative things about the organization, the company might develop a norm against such "sour grapes" behavior.

- *Primacy.* The first behavior pattern that emerges in a group often sets group expectations. This is how Paul Pressler set the norm for informality, creativity, and questioning when he took over as CEO of Gap, the clothing retailer that owns the Old Navy and Banana Republic stores: Pressler started by telling employees, "I've got a gazillion ideas, many of which are really stupid. But what the hell—you'll let me know!"[22]
- *Carryover behaviors from past situations.* Carrying over individual behaviors from past situations can increase the predictability of group members' behaviors in new settings and facilitate task accomplishment. For instance, students and professors carry fairly constant sets of expectations from class to class.[23]

Think about the norms that are currently in effect in your classroom. Do these norms help or hinder your ability to learn? Norms can affect performance either positively or negatively.

Group members tend to enforce norms under certain circumstances. Norms tend to be enforced when they help the group or organization survive, clarify or simplify behavioral expectations, help individuals avoid embarrassing situations, and clarify the group's or organization's central values and/or unique identity.[24]

TEAMS, TRUST, AND TEAMWORK

The team approach to managing organizations is having substantial impact on organizations and individuals. Teams promise to be a cornerstone of progressive management for the foreseeable future. General Electric's CEO, Jeffrey Immelt, offers this blunt overview for managers: "You lead today by building teams and placing others first. It's not about you."[25] So, virtually all employees will need to polish their team skills. Southwest Airlines, a company that credits a strong team spirit for its success, puts team skills above all else, in the belief that they are more difficult to acquire than technical skills.[26] Fortunately, the trend toward teams has a receptive audience today. Women and younger employees, according to research, thrive in team-oriented organizations.[27] Other evidence suggests that managers' desire to see teamwork outstrips employees' experience in the trenches. In a survey of 13 companies, 65% of upper-level managers agreed that "Teamwork and cooperation exist among departments," but less than half of the nonmanagement employees witnessed that teamwork.[28]

Teams: More Than Just a Group

Jon R Katzenbach and Douglas K Smith, management consultants at McKinsey & Company, say it is a mistake to use the terms *group* and *team* interchangeably. After studying many different kinds of teams—from athletic to corporate to military—they concluded that successful teams tend to take on a life of their own. Katzenbach and Smith define a **team** as "a small number of people with complementary skills who are committed to a common purpose, performance goals, and approach for which they hold themselves mutually accountable."[29] A group becomes a team when the following criteria are met:

Team
Experiential learning aimed at better internal functioning of groups.

- *Leadership* becomes a shared activity.
- *Accountability* shifts from strictly individual to both individual and collective.

- The group develops its own *purpose* or mission.
- *Problem solving* becomes a way of life, not a part-time activity.
- *Effectiveness* is measured by the group's collective outcomes and products.[30]

In terms of Tuckman's five-stage model of group development—forming, storming, norming, performing, and adjourning—teams are task groups that have matured to the *performing* stage. Many work groups fail to reach this stage because of conflicts over power and authority and unstable interpersonal relations, so they never qualify as a real team.[31] Katzenbach and Smith clarified the distinction this way: "The essence of a team is common commitment. Without it, groups perform as individuals; with it, they become a powerful unit of collective performance."[32]

When Katzenbach and Smith refer to "a small number of people" in their definition, they mean between 2 and 25 team members. According to their findings, effective teams typically have fewer than 10 members. In a survey of 400 workplace team members in the United States and Canada, the average team size was 10 members, and the most common size was 8 members.[33]

Developing Teamwork Competencies

Forming workplace teams and urging employees to be good team players are good starting points on the road to effective teams. But they are not enough today. Managers need to model and teach a variety of teamwork skills and competencies:

- Helping the team understand its problem-solving situation—understanding the issue to be addressed, researching the situation and possible solutions, helping the group arrive at a common understanding.
- Helping the team get organized and measure its performance—participating in goal setting, monitoring and providing feedback on performance, responding to feedback.
- Promoting a positive team environment—helping create and reinforce norms for respectful treatment and excellent work, praising other team members' work, supporting other team members.
- Handling conflict—encouraging constructive debate, discouraging destructive conflict, understanding the sources of conflict, negotiating win-win solutions.
- Promoting one's point of view appropriately—defending a legitimate point of view, modifying positions in response to good arguments, using a courteous manner in debates.[34]

Notice the importance of skills that are discussed and emphasized in this book, including group problem solving, mentoring, conflict management, and emotional intelligence.

Organizations focus on building teamwork competencies by the way they hire and reward employees. Internet equipment maker Cisco Systems includes an assessment of applicants' teamwork and collaboration skills in all hiring decisions. The company also rewards teamwork and collaboration by basing as much as 20% of a manager's annual bonus on an assessment of these important skills.[35]

Trust: A Key Ingredient of Teamwork

In recent years, the combination of mergers, layoffs, bloated executive bonuses, and corporate criminal proceedings has left many people cynical about trusting management.

Trust
Reciprocal faith in others' intentions and behavior.

A 2004 survey by Harris Interactive found that almost three-quarters of respondents rated American corporations' reputations as "not good" or "terrible."[36] In this business environment, it is difficult for organizations to cultivate **trust**—that is, reciprocal faith in others' intentions and behavior.[37] According to experts on the subject, the reciprocal (give-and-take) nature of trust means that "when we see others acting in ways that imply that they trust us, we become more disposed to reciprocate by trusting in them more," and "we come to distrust those whose actions appear to violate our trust or to distrust us."[38] In short, we tend to give what we get: trust begets trust; distrust begets distrust.

Trust is expressed in different ways. It has several dimensions, including *overall trust* (expecting fair play, the truth, and empathy), *emotional trust* (having faith that someone will not misrepresent you to others or betray a confidence), and *reliableness* (believing that promises and appointments will be kept and commitments met).[39] These dimensions contribute to a wide and complex range of trust, from very low to very high.

Experts advised readers of the *Harvard Business Review,* "No one can manufacture trust or mandate it into existence."[40] Their point was that leaders can't use assertions and arguments to convince someone to trust them. Rather, people build trust through actions such as rewarding integrity and trust, as well as behaving with integrity and trust themselves. Management professor and consultant Fernando Bartolomé offers the following six guidelines for building and maintaining trust:[41]

1. *Communication.* Keep team members and employees informed by explaining policies and decisions and providing accurate feedback. Be candid about your own problems and limitations. Tell the truth.[42]
2. *Support.* Be available and approachable. Provide help, advice, coaching, and support for team members' ideas.
3. *Respect.* Delegation, in the form of real decision-making authority, is the most important expression of managerial respect. Actively listening to the ideas of others is a close second.[43]
4. *Fairness.* Be quick to give credit and recognition to those who deserve it. Make sure all performance appraisals and evaluations are objective and impartial.
5. *Predictability.* Be consistent and predictable in your daily affairs. Keep both expressed and implied promises.
6. *Competence.* Enhance your credibility by demonstrating good business sense, technical ability, and professionalism.

In sum, trust needs to be earned; it cannot be demanded.

Self-Managed Teams

Have you ever thought you could do a better job than your boss? If the trend toward self-managed work teams continues to grow as predicted, you just may get your chance. Entrepreneurs and artisans often boast of not having a supervisor. The same generally cannot be said for employees working in offices and factories. But the workplace is changing. In fact, by the end of the last decade, an estimated half of the employees at *Fortune* 500 companies were working on teams.[44] More and more of those teams are self-managing, including production teams at a General Mills cereal plant in Lodi, California, which handle schedules and operations so effectively that no managers are scheduled to work during the night shift.[45] More typically, managers are present to serve as trainers and facilitators.

Self-managed teams

Groups of employees granted administrative oversight for their work.

Self-managed teams are groups of workers who are given administrative oversight for their task domains. Administrative oversight involves delegated activities such as planning, scheduling, monitoring, and staffing—chores normally performed by managers. In short, employees in these unique work groups act as their own supervisor. Accountability is maintained indirectly by outside managers and leaders. According to a recent study of a company with 300 self-managed teams, 66 "team advisors" relied on several indirect influence tactics:

- *Relating.* Understanding the organization's power structure, building trust, showing concern for individual team members.
- *Scouting.* Seeking outside information, diagnosing teamwork problems, facilitating group problem solving.
- *Persuading.* Gathering outside support and resources, influencing team to be more effective and pursue organizational goals.
- *Empowering.* Delegating decision-making authority, facilitating the team's decision-making process, coaching.[46]

Self-managed teams are variously referred to as semiautonomous work groups, autonomous work groups, and superteams.

Although the term *self-managed* may sound simple, it does not mean simply turning workers loose with no direction. Management is necessary, but in a new way. An organization embracing self-managed teams should be prepared to undergo revolutionary changes in management philosophy, structure, staffing and training practices, and reward systems. In addition, the traditional notions of managerial authority and control are turned on their heads. Not surprisingly, many managers strongly resist these changes and fear giving up the reins of power as a threat to their job security.

Among companies with self-managed teams, the most commonly delegated tasks are work scheduling and dealing directly with outside customers. The least common team chores are hiring and firing.[47] Most of today's self-managed teams remain bunched at the shop-floor level in factory settings. But experts predict growth of the practice in the managerial ranks and in service operations.[48]

Cross-Functionalism

Cross-functionalism

Team made up of technical specialists from different areas.

A common feature of self-managed teams, particularly among those above the shop-floor or clerical level, is **cross-functionalism,**[49] an arrangement in which specialists from different areas are put on the same team. Mark Stefik, a manager at the world-renowned Palo Alto Research Center in California, praises cross-functionalism as a method for stimulating breakthrough ideas that seem "magical." Says Stefik, "The idea is to start a team on a problem—a hard problem, to keep people motivated. When there's an obstacle, instead of dodging it, bring in another point of view: an electrical engineer, a user interface expert, a sociologist, whatever spin on the market is needed. Give people new eyeglasses to cross-pollinate ideas."[50]

Cross-functionalism has been incorporated into university programs to help students learn to think broadly and polish their team skills. At Carnegie Mellon University's business school, for example, a class called Integrated Product Development brings business students together with students in engineering and fine arts to create product ideas.[51]

Effectiveness of Self-Managed Teams

Much of what we know about self-managed teams comes from testimonials and case studies. Fortunately, a body of higher-quality field research is slowly developing. A review of three meta-analyses covering 70 individual studies concluded that self-managed teams had a positive effect on productivity and on specific attitudes relating to self-management (e.g., responsibility and control). No significant effect was found on general attitudes (e.g., job satisfaction and organizational commitment) or on absenteeism or turnover.[52] Although encouraging, these results do not qualify as a sweeping endorsement of self-managed teams. Yet, experts say the trend toward self-managed work teams will continue to grow in North America because of a strong cultural bias in favor of direct participation. Managers need to be prepared for the resulting shift in organizational administration, however.

Virtual Teams

Virtual teams are a product of modern times. They take their name from *virtual reality* computer simulations, where "it's almost like the real thing." Thanks to evolving information technologies such as the Internet, e-mail, videoconferencing, groupware, and fax machines, you can be a member of a work team without really being there.[53] Traditional team meetings are location specific. Team members are either physically present or absent. Virtual teams, in contrast, convene electronically, with members reporting in from different locations, different organizations, and even different time zones. By one estimate, more than 1 out of 10 workers are "distributed workers," meaning they have no permanent work location but plug in their computers or talk to co-workers and clients wherever is most convenient for a particular task.[54]

Virtual team
Information technology allows group members in different locations to conduct business.

Because virtual teams are so new, there is no consensual definition. Our working definition of a virtual team is a physically dispersed task group that conducts its business through modern information technology.[55] Advocates say virtual teams are very flexible and efficient because they are driven by information and skills, not by time and location.[56] People with needed information and skills can be team members, regardless of where or when they actually do their work. For example, Volvo recently developed a station wagon through a global collaboration among designers in Sweden, Spain, and the United States. Software called Alias allowed designers to share and edit images; they could even view full-size 3-D images projected in special theaters on both continents.[57] Virtual teamwork, such as Volvo uses, can allow work to progress around the clock, as employees in different time zones keep the task progressing. Still, one negative consequence is a lack of face-to-face interaction, which can weaken trust, communication, and accountability.

As you might expect with a practice as new and ill-defined as virtual teams, research evidence to date of its functioning and effectiveness is a bit spotty. However, recent studies of computer-mediated groups offer several insights. First, virtual groups formed over the Internet follow a group development process similar to that for face-to-face groups.[58] Also, Internet chat rooms create more work and yield poorer decisions than face-to-face meetings and telephone conferences.[59] Successful use of groupware—software that facilitates interaction among virtual group members—requires training and hands-on experience.[60] And finally, inspirational leadership has a positive impact on creativity in electronic brain-storming groups.[61]

Virtual teams may be in fashion, but they are not a cure-all. In fact, they may be a giant step backward for those not well versed in modern information technology and group dynamics.[62] Managers who rely on virtual teams agree on one point: *Meaningful face-to-face contact, especially during early phases of the group development process, is absolutely essential.* Virtual group members need "faces" in their minds to go with names and elec-tronic messages.[63] Additionally, virtual teams cannot succeed without some old-fashioned requirements such as top-management support, hands-on training, a clear mission and spe-cific objectives, effective leadership, and schedules and deadlines.[64]

THREATS TO GROUP AND TEAM EFFECTIVENESS

No matter how carefully managers staff and organize task groups, group dynamics can still go haywire. Forehand knowledge of two major threats to group effectiveness—groupthink and social loafing—can help managers and team members alike take necessary preventive steps.

Groupthink

Systematic analysis of the decision-making processes underlying the war in Vietnam and other U.S. foreign-policy fiascoes prompted Yale University's Irving Janis to coin the term *groupthink*.[65] Like professional politicians, modern managers can all too easily become victims of groupthink if they passively ignore the danger. Janis defines **groupthink** as "a mode of thinking that people engage in when they are deeply involved in a cohesive in-group, when members' strivings for unanimity override their motivation to realistically appraise alternative courses of action."[66] He says groupthink results when pressure within the group causes "a deterioration of mental efficiency, reality testing, and moral judgment."[67] In groups victimized by groupthink, members tend to be friendly and tightly knit.

Groupthink
Janis's term for a cohesive in-group's unwill-ingness to realistically view alternatives.

According to Janis's model, groupthink has eight classic symptoms:

1. An illusion of *invulnerability,* which breeds excessive optimism and risk taking.
2. A belief in the group's *inherent morality,* which encourages group members to ignore ethical implications.
3. Use of *rationalization* to protect pet assumptions.
4. *Stereotyped views of opposition,* which cause the group to underestimate opponents.
5. *Self-censorship,* or stifling of critical debate.
6. An *illusion of unanimity,* in which silence is interpreted to mean consent.
7. *Peer pressure* that questions the loyalty of any dissenters.
8. *Mindguards,* or people who appoint themselves to protect the group against adverse information.[68]

The more symptoms there are, the higher the probability of groupthink.

These symptoms thrive in the sort of climate outlined in management consultant Victor H Palmieri's critique of corporate directors in the United States: "No one likes to be the skunk at the garden party. . . . One does not make friends and influence people in the board-room or elsewhere by raising hard questions that create embarrassment or discomfort for management."[69] In short, policy- and decision-making groups can become so cohesive that strong-willed executives are able to gain unanimous support for poor decisions.[70]

To combat groupthink, Janis believes that prevention is better than the cure. Prevention begins by assigning each group member the role of critical evaluator, which involves actively voicing objections and doubts. Also, top-level executives should not use policy committees to rubber-stamp decisions that have already been made. Another technique is to have different groups with different leaders explore the same policy questions. Methods to introduce fresh perspectives include scheduling debates among subgroups and inviting participation from outside experts. When the group discusses major alternatives, someone should be given the role of devil's advocate, a person who tries to uncover every conceivable negative factor. Finally, once the group has reached a consensus, all the group members should be encouraged to rethink their position to check for flaws.[71]

Social Loafing

Is group performance less than, equal to, or greater than the sum of its parts? For example, can three people working together accomplish less than, the same amount as, or more than they would working separately? An interesting study conducted more than a half century ago by a French agricultural engineer named Ringelmann found the answer to be "less than."[72] In a rope-pulling exercise, Ringelmann reportedly found that three people pulling together could achieve only two and a half times the average individual rate. Eight pullers achieved less than four times the individual rate. This tendency for individual effort to decline as group size increases has come to be called **social loafing.**[73]

Social loafing
Decrease in individual effort as group size increases.

Several theoretical explanations have been offered for the social-loafing effect: equity of effort ("Everyone else is goofing off, so why shouldn't I?"), loss of personal accountability ("I'm lost in the crowd, so who cares?"), motivational loss due to the sharing of rewards ("Why should I work harder than the others when everyone gets the same reward?"), and coordination loss as more people perform the task ("We're getting in each other's way."). Laboratory studies refined these theories by identifying situational factors that moderated the social-loafing effect. Social loafing occurred under the following circumstances:

- The task was perceived to be unimportant, simple, or uninteresting.[74]
- Group members thought their individual output was not identifiable.[75]
- Group members expected their co-workers to loaf.[76]

In contrast, social loafing did not occur when group members in two laboratory studies expected to be evaluated.[77] Also, research suggests that self-reliant "individualists" are more prone to social loafing than are group-oriented "collectivists." Individualists are more cooperative, however, if the group is small and each member is held personally accountable for results.[78]

These findings demonstrate that social loafing is not an inevitable part of group effort. Management can curb this threat to group effectiveness by making sure the task is challenging and that group members perceive it as important. Additionally, it is a good idea to hold group members personally accountable for identifiable portions of the group's task.[79] Recall our discussion of the power of goal setting in Chapters 4 and 5.

Chapter **Seven**

Decision Making: How Individuals and Groups Arrive at Decisions

Learning Objectives

After reading the material in this chapter, you should be able to:

- Compare the rational model of decision making with Simon's normative model.
- Discuss knowledge management and ways that companies increase knowledge sharing.
- Explain the model of decision-making styles and the stages of the creative process.
- Summarize pros and cons of involving groups in the decision-making process.
- Explain how participative management affects performance.
- Describe techniques used to improve the quality of group decisions.

Many stories circulate about high-profile executives' work habits, and one that has recently been discussed concerns Microsoft's cofounder, Bill Gates. To set a course or correct it for his company during his years as chief executive, Gates would solicit ideas—no matter how off-the-wall—from any employees who wanted to share their ideas. Then he would go to a retreat in the woods by himself to read and consider the suggestions. Gates called this period of reflection his "think week," and the resulting decisions drove the strategy of Microsoft. This dedicated week of decision making worked for Bill Gates, but what process do other managers use?

Continuing our exploration of the collective or social dimensions of organizational behavior, this chapter focuses on individual and group decision making. Decision making is one of a manager's primary responsibilities. The quality of a manager's decisions directly affects his or her own career opportunities, rewards, and job satisfaction while also contributing to the organization's success or failure. **Decision making** is a means to an end; it entails identifying and choosing alternative solutions that lead to a desired state of affairs. The process begins with a problem and ends when a solution has been chosen. This chapter focuses on three aspects of decisions in

Decision making
Identifying and choosing solutions that lead to a desired end result.

organizations: models of decision making, the dynamics of decision making, and group decision making.

MODELS OF DECISION MAKING

How do people make decisions? Two fundamental ways to describe this process are the rational model and Simon's normative model. Each is based on a different set of assumptions and offers unique insights into the decision-making process.

The Rational Model

Rational model
Logical four-step approach to decision making.

Problem
Gap between an actual and desired situation.

The **rational model** proposes that managers use a rational, four-step sequence when making decisions:

1. *Identifying the problem.* A **problem** exists when the actual situation and the desired situation differ. Suppose you have to pay rent at the end of the month and don't have enough money. You have a problem: not that you have to pay rent, but that you must obtain the needed funds. Likewise, after the merger of pharmaceutical giants Glaxo Wellcome and SmithKline Beecham, management observed that the company had enormous revenues but no major new drugs in development to propel future profits as the company's popular drugs neared the end of their patent protection. The company's problem was the lack of new drugs, possibly caused by poor drug discovery facilities and processes, lack of resources for research and development, and lack of inventors.[1]

2. *Generating solutions.* After identifying a problem, the next logical step is generating alternative solutions. For repetitive and routine decisions such as deciding when to send customers a bill, alternatives are readily available through decision rules, such as a company's policy of billing customers three days after shipping a product. This automatic response is not the case for novel and unstructured decisions. Novel problems lack routine procedures, so decision makers must creatively generate alternatives.

3. *Selecting a solution.* Optimally, decision makers want to choose the alternative with the greatest value, which decision theorists call "maximizing the expected utility" of an outcome. This task is not easy. First, assigning values to alternatives is complicated and prone to error because values are subjective and vary according to the preferences of the decision maker. In addition, evaluating alternatives assumes they can be judged according to some standards or criteria. This view further assumes that valid criteria exist, each alternative can be compared against these criteria, and the decision maker actually uses the criteria.

4. *Implementing and evaluating the solution.* Once a solution has been chosen, it must be implemented. Then the evaluation phase is used to assess its effectiveness. If the solution is effective, it should reduce the difference between the actual and desired states that created the problem. If the gap has not closed, the implementation was not successful, meaning that the problem was incorrectly identified or the solution was inappropriate.

According to this model, managers are completely objective and possess complete information to make a decision. Despite criticism for being unrealistic, the rational model is instructive because it analytically breaks down the decision-making process and serves as a conceptual anchor for newer models.[2]

Optimizing
Choosing the best possible solution.

The rational model is based on the premise that managers optimize when they make decisions. **Optimizing** involves solving problems by producing the best possible solution. But as Herbert Simon, a decision theorist who in 1978 earned the Nobel Prize for his work on decision making, points out, real-world decision makers aren't perfectly rational; they don't even approximate rationality. In fact, said Simon, "The assumptions of perfect rationality . . . do not even remotely describe the processes that human beings use for making decisions in complex situations."[3] In a recent study of 400 strategic decisions, researchers found that decision makers often rushed to judgment, selected readily available ideas or solutions, and poorly allocated resources to study alternatives.[4] As a result, the rational model is at best an instructional tool.

Simon's Normative Model

Bounded rationality
Constraints that restrict decision making.

Considering that decision makers do not follow rational procedures, Simon proposed a normative model of decision making, which attempts to identify the process that managers actually use when making decisions. The process is guided by a decision maker's **bounded rationality,** meaning the notion that decision makers are restricted ("bounded") by a variety of constraints when making decisions. These constraints include any personal or environmental characteristics that reduce rational decision making, such as the limited capacity of the human mind, the complexity and uncertainty of the problem, the amount and timeliness of information at hand, the criticality of the decision, and time demands.[5] Because of these constraints, Simon's normative model suggests that decision making is characterized by limited information processing, the use of judgmental heuristics, and satisficing.

Limited Information Processing

Managers tend to acquire manageable rather than optimal amounts of information. This practice makes it difficult for managers to identify all possible alternative solutions. So, in the long run, the constraints of bounded rationality cause decision makers to fail to evaluate all potential alternatives.

Judgmental Heuristics

Judgmental heuristics
Rules of thumb or shortcuts that people use to reduce information-processing demands.

To reduce information-processing demands, people use **judgmental heuristics,** which are rules of thumb or shortcuts to simplify making judgments.[6] Research also shows that we tend to use these heuristics when confronted with excessive amounts of choice or information, and we use them without conscious awareness.[7] The use of heuristics helps decision makers reduce the uncertainty inherent in the decision-making process. Because these shortcuts represent knowledge gained from experience, they can help decision makers evaluate current problems. But they also can lead to systematic errors that erode the quality of decisions.

Availability heuristic
Tendency to base decisions on information readily available in memory.

Two common categories of heuristics are important: the availability heuristic and the representativeness heuristic. The **availability heuristic** represents a decision maker's tendency to base decisions on information that is readily available in memory. Information is more accessible in memory when it involves an event that recently occurred, is salient (noticeable and significant), and evokes strong emotions. Because people use this heuristic, they tend to overestimate the occurrence of unlikely but dramatic events such as a plane crash or a high school shooting. This bias also is partially responsible for the recency effect

HOT SEAT VIDEO
Office Romance: Groping for Answers

(discussed in Chapter 2). A manager is more likely to give an employee a positive performance evaluation if the employee did something exceptional near the time of the review.

Representativeness heuristic
Tendency to assess the likelihood of an event occurring based on impressions about similar occurrences.

When people estimate the probability of an event occurring, they use the **representativeness heuristic,** which is the tendency to assess the likelihood of an event based on their impressions about similar occurrences. A manager may hire a graduate from a particular university because the past three people hired from that school turned out to be good performers. In this case, the manager uses the "school attended" criterion to simplify complex information processing needed for employment interviews. Unfortunately, this shortcut can result in a biased decision.

Satisficing

Satisficing
Choosing a solution that meets a minimum standard.

People lack the time, information, or ability to handle the complexity associated with following a rational process. So, they engage in **satisficing,** or choosing a solution that meets some minimum qualifications—one that is "good enough." This method is not necessarily undesirable. Satisficing resolves problems by producing solutions that are satisfactory, if not optimal. An example is finding a radio station to listen to in your car. You cannot know what is playing on every station at the time, because it is impossible to listen to all stations at once, so you cannot optimize. Rather, you stop searching for a station when you find one playing a song you like or do not mind hearing.

Settling

DYNAMICS OF DECISION MAKING

Decision making is part science and part art. In general, a decision-making expert says people can best carry out this process when they are in a state of "clarity," meaning they have prepared themselves physically, emotionally, and mentally to be "relaxed, positive, and focused."[8] Regarding the "science" component of decision making, several dynamics come into play: knowledge management, decision-making styles, escalation of commitment, and creativity. Understanding these dynamics can help managers make better decisions.

Improving Decision Making through Effective Knowledge Management

Knowledge management (KM)
Implementing systems and practices that increase the sharing of knowledge and information throughout an organization.

People who have tried to make a decision with incomplete information know that the quality of a decision is only as good as the information used to make it. In the case of managerial decision making, managers frequently need information or knowledge that people working in other parts of the organization possess. This realization has spawned a growing interest in the concept of **knowledge management (KM),** which is "the development of tools, processes, systems, structures, and cultures explicitly to improve the creation, sharing, and use of knowledge critical for decision making."[9] Effective use of KM helps organizations improve the quality of their decision making and correspondingly reduce costs and increase efficiency. For example, when weather forecasts predict storms in areas traveled by American Airlines, employees use computer software to identify how many passengers will be affected if particular flights are canceled. The information helps them select cancellations that will affect the fewest passengers.[10] In contrast, ineffective knowledge management can be very costly. Experts estimate that *Fortune* 500 companies lose at least $31.5 billion a year by failing to share knowledge.[11]

Forms of Knowledge

Tacit knowledge
Information gained through experience that is difficult to express and formalize.

The quality of decisions depends on two types of knowledge: tacit knowledge and explicit knowledge. **Tacit knowledge** consists of "information that is difficult to express, formalize, or share" and "is unconsciously acquired from the experiences one has while immersed in an environment."[12] Many skills, such as swinging a golf club or writing a speech, are difficult to describe in words because they involve tacit knowledge. Tacit knowledge is intuitive and is acquired by having considerable experience and expertise at some task or job. Executive testimonies and research results increasingly reveal that the intuitive component of tacit knowledge is a key component of effective decision making.[13] Richard Abdoo, chair and CEO of Wisconsin Energy Corporation, explains it this way: "You end up consuming more Rolaids, but you have to learn to trust your intuition. Otherwise, at the point when you've gathered enough data to be 99.99% certain that the decision you're about to make is the correct one, that decision has become obsolete."[14]

Explicit knowledge
Information that can be easily put into words and shared with others.

In contrast, **explicit knowledge** can easily be put into words and explained to others. This type of knowledge is shared orally or in written documents or numerical reports. In summary, tacit knowledge represents private information that is difficult to share, whereas explicit knowledge is external or public and is more easily communicated. Although both types of knowledge affect decision making, experts suggest that competitive advantages are created when employees share tacit knowledge.[15]

Knowledge Sharing

Organizations increasingly rely on sophisticated KM software to share explicit knowledge. This software allows companies to amass large amounts of information that can be accessed quickly from around the world. For example, Procter & Gamble uses scientific networks from outside the company to obtain information needed for developing new products. The company gets more than one-third of its new products from outside sources, so it has increased its level of sales per R&D employee by 40%.[16] In contrast, tacit knowledge is shared most directly by observing, participating, or working with experts, coaches, or mentors (discussed later in Chapter 12). Finally, informal networking, periodic meetings, and the design of office space can be used to facilitate KM. Alcoa, for example, designed its headquarters with the aim of increasing information sharing among its executives, by providing opportunities to interact in open offices, centrally located kitchens, and other shared space.[17]

KM plans are unlikely to succeed without the proper organizational culture (see Chapter 12). Effective KM requires that the values of the organization encourage and reinforce the spread of tacit knowledge. At IBM Global Services, the creation and sharing of knowledge are rewarded in the company's performance evaluations, especially at the executive level, and are included in the goals that managers must meet to be promoted.[18]

General Decision-Making Styles

Decision-making style
A combination of how individuals perceive and respond to information.

Individuals may differ in their approach to decision making. They have a **decision-making style,** which reflects the combination of how an individual perceives and comprehends stimuli and the general manner in which he or she chooses to respond to such information.[19] A team of researchers developed a model of decision-making styles based on the idea that styles vary along two different dimensions: value orientation and tolerance for ambiguity.[20] *Value orientation* reflects the extent to which an individual focuses on either task and technical concerns or people and social concerns when making decisions. The second dimension, a person's *tolerance for ambiguity,* indicates the extent to which a person has a high need for structure or control in his or her life. Combining these dimensions yields the four styles of decision making shown in Figure 7–1:

1. *Directive.* People with a directive style have a low tolerance for ambiguity and are oriented toward task and technical concerns when making decisions. They are efficient, logical, practical, and systematic in their approach to solving problems. People with this style are action-oriented and decisive and like to focus on facts. In their pursuit of speed and results, however, these individuals tend to be autocratic, exercise power and control, and focus on the short run.

2. *Analytical.* This style has a much higher tolerance for ambiguity and is characterized by the tendency to overanalyze a situation. People with this style like to consider more information and alternatives than do directives. Analytic individuals are careful decision makers who take longer to make decisions but also respond well to new or uncertain situations. They can often be autocratic.

3. *Conceptual.* People with a conceptual style have a high tolerance for ambiguity and tend to focus on the people or social aspects of a work situation. They take a broad perspective to problem solving and like to consider many options and future possibilities. Conceptual types adopt a long-term perspective and rely on intuition and discussions with others to acquire information. They also are willing to take risks and are good at finding creative solutions to problems. On the downside, a conceptual style can foster an idealistic and indecisive approach to decision making.

FIGURE 7–1
Decision-Making Styles

Source: Based on discussion contained in A J Rowe and R O Mason, *Managing with Style: A Guide to Understanding, Assessing, and Improving Decision Making* (San Francisco: Jossey-Bass, 1987), pp 1–17.

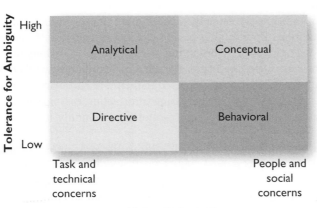

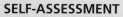

4. *Behavioral.* People with this style work well with others and enjoy social interactions in which opinions are openly exchanged. Behavioral types are supportive and receptive to suggestions, show warmth, and prefer verbal to written information. Although they like to hold meetings, people with this style have a tendency to avoid conflict and can be too concerned about others. This situation can lead behavioral types to adopt a wishy-washy approach to decision making, to have a hard time saying no to others, and to struggle with making difficult decisions.

Research shows that very few people have only one dominant decision-making style. Rather, most managers have characteristics that fall into two or three styles. Studies also show that decision-making styles vary by age, occupation, job level, and country.[21]

You can use knowledge of decision-making styles in three ways. First, knowledge of styles helps you to understand yourself. Awareness of your style assists you in identifying your strengths and weaknesses as a decision maker and facilitates the potential for self-improvement. Second, you can increase your ability to influence others by being aware of styles. For example, if you are dealing with an analytical person, you should provide as much information as possible to support your ideas. This same approach is more likely to frustrate a directive type. Finally, knowledge of styles gives you an awareness of how people can take the same information and yet arrive at different decisions by using a variety of decision-making strategies. But keep in mind that there is not a best decision-making style that applies in all situations.

Escalation of Commitment

Escalation of commitment
Sticking to an ineffective course of action too long.

Under circumstances in which things have gone wrong, decision makers have to weigh whether investing additional time, money, or effort can turn the situation around. This dilemma is known as an escalation situation.[22] In practice, even when it is unlikely that the bad situation can be reversed, people tend to engage in **escalation of commitment,** sticking to an ineffective course of action. Buying a new transmission for an old car "because I just replaced the brakes and tie rods" is an example. The financial commitment of the earlier repairs supposedly justifies the additional repairs, rather than a rational analysis of the cost to repair versus the cost to replace the vehicle. Case studies indicate that escalation of commitment is partly responsible for some of the worst financial losses experienced by organizations. From 1966 to 1989 the Long Island Lighting Company escalated its investment in the Shoreham nuclear power plant from $65 million to $5 billion, despite a steady flow of negative feedback. The plant was never opened.[23]

Organizational behavior researchers Jerry Ross and Barry Staw identified four reasons for escalation of commitment:[24]

1. *Psychological and social determinants.* The key psychological contributors to escalation of commitment are ego defense and individual motivations. Individuals "throw good money after bad" because they tend to bias facts so that they support previous decisions, take more risks when a decision is stated in negative terms (to recover losses) rather than positive ones (to achieve gains), and get too ego-involved with the project. Failure threatens an individual's self-esteem or ego, so people tend to ignore negative signs and push forward. Social pressures also can make it difficult for a manager to reverse a course of action (for instance, to drop a course of action that one has publicly supported in the past). Finally, managers may continue to support bad decisions as a way to keep their mistakes from being exposed to others.

2. *Organizational determinants.* Breakdowns in communication, workplace politics, and organizational inertia cause organizations to maintain bad courses of action.

3. *Project characteristics.* The objective features of a project have the greatest impact on escalation decisions. For example, because most projects do not reap benefits until some delayed time period, decision makers are motivated to stay with the project until the end.[25] As a result, there is a tendency to attribute setbacks to temporary causes that are correctable with additional expenditures. Also, escalation is related to whether the project has clearly defined goals and whether people receive clear feedback about performance. In one study, escalation was fueled by ambiguous performance feedback and the lack of performance standards.[26]

4. *Contextual determinants.* The context of an escalation situation includes the culture of the decision makers and the political climate of the escalation situation. Research studying decisions by U.S. and Mexican managers showed that a manager's national culture influenced the amount of escalation in decision making. The Mexican managers exhibited more escalation than the U.S. managers.[27] In the previously discussed case of the Shoreham nuclear power plant, decisions were partly influenced by pressures from other public utilities interested in nuclear power, representatives of the nuclear power industry, and people in the federal government pushing for the development of nuclear power.[28]

It is important to reduce escalation of commitment because it leads to poor decision making. Barry Staw and Jerry Ross, the researchers who originally identified the phenomenon of escalation, recommended several ways to reduce it:

- Set minimum targets for performance, and have decision makers compare their performance with these targets.
- Have different individuals make the initial and subsequent decisions about a project.
- Encourage decision makers to become less ego-involved with a project.
- Provide more frequent feedback about project completion and costs.
- Reduce the risk or penalties of failure.
- Make decision makers aware of the costs of persistence.

Creativity

In light of today's need for fast-paced decisions, an organization's ability to stimulate the creativity and innovation of its employees is becoming increasingly important.[29] Although

Creativity
Process of developing something new or unique.

many definitions have been proposed, **creativity** is defined here as the process of using intelligence, imagination, and skill to develop a new or novel product, object, process, or thought.[30] It can be as simple as locating a new place to hang your car keys or as complex as developing a handheld computer. This definition highlights three broad types of creativity: creating something new (creation), combining or synthesizing things (synthesis), and improving or changing things (modification).

Researchers are not absolutely certain how creativity takes place. Yet, we do know that creativity involves making "remote associations" among unconnected events, ideas, information stored in memory (see Chapter 2), or physical objects. Biologist Napoleone Ferrara made a remote association when he observed a protein in cows' pituitary glands; it seemed to cause growth in blood vessels, and Ferrara thought this could be connected to the idea of cancer cells growing. If he could figure out how to block the protein's growth, he could use the method to fight cancer. His creative thinking eventually led him to create a new type of cancer therapy that extends cancer patients' lives.[31]

Researchers have identified five stages underlying the creative process: preparation, concentration, incubation, illumination, and verification. The *preparation* stage reflects the notion that creativity starts from a base of knowledge, perhaps a convergence between tacit or implied knowledge and explicit knowledge. During the *concentration* stage, an individual focuses on the problem at hand. Research shows that creative ideas at work are often triggered by work-related problems, incongruities, or failures.[32] This was the situation faced by Boeing engineer Walt Gillette as he worked on the modification of a 737 aircraft for Southwest Airlines. Boeing needed to mount powerful engines on relatively small wings, which caused aerodynamic problems. Resolving those problems required travel to study other aircraft, finding ideas that combined to make a completely new installation.[33] Japanese companies encourage this stage as part of a quality improvement process (by one account, the average number of ideas per Japanese employee was 37.4 versus 0.12 for U.S. workers).[34] The next stage, *incubation,* is done unconsciously. During this stage, people engage in daily activities while their minds simultaneously mull over information and make remote associations. These associations ultimately are generated in the *illumination* stage. Finally, *verification* entails going through the entire process to verify, modify, or try out the new idea.

The stages of creativity help to explain why Japanese workers propose and implement more ideas than do American workers. To address this issue, a creativity expert visited and extensively interviewed employees from five major Japanese companies. He observed that Japanese firms have created a management infrastructure that encourages and reinforces creativity. People were taught to identify problems (discontents) on their first day of employment. In turn, discontents were referred to as "golden eggs" to reinforce the notion that it is good to identify problems.

These organizations also promoted the stages of incubation, illumination, and verification through teamwork and incentives. For example, some companies posted the golden eggs on large wall posters in the work area; employees were encouraged to interact with each other to execute the final three stages of the creative process. Employees eventually received monetary awards for any suggestions that passed all five phases of this process.[35] This research underscores the conclusion that creativity can be enhanced by effectively managing the creative process and by fostering a positive and supportive work environment.[36] In contrast, creativity is stifled in organizations where the focus is on short-term results; the organization lacks the time, resources, or staff to identify and try new ideas; leaders are unrealistic about how fast a new idea can deliver results; rewards are not linked to innovation; no system is in place for innovating; and management believes that innovation is inherently risky.[37]

GROUP DECISION MAKING

To overcome the biases of individual decisions, described earlier, Eric Schmidt, CEO and chairman of Google, requires two people to agree on solutions for every important decision. Schmidt told a reporter from *The Wall Street Journal* that this approach provides "a kind of check and balance in the decision-making process."[38] This section explores important advantages and disadvantages of group-aided decision making, as well as group problem-solving techniques.

Group Involvement in Decision Making

Whether groups assemble in face-to-face meetings or rely on technologically based methods to communicate, they can contribute to each stage of the decision-making process. To maximize the value of group-aided decision making, it is important to create an environment in which group members feel free to participate and express their opinions.

A team of researchers conducted two studies to determine whether a group's innovativeness was related to *minority dissent* (the extent to which group members feel comfortable disagreeing with other group members) and the extent to which group members participated in decision making. The most innovative groups in these studies possessed high levels of both minority dissent and participation in decision making.[39] These findings encourage managers to seek divergent views from group members during decision making. They also support the practice of not seeking compliance from group members or punishing group members who disagree with the majority opinion.

These studies reinforce the notion that the quality of group decision making varies across groups. Although experts do not agree on one best measure of a group's decision-making effectiveness, there is agreement that groups need to work through various aspects of decision making to be effective. One expert proposed that the effectiveness of decision making depends on the group's accomplishment of the following tasks:[40]

- Developing a clear understanding of the decision situation.
- Developing a clear understanding of the requirements for an effective choice.
- Thoroughly and accurately assessing the positive qualities of alternative solutions.
- Thoroughly and accurately assessing the negative qualities of alternative solutions.

Meeting these objectives may increase the probability that a group will make high-quality decisions.[41]

Advantages and Disadvantages of Group-Aided Decision Making

Including groups in the decision-making process has both pros and cons (see Table 7–1). On the positive side, groups contain a greater pool of knowledge, provide more varied perspectives, create more comprehension of decisions, increase decision acceptance, and

GROUP EXERCISE
Stranded in the Desert: An Exercise in Decision Making

create a training ground for inexperienced employees. These advantages must be balanced, however, with the disadvantages of social pressure, domination by a few, logrolling, goal displacement, and groupthink (discussed in Chapter 6). In doing so, managers need to determine the extent to which the advantages and disadvantages apply to the decision situation.

Several guidelines may indicate whether group members should be included in the decision-making process. First, if additional information would increase the quality of the decision, managers should involve the people who can provide the needed information. Similarly, if acceptance is important, managers need to involve the individuals whose acceptance and commitment are important. Finally, if people can be developed through their participation, managers may want to involve those whose development is most important.[42]

Do groups make better or worse decisions than individuals? After reviewing 61 years of relevant research, a decision-making expert concluded, "Group performance was generally qualitatively and quantitatively superior to the performance of the average individual."[43] Subsequent research of small-group decision making has generally supported this conclusion, but additional research suggests that managers should use a contingency approach when determining whether to include others in the decision-making process. For decisions that occur frequently, such as deciding who receives promotions or who qualifies for a loan, groups tend to produce more consistent decisions than do individuals.

TABLE 7–1   Advantages and Disadvantages of Group-Aided Decision Making

Source: R Kreitner, *Management,* 10th ed (Boston: Houghton Mifflin, 2007), p 231. Used with permission.

Advantages	Disadvantages
1. *Greater pool of knowledge.* A group can bring much more information and experience to bear on a decision or problem than can an individual acting alone.	1. *Social pressure.* Unwillingness to "rock the boat" and pressure to conform may combine to stifle the creativity of individual contributors.
2. *Different perspectives.* Individuals with varied experience and interests help the group see decision situations and problems from different angles.	2. *Domination by a vocal few.* Sometimes the quality of group action is reduced when the group gives in to those who talk the loudest and longest.
3. *Greater comprehension.* Those who personally experience the give-and-take of group discussion about alternative courses of action tend to understand the rationale behind the final decision.	3. *Logrolling.* Political wheeling and dealing can displace sound thinking when an individual's pet project or vested interest is at stake.
4. *Increased acceptance.* Those who play an active role in group decision making and problem solving tend to view the outcome as "ours" rather than "theirs."	4. *Goal displacement.* Sometimes secondary considerations such as winning an argument, making a point, or getting back at a rival displace the primary task of making a sound decision or solving a problem.
5. *Training ground.* Less experienced participants in group action learn how to cope with group dynamics by actually being involved.	5. *"Groupthink."* Sometimes cohesive "in-groups" let the desire for unanimity override sound judgment when generating and evaluating alternative courses of action.

MASTER YOUR KNOWLEDGE OF GROUP DECISION MAKING
The Vroom/Yetton/Jago Decision Model

Increase your knowledge of group decision making by completing the online quiz at [www.mhhe.com/obcore].

- How many of the scenarios did you assess correctly?
- Which of the decision-making styles recommended by the model would you find easiest to use?

When there are time constraints, the most competent individual, rather than a group, should make the decision. In the face of environmental threats such as time pressure and the potentially serious effects of a decision, groups use less information and fewer communication channels, thereby increasing the probability of a bad decision.[44] In general, the quality of communication strongly affects a group's productivity, so for complex tasks, it is essential to devise mechanisms to enhance communication effectiveness.

Participative Management

Participative management
Involving employees in various forms of decision making.

To compete successfully in the global economy, an organization needs to maximize its workers' potential. Highly touted methods for meeting this productivity challenge are participative management and employee empowerment (see Chapter 10). **Participative management** is the process in which employees play a direct role in setting goals, making decisions, solving problems, and making changes in the organization. Without question, participative management entails much more than simply asking employees for their ideas or opinions.

Participative management (PM) appeals to employees. In a nationwide survey of 2,408 employees, almost 66% desired more influence or decision-making power in their jobs.[45] Advocates of PM claim employee participation increases employee satisfaction, commitment, and performance.

A Model of Participative Management

Consistent with Maslow's need theory and the job characteristics model of job design (see Chapter 4), participative management is predicted to increase motivation because it helps employees fulfill basic needs for autonomy, meaningfulness of work, and interpersonal contact. Satisfaction of these needs enhances feelings of acceptance and commitment, security, challenge, and satisfaction. In turn, these positive feelings supposedly lead to increased innovation and performance.[46]

Participative management does not work in all situations. The design of work, the level of trust between management and employees, and the employees' competence and readiness to participate represent three factors that influence the effectiveness of PM. With respect to the design of work, individual participation is counterproductive when employees are highly interdependent, as on an assembly line. In this case, the interdependent employees generally do not have a broad understanding of the entire production process. Participative management also is less likely to succeed when employees do not trust management.

Finally, PM is more effective when employees are competent, prepared, and interested in participating. Northwest Airlines is a good case in point. Employees responded positively to the company's new employee suggestion system because they were motivated to help the airline reduce operating costs in order to save jobs. The suggestion system resulted in $6 million in annual savings from workers' ideas, such as reducing the number of coffee pots on each flight and improving maintenance procedures.[47]

Research and Applications

Participative management can significantly increase employee job involvement, organizational commitment, creativity, and perceptions of procedural justice and personal control.[48] Two meta-analyses provide additional support for the value of participative management. According to a meta-analysis involving 27 studies and 6,732 individuals, employee participation in the performance appraisal process was positively related to an employee's satisfaction with his or her performance review, perceived value of the appraisal, motivation to improve performance following a performance review, and perceived fairness of the appraisal process.[49] A meta-analysis of 86 studies involving 18,872 people further demonstrated that participation had a small but significant effect on job performance and a moderate relationship with job satisfaction.[50] This later finding questions the widespread conclusion that participative management should be used to increase employee performance.

So what is a manager to do? We believe that PM is not a quick-fix solution for low productivity and motivation, as some enthusiastic supporters claim. Still, because participative management is effective in certain situations, managers can increase their chances of obtaining positive results by using a contingency approach. The effectiveness of participation depends on the type of interactions between managers and employees as they jointly solve problems. Effective participation requires a constructive interaction that fosters cooperation and respect, as opposed to competition and defensiveness. Managers should not use participative programs when they have destructive interpersonal interactions with their employees.

Experiences of companies implementing participative management programs suggest additional practical recommendations. First, supervisors and middle managers tend to resist participative management because it reduces their power and authority. So, it is important to gain the support of and commitment from employees who have managerial responsibility. This conclusion was supported by results of a 15-year study of 41,000 middle and upper-level managers: 35% of the managers surveyed between 1985 and 1987 preferred to make decisions autocratically versus 31% between 1997 and 1999.[51] Second, a longitudinal study of *Fortune* 1000 firms in 1987, 1990, and 1993 indicated that employee involvement was more effective when it was implemented as part of a broader total quality management program.[52] This study suggests that organizations should use participative management and employee involvement as vehicles to help them meet their strategic and operational goals, as opposed to using these techniques as ends in themselves. Finally, the process of implementing participative management must be firmly supported and monitored by top management.[53]

Consensus
Presenting opinions and gaining agreement to support a decision.

Group Problem-Solving Techniques

Using groups to make decisions generally requires that they reach a consensus. According to a decision-making expert, a **consensus** "is reached when all members can say they either agree with the decision or have had their 'day in court' and were unable to convince the others of their viewpoint. In the final analysis, everyone agrees to support the outcome."[54] This definition indicates that consensus does not require unanimous agreement because group members may still disagree with the final decision but are willing to work toward its success.

Groups can experience roadblocks when they try to arrive at a consensus. First, groups may not generate all relevant alternatives to a problem because an individual dominates or intimidates other group members. This influence can be overt or subtle. For instance, group members who possess power and authority, such as a CEO, can be intimidating regardless of their interpersonal style, simply by being in the room. Also, shyness inhibits the generation of alternatives. Shy or socially anxious individuals may withhold their input out of fear of embarrassment or lack of confidence. Another hurdle to effective group decision making is satisficing, as groups restrict their consideration of alternatives because of limited time, information, or ability to handle large amounts of information.[55]

According to a management expert, observing several do's and don'ts can help a group achieve consensus. Groups should use active listening skills, involve as many members as possible, seek out the reasons behind arguments, and dig for the facts. Behaviors to avoid are horse trading ("I'll support you on this decision because you supported me on the last one"), voting, and agreeing just to avoid rocking the boat.[56] Voting is discouraged because it can split the group into winners and losers. In addition, groups can avoid some roadblocks to consensus by using group problem-solving techniques such as brainstorming, the nominal group technique, and the Delphi technique, as well as by employing decision-support technology.

Brainstorming

Brainstorming
Process to generate a quantity of ideas.

To increase creativity, advertising executive A F Osborn introduced a technique called brainstorming.[57] **Brainstorming** is a method used to help groups generate multiple ideas and alternatives for solving problems. This technique is effective because it helps reduce interference caused by critical and judgmental reactions to a person's ideas from other group members. Brainstorming is an effective technique for generating new ideas and alternatives. It is not appropriate for evaluating alternatives or selecting solutions.

When a group convenes for brainstorming, members begin by reviewing the problem at hand. Individual members then are asked to silently generate ideas for solving the problem. Silent idea generation is recommended over the practice of having group members randomly shout out their ideas because it leads to a greater number of unique ideas. Next, these ideas are solicited and written on a board or flip chart. A recent study suggests that managers or team leaders may want to collect the brainstormed ideas anonymously. In that study, anonymous contributions included more controversial ideas and more nonredundant ideas than were generated in brainstorming groups where contributions were not anonymous.[58] Finally, the group meets in a second session to critique and evaluate the alternatives. Managers are advised to follow the seven rules for brainstorming used by IDEO, a successful product design company:[59]

1. *Defer judgment.* Don't criticize during the initial stage of idea generation. Avoid phrases like "we've never done it that way," "it won't work," "it's too expensive," and "our manager will never agree."

2. *Build on the ideas of others*. Encourage participants to extend others' ideas by avoiding "buts" and using "ands."

3. *Encourage wild ideas*. Encourage out-of-the-box thinking. The wilder and more outrageous the ideas, the better.

4. *Go for quantity over quality*. Participants should try to generate and write down as many new ideas as possible. Focusing on quantity encourages people to think beyond their favorite ideas.

5. *Be visual*. Use different-colored pens to write on big sheets of flip chart paper, white boards, or poster board attached to the wall.

6. *Stay focused on the topic*. A facilitator should be used to keep the discussion on target.

7. *One conversation at a time*. The ground rules are that no one interrupts another person, dismisses someone's ideas, shows disrespect, or is rude.

The Nominal Group Technique

Nominal group technique (NGT)
Process to generate ideas and evaluate solutions.

The **nominal group technique (NGT)** helps groups generate ideas and evaluate and select solutions. NGT is a structured group meeting that follows this format:[60] A group is convened to discuss a particular problem or issue. After the problem is understood, individuals silently generate ideas in writing. Each individual, in round-robin fashion, then offers one idea from his or her list. Ideas are recorded on a blackboard or flip chart; they are not discussed at this stage of the process. Once all ideas are elicited, the group discusses them. Anyone may criticize or defend any item. During this step, clarification is provided, as well as general agreement or disagreement with the idea. The "30-second soap box" technique, which gives each participant a maximum of 30 seconds to argue for or against any of the ideas under consideration, can be used to facilitate this discussion. Finally, group members anonymously vote for their top choices with a weighted voting procedure (e.g., first choice = 3 points; second choice = 2 points; third choice = 1 point). Alternatively, group members can vote by placing colored dots next to their top choices. The group leader then adds the votes to determine the group's choice. Before making a final decision, the group may decide to discuss the top-ranked items and conduct a second round of voting.

The nominal group technique reduces the roadblocks to group decision making by separating brainstorming from evaluation, promoting balanced participation among group members, and incorporating mathematical voting techniques to reach consensus. Nominal group technique has been successfully used in many different decision-making situations and has been found to generate more ideas than a standard brainstorming session.[61]

The Delphi Technique

Delphi technique
Process to generate ideas from physically dispersed experts.

The Rand Corporation originally developed a problem-solving method called the Delphi technique for technological forecasting.[62] It now is used as a multipurpose planning tool. The **Delphi technique** is a group process that anonymously generates ideas or judgments from physically dispersed experts. Unlike the NGT, experts' ideas are obtained from questionnaires or via the Internet, as opposed to face-to-face group discussions.

A manager begins the Delphi process by identifying the issue(s) he or she wants to investigate. For example, a manager might want to inquire about customer demand, customers' future preferences, or the effect of locating a plant in a certain region of the country. Next, participants are identified, and a questionnaire is developed. The questionnaire is sent to participants and returned to the manager. In today's computer-networked environments, questionnaires often are e-mailed to participants. The manager then summarizes the responses and sends feedback to the participants. At this stage, participants are asked to review the feedback, prioritize the issues being considered, and return the survey within a specified time period. This cycle repeats until the manager obtains the necessary information.

The Delphi technique is useful in several situations, such as when face-to-face discussions are impractical, when disagreements and conflict are likely to impair communication, when certain individuals might severely dominate group discussion, and when groupthink is a probable outcome of the group process.[63]

Computer-Aided Decision Making

The purpose of computer-aided decision making is to reduce consensus roadblocks while collecting more information in a shorter period of time. Computer-aided decision-making systems may be chauffeur driven or group driven.[64] Chauffeur-driven systems ask participants to answer predetermined questions on electronic keypads or dials. This kind of system is used to poll live television audiences on shows such as *Who Wants to Be a Millionaire?* The computer system tabulates participants' responses in a matter of seconds.

Group-driven electronic meetings are conducted in one of two ways. First, managers can use e-mail systems (discussed in Chapter 9) or the Internet to collect information or brainstorm about a decision that must be made. For example, when employees at Miami Children's Hospital are designing training programs, they use Internet-based collaboration software that links together trainers in 300 different organizations. To gather ideas, Loubna Noureddin, the hospital's director of staff and community education, can simply post a question; she receives feedback from experts in the content and technology of her training materials. Noureddin appreciates not just the efficiency delivered by collaborating online, but also the time it saves.[65]

The second method of computer-aided, group-driven meetings is conducted in a special facility equipped with individual workstations that are networked to each other. Instead of talking, participants type their input, ideas, comments, reactions, or evaluations on their keyboards. The input simultaneously appears on a large projector screen at the front of the room, enabling all participants to see all input. This computer-driven process reduces consensus roadblocks because input is anonymous, everyone gets a chance to contribute, and no one can dominate the process. Research demonstrated that computer-aided decision making produced greater quality and quantity of ideas than either traditional brainstorming or the nominal group technique for both small and large groups of people.[66]

However, another recent study advises caution when determining what forms of computer-aided decision making to use. This meta-analysis of 52 studies compared the effectiveness of face-to-face decision-making groups with "chat" groups. Results revealed that the use of chat groups led to lower group effectiveness and member satisfaction and greater time to complete tasks than in face-to-face groups.[67] These findings underscore the need to use a contingency approach for selecting the best method of computer-aided decision making in a given situation.

With or without a computer, decision making is one of the most essential activities that occur in organizations. As you review the principles in this chapter, consider also the insights into your decision-making style from the earlier Self-Assessment exercise. How would you like to improve the way you make decisions?

Chapter **Eight**

Conflict and Negotiation: Why Conflict Arises and What to Do about It

Learning Objectives

After reading the material in this chapter, you should be able to:

- Distinguish between functional and dysfunctional conflict, and identify desirable outcomes of conflict.
- Define *personality conflicts,* and explain how they should be managed.
- Discuss ways to manage intergroup conflict, including in-group thinking and cross-cultural conflict.
- Describe methods for promoting functional conflict and styles of handling conflict.
- Identify and describe techniques for alternative dispute resolution.
- Summarize basic approaches to negotiation, giving applications.

From the soap opera episodes of *The Apprentice* to daily news of political infighting over budgets and personnel to teachers or flight attendants walking a picket line, we see the continual costs and consequences of organizations in conflict. Uncontrolled conflict is undeniably a force that can destroy a business. But what about an organization that experiences no dissent? Where will it get its creative spark to drive it to the next level? Both ends of the conflict spectrum can harm today's organizations.

Make no mistake about it. Conflict is an unavoidable aspect of life. Today especially, *organizational* conflict is inevitable because of constant change, greater employee diversity, more teams (virtual and self-managed), and less face-to-face communication (more electronic interaction), all in a global economy with increased cross-cultural dealings. Noting that "change begets conflict, conflict begets change," Dean Tjosvold, from Canada's Simon Fraser University, offers this challenging view:

"Managing conflicts well does not insulate us from change, nor does it mean that we will always come out on top or get all that we want. However, effective conflict management helps us keep in touch with new developments and create solutions appropriate for new threats and opportunities."[1] Although the news is full of sobering examples of failure to manage conflict, we must continue to try. As outlined in this chapter, tools and solutions are available, if only we develop the ability and motivation to use them persistently. The choice is ours: Be active managers of conflict and effective negotiators, or be managed by conflict.[2]

A MODERN VIEW OF CONFLICT

Conflict
One party perceives its interests are being opposed or set back by another party.

A comprehensive review of the literature on conflict yielded this consensus definition: "**conflict** is a process in which one party perceives that its interests are being opposed or negatively affected by another party."[3] The word *perceives* reminds us that sources of conflict and issues can be real or imagined. The resulting conflict is the same. Conflict can escalate (strengthen) or deescalate (weaken) over time. In either case, according to the same review of the literature, "the disputants or third parties can attempt to manage it in some manner."[4] Current and future managers need to understand the dynamics of conflict and know how to handle it effectively, both as disputants and as third parties.

A Conflict Continuum

Ideas about managing conflict underwent an interesting evolution during the 20th century. Initially, scientific management experts such as Frederick W Taylor believed all conflict ultimately threatened management's authority and so had to be avoided or quickly resolved.[5] Later, human relationists recognized the inevitability of conflict and advised managers to learn to live with it. Still, emphasis remained on resolving conflict whenever possible. Beginning in the 1970s, OB specialists realized conflict has both positive and negative outcomes, depending on its nature and intensity.

This more recent perspective introduced the revolutionary idea that organizations could suffer from *too little* conflict. Work groups, departments, or organizations experiencing too little conflict tend to be plagued by apathy, lack of creativity, indecision, and missed deadlines. Appropriate types and levels of conflict energize people in constructive directions.[6] Excessive conflict, in contrast, can erode organizational performance because of political infighting, dissatisfaction, lack of teamwork, and turnover. Other manifestations of excessive conflict may include workplace aggression and violence.[7]

Functional versus Dysfunctional Conflict

Functional conflict
Serves organization's interests.

Dysfunctional conflict
Threatens organization's interests.

The distinction between **functional conflict** and **dysfunctional conflict** pivots on whether the organization's interests are served. According to one conflict expert, conflicts are constructive if they "support the goals of the organization and improve performance" and dysfunctional if they "hinder organizational performance."[8] The manager's job logically includes eliminating dysfunctional forms of conflict. In management circles, functional conflict is commonly referred to as constructive or cooperative conflict.[9]

Often, a simmering conflict can be defused in a functional manner or driven to dysfunctional proportions, depending on how it is handled. A few years ago, Southwest Airlines creatively defused a conflict between flight attendants and their schedulers by requiring the feuding employees to switch jobs for a day.[10] In contrast, at computer retailer Gateway, sales fell sharply, and the company's recently appointed CEO, Ted Waitt, tried to paint an optimistic picture, only to have a board member say, "Why should we believe you?" Unable to convince the board, including company founder Jeff Weitzen, to trust his leadership, Waitt left the company.[11]

Antecedents of Conflict

Certain situations produce more conflict than others. Knowing the antecedents of conflict prepares managers to anticipate conflict and take steps to resolve it if it becomes dysfunctional. The following situations tend to produce either functional or dysfunctional conflict:

- Incompatible personalities or value systems.
- Overlapping or unclear job boundaries.
- Competition for limited resources.
- Interdepartment or intergroup competition.
- Inadequate communication.
- Interdependent tasks (so that one person cannot complete an assignment until others have completed their work).
- Organizational complexity (more hierarchical layers and specialized tasks).
- Unreasonable or unclear policies, standards, or rules.
- Unreasonable deadlines or extreme time pressure.
- Collective decision making (the greater the number of people participating in a decision, the greater the potential for conflict).
- Decision making by consensus.
- Unmet expectations (unrealistic expectations about job assignments, pay, or promotions).
- Unresolved or suppressed conflicts.[12]

Proactive managers carefully read these early warnings and take appropriate action. For example, group conflict sometimes can be reduced by making decisions on the basis of majority approval rather than striving for a consensus. Another method is to use the "conflict iceberg" in Figure 8–1. For a given conflict, the manager would work from top to bottom, noting any observations or insights about each level. If all parties to the conflict complete the exercise, they may be able to arrive at a deeper understanding that helps them identify an acceptable resolution.

Why People Avoid Conflict

Are you uncomfortable in situations involving conflict? Do you go out of your way to avoid conflict? If so, you're not alone. Many of us avoid conflict for a variety of both good and bad reasons. Tim Ursiny, in his entertaining and instructive book, *The Coward's Guide to Conflict,* contends that we avoid conflict because we fear various combinations of the following: harm, rejection, loss of relationship, anger, being seen as selfish, saying the wrong thing, failing, hurting someone else, getting what you want, and intimacy.[13] This list is self-explanatory, except for the fear of "getting what you want." By this, Ursiny is referring to

FIGURE 8–1
The Conflict Iceberg

Source: From K Cloke and J Goldsmith, *Resolving Conflicts at Work: A Complete Guide for Everyone on the Job* (San Francisco: Jossey-Bass, 2000), p 114. Copyright © 2000 Jossey-Bass, Inc. This material is used by permission of John Wiley & Sons, Inc.

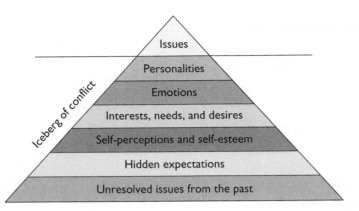

those who, for personal reasons, feel undeserving or fear the consequences of success, so they tend to sabotage themselves. For our present purposes, it is sufficient to become aware of our fears and practice overcoming them. Reading, understanding, and acting on the material in this chapter are steps in a positive direction.

Desired Outcomes of Conflict

Within organizations, conflict management is more than simply a quest for agreement. Making progress and minimizing dysfunctional conflict require a broader agenda. Tjosvold's cooperative conflict model calls for three desired outcomes:

1. *Agreement.* But at what cost? Equitable and fair agreements are best. An agreement that leaves one party feeling exploited or defeated will tend to breed resentment and subsequent conflict.

2. *Stronger relationships.* Good agreements enable conflicting parties to build bridges of goodwill and trust for future use. Moreover, conflicting parties who trust each other are more likely to keep their end of the bargain.

3. *Learning.* Functional conflict can promote greater self-awareness and creative problem solving. Like the practice of management itself, successful conflict handling is learned primarily by doing. Knowledge of the concepts and techniques in this chapter is a necessary first step, but there is no substitute for hands-on practice. In a contentious world, there are plenty of opportunities to practice conflict management.[14]

MAJOR FORMS OF CONFLICT

Certain antecedents of conflict deserve a closer look. This section explores the nature and organizational implications of three common forms of conflict: personality conflict, intergroup conflict, and cross-cultural conflict.

Personality Conflicts

As discussed in Chapter 3, your *personality* is the package of stable traits and characteristics creating your unique identity. According to experts on the subject, personality shapes "whether we are seen as charming, irritating, fascinating, nondescript, approachable, or intimidating."[15]

Personality conflict

Interpersonal opposition driven by personal dislike or disagreement.

Given the many possible combinations of personality traits, it is clear why personality conflicts are inevitable. We define a **personality conflict** as interpersonal opposition based on personal dislike and/or disagreement. This topic is important, as evidenced by a recent survey of 173 managers in the United States. When the managers were asked what makes them most uncomfortable, an overwhelming 73% said "building relationships with people I dislike"—far ahead of "asking for a raise" (25%) and "speaking to large audiences" (24%).[16]

Personality conflicts can involve individuals who have much to contribute but different styles of contributing. The leadership of EMC Corporation, which makes data storage equipment, experienced some of this conflict after Joseph M Tucci, whose background is in sales, replaced Michael C Ruettgers, whose expertise is in operations, as the company's CEO. Ruettgers continued on as the company's executive chairman, and he was not quiet about his displeasure when after a year, the company posted a $508 million loss. Some former EMC executives said Ruettgers slowed Tucci down when he wanted to make changes, and perhaps personality differences were behind some of that resistance. Ruettgers is considered more reserved and slower to make decisions; Tucci is known as a fast decision maker who likes to build relationships. In the end, however, the personality differences faded into the background after new-product development eventually led the company to good financial performance.[17]

Workplace Incivility: The Seeds of Personality Conflict

Somewhat akin to physical pain, chronic personality conflicts often begin with seemingly insignificant irritations. For instance, a manager can grow to deeply dislike someone in the next cubicle who hums along to music from his iPod while drumming his foot on the side of a filing cabinet. Sadly, grim little scenarios such as this are all too common today, given the steady erosion of civility in the workplace.[18] In a recent survey of 612 employees, sizable numbers reported uncivil words, including sexually offensive remarks (reported by 35%), ethnic slurs (29%), and racial slurs (29%).[19] A pair of OB researchers recently offered a cautionary overview of the problem, noting that incivility is costly to employers in a variety of subtle ways. They explain, "Because of their experiences of workplace incivility, employees decrease work effort, time on the job, productivity, and performance," adding that failure to correct the problem causes a decline in job satisfaction and loyalty to the organization—even to employee turnover.[20]

Vicious cycles of incivility need to be avoided (or broken early) with an organizational culture that places a high value on respect for co-workers. This transformation requires managers and leaders to act as caring and courteous role models. A positive spirit of cooperation, as opposed to one based on negativism and aggression, also helps. Some organizations have resorted to workplace etiquette training.[21] More specifically, constructive feedback and skillful positive reinforcement can keep a single irritating behavior from precipitating a full-blown personality conflict (or worse).

Dealing with Personality Conflicts

Personality conflicts are a potential minefield for managers. Personality traits, by definition, are stable and resistant to change. Moreover, according to the American Psychiatric Association's *Diagnostic and Statistical Manual of Mental Disorders,* there are 410 psychological disorders that can and do show up in the workplace.[22] This fact brings up legal issues. Employees in the United States suffering from psychological disorders such as depression and mood-altering diseases such as alcoholism are protected from discrimination by the Americans with Disabilities Act.[23] (Other nations have similar laws.) Also, sexual harassment and other forms of discrimination can grow out of apparent personality conflicts.[24] Finally, personality conflicts can spawn workplace aggression and violence.[25]

Traditionally, managers dealt with personality conflicts by either ignoring them or transferring one party.[26] In view of the legal implications just discussed, both of these options may be open invitations to discrimination lawsuits. Table 8–1 presents practical tips for both nonmanagers and managers who are involved in or affected by personality conflicts. Our later discussions of handling dysfunctional conflict and alternative dispute resolution techniques also apply.

Intergroup Conflict

Conflict among work groups, teams, and departments is a common threat to organizational competitiveness. For example, when Michael Volkema became CEO of Herman Miller in the mid-1990s, he found an inward-focused company with divisions fighting over budgets. He has since curbed intergroup conflict at the Michigan-based furniture maker by emphasizing collaboration and redirecting everyone's attention outward, to the customer.[27] Managers who understand the mechanics of intergroup conflict are better equipped to face this sort of challenge.

In-Group Thinking: The Seeds of Intergroup Conflict

As we mentioned in Chapter 6, *cohesiveness*—a "we feeling" binding group members together—can be a good or bad thing. A certain amount of cohesiveness can turn a group

TABLE 8–1 **How to Deal with Personality Conflicts**

Tips for Employees Having a Personality Conflict	Tips for Third-Party Observers of a Personality Conflict	Tips for Managers Whose Employees Are Having a Personality Conflict
Note: All employees need to be familiar with and *follow* company policies for diversity, antidiscrimination, and sexual harassment.		
• Communicate directly with the other person to resolve the perceived conflict (emphasize problem solving and common objectives, not personalities). • Avoid dragging co-workers into the conflict. • If dysfunctional conflict persists, seek help from direct supervisors or human resource specialists.	• Do not take sides in someone else's personality conflict. • Suggest the parties work things out themselves in a constructive and positive way. • If dysfunctional conflict persists, refer the problem to the parties' direct supervisors.	• Investigate and document conflict. • If appropriate, take corrective action (e.g., feedback or behavior modification). • If necessary, attempt informal dispute resolution. • Refer difficult conflicts to human resource specialists or hired counselors for formal resolution attempts and other interventions.

of individuals into a smooth-running team. Too much cohesiveness, however, can bree groupthink because a desire to get along pushes aside critical thinking. The study of in-groups by small-group researchers has revealed a whole package of changes associated with increased group cohesiveness:

- Members of in-groups view themselves as a collection of unique individuals, while they stereotype members of other groups as being "all alike."
- In-group members see themselves positively and as morally correct, while they view members of other groups negatively and as immoral.
- In-groups view outsiders as a threat.
- In-group members exaggerate the differences between their group and other groups. This typically involves a distorted perception of reality.[28]

Avid sports fans who simply can't imagine how someone would support the opposing team exemplify one form of in-group thinking. Also, this pattern of behavior is a form of ethnocentrism (see Chapter 2), a cross-cultural barrier. Reflect for a moment on evidence of in-group behavior in your life. Does your circle of friends make fun of others because of their race, gender, nationality, weight, sexual preference, or major in college?[29]

In-group thinking is one more fact of organizational life that virtually guarantees conflict. Managers cannot eliminate in-group thinking, but they certainly should not ignore it when handling intergroup conflicts.

Research Lessons for Handling Intergroup Conflict

When advising on how to reduce intergroup conflict, sociologists have long recommended the *contact hypothesis*. According to this hypothesis, the more the members of different groups interact, the less intergroup conflict they will experience. Those interested in improving race, international, and union–management relations typically encourage cross-group interaction. The hope is that *any* type of interaction, short of actual conflict, will reduce stereotyping and combat in-group thinking. But research has shown this approach to be naive and limited. For example, a study of 83 health center employees (83% female) at a midwestern U.S. university probed the specific nature of intergroup relations and concluded, "The number of *negative* relationships was significantly related to higher perceptions of intergroup conflict. So, it seems that negative relationships have a salience that overwhelms any possible positive effects from friendship links across groups."[30]

Intergroup friendships are desirable, as documented in many studies,[31] but they are readily overpowered by negative intergroup interactions. As a result, *priority number 1 for managers faced with intergroup conflict is to identify and root out specific causes of negative relationships between (or among) groups.* A single personality conflict may contaminate the entire intergroup experience. The same goes for an employee who voices negative opinions or spreads negative rumors about another group of individuals.

Based on this and other recent research insights, such as the need to foster positive attitudes toward other groups, we can formulate some general guidelines.[32] Group members are likelier to perceive intergroup conflict when (1) conflict within the group is high, (2) negative interactions occur between groups or members of the groups, and (3) influential third parties engage in negative gossip about the other group. When these situations arise, managers are encouraged to consider the following actions:

- Work to eliminate *specific negative* interactions between groups and their members.
- Conduct team building to reduce *intragroup* conflict and prepare employees for cross-functional teamwork.
- Encourage friendships and good working relationships across groups and departments.
- Foster positive attitudes (empathy, compassion, sympathy) toward members of other groups.
- Avoid or neutralize negative gossip across groups or departments.

Notice that, for minimizing intergroup conflict, conflict within the group and negative gossip from third parties are threats that need to be neutralized.

Cross-Cultural Conflict

Doing business with people from different cultures is commonplace in our global economy, where cross-border mergers, joint ventures, and alliances are commonplace.[33] Because of differing assumptions about how to think and act, the potential for cross-cultural conflict is both immediate and huge.[34] When business is conducted across cultures, success or failure often hinges on avoiding and minimizing actual or perceived conflict. For example, by one account, U.S. businesspeople tend to favor addressing conflicts openly and directly, keeping them objective and not personal, whereas Mexican businesspeople are more inclined to downplay conflicts to preserve everyone's dignity.[35] These different mechanisms are not a matter of who is right and who is wrong but of accommodating cultural differences for a successful business transaction. Awareness of cross-cultural differences is an important first step. Beyond that, cross-cultural conflict can be moderated by using international consultants and building cross-cultural relationships.

In response to broad demand, there is a growing army of management consultants specializing in cross-cultural relations. Competency and fees vary widely, but in general, a carefully selected cross-cultural consultant can be helpful, as Canon learned when its Netherlands division set out to open a subsidiary in Dubai, in the United Arab Emirates. Canon asked a Dubai-based consultant, Sahid Mirza, to help with the process. Mirza determined that the Dutch and Arab business values were similar, but behaviors tended to differ. For instance, Dutch businesspeople tend to be more blunt and direct, while Arab businesspeople would refrain from negative statements to avoid offense. Applying Mirza's research, Canon trained its Dutch and Arab managers before they launched the expansion into Dubai.[36] Consultants also can help untangle possible personality, value, and intergroup conflicts from conflicts rooted in differing national cultures. But although we have discussed these basic types of conflict separately, they typically are encountered in complex, messy bundles.

Rosalie L Tung's study of 409 expatriates from U.S. and Canadian multinational firms is very instructive for building relationships across cultures.[37] Her survey sought to pinpoint success factors for expatriates (14% female) working in 51 different countries. Based on the results, Tung ranked nine specific ways to facilitate interaction with host-country nationals. They are listed from most useful to least useful in Table 8–2. Skillful listening topped the list, followed by a tie between being sensitive to others and emphasizing cooperativeness over competitiveness. Interestingly, U.S. managers often are culturally characterized as just the opposite: poor listeners, blunt to the point of insensitivity, and excessively competitive. Some managers need to add self-management to the list of ways to minimize cross-cultural conflict.

TABLE 8–2
How to Build Cross-Cultural Relationships

Source: Adapted from R L Tung, "American Expatriates Abroad: From Neophytes to Cosmopolitans," *Journal of World Business,* Summer 1998, Table 6, p 136.

Behavior	Rank
Be a good listener	1
Be sensitive to needs of others	2
Be cooperative, rather than overly competitive	2 > Tie
Advocate inclusive (participative) leadership	3
Compromise rather than dominate	4
Build rapport through conversations	5
Be compassionate and understanding	6
Avoid conflict by emphasizing harmony	7
Nurture others (develop and mentor)	8

MANAGING CONFLICT

Managers must actively manage both functional and dysfunctional conflict.[38] This responsibility includes stimulating functional conflict and handling dysfunctional conflict, sometimes as third parties to the conflict.

Programming Functional Conflict

Sometimes committees and decision-making groups become so bogged down in details and procedures that nothing substantive is accomplished. Carefully monitored functional conflict can help get the creative juices flowing once again. Managers basically have two options. They can fan the fires of naturally occurring conflict—although this approach can be unreliable and slow. Alternatively, managers can resort to programmed conflict.[39] Experts in the field define **programmed conflict** as "conflict that raises different opinions *regardless of the personal feelings of the managers.*"[40] The trick is to get contributors to either defend or criticize ideas based on relevant facts rather than on the basis of personal preference or political interests. This give-and-take requires disciplined role playing and effective leadership. Two programmed conflict techniques with proven track records are devil's advocacy and the dialectic method.

Programmed conflict
Encourages different opinions without protecting management's personal feelings.

Devil's Advocacy

The devil's advocacy technique gets its name from a traditional practice within the Roman Catholic Church. When someone's name came before the College of Cardinals for elevation to sainthood, it was absolutely essential to ensure that he or she had a spotless record. Consequently, one individual was assigned the role of *devil's advocate* to uncover and air all possible objections to the person's canonization. In accordance with this practice, **devil's advocacy** in today's organizations involves assigning someone the role of critic.[41] Assigning this role to a group member was one of the methods that Irving Janis recommended for preventing groupthink (see Chapter 7).

Devil's advocacy
Assigning someone the role of critic.

In the left half of Figure 8–2, note how devil's advocacy alters the usual decision-making process in steps 2 and 3. This approach to programmed conflict is intended to generate critical thinking and reality testing.[42] It is a good idea to rotate the job of devil's advocate so that no one person or group develops a strictly negative reputation. Moreover, periodic devil's advocacy role-playing is good training for developing analytical and communication skills and emotional intelligence.

FIGURE 8–2
Techniques for Stimulating Functional Conflict: Devil's Advocacy and the Dialectic Method

Source: R A Cosier and C R Schwenk, "Agreement and Thinking Alike: Ingredients for Poor Decisions," *Academy of Management Executive: The Thinking Manager's Source,* February 1990, pp 72–73. Copyright 1990 by Academy of Management. Reproduced with permission of Academy of Management via Copyright Clearance Center.

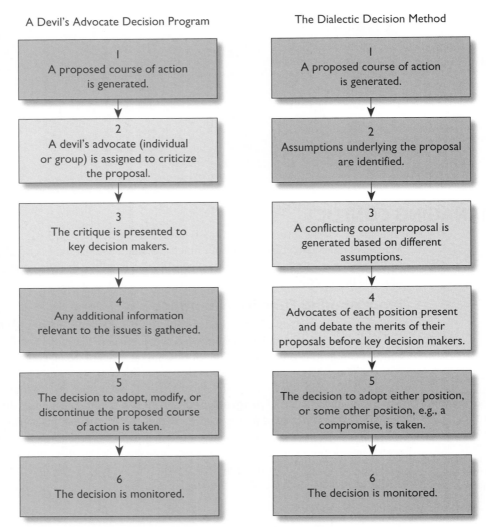

A Devil's Advocate Decision Program

1 A proposed course of action is generated.

2 A devil's advocate (individual or group) is assigned to criticize the proposal.

3 The critique is presented to key decision makers.

4 Any additional information relevant to the issues is gathered.

5 The decision to adopt, modify, or discontinue the proposed course of action is taken.

6 The decision is monitored.

The Dialectic Decision Method

1 A proposed course of action is generated.

2 Assumptions underlying the proposal are identified.

3 A conflicting counterproposal is generated based on different assumptions.

4 Advocates of each position present and debate the merits of their proposals before key decision makers.

5 The decision to adopt either position, or some other position, e.g., a compromise, is taken.

6 The decision is monitored.

The Dialectic Method

Like devil's advocacy, the dialectic method is a time-honored practice. This particular approach to programmed conflict traces back to the dialectic school of philosophy in ancient Greece. Plato and his followers attempted to synthesize truths by exploring opposite positions (called *thesis* and *antithesis*). Court systems in the United States and elsewhere rely on directly opposing points of view for determining guilt or innocence. Accordingly, today's **dialectic method** calls for managers to foster a structured debate of opposing viewpoints prior to making a decision.[43] Steps 3 and 4 in the right half of Figure 8–2 set the dialectic approach apart from the normal decision-making process. Anheuser-Busch's corporate policy committee uses the dialectic method by assigning teams to argue both sides of a major decision. Sometimes people are assigned to argue a position opposite their

Dialectic method

Fostering a debate of opposing viewpoints to better understand an issue.

actual opinion. The result is creative discussion, with thorough consideration of the possible arguments.[44]

A major drawback of the dialectic method is that "winning the debate" may overshadow the issue at hand. Also, the dialectic method requires more skill training than does devil's advocacy.

Choosing a Method

Which of these two approaches to stimulating functional conflict is more effective? A laboratory study addressing this question ended in a tie. Compared with groups that strived to reach a consensus, decision-making groups using either devil's advocacy or the dialectic method yielded decisions of equally higher quality.[45] But in a more recent laboratory study, groups using devil's advocacy produced more potential solutions and made better recommendations for a case problem than did groups using the dialectic method.[46]

Managers, in light of this mixed evidence, have some latitude in using either devil's advocacy or the dialectic method for pumping creative life back into stalled deliberations. Personal preference and the role players' experience may well be the deciding factors in choosing one approach over the other. The important point is to actively stimulate functional conflict when necessary, such as when the risk of blind conformity or groupthink is high. Joseph M Tucci, CEO of EMC, a leading data storage equipment company, fosters functional conflict by creating a supportive climate for dissent. In Tucci's opinion, "Every company needs a healthy paranoia. It's the CEO's job to keep it on the edge, to put tension in the system. You have to do the right thing for the right circumstances."[47] This practice meshes well with the results of a pair of recent laboratory studies that found a positive relationship between the degree of minority dissent and team innovation, *but only when participative decision making was used*.[48]

Alternative Styles for Handling Dysfunctional Conflict

People tend to handle negative conflict in patterned ways referred to as *styles*. Several conflict styles have been categorized over the years. According to conflict specialist Afzalur Rahim, five different conflict-handling styles can be plotted on a 2 × 2 grid, as shown in Figure 8–3. High to low concern for *self* is found on the horizontal axis of the grid, while low

FIGURE 8–3   **Five Conflict-Handling Styles**

Source: Reprinted by permission of Sage Publications Ltd from M A Rahim, "A Strategy for Managing Conflict in Complex Organizations," *Human Relations,* January 1985, p 84. Copyright © 1985 The Tavistock Institute.

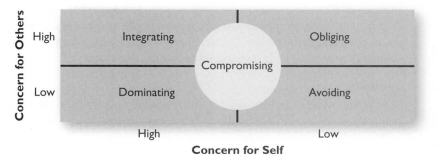

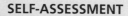

SELF-ASSESSMENT
What Is Your Preferred Conflict-Handling Style?

Go online at [www.mhhe.com/obcore] to discover which of these conflict management styles you tend to prefer.

- What are the strengths and weaknesses of your conflict-handling style?
- Is your conflict-handling style more suited to certain situations than others?

Read on to examine the advantages and disadvantages of each conflict-handling style.

to high concern for *others* forms the vertical axis. Various combinations of these variables produce the five different conflict-handling styles: integrating, obliging, dominating, avoiding, and compromising.[49] There is no single best style; each has strengths and limitations and is subject to situational constraints.

Integrating (Problem Solving)

In the integrating style, interested parties confront the issue and cooperatively identify the problem, generate and weigh alternative solutions, and select a solution. Integrating is appropriate for complex issues plagued by misunderstanding. However, it is inappropriate for resolving conflicts rooted in opposing value systems. Its primary strength is its longer-lasting impact because it deals with the underlying problem rather than merely with symptoms. The primary weakness of this style is that it is very time-consuming.

Obliging (Smoothing)

"An obliging person neglects his or her own concern to satisfy the concern of the other party."[50] This style, often called *smoothing,* involves playing down differences while emphasizing commonalities. Obliging may be an appropriate conflict-handling strategy when it is possible to eventually get something in return. But it is inappropriate for complex or worsening problems. Its primary strength is that it encourages cooperation. Its main weakness is that it's a temporary fix that fails to confront the underlying problem.

Dominating (Forcing)

High concern for self and low concern for others encourages "I win, you lose" tactics. The other party's needs are largely ignored. The dominating style is often called *forcing* because it relies on formal authority to force compliance. Dominating is appropriate when an unpopular solution must be implemented, the issue is minor, or a deadline is near. It is inappropriate in an open and participative climate. Speed is its primary strength. The primary weakness of this domineering style is that it often breeds resentment.[51]

Avoiding

The tactic of avoiding may involve either passive withdrawal from the problem or active suppression of the issue. Avoidance is appropriate for trivial issues or when the costs of confrontation outweigh the benefits of resolving the conflict. It is inappropriate for difficult and worsening problems. The main strength of this style is that it buys time in unfolding or ambiguous situations. The primary weakness is that the tactic provides a temporary fix that sidesteps the underlying problem.

Compromising

The final alternative is compromising, a give-and-take approach that involves moderate concern for both self and others. Compromise is appropriate when parties have opposite goals or possess equal power. But compromise is inappropriate when overuse would lead to inconclusive action (e.g., failure to meet production deadlines). The primary strength of this tactic is that everyone gets something, but it's a temporary fix that can stifle creative problem solving.[52]

Third-Party Interventions: Alternative Dispute Resolution

Disputes between employees, between employees and their employer, and between companies too often end up in lengthy and costly court battles. A more constructive, less expensive approach called *alternative dispute resolution* has enjoyed enthusiastic growth in recent years.[53] In fact, the widely imitated *People's Court*–type television shows operating outside the formal judicial system are part of this trend toward what one writer calls "do-it-yourself justice."[54] **Alternative dispute resolution (ADR),** according to a pair of Canadian labor lawyers, "uses faster, more user-friendly methods of dispute resolution, instead of traditional, adversarial approaches (such as unilateral decision making or litigation)."[55] The following ADR techniques represent a progression of steps third parties can take to resolve organizational conflicts.[56] They are ranked from easiest and least expensive to most difficult and costly. A growing number of organizations have formal ADR policies that involve an established sequence of various combinations of these techniques:

Alternative dispute resolution (ADR)
Avoiding costly lawsuits by resolving conflicts informally or through mediation or arbitration.

- *Facilitation.* A third party, usually a manager, informally urges disputing parties to deal directly with each other in a positive and constructive manner.
- *Conciliation.* A neutral third party informally acts as a communication conduit between disputing parties. This alternative is appropriate when conflicting parties refuse to meet face to face. The immediate goal is to establish direct communication, with the broader aim of finding common ground and a constructive solution.
- *Peer review.* A panel of trustworthy co-workers, selected for their ability to remain objective, hears both sides of a dispute in an informal and confidential meeting. Any decision by the review panel may or may not be binding, depending on the company's ADR policy. Membership on the peer review panel often is rotated among employees.[57]
- *Ombudsman.* Someone who works for the organization and is widely respected and trusted by his or her co-workers hears grievances on a confidential basis and attempts to arrange a solution. This approach, more common in Europe than North America, permits someone to get help from above without relying on the formal hierarchy chain.

MASTER YOUR KNOWLEDGE
Styles of Handling Conflict

Increase your knowledge of conflict management by completing the online quiz at [www.mhhe.com/obcore].

- Now that you've gained experience identifying conflict-handling styles, think of a conflict you have experienced. What method did you use? Was it helpful or harmful in resolving the conflict?
- Think of a conflict you have witnessed—a dispute between friends, a situation in the news, or a problem between co-workers. What conflict-handling method was involved? Did it resolve the conflict completely and to the satisfaction of both parties? If not, think through a scenario using one of the conflict-handling styles that could result in a better outcome.

- *Mediation.* "The mediator—a trained, third-party neutral—actively guides the disputing parties in exploring innovative solutions to the conflict. Although some companies have in-house mediators who have received ADR training, most also use external mediators who have no ties to the company."[58] Unlike an arbitrator, a mediator does *not* render a decision. It is up to the disputants to reach a mutually acceptable decision.
- *Arbitration.* Disputing parties agree ahead of time to accept the decision of a neutral arbitrator in a formal courtlike setting, often complete with evidence and witnesses. Statements are confidential. Decisions are based on legal merits. Trained arbitrators, typically from outside agencies such as the American Arbitration Association, are versed in relevant laws and case precedents. Historically, employee participation in arbitration was voluntary. A 2001 U.S. Supreme Court decision changed this. As part of the employment contract with nonunion workers, employers in the United States now have the legal right to insist on *mandatory* arbitration in lieu of a court battle. A vigorous debate now rages over the fairness and quality of mandatory arbitration.[59]

NEGOTIATING

Negotiation
Give-and-take process between conflicting inter-dependent parties.

Formally defined, **negotiation** is a give-and-take decision-making process involving interdependent parties with different preferences.[60] Common examples include labor–management negotiations over wages, hours, and working conditions and negotiations between supply chain specialists and vendors involving price, delivery schedules, and credit terms. Self-managed work teams with overlapping task boundaries also need to rely on negotiated agreements. Negotiating skills are more important than ever today.[61]

Basic Types of Negotiation

Negotiation experts distinguish between two types of negotiation—*distributive* and *integrative.* Understanding the difference requires a change in traditional "fixed-pie" thinking. A fixed pie is a metaphor for situations in which any gains to one person come at the expense of another. If the one person gets a large slice of the pie, the other person must make do with a smaller slice. This type of situation characterizes distributive negotiations. The classic example is haggling over the price of a purchase: the buyer wants a low price, and the seller wants a high price.

Integrative negotiation, in contrast, applies to situations where many issues are at stake, not just price or some other single concern. In these situations, the parties may determine a situation in which they are both better off. In fact, the result of integrative negotiation may be superior to the outcome of distributive negotiation. Two experts on negotiation note, however, that this is not always the case: "Parties in a negotiation often don't find these beneficial trade-offs because each *assumes* its interests *directly* conflict with those of the other party. 'What is good for the other side must be bad for us' is a common and unfortunate perspective that most people have. This is the mind-set we call the *mythical* 'fixed-pie.'"[62] Another way to think of this concept is that distributive negotiation involves traditional win–lose thinking, whereas integrative negotiation calls for a progressive win–win strategy.[63]

Added-Value Negotiation

Added-value negotiation (AVN)
Cooperatively developing multiple-deal packages while building a long-term relationship.

One practical application of the integrative approach is **added-value negotiation (AVN).** During AVN, the negotiating parties cooperatively develop multiple deal packages while building a productive long-term relationship. AVN consists of these five steps:

1. *Clarify interests.* After each party identifies its tangible and intangible needs, the two parties meet to discuss their respective needs and find *common ground* for negotiation.
2. *Identify options.* A *marketplace of value* is created when the negotiating parties discuss desired elements of value (such as property, money, behavior, rights, and risk reduction).
3. *Design alternative deal packages.* While aiming for *multiple deals,* each party mixes and matches elements of value from both parties in workable combinations.
4. *Select a deal.* Each party analyzes deal packages proposed by the other party. Jointly, the parties discuss and select from feasible deal packages, with a spirit of *creative agreement.*
5. *Perfect the deal.* Together the parties discuss unresolved issues, develop a written agreement, and *build relationships* for future negotiations.[64]

Applying Negotiation Skills: How to Negotiate Your Pay and Benefits

Few negotiating situations are as personally important as negotiating fair compensation on the job. Women and other minorities too often come up short in this regard, in addition to being underrepresented in top-management positions. Looking specifically at the situation of women, *Harvard Business Review* recently offered this interpretation: "Research has shown that both conscious and subconscious biases contribute to this problem. But we've discovered another, subtler source of inequality: Women often don't get what they want and deserve because they don't ask for it."[65] The authors attribute this pattern to the socialization of girls to focus on others more than on themselves and to women's tendency to assume their hard work will be noticed and rewarded. They also believe that organizational cultures often penalize women who are assertive about what they want.

Consequently, women (and any other employees) who think they are being short-changed in pay or promotions need to polish their integrative negotiation skills. Several tactics are associated with successful pay negotiations:

1. Know the market rate of pay for your type of work in your geographic area.
2. Be honest about your current earnings.
3. Figure out how to measure the value you provide, and deliver that evidence.
4. Avoid specifying the exact amount. Let the other party offer a number, or if you must, give a general range of pay.
5. Aim high, but don't get caught up in haggling over small differences.
6. Don't go overboard in requesting luxuries, like a big office.
7. If the salary offered isn't what you hoped for, see if you can get additional incentive pay.[66]

Employers, meanwhile, need to cultivate a diversity ethic, grant rewards equitably, and foster a culture of dignity and fair play.

Part **Three**

Managing Processes of Organizations

Chapter Nine

Communication: How to Get Messages Across— Online and Off

Learning Objectives

After reading the material in this chapter, you should be able to:

- Describe the elements and steps of the communication process.
- Identify situations that can distort communication between managers and employees.
- Contrast assertive, aggressive, and nonassertive communication styles.
- Discuss the skills of nonverbal communication and effective listening.
- Summarize how information technology has affected communication in organizations.
- Give examples of barriers to effective communication and ways to overcome them.

The aftermath of Hurricane Katrina demonstrates the critical importance of communication. Rescuers on the ground could not relay information to their co-workers to evacuate people quickly or get them life-saving supplies, and higher-ups did not know what resources and personnel were needed and where to send them. As we know, the crisis grew day by day to tragic proportions. If only the lines of communication had been open, who knows how many people could have been saved or spared their hardships and heartbreak. Messages during a crisis are a dramatic example of why communication is so important to organizations.

Every managerial function and activity involves some form of direct or indirect communication. Whenever managers are planning, organizing, directing, and leading, they communicate with and through others. Managerial decisions and organizational policies are ineffective unless those responsible for carrying them out understand their meaning. But beyond simple implementation issues, effective communication is critical for employee motivation and job satisfaction. This chapter explores how managers can improve their own communication skills and design more effective communication programs.

DIMENSIONS OF THE COMMUNICATION PROCESS

Communication
Interpersonal exchange of information and understanding.

A general definition of **communication** is "the exchange of information between a sender and a receiver, and the inference (perception) of meaning between the individuals involved."[1] Analyzing this exchange shows that communication is a two-way process consisting of consecutively linked elements such as sending, receiving, and inferring a message. Managers who understand this process can evaluate their own communication patterns and design communication programs that fit their organization's needs.

A Perceptual Process Model of Communication

Communication is subject to many errors. Recognizing this, researchers have examined communication as a form of social information processing (see Chapter 2) in which receivers interpret messages by cognitively processing information. This view led to development of a perceptual model, shown in Figure 9–1, which depicts communication as a process in which receivers create meaning in their own minds. Let us briefly examine the elements of this perceptual process model:

- *Sender and receiver.* The sender—an individual, group, or organization—desires or attempts to communicate with a particular receiver. Receivers also may be individuals, groups, or organizations.

- *Encoding.* Communication begins when a sender encodes an idea or thought by translating it into a code or language that others can understand. Managers typically encode using words, numbers, pictures, and nonverbal cues such as gestures and facial expressions. Different methods of encoding can portray similar ideas.

- *Message.* The output of encoding is a message. Messages contain more than meets the eye; they may contain hidden agendas and trigger affective (emotional) reactions. Also, messages need to match the medium used to transmit them.

FIGURE 9–1
A Perceptual Model of Communication

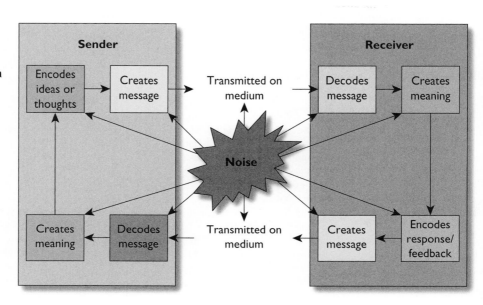

- *Selecting a medium.* Managers can communicate through a variety of media, including face-to-face conversations, telephone calls, electronic mail, voice mail, videoconferencing, written memos or letters, photographs or drawings, meetings, bulletin boards, computer output, and charts or graphs. The appropriateness of a medium depends on many factors, including the nature of the message, its intended purpose, the type of audience, proximity to the audience, time horizon for disseminating the message, personal preferences, and the complexity of the situation at hand.[2] Several years ago, Tower Snow, chairman of the law firm Brobeck, Phleger & Harrison, learned that he had been fired. The message came to him as a note delivered to him at the airport by a gate agent.[3] Most people would criticize this choice of a communication medium as being inappropriate for the sensitive content of the message. Managers can seem thoughtless when they do not carefully consider the interplay between a message and the medium used to convey it. In contrast, when Thomas Swidarski became chief executive of Diebold, he sent an e-mail to the company's 14,500 employees, explaining his goals and inviting their comments. This easy and democratic medium helped to encourage more than 1,000 responses.[4] Table 9–1 lists some advantages and disadvantages to consider when choosing a medium for communication.

- *Decoding.* During decoding, the receiver reverses the process of encoding by translating verbal, oral, or visual aspects of a message into a form that can be interpreted. Receivers rely on social information processing to determine the meaning of the message. This process is subject to social and cultural values that may not be understood by the sender, so decoding is a key contributor to misunderstanding in interracial and intercultural communication.[5]

- *Creating meaning.* The receiver creates the meaning of a message in his or her head. A receiver's interpretation of a message can differ from that intended by the sender. Receivers act according to their own interpretations, not the sender's.

- *Feedback.* The feedback loop provides the receiver's response to a message. At this point in the communication process, the receiver becomes a sender by encoding a response and then transmitting it to the original sender, who decodes the new message

circle

TABLE 9–1   **Pros and Cons of Communication Media**

Medium	Advantages	Disadvantages
Face-to-face conversation	Visual cues; appropriate for sensitive messages where feedback is important; encourages interaction for making decisions and building commitment	Can be time-consuming, expensive, and inconvenient
Phone call	Convenient, fast, and private; can express tone of voice	No nonverbal (visual) information
Memo or letter	Provides formality and a written record; useful for detailed information	No information from tone of voice or nonverbal cues; time-consuming; feedback is delayed
E-mail	Fast and efficient; can be sent to many people at once; best for factual rather than sensitive topics	Impersonal; possible misunderstanding from hastily written messages without tone of voice and nonverbal cues

and interprets it. So, feedback provides a comprehension check; it gives senders an idea of how accurately their message is understood. A Wal-Mart employee received feedback to an e-mail asking the company's chief executive why "the largest company on the planet" could not offer its employees "medical retirement benefits." The reply from CEO H Lee Scott Jr said the benefits would put Wal-Mart at a competitive disadvantage and that the apparently disloyal employee should consider leaving the company.[6] How do you think the employee would have interpreted this feedback?

Noise
Interference with the transmission and understanding of a message.

- *Noise.* Anything that interferes with the transmission and understanding of a message is called **noise.** Noise affects all links of the communication process. It includes speech impairments, poor telephone connections, illegible handwriting, inaccurate statistics in a memo or report, poor hearing and eyesight, physical distance between sender and receiver, and distractions during conference calls.[7] Managers can improve communication by reducing noise.

Communication Distortion between Managers and Employees

Communication distortion
Purposely modifying the content of a message.

Purposely modifying the content of a message, thus reducing the accuracy of communication between managers and employees, is called **communication distortion.** Employees tend to engage in this practice because of workplace politics, a desire to manage impressions, or fear of how a manager might respond to a message.[8] According to communication experts, distortion causes "misdirectives to be transmitted, nondirectives to be issued, incorrect information to be passed on, and a variety of other problems related to both the quantity and quality of information."[9]

Knowledge of the antecedents or causes of communication distortion can help managers avoid or limit these problems. Studies have identified several antecedents of distortion in upward communication. Distortion tends to increase when supervisors have high upward influence and/or power. Employees also tend to modify or distort information when they aspire to move upward and when they do not trust their supervisors.[10]

Of course, managers generally do not want to reduce their upward influence or curb their direct reports' desire for upward mobility. However, they can reduce distortion in several ways:

- Managers can deemphasize power differences between themselves and their direct reports.
- They can enhance trust through a meaningful performance review process that rewards actual performance.
- They can encourage staff feedback by conducting smaller, more informal meetings. For example, employees of the Lodge at Vail participate in a "lunch with the boss" program in which groups of employees meet with the hotel manager, Wolfgang Triebnig, for lunch in the hotel's five-star restaurant, where they are invited to share any comments or concerns they might have. According to Mandy Wulfe, the lodge's human resources director, "Some come prepared with questions, some come because they were invited and prefer to listen quietly, and some are moved to ask questions because of what they are hearing."[11]
- Managers can establish performance goals that encourage employees to focus on problems rather than personalities.
- They can encourage dialogue between individuals or groups with opposing viewpoints.

INTERPERSONAL COMMUNICATION

The quality of interpersonal communication within an organization is very important. Research has found that people with good communication skills helped groups make more innovative decisions and were promoted more frequently than individuals with less developed abilities.[12] We can think of these skills as elements of **communication competence,** a performance-based index of an individual's abilities to effectively use communication behaviors in a given context.[13] For example, one component of communication competence is business etiquette.

Communication competence
Ability to effectively use communication behaviors in a given context.

Communication competence is determined by the three sets of criteria shown in Figure 9–2: communication abilities and traits, situational factors, and the individuals involved in the interaction. Important communication abilities and traits include cross-cultural awareness and active listening. Situational factors include the organization's openness, procedures, and policies. Individuals involved in an interaction shape it depending on their rank in the organization and the level of trust and friendship in their relationships. For example, people tend to withhold information and react emotionally or defensively when interacting with someone they dislike or distrust. You can improve your communication competence through your use of five communication styles, abilities, or traits under your control: assertiveness, aggressiveness, nonassertiveness, nonverbal communication, and active listening. As we will discuss later in the section, some of these traits are shaped in part by gender roles.

Assertiveness, Aggressiveness, and Nonassertiveness

The saying "You can attract more flies with honey than with vinegar" captures the difference between an assertive communication style and an aggressive style. Research indicates that assertiveness is more effective than aggressiveness in work-related and consumer

FIGURE 9–2
Criteria Shaping Communication Competence

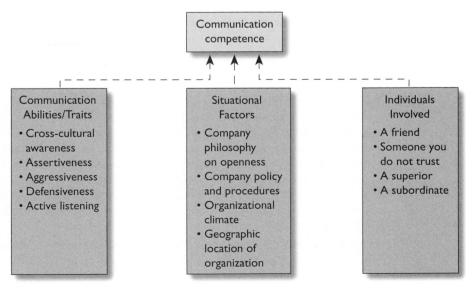

Assertive style
Expressive and self-enhancing, but does not take advantage of others.

Aggressive style
Expressive and self-enhancing, but takes unfair advantage of others.

Nonassertive style
Timid and self-denying behavior.

contexts.[14] An **assertive style** is expressive and self-enhancing and is based on the "ethical notion that it is not right or good to violate our own or others' basic human rights, such as the right to self-expression or the right to be treated with dignity and respect."[15] In contrast, an **aggressive style** is expressive and self-enhancing and strives to take unfair advantage of others. At the opposite extreme is a **nonassertive style,** characterized by timid and self-denying behavior. Nonassertiveness is ineffective because it gives the other person an unfair advantage.

Managers may improve their communication competence by being more assertive and less aggressive or nonassertive. This improvement can be achieved by using the appropriate nonverbal and verbal behaviors listed in Table 9–2. Managers should attempt to use the nonverbal behaviors of good eye contact; a strong, steady, and audible voice; and selective interruptions. They should avoid nonverbal behaviors such as glaring or little eye contact, threatening gestures, slumped posture, and a weak or whiny voice. Appropriate verbal behaviors include direct and unambiguous language and use of "I" messages instead of "you" statements. Defensiveness is likely to result from an aggressive "you" statement like "Mike, you messed up your report." The manager can reduce defensiveness with a more assertive "I" statement: "Mike, I was disappointed with your report because it contained typographical errors." "I" statements describe your own reaction to someone's performance or behavior instead of laying blame on the other person.

TABLE 9–2   **Communication Styles**

Source: Adapted in part from J A Waters, "Managerial Assertiveness," *Business Horizons,* September/October 1982, pp 24–29.

Communication Style	Description	Nonverbal Behavior Pattern	Verbal Behavior Pattern
Assertive	Pushing hard without attacking; permits others to influence outcome; expressive and self-enhancing without intruding on others'	Good eye contact Comfortable but firm posture Strong, steady, and audible voice Facial expressions matched to message Appropriately serious tone Selective interruptions to ensure understanding	Direct and unambiguous language No attributions or evaluations of others behavior Use of "I" statements and cooperative "we" statements
Aggressive	Taking advantage of others; expressive and self-enhancing at others' expense	Glaring eye contact Moving or leaning too close Threatening gestures (pointed finger; clenched fist) Loud voice Frequent interruptions	Swear words and abusive language Attributions and evaluations of others' behavior Sexist or racist terms Explicit threats or put-downs
Nonassertive	Encouraging others to take advantage of us; inhibited; self-denying	Little eye contact Downward glances Slumped posture Constantly shifting weight Wringing hands Weak or whiny-voice	Qualifiers ("maybe"; "kind of") Fillers ("uh," "you know," "well") Negaters ("It's not really that important"; "I'm not sure")

GROUP EXERCISE
Nonverbal Communication: A Twist on Charades

Sources of Nonverbal Communication

Nonverbal communication

Messages sent outside of the written or spoken word.

Much of our communication is actually **nonverbal communication,** that is, messages sent and received without the use of written and spoken words. Nonverbal communication takes many forms, including "use of time and space, distance between persons when conversing, use of color, dress, walking behavior, standing, positioning, seating arrangement, office locations and furnishings."[16]

Experts estimate that 65% to 90% of every conversation includes nonverbal messages.[17] Those nonverbal messages need to match the message's words, or the communication will produce noise and misunderstanding.[18] Nonverbal communication affects organizational behavior including perceptions of others, hiring decisions, work attitudes, turnover, and acceptance of a person's ideas in a presentation. As a result, managers need to become conscious of the major sources of nonverbal communication:

• *Body movements and gestures.* Body movements, such as leaning forward or backward, and gestures, such as pointing, provide nonverbal information that can either enhance or detract from the verbal communication process. Open body positions, such as leaning backward, communicate *immediacy,* that is, openness, warmth, closeness, and availability for communication. *Defensiveness* is communicated by gestures such as folding arms, crossing hands, and crossing one's legs. Although interpreting body movements and gestures is fun, keep in mind that the analysis of body language is subjective, easily misinterpreted, and highly dependent on the context and cross-cultural differences.[19] So, managers need to be careful when trying to interpret body movements. Inaccurate interpretations can create additional "noise" in the communication process.

• *Touch.* People tend to touch those they like. Touching conveys an impression of warmth and caring and can be used to create a bond between people. A meta-analysis of gender differences in touching indicated that women do more touching during conversations than men.[20] But be careful about touching people from diverse cultures, as norms for touching vary significantly around the world.[21]

• *Facial expressions.* A person's facial expressions convey a wealth of information. Smiling typically represents warmth, happiness, or friendship, while frowning conveys dissatisfaction or anger. However, a summary of relevant research revealed that the association between facial expressions and emotions varies across cultures.[22] As a result, managers need to be careful when interpreting facial expressions among diverse groups of employees.

• *Eye contact.* Eye contact is a strong nonverbal cue that varies across cultures. Westerners are taught at an early age to look at their parents when spoken to. In contrast, Asians are taught to avoid eye contact with a parent or superior in order to show obedience and subservience.[23] Again, managers should be sensitive to different orientations toward maintaining eye contact with diverse employees.

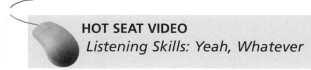

HOT SEAT VIDEO
Listening Skills: Yeah, Whatever

Nonverbal communication skills are related to the development of positive interpersonal relationships, so strong skills in this area are essential. To improve nonverbal communication skills for Western business culture, work on maintaining eye contact, nodding to show interest and agreement, smiling and leaning toward the speaker to show interest, and using a tone of voice that matches your message. Avoid turning away from the message sender, closing your eyes, licking your lips, playing with your hair or moustache, biting your nails, and other distracting behaviors. Also watch your tone of voice and pace of speaking to ensure your voice is pleasant and easy to understand.[24] Honest feedback from your friends about your nonverbal communication style may help, too.

Active Listening

Some communication experts contend that listening is the keystone communication skill for employees involved in sales, customer service, and management. Listening effectiveness has been positively associated with customer satisfaction and negatively associated with employee intentions to quit. Poor communication between employees and management was linked to employee discontent and turnover.[25]

Listening
Actively decoding and interpreting verbal messages.

Listening involves much more than hearing a message. Hearing is merely the physical component of listening. **Listening** is the process of *actively* decoding and interpreting verbal messages. Unlike hearing, listening requires cognitive attention and information processing.

Listening Styles

According to communication experts, people have a preferred listening style. Even though people may lean toward one dominant listening style, they tend to use a combination of two or three.

There are five dominant listening styles: appreciative, empathetic, comprehensive, discerning, and evaluative.[26] An *appreciative* listener listens in a relaxed manner, preferring to listen for pleasure, entertainment, or inspiration. He or she tends to tune out speakers who provide no amusement or humor. *Empathetic* listeners interpret messages by focusing on the emotions and body language displayed by the speaker and the presentation media. They tend to listen without judging. A *comprehensive* listener makes sense of a message by organizing specific thoughts and actions and then integrates this information by focusing on relationships among ideas. These listeners prefer logical presentations without interruptions. *Discerning* listeners attempt to understand the main message and determine important points. They like to take notes and prefer logical presentations. Finally, *evaluative* listeners listen analytically and continually formulate arguments and challenges to what is being said. They tend to accept or reject messages based on personal beliefs, ask a lot of questions, and may interrupt often.

You can improve your listening skills by becoming aware of the effectiveness of the different listening styles you use in various situations. This awareness can help you to modify

SELF-ASSESSMENT
Active Listening Skills

Go online at [www.mhhe.com/obcore] to discover how well you are already apply-ing active listening skills.

- According to your feedback, in which areas of active listening are you strongest and weakest?
- How can you improve your active listening skills?

Review the entries in Table 9–3 to get a head start on polishing your listening skills.

your style to fit a specific situation. For example, a manager with an employee who is upset may want to use an empathetic style initially. As the employee calms down, the discerning and evaluative styles may become appropriate for problem solving.

Becoming a More Effective Listener

Even if there seem to be no rewards for listening, there are penalties when we don't. Think of a time when someone you were speaking to did not pay attention but looked at text messages on a cell phone or typed on a keyboard. How did you feel? Perhaps devalued or offended. Such feelings can erode the quality of interpersonal relationships and fuel job dissatisfaction, lower productivity, and poor customer service. Listening is an important skill for any manager.

Effective listening is a learned skill that requires effort, awareness, and motivation to prac-tice; it does not improve on its own. Ways to improve listening skill include avoiding the 10 habits of bad listeners while cultivating the 10 good listening habits (see Table 9–3).[27] Stephen Covey, author of the best seller *The 7 Habits of Highly Effective People,* offers another good piece of advice about becoming a more effective listener: "Seek first to understand, then to be understood."[28] Additional ways to improve listening skills include focusing on what is being said rather than your next response, allowing others to finish what they are saying, and rephrasing what you heard to be sure you understood correctly.[29]

Communication Styles of Women and Men

Linguistic style
A person's typi-cal speaking pattern.

Women and men tend to communicate differently. Gender-based differences in communi-cation are partly caused by linguistic styles commonly used by women and men. Deborah Tannen, a communication expert, defines **linguistic style** as "a person's characteristic speaking pattern," including "directness or indirectness, pacing and pausing, word choice, and the use of such elements as jokes, figures of speech, stories, questions, and apolo-gies."[30] This culturally based pattern is used for both sending and interpreting messages. Besides helping to explain communication differences between women and men, linguis-tic style influences our perceptions of others' confidence, competence, and abilities. Increased awareness of linguistic styles can improve communication accuracy and skill.

Reasons for Different Linguistic Styles

Although researchers do not completely agree on the cause of communication differ-ences between women and men, there are two competing explanations that involve the

TABLE 9–3   The Keys to Effective Listening

Sources: Derived from N Skinner, "Communication Skills," *Selling Power,* July/August 1999, pp 32–34; and G Manning, K Curtis, and S McMillen, *Building the Human Side of Work Community* (Cincinnati, OH: Thomson Executive Press, 1996), pp 127–54.

Keys to Effective Listening	The Bad Listener	The Good Listener
1. Capitalize on thought speed	Tends to daydream	Stays with the speaker, mentally summarizes the speaker, weighs evidence, and listens between the lines
2. Listen for ideas	Listens for facts	Listens for central or overall ideas
3. Find an area of interest	Tunes out dry speakers or subjects	Listens for any useful information
4. Judge content, not delivery	Tunes out dry or monotone speakers	Assesses content by listening to entire message before making judgments
5. Hold your fire	Gets too emotional or worked up by something said by the speaker and enters into an argument	Withholds judgment until comprehension is complete
6. Work at listening	Does not expend energy on listening	Gives the speaker full attention
7. Resist distractions	Is easily distracted	Fights distractions and concentrates on the speaker
8. Hear what is said	Shuts out or denies unfavorable information	Listens to both favorable and unfavorable information
9. Challenge yourself	Resists listening to presentations of difficult subject matter	Treats complex presentations as exercise for the mind
10. Use handouts, overheads, or other visual aids	Does not take notes or pay attention to visual aids	Takes notes as required and uses visual aids to enhance understanding of the presentation

well-worn debate between *nature and nurture*. Some researchers believe interpersonal differences between women and men arise from inherited biological differences between the sexes. This perspective, also called the *Darwinian perspective* or *evolutionary psychology,* attributes gender differences in communication to drives, needs, and conflicts associated with reproductive strategies used by women and men. For example, proponents would say that males communicate more aggressively, interrupt more than women, and hide their emotions because they have an inherent desire to possess features attractive to females in order to compete with other males for mate selection. In this view, although males are certainly not competing for mate selection during a business meeting, men cannot turn off the biologically based determinants of their behavior.[31]

In contrast, social role theory emphasizes that females and males learn ways of speaking as children growing up. Research shows that girls learn conversational skills and habits focused on rapport and relationships, while boys learn skills and habits that focus on status and hierarchies. So, women come to view communication as a network of connections in which conversations are negotiations for closeness. As a result, women seek and give confirmation and support more than men. Men, in contrast, see conversations as negotiations in which people try to achieve and maintain the upper hand, so they protect themselves from others' attempts to put them down or push them around. This perspective increases a male's need to maintain independence and avoid failure.[32]

Gender Differences in Communication

Research demonstrates that women and men communicate differently in a number of ways.[33] Women are more likely to share credit for success, ask questions for clarification, give feedback tactfully by mitigating criticism with praise, and indirectly tell others what to do. Men are more likely to boast about themselves, give feedback bluntly, and withhold compliments, and they are less likely to ask questions and admit fault or weaknesses.

These patterns raise two important issues. First, the patterns identified cannot be generalized to include all women and men. Some men are less likely to boast about their achievements, while some women are less likely to share the credit. Second, a person's linguistic style influences perceptions about the person's confidence, competence, and authority. These judgments may, in turn, affect future job assignments and subsequent promotability.

Improving Communication between the Sexes

Deborah Tannen recommends becoming aware of how linguistic styles work and how they influence our perceptions and judgments, because knowledge of linguistic styles helps to ensure that people with valuable insights or ideas get heard. Consider how gender-based linguistic differences affect who gets heard at a meeting. People "who are comfortable speaking up in groups, who need little or no silence before raising their hands, or who speak out easily without waiting to be recognized are far more likely to get heard at meetings," and they are less likely to notice those "who refrain from talking until it's clear that the previous speaker is finished, who wait to be recognized, and who are inclined to link their comments to those of others."[34] The style of those who are heard resembles the linguistic patterns observed in men.

Knowledge of these linguistic differences can help managers devise methods to ensure that everyone's ideas are heard and receive fair credit. In addition, it is useful to consider the organizational strengths and limitations of your own linguistic style. You may want to consider modifying a linguistic characteristic that is a detriment to perceptions of your confidence, competence, and authority.

COMMUNICATION IN THE COMPUTERIZED INFORMATION AGE

As organizations use information technology to improve productivity and customer and employee satisfaction, communication patterns at work are radically changing. Internet and wireless technologies connect people anytime, anywhere, at all levels of the organization. Components of information technology that influence communication patterns and management within a computerized workplace include the Internet and its variants (intranets and extranets), electronic mail, blogs, videoconferencing, collaborative computing, and telecommuting.

Internet, Intranets, and Extranets

Internet
A global system of networked computers.

The **Internet** is a network of computer networks—a global network of independently operating but interconnected computers. The Internet links supercomputers used for research, mainframe computers that process data for businesses, government, and universities, and the

Intranet
An organization's private Internet.

Extranet
Connects internal employees with selected customers, suppliers, and strategic partners.

personal computers in our homes and offices. An organization that wants to link employees but protect its data from outsiders may set up an **intranet,** essentially a private Internet that uses *firewalls* to block outside users from accessing private and confidential company documents. Companies that want to expand information sharing beyond employees may use an **extranet,** an extended intranet that connects employees with selected customers, suppliers, and other strategic partners. Ford Motor Company's extranet lets employees share data with its dealers worldwide to support the sales and servicing of cars.

The primary benefit of the Internet, intranets, and extranets is that they can help employees find, create, manage, and distribute information. The effectiveness of these systems depends on how organizations set them up and manage them and how employees use the acquired information. Communication effectiveness actually can decrease if a corporate intranet becomes a dumping ground of unorganized information. In this case, employees will find themselves flailing in a sea of information. Although no rigorous studies have been conducted that directly demonstrate productivity increases from using the Internet, intranets, or extranets, case studies show benefits. For example, the University of Michigan and the University of Louisville saved $200,000 and $90,000 a year, respectively, by asking employees to enroll for employee benefits on their intranets.[35] United Parcel Service estimated that productivity increased 35% after it implemented Wi-Fi (wireless high-speed Internet connectivity).[36] Companies have reported saving millions of dollars by putting some or all of their training programs online.[37]

In contrast to these positive case studies, a survey conducted by Harris Interactive found that 51% admitted using the Internet at work from one to five hours a week for personal matters.[38] All told, International Data Corp. estimated personal use of the Internet during work hours contributes to a 30% to 40% decrease in productivity.[39] Organizations are taking these statistics to heart and attempting to root out cyberslackers by tracking employee behavior with electronic monitoring. Many companies monitor their employees' use of the Internet and check their e-mail.

Electronic Mail and Instant Messaging

Popular applications of the Internet are electronic mail (e-mail) and instant messaging, which use Internet or intranet connections for sending and receiving messages. Most of the e-mail users responding to an informal poll said they receive at least 15 messages a day (and some more than 100); one-fourth of them said they spend at least four hours a day reading, answering, and filing e-mail messages.[40] The use of e-mail is widespread because it is economical, especially when reaching large numbers of people regardless of their location, and has the ability to attach documents to the message. To the extent that it replaces paper, e-mail also saves money on supplies. E-mail provides flexibility as well, because receivers of e-mail messages can retrieve them at their convenience whenever they are near a computer or portable device (such as a cell phone or a personal digital assistant [PDA]) with an Internet connection. Because of these advantages, the use of e-mail can contribute to teamwork. Instant messaging shares similar advantages, except that it is appropriate mainly for short messages, and it operates only between users who are currently logged on to the Internet service provider.

In spite of these benefits, e-mail and instant messaging have drawbacks. The ease of sending messages has contributed to a flood of e-mail, causing many employees to waste time and effort wading through messages. The constant arrival of e-mail and instant messages can distract employees from completing critical job duties. A national survey of U.S.

workers indicated that between 33% and 50% of their e-mail messages were unimportant.[41] Not only do employees receive spam from marketers of investment schemes and herbal remedies, but they also tend to share jokes and chain letters. Copying colleagues on a message is so easy that co-workers routinely receive copies of messages that do not require their action. Besides distracting employees, the flood of messages can cause information overload. According to a study by Nucleus Research, three-quarters of all e-mail traffic in 2004 was spam.[42]

In addition to these drawbacks, people overestimate their ability to communicate effectively via e-mail.[43] Also, preliminary evidence suggests that people are using electronic mail to communicate when they should be using other media. This practice can reduce communication's effectiveness. A four-year study of communication patterns within a university demonstrated that the increased use of electronic mail was associated with decreased face-to-face interactions and a drop in the overall amount of organizational communication. Employees also expressed a feeling of being less connected and less cohesive as a department as the amount of e-mails increased.[44] This interpersonal "disconnection" may be caused by the replacement of everyday face-to-face interactions with electronic messages. Employees satisfy social needs through the many personal interactions that occur at work.

Following some guidelines can make the use of e-mail and instant messaging more effective. When sending messages, keep in mind that the person receiving the message must be able to open it. Most businesspeople today use computers, but not everyone has access to one all the time. The speed of getting a response to an e-mail message depends partly on how frequently the receiver examines his or her messages. If you want responses right away, get to know when receivers of your messages check their mail. Keep messages short and simple, and don't click "Reply to All" unless everyone who received the message will need your viewpoint. Use subject headings that are specific enough for the receiver to know what you are writing about. Because of misuse and potential legal liability, a growing number of companies have policies for using e-mail. Do not assume that e-mail and instant messages sent or received at work are private and confidential. For instance, four female employees working at Chevron filed a suit claiming that they were sexually harassed through e-mail. The company settled for $2.2 million, plus legal fees and court costs.[45]

When you are the receiver of e-mail, you can manage the flood of messages in your in-box by applying the following guidelines:

- Before opening messages, review the list for unfamiliar messages and suspicious subject lines. Learn to recognize and delete spam without opening it.
- Use file folders to sort messages by topic. When you have a series of messages from the same person, read the first message and then the most recent. You may be able to understand and respond to the situation without reading the messages in between.
- Prioritize your list of messages, and respond to them in order of importance.
- Ask colleagues and friends not to send you jokes, chain letters, and other unimportant messages.
- Consider whether a telephone reply will help you resolve a complex situation faster than a series of e-mail messages trying to sort out the details.
- Ask to unsubscribe from lists that send you unimportant messages and e-mail newsletters that are not helpful.[46]

Blogs

Blog

Online journal in which people comment on any topic.

A **blog** is an online journal in which people write whatever they want about any topic. Experts recently estimated that there are more than 23 million blogs in existence, and tens of thousands of new ones are started every day.[47] The benefits of blogs include the opportunity to discuss issues in a casual format. These discussions serve much like a chat group, so they can provide organizations with insights from customers or employees, as well as the general public. Christopher Barger, a blogger at IBM, reads other people's blogs to see what they are saying about IBM's products.[48] Some executives, including Jonathan Schwartz of Sun Microsystems and Paul Otellini of Intel, have used blogs at work as a format for discussing issues related to their businesses.[49]

Blogs give people freedom to air their opinions, grievances, and creative ideas—an ability that can be both an advantage and a pitfall of this medium. Employees who post inappropriate material or negative remarks about their company can hurt the company's image. Google fired one of its employees, Mark Jen, for commenting about its finances in his blog.[50] Another problem with blogs is that, like e-mail, people may waste a great deal of time reading and forwarding unimportant or inaccurate material. One study found that 25% of employees read blogs at work.[51]

Videoconferencing

Videoconferencing, also known as *teleconferencing,* uses video and audio links along with computers to enable people in different locations to see, hear, and talk with one another. This capability enables people from many locations to conduct a meeting without having to travel. Applications of videoconferencing include the sharing of reports among engineers at Harken Energy Corporation, a Houston-based oil and gas exploration company, and the teaching of basic job-hunting skills by the U.S. Department of Labor.[52]

Videoconferencing in place of face-to-face meetings can significantly reduce an organization's travel expenses. Many organizations set up special videoconferencing rooms or booths with specially equipped television cameras. Modern equipment enables people to attach small cameras and microphones to their desks or computer monitors, so employees can participate in long-distance meetings and training classes without leaving their office or cubicle.

Group Support Systems

Group support systems (GSSs)

Using computer software and hardware to help people work better together.

Another computer application related to communication is **group support systems (GSSs),** which use computer software and hardware to help people work together without the constraints of time and space. Computer networks link people using software applications such as messaging and e-mail systems, calendar management, videoconferencing, computer teleconferencing, electronic whiteboards, and the type of computer-aided decision-making systems discussed in Chapter 7.

Group support systems can increase productivity and cut costs. Organizations that use full-fledged group support systems can create virtual teams or operate as a virtual organization (see Chapter 13). As described in Chapter 6, a virtual team represents a physically dispersed task group that conducts its business by using information technology, including Internet/intranet systems, collaborative software, and videoconferencing. These real-time systems enable people to communicate with anyone at any time. Group support systems applications have been associated with productivity growth, cost savings, and during brainstorming a greater quantity of ideas and wider participation.[53]

Although modern information technology enables people to interact virtually, it doesn't guarantee effective communication. A whole host of unique communication problems is associated with using the information technology needed to operate virtually.[54]

Telecommuting

Telecommuting
Doing work that is generally performed in the office away from the office using different information technologies.

Communication challenges also arise with the use of **telecommuting,** a work practice in which an employee does part of his or her job in a remote location using a variety of information technologies such as wireless devices, fax, or a home computer that is linked via modem to an office computer. For example, recent years have seen an explosion of telecommuting among call center employees situated in home offices. A recent survey of U.S. and Canadian call centers found that almost one-fourth of the employees were working from home.[55] Telecommuting is most common for jobs involving computer work, writing, and phone work that require concentration and limited interruptions. Experts have estimated that 41 million people will work from home at least one day a week by 2008.[56]

Telecommuting offers several potential benefits.[57] Companies can save money on the capital required to operate large workplaces for all employees. Sun Microsystems reported saving $50 million in 2002 by letting employees work from home. Workers benefit from greater flexibility and autonomy. Not only can these qualities be motivating (see Chapter 4), but the opportunity to telecommute can also give the employer an edge in recruiting. Some employees like telecommuting because it helps resolve work–family conflicts. AT&T's telecommuters had less absenteeism than traditional employees, and employees who appreciate telecommuting also may experience greater job satisfaction and be more likely to stay with the organization. Some companies have enjoyed growth in productivity. Telecommuting resulted in productivity increases of 25% and 35% for FourGen Software and Continental Traffic Services, respectively. Organizations that struggle to fill positions may appreciate the opportunity to tap nontraditional labor pools, including prison inmates and homebound disabled persons.

Although telecommuting represents an attempt to accommodate employee needs and desires, it requires adjustments and is not for everybody. Many people thoroughly enjoy the social camaraderie that exists within an office setting. These individuals probably would not like to telecommute. Others lack the self-motivation needed to work at home. Finally, organizations must be careful to implement telecommuting in a nondiscriminatory manner. Organizations can easily and unknowingly violate one of several antidiscrimination laws.[58]

BARRIERS TO EFFECTIVE COMMUNICATION

A good starting point to improve the communication process is for management to be aware of communication barriers. Barriers to effective communication include process barriers, personal barriers, cultural barriers, physical barriers, and semantic barriers.

Process Barriers

Every element of the perceptual model of communication (see Figure 9–1) is a potential process barrier

- *Sender barrier.* A customer gets incorrect information from a customer service agent who was just hired and lacks knowledge.

- *Encoding barrier.* An employee for whom English is a second language has difficulty explaining why a delivery was late.
- *Message barrier.* An employee misses a meeting for which she never received a confirmation memo.
- *Medium barrier.* A salesperson gives up trying to make a sales call when the potential customer fails to return three previous phone calls.
- *Decoding barrier.* An employee does not understand how to respond to a manager's request to stop exhibiting "passive aggressive" behavior.
- *Receiver barrier.* A student who is talking to his friend during a lecture asks the professor the same question that was just answered.
- *Feedback barrier.* An interviewer's nonverbal head nodding leads an interviewee to believe she is answering questions well.

Barriers in any of these process elements can distort the transfer of meaning. Reducing these barriers is essential but difficult, given the current diversity of the workforce.

Personal Barriers

Many personal barriers to communication exist.[59] One of the most common is the *ability to communicate effectively;* people possess varying levels of communication skills. Differences in the *way people process and interpret information* create a second barrier. People use different frames of reference and experiences to interpret the world around them (see Chapter 2), and they selectively attend to various stimuli. These differences affect what we say and what we think we hear. In addition, the *level of interpersonal trust between people* can be either a barrier or an enabler of effective communication. Communication is more likely to be distorted when people do not trust each other. *Stereotypes and prejudices* are a fourth barrier. They can powerfully distort what we perceive about others. Our *egos* are a barrier, because egos influence how people treat each other as well as their receptiveness to being influenced by others. Egos can cause political battles, turf wars, and pursuit of power, credit, and resources. *Poor listening skills* are a sixth barrier.

Carl Rogers, a renowned psychologist, identified two more barriers that interfere with interpersonal communication.[60] One of these is a *natural tendency to evaluate or judge a sender's message.* Consider how you might respond to the statement "I like the book you are reading." Your likely response is to approve or disapprove the statement by saying either, "I agree," or, "I disagree; the book is boring." These answers display the tendency to evaluate messages from a personal point of view or frame of reference, especially when the individual has strong feelings or emotions about the issue being discussed. The other barrier identified by Rogers is an *inability to listen with understanding*—that is, to "see the expressed idea and attitude from the other person's point of view, to sense how it feels to him, to achieve his frame of reference in regard to the thing he is talking about."[61] Listening with understanding reduces defensiveness and improves accuracy in perceiving a message.

Cultural Barriers: High- and Low-Context Cultures

High-context cultures Primary meaning derived from nonverbal situational cues.

Significant barriers to communication can arise between people of different cultures, especially when their cultures differ in terms of the importance placed on the context of a message. In **high-context cultures**—including those of China, Korea, Japan, Vietnam, Mexico, and Arabic nations—people rely heavily on situational cues for meaning when perceiving and communicating with others.[62] Nonverbal cues such as a person's official position, status, or family connections convey messages more powerfully than do spoken words. Thus, in the high-context culture of Japan, the ritual of exchanging *and reading* business cards is significant. A business card, listing employer and official position, conveys vital messages about a person's status. People from high-context cultures who are not especially talkative during a first encounter with a stranger are not necessarily being unfriendly; they are simply taking time to collect "contextual" information.

Low-context cultures
Primary meaning derived from written and spoken words.

In **low-context cultures,** written and spoken words carry the burden of shared meanings. Low-context cultures include those found in Germany, Switzerland, Scandinavia, North America, and Great Britain. True to form, Germany has precise written rules for even the smallest details of daily life. In *high*-context cultures, agreements tend to be made on the basis of someone's word or a handshake, after a rather prolonged get-acquainted and trust-building period. Low-context Americans and Canadians, who have cultural roots in Northern Europe, see the handshake as a signal to get a signature on a detailed, lawyer-approved, iron-clad contract.

Misunderstanding and miscommunication often are problems in international business dealings that bring together parties from high- and low-context cultures. A Mexican business professor observed that in the low-context culture of the United States, business reports are expected to be brief and to the point, but in the high-context cultures of Mexico and other parts of Latin America, long explanations are the norm. The professor mentioned that a Latin American friend in the United States received regular criticism from his U.S. boss because "his reports are long, including detailed explanations on the context in which the events he is reporting on occur and the possible interpretations that they might have," which the boss perceives as a waste of his time.[63]

When cultural barriers arise in a workplace that brings together employees from high- and low-context cultures, managers should train employees to recognize these issues and know how to adjust their communication style to communicate more effectively. To welcome a new employee from a high-context culture, it is helpful to arrange for that person to be greeted by a group including the new employees' supervisor, colleagues with similar responsibilities, and someone who will be working near the new employee. People from high-context cultures will want to receive information about the context of their activities, such as the history of a situation and the objectives and processes involved in a project. To succeed in a low-context U.S. business, employees from high-context cultures need encouragement to ask questions and act independently.[64]

Physical Barriers

The distance between employees can interfere with effective communication. It is hard to understand someone who is speaking to you from 20 yards away. Time zone differences between the East and West Coasts also represent physical barriers. Work and office noise are additional barriers. Static-filled telephone lines and crashed computers represent physical barriers that impair our ability to communicate with information technology.

Although physical barriers are widely expected, they can be reduced. For example, employees on the East Coast can agree to call their West Coast peers before leaving for lunch. Distracting or inhibiting walls also can be torn down. It is important that managers attempt to manage this barrier by choosing a medium that optimally reduces the physical barrier at hand.

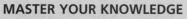

MASTER YOUR KNOWLEDGE
Barriers to Effective Communication

Increase your knowledge of communication basics by completing the online quiz [www.mhhe.com/obcore].

- For a deeper understanding, suggest a way to overcome each barrier described in the online exercise.
- Which barriers might be hardest to overcome?

Semantic Barriers

Semantics is the study of words. Semantic barriers show up as encoding and decoding errors because these phases of communication involve transmitting and receiving words and symbols. Semantic barriers have been a challenge for employees working in India's call centers as they try to communicate with English-speaking customers. Sabira Merchant, a speech-voice consultant, notes that these employees generally have excellent skill in written English, but it is not their first language. Thus, says Merchant, "While Americans think in English, we think in our mother tongue and translate it while speaking." This makes fluent communication more difficult for these employees than for a native speaker of English.[65] Even among people who speak the same language, semantic barriers can occur as a result of different expectations and values. Ann Garcia once worked at a company where the top executive hated profanity but the second in command viewed occasional swear words as a sign of desirable passion. Garcia and her co-workers learned to choose their words accordingly.[66]

Semantic barriers also are related to the choice of words we use when communicating. Consider the following statement: *Crime is ubiquitous.* Do you understand this message? Even if you do, would it not be simpler to say, "Crime is everywhere"? Similarly, semantic barriers arise when people overload their messages with jargon and acronyms.[67] Choosing words that the receiver will understand is the easiest way to reduce semantic barriers. This barrier can also be decreased by attentiveness to mixed messages and cultural diversity. Mixed messages occur when a person's words imply one message while his or her actions or nonverbal cues suggest something different. Obviously, understanding is enhanced when a person's actions and nonverbal cues match the verbal message.

r Ten

Power and Politics: How People Influence One Another

Learning Objectives

After reading the material in this chapter, you should be able to:

- List influence tactics and outcomes, and summarize research conclusions about the effectiveness of the tactics.
- Describe five bases of power, and give examples of how they are related to work outcomes.
- Discuss how to make employee empowerment succeed.
- Define organizational politics, explain what triggers it, and describe its use in organizations.
- Distinguish between favorable and unfavorable impression management tactics.
- Explain how to manage organizational politics.

We see the role that power plays in organizations when top executives lose the confidence of the board of directors and are forced to resign. Such dramatic events make headlines. But day-to-day activities that receive little notice in organizations also involve influence and power. A manager lobbies the CEO for funding for a pet project, an employee reaches set goals and argues for a raise, a marketing team gets support from manufacturing to produce a new product line. All of these actions involve influence, power, and politics.

In a perfect world, individual and collective interests would be closely aligned, and everyone would move forward together. Instead, we typically find messy situations in which self-interests often override the collective mission. Organization members pursue personal hidden agendas, form political coalitions, make false impressions, and end up working at cross purposes. Managers need to be able to guide diverse individuals, who are often powerfully motivated to put their own self-interests first, to pursue common objectives.[1] At stake in this tug-of-war between individual and collective interests is the ultimate survival of the organization. This chapter offers a survival kit for the rough-and-tumble side of organizational life by exploring the interrelated topics of organizational influence, social power, employee empowerment, organizational politics, and impression management.

INFLUENCING OTHERS

How do you get others to carry out your wishes? Do you simply tell them what to do? Or do you prefer a less direct approach, such as promising to return the favor? Whatever approach you use, the crux of the issue is *social influence.* A large measure of interpersonal interaction involves attempts to influence others, including parents, bosses, co-workers, spouses, teachers, friends, and children.

Generic Influence Tactics

A particularly fruitful stream of research, initiated by David Kipnis and his colleagues in 1980, reveals how people influence each other in organizations. The Kipnis methodology involved asking employees how they managed to get their bosses, co-workers, or subordinates to do what they wanted them to do.[2] Statistical refinements and replications by other researchers over a 13-year period eventually yielded the following nine influence tactics, ranked in diminishing order of use in the workplace:

1. *Rational persuasion.* Trying to convince someone with reason, logic, or facts.
2. *Inspirational appeals.* Trying to build enthusiasm by appealing to others' emotions, ideals, or values.
3. *Consultation.* Getting others to participate in planning, making decisions, and changes.
4. *Ingratiation.* Getting someone in a good mood before making a request; being friendly, helpful, and using praise, flattery, or humor.[3]
5. *Personal appeals.* Referring to friendship and loyalty when making a request.
6. *Exchange.* Making express or implied promises and trading favors.
7. *Coalition tactics.* Getting others to support your effort to persuade someone.
8. *Pressure.* Demanding compliance or using intimidation or threats.
9. *Legitimating tactics.* Basing a request on one's authority or right, organizational rules or policies, or express or implied support from superiors.[4]

These approaches can be considered *generic* influence tactics because they characterize social influence in all directions. Researchers have found this ranking to be fairly consistent regardless of whether the direction of influence is downward, upward, or lateral.[5]

Some call the first five influence tactics—rational persuasion, inspirational appeals, consultation, ingratiation, and personal appeals—"soft" tactics because they are friendlier and less coercive than the last four tactics. Exchange, coalition, pressure, and legitimating tactics accordingly are called "hard" tactics because they involve more overt pressure.

Influence Outcomes

According to researchers, an influence attempt has three possible outcomes:

1. *Commitment.* Substantial agreement followed by initiative and persistence in pursuit of common goals.
2. *Compliance.* Reluctant or insincere agreement requiring subsequent prodding to satisfy minimum requirements.
3. *Resistance.* Stalling, unproductive arguing, or outright rejection.[6]

The best outcome in the workplace is commitment, because the target person's intrinsic motivation will energize good performance.[7]

A G Lafley, the highly respected CEO of Procter & Gamble, made commitment the cornerstone of his growth plan after taking charge in 2000. He identified every level of commitment, from the highest ("disciples") to those who were completely hostile to change ("saboteurs") and built his team around the disciples, who could win others over to his way of thinking. The painful reality was that he had to ask the saboteurs to leave so they would not derail the growth plans. Lafley needed his best powers of influence for the fence sitters, whom he addressed in a hectic schedule of face-to-face meetings with P&G's 100,000 employees worldwide.[8] Too often in today's fast-paced workplaces, managers must settle for compliance or face resistance because they do not invest themselves in the situation, as Lafley did.

Practical Research Insights

Laboratory and field studies have taught us useful lessons about the relative effectiveness of influence tactics along with other instructive insights. One lesson is that commitment is more likely when people rely on consultation, strong rational persuasion, and inspirational appeals and *do not* rely on pressure and coalition tactics.[9] In one study, managers were not very effective at *downward* influence. They relied most heavily on inspiration (an effective tactic), ingratiation (a moderately effective tactic), and pressure (an ineffective tactic).[10]

Ingratiation may help achieve some goals. A review of 69 studies suggests ingratiation— in this case, making the boss feel good—can slightly improve your performance appraisal results and make your boss like you significantly more.[11]

Influence also is affected by relationships. Commitment is more likely when the influence attempt involves something *important* and *enjoyable* and is based on a *friendly* relationship.[12] Credible (believable and trustworthy) people tend to be the most persuasive.[13] In a survey, 214 employed MBA students (55% female) tended to perceive their superiors' soft influence tactics as fair and hard influence tactics as unfair. Unfair influence tactics were associated with greater resistance among employees.[14]

Some researchers have looked for male–female differences in influencing work groups. Building on prior findings that women are perceived as being less competent and are less influential in work groups than men, one study had male and female work group leaders engage in either task behavior (demonstrating ability and task competence) or dominating behavior (threats). For leaders of both sexes, task behavior was associated with perceived competence and effective influence. Dominating behavior was not effective. The researchers concluded that male and female managers seeking to influence their employees will find displays of their task competence "an effective means to enhance one's status in groups" and threats "a poorly received strategy."[15]

Other research suggests that the success of influence tactics varies according to the culture of the people involved. The research described is based on the norms of Europeans and North Americans. Much remains to be learned about how to effectively influence others (without unintended insult) in today's diverse labor force and cross-cultural economy.[16] This cross-cultural challenge is merely one application of a broad principle: Influence is most likely to be effective if you understand the person you are trying to influence. In the context of influencing your boss, author and consultant Barbara Moses writes, "You can't make change; you have to sell it. And the key to selling anything is to understand where the other person is coming from—rather than to assume that your boss is a complete jerk."[17] Moses advises that employees identify what is most important to their boss and focus their influence efforts accordingly.

Strategic Alliances and Reciprocity

In their book *Influence without Authority,* Allan R Cohen and David L Bradford extended the concept of corporate strategic alliances to interpersonal influence.[18] Hardly a day goes by without another mention in the business press of a new strategic alliance between two global companies intent on staying competitive. These win–win relationships are based on complementary strengths. According to Cohen and Bradford, managers need to adopt that model and form some strategic alliances of their own with anyone who has a stake in their area. This strategy is particularly true in today's rapidly changing, cross-functional work teams, with diminished reliance on traditional authority structures.

While admitting the task is challenging, Cohen and Bradford recommend several types of behavior for creating strategic allies:

- *Mutual respect.* Assume co-workers are intelligent and competent.
- *Openness.* Talk to co-workers honestly and directly. Rather than assuming they know everything, share information so that you can more effectively help one another.
- *Trust.* Start with the assumption that your co-workers have good intentions. Even if sharing information doesn't help you immediately, cooperate for long-term benefits.
- *Mutual benefit.* When you make plans or decisions, look for alternatives in which both parties win. Unless you and your co-workers both benefit, the alliance will break up. Even if you arrive at the last resort—dissolving a partnership—try to do it without angering co-workers. After all, the situation may change so that you need them as allies later on.[19]

Reciprocity
A mutual exchange of benefits.

True, these tactics involve taking some personal risks. But the effectiveness of interpersonal strategic alliances is anchored to the concept of **reciprocity:** "the almost universal belief that people should be paid back for what they do—that one good (or bad) turn deserves another."[20] In short, people tend to get what they give when attempting to influence others.

SOCIAL POWER AND EMPOWERMENT

The term *power* evokes mixed and often passionate reactions. To skeptics of the benefits of power, Lord Acton's time-honored declaration that "power corrupts and absolute power corrupts absolutely" is as true as ever.[21] However, OB specialists remind us that, like it or not, power is a fact of life in modern organizations. According to one management writer, power is necessary and natural as a way for managers to "influence those they depend on" and to develop their "self-confidence and willingness to support subordinates," so "it is powerlessness, not power, that undermines organizational effectiveness."[22]

Power is a necessary and generally positive force in organizations.[23] More specifically, members of an organization exert **social power,** which in the context of organizational behavior is "the ability to marshal the human, informational, and material resources to get something done."[24]

Social power
Ability to get things done with human, informational, and material resources.

Note that social power in organizations does not necessarily flow downward. Employees can and do exercise power upward and laterally. An example of an upward power play occurred at Alberto-Culver Company, which sells personal care products. Leonard Lavin, founder of the company, was under pressure to revitalize the firm because key employees were departing for more innovative competitors. Lavin's daughter Carol Bernick, and her husband Howard, both long-time employees, took matters into their own hands by informing Lavin that they, too, would leave if he continued to serve as CEO. Lavin conceded and surrendered his position to his son-in-law, who made changes that all three parties came to accept as beneficial.[25]

Bases of Power

A popular classification scheme for social power traces back to the landmark work of John French and Bertram Raven. They proposed that power arises from five different bases, each involving a different approach to influencing others and each with advantages and drawbacks:[26]

Reward power
Obtaining compliance with promised or actual rewards.

- *Reward power.* Managers have **reward power** if they can obtain compliance by promising or granting rewards. Pay-for-performance plans and positive reinforcement programs attempt to exploit reward power.

Coercive power
Obtaining compliance through threatened or actual punishment.

- *Coercive power.* Threats of punishment and actual punishment give an individual **coercive power.** A sales manager who threatens to fire any salesperson who uses a company car for family vacations is relying on coercive power.[27]

Legitimate power
Obtaining compliance through formal authority.

- *Legitimate power.* This base of power is anchored to a person's formal position or authority.[28] So, managers who obtain compliance primarily because of their formal authority to make decisions have **legitimate power.** Legitimate power may be expressed either positively or negatively. Positive legitimate power focuses constructively on job performance. Negative legitimate power tends to be threatening and demeaning to those being influenced. Its main purpose is to build the power holder's ego.

Expert power
Obtaining compliance through one's knowledge or information.

- *Expert power.* Valued knowledge or information gives an individual **expert power** over those who need that knowledge or information. The power of supervisors is enhanced because they know about work assignments and schedules before their employees do. Skillful use of expert power played a key role in the effectiveness of team leaders in a study of three physician medical diagnosis teams.[29] Knowledge *is* power in today's high-tech workplaces.

Referent power
Obtaining compliance through charisma or personal attraction.

- *Referent power.* Also called *charisma,* **referent power** comes into play when a person's personality becomes the reason for compliance. Role models have referent power over those who identify closely with them.[30]

MASTER YOUR KNOWLEDGE
Sources of Power

Increase your knowledge of the sources of social power (power bases) by completing the online quiz at [www.mhhe.com/obcore].

- For a deeper understanding, think of your own example of each source of power. Try to think of examples from your own work experience.
- Review the examples given for each question in the online exercise, and decide whether each example shows a use of power that is in line with the organization's objectives.

Practical Lessons from Research

Researchers have investigated relationships between power bases and work outcomes such as job performance, job satisfaction, and turnover.[31] In these studies, expert and referent power had a generally positive effect, while reward and legitimate power had a slightly positive effect. Coercive power, by contrast, had a slightly negative effect.

A follow-up study involving 251 employed business seniors looked at the relationship between influence styles and bases of power. This was a bottom-up study, meaning that it focused on employee perceptions of managerial influence and power. Rational persuasion was found to be a highly acceptable managerial influence tactic. The reason was that employees perceived it to be associated with the three bases of power they viewed positively: legitimate, expert, and referent.[32]

In summary, expert and referent power appear to get the best *combination* of results and favorable reactions from lower-level employees.[33]

Employee Empowerment

An exciting trend in today's organizations centers on giving employees a greater say in the workplace. This trend wears various labels, including "participative management" and "open-book management."[34] Regardless of the term used, what people are discussing is empowerment. One management writer defines **empowerment** in terms of serving the customer: "Empowerment quite simply means granting supervisors or workers permission to give the customer priority over other issues in the operation. In practical terms, it relates to the resources, skill, time and support to become leaders rather than controllers or mindless robots."[35] Steve Kerr, a pioneer in the field of employee empowerment, explains: "We say empowerment is moving decision making down to the lowest level *where a competent decision can be made.*"[36] Of course, it is naive and counterproductive to hand power over to unwilling or unprepared employees.

Empowerment
Sharing varying degrees of power with lower-level employees to better serve the customer.

The concept of empowerment requires some adjustment in traditional thinking. First and foremost, power is *not* a zero-sum situation in which one person's gain is another's loss. Social power is unlimited, and empowering employees requires win–win thinking. Authoritarian managers who view employee empowerment as a threat to their personal power are missing the point because of their win–lose thinking.[37] In contrast, a role model

GROUP EXERCISE
The Effects of Abusing Power

for using win–win thinking is Motorola executive Greg Brown, whose management philosophy is "listen, learn, lead." Brown listens to employees to learn the details of the business, expects them to know more than he does about some issues, and focuses on tracking performance in terms of only a few key measures.[38]

We believe empowerment shows promise if managers go about it properly. Empowerment is a sweeping concept with many different definitions. Consequently, researchers use inconsistent measurements, and cause-effect relationships are fuzzy.[39] Managers committed to the idea of employee empowerment need to follow the path of continuous improvement, learning from their successes and failures. Eight years of research with 10 "empowered" companies led consultant W Alan Randolph to formulate the three-pronged empowerment plan shown in Figure 10–1. Notice how open-book management and active information sharing are needed to build the necessary foundation of trust. Beyond that, clear goals and lots of relevant training are needed. Randolph adds that the process requires managers to have courage to share information, as well as a strong commitment and perseverance.[40]

FIGURE 10–1 Randolph's Empowerment Model

Source: Reprinted from *Organizational Dynamics,* W Alan Randolph, "Navigating the Journey to Empowerment," Spring 1995. Copyright © 1995, with permission from Elsevier.

The Empowerment Plan

Share Information
- Share company performance information.
- Help people understand the business.
- Build trust through sharing sensitive information.
- Create self-monitoring possibilities.

Create Autonomy through Structure	Let Teams Become the Hierarchy
• Create a clear vision and clarify the little pictures.	• Provide direction and training for new skills.
• Create new decision-making rules that support empowerment.	• Provide encouragement and support for change.
• Clarify goals and roles collaboratively.	• Gradually have managers let go of control.
• Establish new empowering performance management processes.	• Work through the leadership vacuum stage.
• Use heavy doses of training.	• Acknowledge the fear factor.

Remember: Empowerment is not magic;
it consists of a few simple steps and a lot of persistence.

ORGANIZATIONAL POLITICS AND IMPRESSION MANAGEMENT

Most students of OB find the study of organizational politics intriguing. Perhaps this topic owes its appeal to the antics of Hollywood's corporate villains and contestants on *The Apprentice,* who step on each other to avoid Donald Trump's dreaded words, "You're fired!"[41] As we will see, however, organizational politics includes, but is not limited to, dirty dealing. Organizational politics is an ever-present and sometimes annoying feature of modern work life. Results from a survey of 150 executives at large U.S. companies estimated that "office politics wastes an average of 20% of their time."[42] Even so, organizational politics is often a positive force in modern work organizations. Skillful and well-timed politics can help you get your point across, neutralize resistance to a key project, relieve stress, or get a choice job assignment.[43]

Definition and Domain of Organizational Politics

Organizational politics
Intentional enhancement of self-interest.

Formally defined, **organizational politics** refers to "intentional acts of influence to enhance or protect the self-interest of individuals or groups."[44] This form of social influence is distinguished by its emphasis on self-interest. Managers are continually challenged to achieve a workable balance between employees' self-interests and organizational interests. When a proper balance exists, the pursuit of self-interest may serve the organization's interests. In contrast, political behavior becomes a negative force when self-interests erode or defeat organizational interests. For example, researchers have documented the political tactic of filtering and distorting information flowing up to the boss. This self-serving practice put the reporting employees in the best possible light.[45]

Political Behavior Triggered by Uncertainty

Political maneuvering is triggered primarily by *uncertainty*. Sources of uncertainty within organizations include unclear objectives, vague performance measures, ill-defined decision processes, strong individual or group competition, and any type of change.[46] Performance measures trigger political behavior not only when they are vague but also when the linkage between performance and rewards is unclear (see expectancy theory in Chapter 4). This is a significant problem, according to a recent survey of 10,000 employees. Regarding the statement "Employees who do a better job get paid more," 48% of the managers agreed, while only 31% of the nonmanagers agreed.[47] When employees are unsure about what it takes to get ahead, they tend to resort to political games.

Based on these factors of uncertainty, we would expect that a field sales representative who is striving to achieve an assigned quota will be less political than a management trainee working on a variety of projects. While some management trainees stake their career success on hard work, competence, and a bit of luck, many do not. These people attempt to gain a competitive edge through a combination of the political tactics discussed later in this section. Meanwhile, the salesperson's performance is measured in actual sales, not in terms of being friends with the boss or taking credit for others' work. As a result, the management trainee would tend to be more political than the field salesperson because of greater uncertainty about management's expectations.

Because employees generally experience greater uncertainty during the earlier stages of their careers, the question arises whether junior employees are more political than more senior ones. According to a survey of 243 employed adults in upstate New York, the answer

FIGURE 10–2
Levels of
Political Action
in Organizations

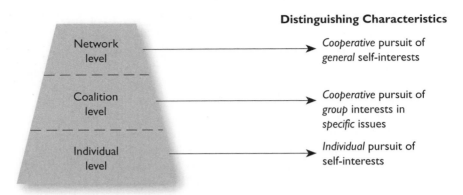

is yes. In fact, one senior employee nearing retirement told the researcher, "I used to play political games when I was younger. Now I just do my job."[48]

Three Levels of Political Action

Although much political maneuvering occurs at the individual level, it also can involve group or collective action. Figure 10–2 illustrates three different levels of political action: the level of the individual, the coalition, and the network.[49] Each level has its distinguishing characteristics. At the individual level, personal self-interests are pursued by the individual. The political aspects of coalitions and networks are less obvious.

People with a common interest can become a political coalition. In an organizational context, a **coalition** is an informal group bound together by the *active* pursuit of a *single* issue. Coalitions may or may not coincide with formal group membership. When the target issue is resolved (say, a sexually harassing supervisor is fired), the coalition disbands. Experts note that political coalitions have "fuzzy boundaries," meaning they are fluid in membership, flexible in structure, and temporary in duration.[50] Coalitions are a potent political force in organizations. Chief executives frequently must bow to this force when corporate board members form a coalition that withdraws support and brings about their resignation, as has happened recently at Hewlett-Packard, Disney, and many other corporations.[51]

A third level of political action involves networks.[52] Unlike coalitions, which pivot on specific issues, networks are loose associations of individuals seeking social support for their general self-interests. Politically, networks are people-oriented, while coalitions are issue-oriented. Networks have broader and longer-term agendas than do coalitions. For instance, Avon's Hispanic and Latino employees have built a network to enhance the members' career opportunities.

Political Tactics

Anyone who has worked in an organization has firsthand knowledge of blatant politicking. Blaming someone else for your mistake is an obvious political ploy. So are these self-serving games that an analyst for several investment banks shared with a *Wall Street Journal* reporter: The analyst would set herself easy goals so she could report that she had exceeded them, filled folders with evidence of accomplishments and praise from others, and was not above mentioning during performance reviews that her behavior was more frugal than that of her colleagues.[53] Other political tactics are more subtle.

Coalition
Temporary
groupings of
people who
actively pursue
a single issue.

Researchers have identified a range of political behavior. One landmark study involved in-depth interviews with 87 managers from 30 electronics companies in Southern California, including a roughly equal mix of top-, middle-, and low-level managers. The researchers asked these managers to consider all organizations in which they had worked and to "describe organizational political tactics and personal characteristics of effective political actors" they had witnessed in those organizations.[54] Based on those answers, the researchers identified eight political tactics, listed here in descending order of occurrence:

1. Attacking or blaming others.
2. Using information as a political tool.
3. Creating a favorable image (also known as *impression management*).[55]
4. Developing a base of support.
5. Praising others (ingratiation).
6. Forming power coalitions with strong allies.
7. Associating with influential people.
8. Creating obligations (reciprocity).

The researchers distinguished between reactive and proactive political tactics, based on the objectives of each tactic. The intent of a reactive tactic is to *defend* one's self-interest. An example is scapegoating. A proactive tactic, in contrast, seeks to *promote* the individual's self-interest. Developing a base of support is proactive.

Impression Management

Impression management
Getting others to see us in a certain manner.

In organizations, an important form of political behavior is **impression management,** "the process by which people attempt to control or manipulate the reactions of others to images of themselves or their ideas."[56] This process encompasses how someone talks, behaves, and looks. Most attempts at impression management are directed toward making a *good* impression on relevant others, but some employees strive to make a *bad* impression. For purposes of conceptual clarity, we will focus on *upward* impression management—trying to impress your immediate supervisor—because it is most relevant for managers. However, anyone can be the target of impression management. Parents, teachers, peers, employees, and customers are all fair game when it comes to managing the impressions of others.

Good Impressions

If you "dress for success," project an upbeat attitude at all times, and avoid offending others, you are engaging in favorable impression management—particularly if your motive is to improve your chances of getting what you want in life.[57] There are questionable ways to create a good impression as well. For instance, Stewart Friedman, director of the University of Pennsylvania's Leadership Program, offered this gem, an anecdote he heard while consulting with a bank: "After 7 PM, people would open the door to their office, drape a spare jacket on the back of their chair, lay a set of glasses down on some reading material on their desk—and then go home for the night. The point of this elaborate gesture was to create the illusion that they were just out grabbing dinner and would be returning to burn the midnight oil."[58] Impression management often strays into unethical territory. Do you think this example is unethical?

Tactics for favorable upward impression management fell into three categories in a statistical analysis of influence attempts reported by a sample of 84 bank employees, mostly women.[59] These tactics were either *job-focused* (manipulating information about a person's job performance), *supervisor-focused* (praising and doing favors for a supervisor), or *self-focused* (presenting an image of being a polite and nice person).

A moderate amount of upward impression management is necessary for the average employee. If you engage in too little, busy managers are liable to overlook some of your valuable contributions when they make decisions about job assignments, pay, and promotions. Using it too much runs the risk of co-workers branding you a "schmoozer," a "phony," and other unflattering labels.[60] Excessive flattery and ingratiation can backfire by embarrassing the target person and damaging a person's credibility. Also, the risk of unintended insult is very high when impression management tactics cross gender, racial, ethnic, and cultural lines.[61] International management experts further warn that tactics will be effective only if they dovetail with cultural norms about how people should behave. Norms for praise, physical contact, and tone of voice vary from culture to culture.[62]

Bad Impressions

At first glance, the idea of consciously trying to make a bad impression in the workplace seems absurd.[63] But an interesting new line of impression management research has uncovered both motives and tactics for this behavior. In a survey of the work experiences of business students at a large northwestern U.S. university, more than half said they had observed someone trying to look bad at work.[64]

Why would anyone want to create a negative impression? The study uncovered several motives.[65] First, some employees wanted to look bad to avoid something negative, such as receiving more work, stress, or an undesirable job change. Others used bad behavior as a way to obtain a desired outcome, such as a pay increase or a desired job change—sometimes even a desired demotion. Employees who were unhappy with their jobs used bad behavior as a way to have their jobs terminated, ideally with compensation such as unemployment compensation or workers' compensation, which are unavailable to employees who simply quit. Finally, negative impression management can be used as a way to obtain and exert power, say, by intimidating others or getting revenge. Within the context of these motives, unfavorable upward impression management makes sense.

In the same study, the researchers identified five tactics for unfavorable upward impression management:

1. *Decreasing performance.* Restricting productivity, making more mistakes than usual, lowering quality, neglecting tasks.
2. *Not working to potential.* Pretending ignorance or having unused capabilities.
3. *Withdrawing.* Being tardy, taking excessive breaks, faking illness.
4. *Displaying a bad attitude.* Complaining, getting upset and angry, acting strangely, or not getting along with co-workers.
5. *Broadcasting limitations.* Letting co-workers know about your physical problems and mistakes, both verbally and nonverbally.[66]

In general, managers need to intervene to discourage negative impression management. To redirect employees who try to make a bad impression, managers can employ a variety of motivational and leadership principles found throughout this book, such as providing more challenging work, greater autonomy, better feedback, supportive leadership, clear and reasonable goals, and a less stressful work setting.[67]

Keeping Organizational Politics in Check

Organizational politics cannot be eliminated. A manager would be naive to expect such an outcome. But political maneuvering can and should be managed to keep it constructive and within reasonable bounds. Harvard's Abraham Zaleznik put the issue this way: "People can focus their attention on only so many things. The more it lands on politics, the less energy—emotional and intellectual—is available to attend to the problems that fall under the heading of real work."[68]

An individual's degree of politicalness is a matter of personal values, ethics, and temperament. People who are either strictly nonpolitical or highly political generally pay a price for their behavior. The former may experience slow promotions and feel left out, while the latter may run the risk of being called self-serving and lose their credibility. People at both ends of the political spectrum may be considered poor team players. A moderate amount of prudent political behavior generally is considered a survival tool in complex organizations.

With this perspective in mind, managers can take several practical steps to keep organizational politics within reasonable bounds:

- Screen out overly political individuals at hiring time.
- Create an open-book management system.
- Make sure every employee knows how the business works and has a personal line of sight to key results with corresponding measurable objectives for individual accountability.
- Have nonfinancial people interpret periodic financial and accounting statements for all employees.
- Establish formal conflict resolution and grievance processes.
- As an ethics filter, do only what you would feel comfortable doing on national television.
- Publicly recognize and reward people who get real results without political games.[69]

Notice the importance of reducing uncertainty through clear performance-reward linkages. Measurable objectives are management's first line of defense against negative expressions of organizational politics. General Electric has achieved business success and a top ranking on *Fortune* magazine's list of "Most Admired Companies" by adhering to a focus on performance targets that are measurable and ambitious. This focus, according to Kevin Sharer, a former GE executive who now heads Amgen, has created a culture that emphasizes candor and facts. Sharer said that, in this culture, "Everybody has a real chance to know exactly where they are."[70]

Chapter **Eleven**

Leadership: What Makes an Effective Leader

Learning Objectives

After reading the material in this chapter, you should be able to:

- Discuss theories that look for ideal leadership traits and one best style of leadership.
- Explain how leadership style interacts with situational control and other situational variables.
- Describe the difference between transactional and transformational leadership.
- Identify leadership styles and traits that are most effective cross-culturally.
- Describe the leader–member exchange (LMX) model of leadership.
- Summarize the alternative views of shared leadership, servant-leadership, and Level 5 leadership.

Business observers often comment on an organization's leader and his or her effectiveness. They speculate on what made Jack Welch of General Electric so successful that he was given accolades when he retired, while Carleton Fiorina, former CEO of Hewlett-Packard, worked hard, cared about her staff but ultimately failed and was forced out. Why does Meg Whitman of eBay continue to motivate her staff and keep her company rolling along in the very uncertain environment of the Internet, while Steve Case, former CEO of Time Warner, failed to win the confidence of his employees? Do they have different characteristics that help or hinder their success, or do their organizations and competitive challenges make them more or less likely to prevail?

Someone once observed that a leader is a person who finds out which way the parade is going, jumps in front, and yells "Follow me!" This approach to leadership has little chance of working in today's rapidly changing world. Leaders do far more than simply take charge. This chapter describes the principles behind what leaders do. After defining *leadership,* this chapter examines research into the traits and behaviors associated with effective leaders, describes how leaders behave in different situations, explores how they can transform organizations, and summarizes additional perspectives on leadership. Each topic has been the subject of many different leadership theories, so it is impossible to discuss them all. This chapter reviews the theories with the most research support.

WHAT DOES LEADERSHIP INVOLVE?

Leading involves a complex interaction among the leader, the followers, and the situation. Definitions of leadership emphasize different aspects of this interaction. Some researchers define leadership in terms of personality and physical traits, while others refer to a set of prescribed behaviors. Still others believe that leadership is a temporary role that anyone can fill.

Leadership
Influencing employees to voluntarily pursue organizational goals.

As the term is used in this chapter, **leadership** is "a process whereby an individual influences a group of individuals to achieve a common goal."[1] This definition is based on some common assumptions made by those who write about leadership. First, leadership is a process involving a leader and followers. Second, leadership involves social influence. Also, leadership is exhibited on different levels. At the individual level, leadership involves mentoring, coaching, inspiring, and motivating. Leaders build teams, create cohesion, and resolve conflict at the group level, and they build culture and create change at the organizational level.[2] Finally, leadership focuses on goal accomplishment.

This definition of leadership excludes a moral component; that is, leadership is not a moral concept. History is filled with examples of successful leaders who were killers, corrupt, and morally bankrupt. Barbara Kellerman, a leadership expert, commented on this notion: "Leaders are like the rest of us: trustworthy and deceitful, cowardly and brave, greedy and generous. To assume that all good leaders are good people is to be willfully blind to the reality of the human condition, and it more severely limits our scope for becoming more effective at leadership."[3] Good leaders develop a keen sense of their strengths and weaknesses and build on their positive attributes.[4]

Our definition also omits an important perspective on leading: that of the follower. Research on the follower perspective reveals that people seek, admire, and respect leaders who create feelings of *significance* (what someone does at work is important and meaningful), *community* (a sense of unity encourages people to treat others with respect and dignity and to work together in pursuit of organizational goals), and *excitement* (people are engaged and feel energy at work).[5]

Successful leaders step into a difficult situation and make a noticeable difference. Organizational behavior researchers have discovered that leaders can indeed make a difference in modern organizations. According to one study, leadership was positively associated with net profits at 167 companies over a time span of 20 years.[6] In another study, teams in Major League Baseball and college basketball won more games when players perceived the coach to be an effective leader.[7] Rest assured, leadership matters! Fortunately, people can be taught to be more effective leaders.[8]

TRAIT AND BEHAVIORAL THEORIES OF LEADERSHIP

The two earliest approaches to explaining leadership were trait theories, which focused on identifying the personal traits that differentiated leaders from followers, and behavioral theories aimed at describing the leader behaviors that result in higher work-group performance. Both approaches to leadership can teach valuable lessons about leading.

GROUP EXERCISE
What Is Your Motivation to Lead?

Trait Theory

What made Abraham Lincoln, Martin Luther King Jr, and former General Electric CEO Jack Welch such effective leaders? Many people think such great leaders must have been born with the ability to lead. In contrast to this "great man" theory of leadership, more recent theorists have proposed that leadership traits are not innate but can be developed through experience and learning. A **leader trait** is a physical or personality characteristic that can be used to differentiate leaders from followers.

Leader trait
Personal characteristic that differentiate leaders from followers.

Before World War II, hundreds of studies were conducted to pinpoint the traits of successful leaders. Dozens of leadership traits were identified. During the postwar period, however, enthusiasm was replaced by widespread criticism. Researchers simply were unable to uncover a consistent set of traits that accurately predicted which individuals became leaders in organizations.

Contemporary Trait Research

Leadership prototype
Mental representation of the traits and behaviors possessed by leaders.

Even so, **leadership prototypes**—the ways we mentally represent the traits and behaviors we associate with a leader—are important because they determine whether individuals perceive someone as a leader. Two OB researchers concluded in 1983 that past trait data may have been incorrectly analyzed. By applying modern statistical techniques to an old database, they demonstrated that the majority of a leader's behavior could be attributed to stable underlying traits.[9] Unfortunately, their methodology did not single out specific traits.

More recently, two meta-analytic studies conducted by Timothy Judge and his colleagues shed light on which traits are associated with leadership effectiveness. The first study examined 94 studies to assess the relationship between the Big Five personality traits (see Table 3–1) and leadership emergence and effectiveness. Extraversion was most consistently and positively related to both leadership emergence and effectiveness. Conscientiousness and openness to experience also were positively correlated with leadership effectiveness.[10] In Judge's second meta-analysis, which involved 151 samples, intelligence was modestly related to leadership effectiveness. Judge concluded that for selecting leaders, personality is more important than intelligence.[11]

This conclusion is supported by research that examined emotional and political intelligence. Given that leadership is an influence process, it makes sense that emotional intelligence—the ability to manage oneself and one's relationships in mature and constructive ways (see Chapter 3)—is associated with leadership effectiveness.[12] Political intelligence, a recently proposed leadership trait, represents an offshoot of emotional intelligence. Politically intelligent leaders use power and intimidation to push followers in the pursuit of an inspiring vision and challenging goals. Although these leaders can be insensitive, hard to work with, and demanding, they tend to be effective in stagnant and change-resistant situations.[13] Famous examples include Martha Stewart (described as "amazing, [with a] well-organized and disciplined mind" but also "incredibly impatient and brusque") and

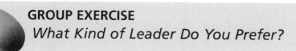

Michael Eisner (who is credited with turning around an ailing Disney Corporation in spite of being considered arrogant and insensitive).[14] Politically intelligent leaders seem to walk a fine line between using intimidation to achieve organizational goals and humiliation and bullying to make themselves feel good. Further research is needed to examine the long-term effectiveness of leaders with political intelligence.

Gender and Leadership

The increase of women in the workforce has generated much interest in comparing female and male leaders. Research has uncovered several patterns. Men were seen as displaying more task leadership and women as displaying greater social leadership.[15] Women used a more democratic or participative style than men, and men used a more autocratic and directive style than women.[16] However, men and women were equally assertive.[17] Women executives, when rated by their peers, managers, and direct reports, scored higher than their male counterparts on a variety of effectiveness criteria.[18]

Trait Theory in Perspective

The implications of leadership traits are important. Traits play a central role in how we perceive leaders and determine the characteristics of effective leaders. Organizations should consider selected leadership traits when choosing among candidates for leadership positions. Gender and race are poor—and illegal—substitutes for meaningful leadership traits. Relevant traits to consider include those listed in Table 11–1. Would-be leaders should consider using trait assessments and cultivating traits associated with good leadership. They can approach this effort systematically by preparing a personal development plan and seeking help from an executive coach.[19] Organizations can use management development programs to enhance employees' leadership traits. Hasbro, for example, has been pleased with the results of sending a group of managers to a program that included a combination of 360-degree feedback, trait assessments, executive coaching, classroom training, and problem-solving assignments.[20]

Behavioral Styles Theory

Research into behavioral styles of leadership began during World War II as part of an effort to develop better military leaders. This research stemmed from the human relations movement

TABLE 11–1
Key Positive Leadership Traits

Positive Traits	
Intelligence	Sociability
Self-confidence	Emotional intelligence
Determination	Extraversion
Honesty/integrity	Conscientiousness

(see Chapter 1) and the seeming inability of trait theory to explain leadership effectiveness. The early behavioral leadership theory shifted the focus from traits to the way leaders behave, on the assumption that leader behavior directly affects work-group effectiveness. Researchers looked for patterns of behavior (called *leadership styles*) that enabled leaders to effectively influence others.

The Ohio State and University of Michigan Studies

Consideration
Creating mutual respect and trust with followers.

Initiating structure
Organizing and defining what group members should be doing.

Researchers at Ohio State University began by generating a list of behaviors exhibited by leaders. Ultimately, these researchers concluded there are only two independent dimensions of leader behavior: **Consideration** involves leader behavior associated with creating mutual respect or trust and focuses on a concern for group members' needs and desires. **Initiating structure** is leader behavior that organizes and defines what group members should be doing to maximize output. By graphing these two dimensions of leader behavior at right angles, they modeled four behavioral styles of leadership: low structure–high consideration, high structure–high consideration, low structure–low consideration, and high structure–low consideration.

The initial hypothesis was that a high-structure–high-consideration style would be the one best style of leadership. Through the years, the effectiveness of the high–high style has been tested many times, with mixed results. As a result, researchers concluded that there is not one best style of leadership. Rather, the effectiveness of a given leadership style depends on situational factors.

As in the Ohio State studies, researchers at the University of Michigan sought to identify behavioral differences between effective and ineffective leaders. The researchers identified two styles of leadership: employee-centered and job-centered. These behavioral styles parallel the consideration and initiating-structure styles identified by the Ohio State group.

The Leadership Grid

Another attempt to define one best style of leadership is the Leadership Grid developed by Robert Blake and Jane Srygley Mouton. The grid is formed by the intersection of two dimensions of leader behavior: concern for production (horizontal axis) and concern for people (vertical axis). By scaling each axis of the grid from 1 (low) to 9 (high), Blake and Mouton plotted five leadership styles: impoverished management (1, 1), country club management (1, 9), authority-compliance (9, 1), middle-of-the-road management (5, 5), and team management (9, 9). The team management style is considered to be the best style, regardless of the situation.

Behavioral Styles in Perspective

By emphasizing leader *behavior,* something that is learned, the behavioral style approach supposes that leaders are made, not born. Given what we know about behavior shaping and model-based training, leader *behaviors* can be systematically improved and developed.[21]

Behavioral styles research also revealed that there is no one best style of leadership. The effectiveness of a particular leadership style depends on the situation at hand. For instance, employees prefer structure over consideration when faced with role ambiguity.[22]

Research also reveals that it is important to consider the difference between how frequently and how effectively managers exhibit various leader behaviors. For example, a manager might ineffectively display a lot of considerate leader behaviors. Such a style is likely to frustrate employees and possibly lower job satisfaction and performance. Because effectiveness is more important than the frequency of exhibiting leadership behaviors, managers should concentrate on what is effective.[23]

SITUATIONAL THEORIES

Situational theories
Propose that leader styles should match the situation at hand.

Attempts to explain the inconsistent findings about traits and styles resulted in situational leadership theories. **Situational theories** propose that the effectiveness of a particular style of leader behavior depends on the situation. As situations change, different styles become appropriate.

Fiedler's Contingency Model

Fred Fiedler, an OB scholar, developed a situational model that is the oldest and one of the most widely known models of leadership. Fiedler's model assumes that a leader's performance depends on two things: "the degree to which the situation gives the leader control and influence" and "the leader's basic motivation—that is, whether [the leader's] self-esteem depends primarily on accomplishing the task or on having close supportive relations with others."[24] The basic motivations of being either task-motivated or relationship-motivated are similar to the leader's concerns in behavioral styles theories (initiating structure–concern for production and consideration–concern for people).

Fiedler's theory also is based on the premise that leaders have one dominant leadership style that is resistant to change. He suggests that leaders must learn to manipulate or influence the leadership situation so it better matches their leadership style and the amount of control within the situation.[25]

Situational Control

In Fiedler's model, the amount of control and influence the leader has in her or his immediate work environment is called *situational control,* which ranges from high to low. High control implies that the leader's decisions will produce predictable results because the leader can influence work outcomes. Low control implies that the leader's decisions may not influence work outcomes because the leader has very little influence. Situational control has three dimensions:

1. *Leader–member relations.* The extent to which the leader has the group's support, loyalty, and trust.
2. *Task structure.* The amount of structure contained within tasks performed by the workgroup.
3. *Position power.* The degree to which the leader has formal power to reward, punish, or otherwise obtain compliance from employees.

These dimensions vary independently, forming the eight combinations of situational control shown at the bottom of Figure 11–1, which shows Fiedler's complete contingency model.

Linking Leadership Motivation and Situational Control

In Fiedler's model (Figure 11–1), each of the eight possible leadership situations, shown in the last row, represents a unique combination of leader–member relations, task structure,

FIGURE 11–1 **Representation of Fiedler's Contingency Model**

Source: Adapted from F E Fiedler, "Situational Control and a Dynamic Theory of Leadership," in *Managerial Control and Organizational Democracy,* eds B King, S Streufert, and F E Fiedler (New York: John Wiley & Sons, 1978), p 114.

Situational Control	High Control Situations			Moderate Control Situations				Low Control Situations
Leader–member relations	Good	Good	Good	Good	Poor	Poor	Poor	Poor
Task structure	High	High	Low	Low	High	High	Low	Low
Position power	Strong	Weak	Strong	Weak	Strong	Weak	Strong	Weak
Situation	I	II	III	IV	V	VI	VII	VIII

Optimal Leadership Style	**Task-Motivated Leadership**	**Relationship-Motivated Leadership**	**Task-Motivated Leadership**

and position power. Situations I, II, and III represent high-control situations. Task-motivated leaders are hypothesized to be most effective in these situations. Under conditions of moderate control (situations IV, V, VI, and VII), relationship-motivated leaders are expected to be more effective. The results orientation of task-motivated leaders is predicted to be more effective under the condition of very low control (situation VIII).

Research and Managerial Implications

Research has provided mixed support for Fiedler's model, suggesting that the model needs theoretical refinement.[26] The major contribution of this model is that it prompted others to examine the contingency nature of leadership. Their research, in turn, reinforced the notion that there is no one best style of leadership. Leaders should alter their task and relationship orientation to fit the demands of the situation at hand. Consider, for example, the different leadership styles of IBM's current CEO, Sam Palmisano, and former CEO, Lou Gerstner. A *Fortune* reporter describes Palmisano as extraverted, approachable, and focused on results, in sharp contrast to Gerstner's style, which was "gruff and intimidating." However, the reporter adds, "Gerstner's role wasn't to be nice; it was to keep IBM from disintegrating. He took over just as it was about to split itself up into 13 distinct, loosely affiliated entities."[27] Palmisano and Gerstner used different leadership styles to lead IBM employees. As suggested by Fiedler, they both were effective because their respective leadership styles were appropriate for the situation at the time.

MASTER YOUR KNOWLEDGE
Fiedler's Contingency Model of Leadership

Increase your knowledge of contingency leadership by completing the online quiz at [www.mhhe.com/obcore].

- Was it difficult for you to categorize these situations? Do you think this type of assessment would be difficult for managers in the workplace?
- Fiedler's model assumes that leaders have a dominant style, so the leader whose style does not match a situation will try to manipulate the situation rather than his or her leader behaviors. Choose one of the scenarios from the exercise, and discuss how a manager with a less than optimal leadership style might try to change the situation. Is this effort likely to succeed?

Path–Goal Theory

Another situational leadership model is path–goal theory, proposed by Robert House in the 1970s.[28] About 50 studies have tested various predictions derived from House's original model. Results have been mixed, with some studies supporting the theory and others not.[29] House thus proposed a new version of his theory in 1996, based on these results and the accumulation of new knowledge about OB. Figure 11–2 illustrates the reformulated model.

Contingency factors
Variables that influence the appropriateness of a leadership style.

House's model describes how leadership effectiveness is influenced by the interaction between leadership behaviors and a variety of contingency factors. **Contingency factors** are situational variables that cause one style of leadership to be more effective than another. The contingency factors in path–goal theory are employee characteristics and environmental

FIGURE 11–2
A General Representation of House's Revised Path–Goal Theory

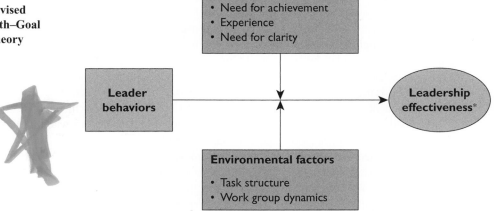

*Leadership effectiveness includes employee motivation, employee satisfaction, employee performance, leader acceptance, and work unit performance.

factors. Important employee characteristics include locus of control, task ability, need for achievement, experience, and need for clarity. Two relevant environmental factors are task structure (independent versus interdependent tasks) and work group dynamics. These contingency factors influence the effectiveness of each type of leader behavior:

- *Path–goal clarifying behaviors.* Clarifying employees' performance goals; guiding employees in how to complete tasks; clarifying performance standards and expectations; rewarding performance.
- *Achievement-oriented behaviors.* Setting challenging goals; emphasizing excellence; demonstrating confidence in employees' abilities.
- *Work facilitation behaviors.* Planning, scheduling, organizing, and coordinating work; providing coaching and feedback; eliminating roadblocks; providing resources; empowering employees.
- *Supportive behaviors.* Showing concern for the employees' well-being and needs; being friendly and approachable; treating employees as equals.
- *Interaction facilitation behaviors.* Resolving disputes; facilitating communication; encouraging expression of minority views; emphasizing collaboration; encouraging positive work relationships.
- *Group-oriented decision-making behaviors.* Posing problems rather than solutions to the group; encouraging group members' participation in decision making; sharing information with the group.
- *Representation and networking behaviors.* Presenting the group in a positive light; maintaining relationships with influential persons; doing favors; participating in organizational functions.
- *Value-based behaviors.* Establishing a vision, displaying passion for it, and supporting its accomplishment; demonstrating self-confidence; communicating high expectations of others; giving frequent positive feedback.[30]

To illustrate how the contingency factors influence leadership effectiveness, we consider locus of control (see Chapter 3), task ability, and experience. Employees with an internal locus of control may prefer achievement-oriented leadership because they believe they have control over the work environment. Such individuals are unlikely to be satisfied with leader behaviors that exert additional control over their activities. In contrast, employees with an external locus tend to view the environment as uncontrollable, so they may prefer the structure provided by work facilitation. An employee with high task ability and experience is less apt to need additional direction and so would respond negatively to path–goal clarifying behaviors. This person is more likely to be motivated and satisfied by group-oriented decision-making and achievement-oriented behaviors. In opposition, an inexperienced employee would find achievement-oriented leadership overwhelming as he or she confronts challenges associated with learning a new job.

The revised theory presented in Figure 11–2 makes three key changes.[31] First, in the belief that leadership is more complex and involves a greater variety of leader behavior, House expanded four leadership styles into eight categories of leadership behavior: path–goal clarifying, achievement-oriented, work facilitation, supportive, interaction facilitation, group-oriented decision making, representation and networking, and value-based. The need for an expanded list of leader behaviors is supported by current research and descriptions of business leaders.[32] For example, Jamie Dimon, CEO of JPMorgan Chase, has been described as blunt, focused on performance, actively involved in decision making, and passionate.[33] Dimon exhibits path–goal clarifying behaviors, achievement-oriented behaviors, group-oriented decision-making behaviors, and value-based behaviors—and apparently relies on intimidation to get others to do what he wants. The second key change in the theory is that House places much more emphasis on the need for leaders to foster intrinsic motivation (see Chapter 4) through empowerment (Chapter 10). Finally, the revised theory incorporates shared leadership. Rather than assuming an employee has to be a supervisor or manager to engage in leader behavior, House believes leadership is shared among all employees within an organization, as discussed in the final section of this chapter.

Without more direct tests of House's revised path–goal theory using appropriate research methods and statistical procedures, we cannot draw overall conclusions. Future research is clearly needed to assess this model's accuracy. That said, we can conclude that effective leaders possess and use more than one style of leadership. Managers should familiarize themselves with the different categories of leader behavior outlined in path–goal theory and try new behaviors when the situation calls for them. Also, a small set of employee characteristics (ability, experience, and need for independence) and environmental factors (task characteristics of autonomy, variety, and significance) are relevant contingency factors.[34] Managers should modify their leadership style to fit these various employee and task characteristics.

THE FULL-RANGE MODEL OF LEADERSHIP: FROM TRANSACTIONAL TO TRANSFORMATIONAL LEADERSHIP

One of the most recent approaches to leadership is known as a full-range model of leadership.[35] The authors of this theory, Bernard Bass and Bruce Avolio, proposed that leadership behavior varies along a continuum from laissez-faire leadership (a general failure to take responsibility for leading) to transactional leadership to transformational leadership. Of course, laissez-faire leadership is a terrible way for any manager to behave and should be avoided. In contrast, transactional and transformational leadership are both positively related to a variety of employee attitudes and behaviors and represent different aspects of being a good leader.

Transactional leadership
Focuses on clarifying employees' roles and providing rewards contingent on performance.

Transactional leadership focuses on clarifying employees' role and task requirements and providing followers with positive and negative rewards contingent on performance. In addition, transactional leadership encompasses the fundamental managerial activities of setting goals, monitoring progress toward goal achievement, and rewarding and punishing people for their level of goal accomplishment.[36] Transactional leadership is thus based on using extrinsic motivation (see Chapter 4) to increase employee productivity. For instance, it was transactional leadership when Norman Adami, CEO of Miller Brewing, instituted a performance management system that requires individuals to meet challenging goals in order to earn a top performance rating.[37]

Transformational leadership
Transforms employees to pursue organizational goals over self-interests.

In contrast, **transformational leaders** "engender trust, seek to develop leadership in others, exhibit self-sacrifice and serve as moral agents, focusing themselves and followers on objectives that transcend the more immediate needs of the work group."[38] Transformational leaders can produce significant organizational change and results because this form of leadership fosters higher levels of intrinsic motivation, trust, commitment, and loyalty from followers than does transactional leadership.

Transactional leadership is a prerequisite to effective leadership, and the best leaders learn to display various degrees of both transactional and transformational leadership. In support of this proposition, research has found that transformational leadership leads to superior performance when it "augments," or adds to, transactional leadership.[39] Norman Adami augmented transactional leadership with transformational leadership shortly after taking the CEO post at Miller. He combined his focus on results with efforts to create a more positive climate at the struggling company. A particularly colorful move was converting a group of offices and storerooms into "Fred's Pub," named after the company's founder, Frederick J Miller. Adami envisioned that the pub would serve as a meeting place for teams, where employees at various levels in the corporation might come into contact.[40]

How Transformational Leadership Transforms Followers

Transformational leaders transform followers by changing their goals, values, needs, beliefs, and aspirations. Leaders accomplish this transformation by appealing to followers' self-concepts—namely their values and personal identity.

As shown in Figure 11–3, transformational leader behavior is first influenced by various individual and organizational characteristics. For example, research shows that transformational leaders tend to have personalities that are more extraverted, agreeable, proactive, and less neurotic than nontransformational leaders, with female leaders using

FIGURE 11–3   **A Transformational Model of Leadership**

Source: Based in part on D A Waldman and F J Yammarino, "CEO Charismatic Leadership: Levels-of-Management and Levels-of-Analysis Effects," *Academy of Management Review,* April 1999, pp 266–85; and B Shamir, R J House, and M B Arthur, "The Motivational Effects of Charismatic Leadership: A Self-Concept Based Theory," *Organization Science,* November 1993, pp 577–94.

Individual and organizational characteristics	Leader behaviors	Effects on followers and work groups	Outcomes
• Traits • Organizational culture	• Inspirational motivation	• Increased intrinsic motivation, achievement orientation, and goal pursuit	• Personal commitment to leader and vision
	• Idealized influence	• Increased identification and trust with the leader	• Self-sacrificial behavior
	• Individualized consideration	• Increased identification and cohesion with work group members	• Organizational commitment
	• Intellectual stimulation	• Increased self-esteem, self-efficacy, and intrinsic interests in goal accomplishment	• Task meaningfulness and satisfaction
		• Increased role modeling of transformational leadership	• Increased individual, group, and organizational performance

transformational leadership more than male leaders.[41] However, the relationship between personality traits and transformational leadership is relatively weak. This suggests that transformational leadership is less traitlike and more susceptible to managerial influence, reinforcing the idea that transformational leadership can be learned.[42] Organizational culture also influences the extent to which leaders are transformational. In cultures that are adaptive and flexible rather than rigid and bureaucratic, work environments are more likely to foster the opportunity for exhibiting transformational leadership.

Transformational leaders engage in four key sets of leader behavior.[43] The first set, known as *inspirational motivation,* involves establishing an attractive vision of the future, the use of emotional arguments, and exhibition of optimism and enthusiasm. A vision is "a realistic, credible, attractive future for your organization."[44] According to leadership expert Burt Nanus, the "right" vision unleashes human potential because it serves as a beacon of hope and common purpose. It does this by attracting commitment, energizing workers, creating meaning in employees' lives, establishing a standard of excellence, promoting high ideals, and bridging the gap between an organization's present problems and its future goals and aspirations. Anne Mulcahy, Xerox's CEO, understands the importance of using a vision to energize the workforce. She successfully used a vision, created by asking top managers to write a story about how various constituents would describe the company in five years, to gain employees' commitment to difficult but necessary organizational changes that brought the company back from near bankruptcy.[45]

The second set of leader behaviors, *idealized influence,* includes sacrificing for the good of the group, being a role model, and displaying high ethical standards. Through their actions, transformational leaders model the desired values, traits, beliefs, and behaviors needed to realize their vision. The third set, *individualized consideration,* entails behaviors associated with providing support, encouragement, empowerment, and coaching to employees. Finally, *intellectual stimulation* involves encouraging employees to question the status quo and seek innovative, creative solutions to organizational problems.

Research and Managerial Implications

Components of the transformational model of leadership have been the most widely researched leadership topic over the last decade. Overall, previous research supported the relationships outlined in Figure 11–3. For example, transformational leader behaviors were positively associated with the extent to which employees identified with their leaders and their immediate work-groups.[46] Followers of transformational leaders were found to set goals consistent with those of the leader, to be more engaged in their work, to have higher levels of intrinsic motivation, and to have higher levels of group cohesion.[47] Regarding the direct relationship between transformational leadership and work outcomes, a meta-analysis indicated that transformational leadership was positively associated with measures of leadership effectiveness and employees' job satisfaction.[48] At the organizational level, a second meta-analysis found a positive correlation between transformational leadership and measures of job satisfaction and organizational effectiveness.[49]

These results underscore several important managerial implications. First, the best leaders are not just transformational; they are both transactional and transformational. Leaders should attempt to use these two types of leadership while avoiding a laissez-faire or wait-and-see style.

In addition, transformational leadership not only affects individual-level outcomes like job satisfaction, organizational commitment, and performance but also influences group dynamics and group-level outcomes. Managers can use the four types of transformational leadership shown in Figure 11–3 to improve group dynamics and work-unit outcomes. This is important in today's organizations because employees tend to rely on the input and collaboration of others, and many organizations are structured around teams.

Third, employees at any level in an organization can be trained to be more transactional and transformational.[50] This reinforces the organizational value of developing and rolling out a combination of transactional and transformational leadership training for all employees. Organizations can effectively develop leadership talent by preparing a formal plan for leadership succession, identifying the leadership competencies that can help the organization meet its goals, setting up programs that fill gaps between the current competencies and the ones desired, holding leaders accountable for meeting leadership development goals (for their teams or themselves), and giving managers a role in teaching the development programs.[51]

Finally, transformational leaders can be ethical or unethical. Whereas ethical transformational leaders enable employees to enhance their self-concepts, unethical ones select or produce obedient, dependent, and compliant followers. Top management can create and maintain ethical transformational leadership by creating and enforcing a clearly stated code of ethics; recruiting, selecting, and promoting people who display ethical behavior; developing performance expectations for the treatment of employees and measuring them in performance appraisals; training employees to value diversity; and identifying, rewarding, and publicly praising employees who exemplify high moral conduct.[52]

ADDITIONAL PERSPECTIVES ON LEADERSHIP

Some additional perspectives have influenced thinking about leadership: research into cultural differences, leader–member exchange theory, shared leadership, servant-leadership, and Level 5 leadership.

International Leadership: Lessons from the GLOBE Project

Project GLOBE (Global Leadership and Organizational Behavior Effectiveness) is the brainchild of University of Pennsylvania professor Robert J House.[53] It is a massive and ongoing attempt to "develop an empirically based theory to describe, understand, and predict the impact of specific cultural variables on leadership and organizational processes and the effectiveness of these processes."[54] GLOBE has evolved into a network of more than 160 scholars from 62 societies since the project was launched in Calgary, Canada, in 1994. Most of the researchers are native to the particular cultures they study, thus greatly enhancing the credibility of the project. To investigate which, if any, attributes of leadership are universally liked or disliked, researchers from the GLOBE project surveyed 17,000 middle managers from 951 different organizations in 62 societies/cultures. As shown in Table 11–2, 23 leader attributes were found to be universally liked, and 8 were universally disliked.

This study represents a refreshing redirection in cross-cultural management research by staking out some *common* cultural ground in the important area of leadership. Among the

TABLE 11–2
Leader
Attributes
Universally
Liked and
Disliked across
62 Nations

Source: Excerpted and adapted from P W Dorfman, P J Hanges, and F C Brodbeck, "Leadership and Cultural Variation: The Identification of Culturally Endorsed Leadership Profiles," in *Culture, Leadership, and Organization: The GLOBE Study of 62 Societies,* eds R J House, P J Hanges, M Javidan, P W Dorfman, and V Gupta (Thousand Oaks, CA: Sage, 2004), Tables 21.2 and 21.3, pp 677–78.

Universally Positive Leader Attributes	Universally Negative Leader Attributes
• Trustworthy	• Loner
• Just	• Asocial
• Honest	• Noncooperative
• Foresight	• Irritable
• Intelligent	• Nonexplicit
• Plans ahead	• Egocentric
• Encouraging	• Ruthless
• Positive	• Dictatorial
• Dynamic	
• Motive arouser	
• Confidence builder	
• Motivational	
• Dependable	
• Decisive	
• Effective bargainer	
• Win–win problem solver	
• Administrative skilled	
• Communicative	
• Informed	
• Coordinator	
• Team builder	
• Excellence oriented	

findings were that leader attributes associated with the charismatic/transformational leadership style are globally applicable. In contrast, certain leader attributes, listed in the right column of Table 11–2, should be avoided in all cultures. Local and foreign managers who heed these results are still advised to use a contingency approach to leadership after using their cultural intelligence to read the local people and culture.[55]

The Leader–Member Exchange Model of Leadership

In contrast to leadership models previously discussed, the leader–member exchange (LMX) model of leadership focuses on the quality of relationships between managers and subordinates, not the behaviors or traits of either leaders or followers. The LMX model revolves around the development of dyadic relationships between managers and their direct reports. Unlike the Leadership Grid and Fiedler's contingency theory, it does not assume that leader behavior is characterized by a stable or average leadership style. Instead of assuming that a leader treats all employees in about the same way, the LMX model assumes that leaders develop unique one-to-one relationships with each of the people reporting to them. Behavioral scientists call this sort of relationship a *vertical dyad*.

The forming of vertical dyads is said to be a naturally occurring process, resulting from the leader's attempt to delegate and assign work roles. As a result of this process, two distinct types of leader–member exchange relationships are expected to evolve.[56] One type is called the **in-group exchange.** In this relationship, leaders and followers

In-group exchange
A partnership characterized by mutual trust, respect, and liking.

SELF-ASSESSMENT

Assessing Your Leader-Member Exchange

Go online at [www.mhhe.com/obcore] to assess the quality of your leader–member exchange with your current supervisor or one you recently worked for.

- What is the overall quality of your LMX? Do you agree with this assessment?
- Which dimensions of your LMX were high? Which were low?

opposite

Out-group exchange
A partnership characterized by a lack of mutual trust, respect, and liking.

develop a partnership characterized by reciprocal influence, mutual trust, respect and liking, and a sense of common fates. In the second type of exchange, an **out-group exchange,** leaders are characterized as overseers who fail to create a sense of mutual trust, respect, or common fate.[57]

Research Findings

If the leader–member exchange model is correct, there should be a significant relationship between the type of leader–member exchange and job-related outcomes. Research supports this prediction. For example, a positive leader–member exchange was positively associated with positive results such as job satisfaction and job performance, and the type of leader–member exchange predicted turnover and career outcomes such as salary level.[58] Studies also have identified variables that influence the quality of an LMX; these include personality similarity, demographic similarity, the extent to which leaders and followers like each other, the leaders' positive expectations of their subordinates, and the frequency of communications between managers and their direct reports.[59]

Managerial Implications

The LMX model of leadership has several implications for managers. First, leaders should establish high performance expectations for all of their direct reports because setting high performance standards fosters high-quality LMXs. Also, because personality and demographic similarity between leaders and followers is associated with higher LMXs, managers need to be careful that they don't create a homogeneous work environment in the spirit of having positive relationships with their direct reports. At the same time, they have to be aware of the challenges posed by leading when they have personality or other differences. Several years ago, Hewlett-Packard was looking to breathe new life into its struggling operations by hiring an articulate and dynamic CEO, Carleton S "Carly" Fiorina. Many observers were initially impressed with Fiorina's apparently endless energy and optimistic vision for the company, but her leadership style alienated members of her management team and board of directors, who were used to a culture that valued engineering innovation and careful analysis. After H-P missed several earnings targets, board members lost patience; without their willingness to follow her lead, Fiorina was forced to resign.[60] Periodically evaluating one's LMX can therefore be helpful.

If you should experience a poor LMX, part of the relationship with your manager may need improvement. A management consultant offers the following tips for improving the quality of leader-member exchanges:[61]

- Stay focused on your department's goals, and remain positive about your ability to accomplish your goals. An unsupportive boss is just another obstacle to overcome.
- Do not fall prey to feeling powerless; empower yourself to get things done.
- Exercise the power you have by focusing on circumstances you can control, and avoid dwelling on circumstances you cannot control.
- Work on improving your relationship with your manager. Try to raise the trust level between the two of you by frequently and effectively communicating, following through on your commitments, and achieving your goals.
- Use an authentic, respectful, and assertive approach to resolve differences with your manager. When disagreements arise, focus on problem solving.

Shared Leadership

A pair of OB scholars noted, "There is some speculation, and some preliminary evidence, to suggest that concentration of leadership in a single chain of command may be less optimal than shared leadership responsibility among two or more individuals in certain task environments."[62] This perspective differs from other leadership models, which assume that leadership is a vertical, downward-flowing process. Shared leadership is based on the idea that people need to share information and collaborate to get work done. This in turn underscores the need for employees to adopt a horizontal process of influence or leadership.
Shared leadership entails a simultaneous, ongoing, mutual influence process in which individuals share responsibility for leading regardless of formal roles and titles. Mayo Clinic, with more than 42,000 employees in various facilities, relies on shared leadership to provide high-quality health care and customer service. The organization hires and rewards people who collaborate and emphasize teamwork as they regularly deal with life-and-death situations.[63]

Shared leadership
Simultaneous, ongoing, mutual influence process in which people share responsibility for leading.

Shared leadership is most likely to be needed when people work in teams, are involved in complex projects involving interdependence and creativity, and are doing knowledge work—work that requires intellectual capital contributed by skilled professionals.[64] Marv Levy, the former head coach of the Buffalo Bills football team, is a strong believer in shared leadership. He concluded that a head coach "must be willing and desirous of forming a relationship with others in the organization that results in their working together productively and even enjoyably," adding, "A head honcho who thinks he can do it all by himself is fooling no one but himself." In Levy's view, cooperation lets all participants contribute fully.[65]

Researchers are just beginning to explore the process of shared leadership, and results are promising. For example, shared leadership in teams was positively associated with group cohesion, group citizenship, and group effectiveness.[66]

When determining how to develop shared leadership, managers should consider several criteria. Shared leadership is most appropriate for tasks that are highly interdependent, require creativity, and are complex. The leader's role in developing shared leadership includes designing the team (clarifying its purpose, securing resources, articulating a vision, selecting team members, and defining team processes) and managing the team's boundaries. At the organizational level, systems are needed to facilitate the development of shared leadership. These systems include training and development of leaders and team members, reward systems that reinforce shared leadership, and cultural systems that express and demonstrate the value of shared leadership. Four categories of leadership behaviors, both vertical and shared, support positive team outcomes: (1) directive leadership to provide task-focused outcomes; (2) transactional leadership to reward good performance; (3) transformational leadership to stimulate commitment and emotional engagement; and (4) empowering leadership to reinforce the importance of self-motivation. Finally, the vertical leader has some ongoing responsibilities, even with shared leadership. The vertical leader must be able to step in and fill any voids in the team and should continue to emphasize the importance of the shared-leadership approach.[67]

Servant-Leadership

Servant-leadership is more a philosophy of managing than a testable theory. The term was coined in 1970 by Robert Greenleaf, who believes that great leaders act as servants, making the needs of others, including employees, customers, and community, their first priority. **Servant-leadership** focuses on increased service to others rather than to oneself.[68] A servant-leader displays the following characteristics:

> **Servant-leadership**
> Focuses on increased service to others rather than to oneself.

- *Listening.* Active listening to identify and clarify the group's needs and desires.
- *Empathy.* Understanding others' feelings and emotions and assuming they have good intentions.
- *Healing.* Trying to make people whole when they suffer or have failed.
- *Awareness.* Recognizing your own strengths and limitations.
- *Persuasion.* Relying more on persuasion than positional authority for influence and decision making.
- *Conceptualization.* Developing broader-based thinking to balance short-term and long-term views.
- *Foresight.* Predicting future outcomes associated with a course of action.
- *Stewardship.* Assuming they are stewards of the people and resources they manage.
- *Commitment to people's growth.* Fostering an environment that encourages personal, professional, and spiritual development.
- *Building community.* Striving to create a sense of community in and outside the organization.[69]

Steve Sanghi, CEO of Microchip Technology, is a good example of a servant-leader. He sees his place in the organization as being at the bottom of a pyramid resting on its point. His role is to support "internal customers": the employees who design and sell the company's products. Of management, Sanghi says, "We serve our internal customers so that external customers are served to the best of our ability."[70] Sanghi's approach to leadership has helped Microchip Technology increase its stock price 5,700% from 1990 to 2006.

According to Jim Stuart, cofounder of the leadership circle in Tampa, Florida, "Leadership derives naturally from a commitment to service. You know that you're practicing servant-leadership if your followers become wiser, healthier, more autonomous—and more likely to become servant-leaders themselves."[71] Servant-leadership is not a quick-fix approach to leadership. Rather, it is a long-term, transformational approach to life and work.

Level 5 Leadership

The model of Level 5 leadership was not derived from any particular theory or model of leadership but instead from a longitudinal study investigating whether a good company can become a great company and, if so, how. The study was conducted by a research team headed by Jim Collins, a former university professor who started his own research-based consulting company. He summarized his work in the best seller *Good to Great*.[72]

To answer the research question, Collins identified a set of companies that shifted from good performance to great performance, defined as "cumulative stock returns at or below the general stock market for 15 years, punctuated by a transition point, then cumulative returns at least three times the market over the next 15 years."[73] Beginning with a sample of 1,435 companies on the *Fortune* 500 from 1965 to 1995, Collins identified 11 good-to-great companies. To uncover the drivers of good-to-great transformations, he compared these 11 companies with a targeted set of direct-comparison companies. One of the key drivers was called Level 5 leadership (see Figure 11–4). In other words, every company that experienced good-to-great performance was led by an individual possessing the characteristics associated with Level 5 leadership.

As shown in Figure 11–4, a Level 5 leader possesses the characteristics of humility and a fearless will to succeed. American president Abraham Lincoln is an example of such an

FIGURE 11–4
The Level 5 Hierarchy

Source: Figure from *Good to Great: Why Some Companies Make the Leap and Others Don't* by J Collins. Copyright © 2001 by J Collins. Reprinted with permission from Jim Collins.

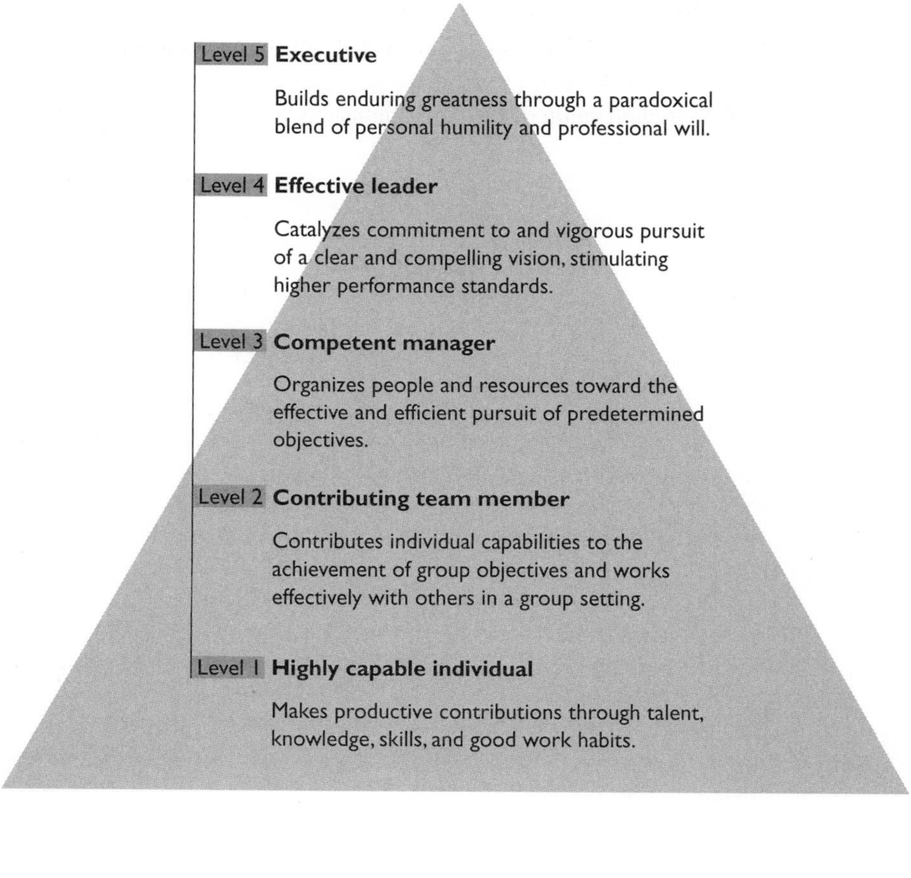

Level 5 **Executive**
Builds enduring greatness through a paradoxical blend of personal humility and professional will.

Level 4 **Effective leader**
Catalyzes commitment to and vigorous pursuit of a clear and compelling vision, stimulating higher performance standards.

Level 3 **Competent manager**
Organizes people and resources toward the effective and efficient pursuit of predetermined objectives.

Level 2 **Contributing team member**
Contributes individual capabilities to the achievement of group objectives and works effectively with others in a group setting.

Level 1 **Highly capable individual**
Makes productive contributions through talent, knowledge, skills, and good work habits.

individual. Although he was soft-spoken and shy, he possessed great will to accomplish his goal of uniting his country during the Civil War in the 1860s. This determination resulted in the loss of 250,000 Confederates, 360,000 Union soldiers, and ultimately to a united country. Being humble and determined, however, was not enough for Lincoln to succeed at his quest. Rather, a Level 5 leader must also possess the capabilities associated with the other levels in the hierarchy. Although an individual does not move up the hierarchy in a stair-step fashion, a Level 5 leader must possess the capabilities contained in Levels 1 through 4 before he or she can use the Level 5 characteristics to transform an organization.

The capabilities represented in this model overlap with other leadership theories. Level 1 is consistent with research on trait theory, which says leaders are intelligent and possess the personality characteristics of extraversion, conscientiousness, and openness to experience. Levels 3 and 4 contain behaviors associated with transactional and transformational leadership. Level 5 leadership thus appears to integrate components of trait theory and the full-range theory of leadership. The theory's novel and unexpected component is the conclusion that good-to-great leaders are not only transactional and transformational but, most importantly, also humble and fiercely determined. Michael Dell, chairman of Dell Inc., is an example. In response to being told that *Fortune* magazine had named his company Most Admired in 2005, Dell told a reporter, "I'm humbled by that, but we've got a lot of work to do."[74]

To apply Level 5 leadership, keep in mind that Collins observed additional drivers for taking a company from good to great.[75] Level 5 leadership enables the implementation of these additional drivers. Also, according to Collins, some people will never become Level 5 leaders because their narcissistic and boastful tendencies do not allow them to subdue their own ego and needs for the greater good of others. To date, there has not been any additional research testing Collins's conclusions. Future research is clearly needed to confirm the Level 5 hierarchy.

Part **Four**

Meeting Organizational Challenges

Chapter Twelve

Organizational Culture: How Organizations Create and Transmit a Culture

---

Learning Objectives

After reading the material in this chapter, you should be able to:

- Describe the layers and functions of organizational culture.
- Define the general types of organizational culture, and identify their associated normative beliefs.
- Explain how organizations embed their cultures.
- Summarize the process of organizational socialization in terms of three phases.
- Describe methods for socializing employees.
- Discuss the role of mentors in organizations.

Competition among the big-box retailers is fierce. Because of their everyday low pricing policies, profit margins are slim. So, the chains look for every opportunity to gain an edge. Analysts have noted that, by some measures, Costco seems to be outperforming its biggest rival, Wal-Mart. Costco's labor costs, measured as a percentage of sales, are lower than Wal-Mart's. Also, its operating profit per hourly employee exceeds that of Sam's Club, the Wal-Mart division that directly competes with Costco. And Costco's rate of employee turnover is one of the lowest in the industry.[1] One explanation for these performance differences is that Costco has a culture that places greater value on employees and their contributions. Evidence of this focus includes Costco's higher pay, relatively generous benefits, and tolerance for risk taking.

This chapter will explain how an organization's culture can provide a competitive advantage. After defining and discussing the context of organizational culture, we examine how it works, how organizations socialize employees, and how mentors play a role in embedding organizational culture.

FIGURE 12–1   A Conceptual Framework for Understanding Organizational Culture

Source: Adapted in part from C Ostroff, A Kinicki, and M Tamkins, "Organizational Culture and Climate," in *Handbook of Psychology*, Vol 12, eds W C Burman, D R Iigen, and R J Klimoski (New York: Wiley and Sons, 2003), pp 565–93.

ORGANIZATIONAL CULTURE: DEFINITION AND CONTEXT

Organizational culture
Shared values and beliefs that underlie a company's identity.

Organizations tend to develop their own culture. **Organizational culture** is "the set of shared, taken-for-granted implicit assumptions that a group holds and that determines how it perceives, thinks about, and reacts to its various environments."[2] Organizational culture is passed on to new employees through the process of socialization, a topic discussed later in this chapter. This culture, which operates at different levels, influences people's behavior at work.

Organizational culture has a widespread impact on organizational behavior, as illustrated by the conceptual framework in Figure 12–1.[3] Its influence occurs through its linkage with other key topics in this book. The antecedents that shape organizational culture are the founders' values, the industry and business environment, the national culture, and the senior leaders' vision and behavior. In turn, organizational culture influences the type of structure adopted by the organization and a host of practices, policies, and procedures implemented in pursuit of organizational goals. These characteristics then affect a variety of group and social processes. This sequence ultimately affects employees' attitudes and behavior and a variety of organizational outcomes. All told, Figure 12–1 reveals that organizational culture is a contextual variable influencing individual, group, and organizational behavior.

DYNAMICS OF ORGANIZATIONAL CULTURE

To show how organizational culture is formed and used by employees, this section begins by discussing the layers of organizational culture. It then reviews functions and types of organizational culture, outcomes associated with organizational culture, and the way cultures are embedded in organizations.

Layers of Organizational Culture

As shown in Figure 12–1, organizational culture operates in three fundamental layers, distinguished by their outward visibility and resistance to change. Each level influences another level.[4]

Observable Artifacts

At the most visible level, culture represents observable artifacts, that is, the physical manifestation of an organization's culture. Organizational examples include acronyms, manner of dress, awards, myths and stories told about the organization, published lists of values, observable rituals and ceremonies, special parking spaces, decorations, and so on. This level also includes visible behaviors exhibited by people and groups. Artifacts are easier to create and change than the less visible aspects of organizational culture. To move from a culture based on tradition and hierarchy to one that is less formal and flexible, JCPenney has been making changes in its artifacts. The company is encouraging people at all levels to use first names, reinforcing the wearing of business-casual clothing, giving employees access to all areas of headquarters, even the executive suite, and replacing its expensive art collection with photos of employees.[5]

Espoused Values

Values
Enduring belief in a mode of conduct or end-state.

Culture also encompasses a set of values. A formal definition of values comprises five dimensions: "**Values** (1) are concepts or beliefs, (2) pertain to desirable end-states or behaviors, (3) transcend situations, (4) guide selection or evaluation of behavior and events, and (5) are ordered by relative importance."[6] Organizations subscribe to a constellation of values rather than to only one. They can be profiled according to their values, which can guide an assessment of whether the values are consistent and supportive of the organization's goals.[7] The culture's values may be merely espoused or also enacted.

Espoused values
The stated values and norms that are preferred by an organization.

Espoused values represent the explicitly stated values and norms that are preferred by an organization. They are generally established by the founder of a new or small company and by the top management team in a larger organization. For example, J. M. Smucker is a 107-year-old family-run business that is headed by co-CEOs Tim and Richard Smucker. The brothers encourage all Smucker employees to adhere to a set of values created by their father, Paul Smucker. For example, one value says, "Listen with your full attention, look for the good in others, have a sense of humor, and say thank you for a job well done."[8] Because espoused values constitute aspirations that are explicitly communicated to employees, managers such as Tim and Richard Smucker hope that espoused values will directly influence employee behavior. Unfortunately, aspirations do not automatically produce the desired behaviors because people do not always "walk the talk."

Enacted values
The values and norms that are exhibited by employees.

Enacted values represent the values and norms that actually are exhibited or converted into employee behavior. Employees ascribe these values to the organization based on their observations of what actually occurs. Thus, they may or may not match the espoused values. At one large corporation, signs in the hallways announced that one of the company's key values was trust, but as employees entered and exited the building each day, their belongings were searched. In contrast, at a company that included work/life balance among its espoused values, managers were given a plan designed to help them work with employees to achieve that balance. Unfortunately, the meeting to discuss that plan was scheduled for a weekend.[9]

Any gaps between an organization's espoused and enacted values should be reduced because they can significantly influence employee attitudes and organizational performance. In a study of 312 British rail drivers, employees said they were more cynical about safety when they believed that senior managers' behaviors were inconsistent with the stated values regarding safety.[10] Managers can use surveys to assess the match between espoused and enacted values. In Indianapolis, Guidant Corp. used a survey titled "Vital Signs" to assess employees' opinions about the organizational culture, work activities, and total compensation. Management used the results of the survey to improve the work environment and to align Guidant's espoused and enacted values.[11]

Basic Assumptions

At the core of organizational culture are basic underlying assumptions, which are unobservable. They constitute organizational values that have become so taken for granted over time that they become assumptions that guide organizational behavior. They thus are highly resistant to change. When basic assumptions are widely held among employees, people will find behavior based on an inconsistent value inconceivable. Google, for example, is noted for innovation. Employees at Google would be shocked to see management act in ways that did not value creativity and new ideas.[12]

Functions of Organizational Culture

An organization's culture fulfills four functions.[13] To help bring these four functions to life, let us consider how each of them has taken shape at Southwest Airlines, which has grown to be the fourth-largest U.S. airline since its inception in 1971 and has achieved 33 consecutive years of profitability. Southwest also was ranked as the third most admired company in the United States by *Fortune* in 2006, partly due to its strong and distinctive culture.[14]

1. *Give members an organizational identity.* Southwest Airlines is known as a fun place to work that values employee satisfaction and customer loyalty over corporate profits. Herb Kelleher, board chairman and former CEO, commented on this issue: "The employees come first. If they're happy, satisfied, dedicated, and energetic, they'll take real good care of the customers. When the customers are happy, they come back. And that makes the shareholders happy."[15] Southwest's people-focused identity is reinforced by the fact that it is an employer of choice. In one recent year, the company received 260,109 résumés from which to select 2,766 new employees. The company also was noted as an employer of choice among college students by *Fortune.*

2. *Facilitate collective commitment.* The mission of Southwest Airlines is "dedication to the highest quality of Customer Service delivered with a sense of warmth, friendliness, individual pride, and Company Spirit."[16] Southwest's more than 31,000 employees are committed to this mission. The Department of Transportation's *Air Travel Consumer Report* reported Southwest was ranked as having the fewest customer complaints for nearly two decades.

3. *Promote social system stability.* Social system stability reflects the extent to which the work environment is perceived as positive and reinforcing, and the extent to which conflict and change are effectively managed. Southwest is noted for its philosophy of having fun, having parties, and celebrating. For example, each city in which the firm operates is given a budget for parties. Southwest also uses a variety of performance-based awards and

service awards to reinforce employees. Evidence of the company's positive and enriching environment is the lowest turnover rate in the airline industry.

4. *Shape behavior by helping members make sense of their surroundings.* This function of culture helps employees understand why the organization does what it does and how it intends to accomplish its long-term goals. Keeping in mind that Southwest's leadership originally viewed ground transportation as the main competitor in 1971, employees come to understand why the airline's primary vision is to be the best primarily short-haul, low-fare, high-frequency, point-to-point carrier in the United States. Employees understand they must achieve exceptional performance, such as turning a plane in 20 minutes, because they must keep costs down in order to compete against Greyhound and the use of automobiles. In turn, the company reinforces the importance of outstanding customer service and high performance expectations by using performance-based awards and profit sharing. Employees own at least 10% of the company stock.

Types of Organizational Culture

Researchers have tried to identify and measure various types of organizational culture in order to study the relationship between types of culture and organizational effectiveness. This pursuit was motivated by the possibility that certain cultures were more effective than others. Unfortunately, research has not uncovered a universal typology of cultural styles that everyone accepts.[17] One effort at classification resulted in the types of organizational culture defined in Table 12–1. Although this example is not a definitive conclusion about the types of organizational culture that exist, awareness of these types contributes to an understanding of the manifestations of culture.

The types of organizational culture in Table 12–1 fall into three categories: constructive, passive–defensive, and aggressive–defensive.[18] Each type is associated with a different set of **normative beliefs,** which are principles about how members of a particular group or organization are expected to approach their work and interact with others. A *constructive culture* is one in which employees are encouraged to interact with others and to work on tasks and projects in ways that will help them satisfy their need to grow and develop. This type of culture endorses normative beliefs associated with achievement, self-actualizing, humanistic-encouraging, and affiliative behavior. In contrast, a *passive–defensive culture* is characterized by an overriding belief that employees must interact with others in ways that do not threaten their own job security. This culture reinforces the normative beliefs associated with approval, conventional, dependent, and avoidance behavior. *BusinessWeek* reporters have described Mitsubishi in a way that suggests the company has a passive–defensive culture: "Managers were so reluctant to relay bad news to higher-ups that they squelched complaints about quality defects for decades to avoid costly product recalls."[19] Finally, companies with an *aggressive–defensive culture* encourage employees to approach tasks in forceful ways to protect their status and job security. This type of culture is more characteristic of normative beliefs favoring oppositional, power, competitive, and perfectionistic behavior. A change to a more aggressive–defensive culture helped save a young high-tech company, SciQuest, which started out selling scientific equipment online—an arrangement that generated sales but not profits. SciQuest hired Stephen J Wiehe as chief executive, and he determined to do whatever was necessary to keep the failing business

Normative beliefs

Thoughts and beliefs about expected behavior and modes of conduct.

TABLE 12–1 Types of Organizational Culture

Source: Adapted from R A Cooke and J L Szumal, "Measuring Normative Beliefs and Shared Behavioral Expectations in Organizations: The Reliability and Validity of the Organizational Culture Inventory," *Psychological Reports,* 1993, Vol. 72, pp 1299–1330.

General Types of Culture	Normative Beliefs	Organizational Characteristics
Constructive	Achievement	Organizations that do things well and value members who set and accomplish their own goals. Members are expected to set challenging but realistic goals, establish plans to reach these goals, and pursue them with enthusiasm. (Pursuing a standard of excellence)
Constructive	Self-actualizing	Organizations that value creativity, quality over quantity, and both task accomplishment and individual growth. Members are encouraged to gain enjoyment from their work, develop themselves, and take on new and interesting activities. (Thinking in unique and independent ways)
Constructive	Humanistic-encouraging	Organizations that are managed in a participative and person-centered way. Members are expected to be supportive, constructive, and open to influence in their dealings with one another. (Helping others to grow and develop)
Constructive	Affiliative	Organizations that place a high priority on constructive interpersonal relationships. Members are expected to be friendly, open, and sensitive to the satisfaction of their work group. (Dealing with others in a friendly way)
Passive–defensive	Approval	Organizations in which conflicts are avoided and interpersonal relationships are pleasant—at least superficially. Members feel that they should agree with, gain the approval of, and be liked by others. ("Going along" with others)
Passive–defensive	Conventional	Organizations that are conservative, traditional, and bureaucratically controlled. Members are expected to conform, follow the rules, and make a good impression. (Always following policies and practices)
Passive–defensive	Dependent	Organizations that are hierarchically controlled and nonparticipative. Centralized decision making in such organizations leads members to do only what they are told and to clear all decisions with superiors. (Pleasing those in positions of authority)
Passive–defensive	Avoidance	Organizations that fail to reward success but nevertheless punish mistakes. This negative reward system leads members to shift responsibilities to others and avoid any possibility of being blamed for a mistake. (Waiting for others to act first)
Aggressive–defensive	Oppositional	Organizations in which confrontation and negativism are rewarded. Members gain status and influence by being critical and thus are reinforced to oppose the ideas of others. (Pointing out flaws)
Aggressive–defensive	Power	Nonparticipative organizations structured on the basis of the authority inherent in members' positions. Members believe they will be rewarded for taking charge, controlling subordinates and, at the same time, being responsive to the demands of superiors. (Building up one's power base)
Aggressive–defensive	Competitive	Winning is valued, and members are rewarded for outperforming one another. Members operate in a "win–lose" framework and believe they must work against (rather than with) their peers to be noticed. (Turning the job into a contest)
Aggressive–defensive	Perfectionistic	Organizations in which perfectionism, persistence, and hard work are valued. Members feel they must avoid any mistake, keep track of everything, and work long hours to attain narrowly defined objectives. (Doing things perfectly)

SELF-ASSESSMENT
Corporate Culture Preference Scale

Go online at [www.mhhe.com/obcore] to discover the kind of corporate culture you prefer.

- Which type of culture did the quiz results indicate you prefer?
- Have you ever held a job in an organization with that type of culture? If so, did you enjoy working there? Were you successful in your work?
- When you are job hunting, how might you identify employers with the type of culture you prefer?

afloat. He insisted that everything be justified, from the business plan to the need for each job. SciQuest cut its work force by half and shifted to selling software that enabled educational institutions to shop more efficiently for scientific equipment on their own. By holding everyone accountable for results, Wiehe led SciQuest to profitability.[20] Such a culture might feel exciting and challenging to one individual but risky and oppressive to another. Managers and employees can benefit from being able to identify the types of culture in which they are likely to flourish.

Although an organization may predominantly represent one cultural type, it can manifest normative beliefs and characteristics from the others. Research demonstrates that organizations can have functional subcultures, hierarchical subcultures based on a person's level in the organization, geographical subcultures, occupational subcultures based on an individual's title or position, social subcultures derived from social activities such as a bowling or golf league and a reading club, and counter-cultures.[21] Managers need to be aware of the possibility that conflict between subgroups representing subcultures can undermine an organization's overall performance.

Outcomes Associated with Organizational Culture

Managers and academic researchers believe that organizational culture can be a driver of employee attitudes and organizational effectiveness and performance. Various measures of organizational culture have been correlated with a variety of individual and organizational outcomes. Several studies demonstrated that organizational culture was significantly correlated with employee behavior and attitudes. For example, a constructive culture was negatively associated with work avoidance and was positively related to job satisfaction, innovation, and intentions to stay at the company. In contrast, passive–defensive and aggressive–defensive cultures were negatively correlated with job satisfaction and intentions to stay at the company.[22] These results suggest that employees seem to prefer organizations that encourage people to interact and work with others in ways that help them satisfy their needs to grow and develop. Also, several studies found that congruence between an individual's values and the organization's values was significantly associated with organizational commitment, job satisfaction, intention to quit, and turnover.[23]

However, a summary of 10 quantitative studies showed that organizational culture did not predict an organization's financial performance.[24] This finding means that no single type of organizational culture fuels financial performance. But in an apparent contradiction, a study of 207 companies from 22 industries for an 11-year period demonstrated that financial performance was higher among companies that had adaptive and flexible cultures.[25]

Studies of mergers have indicated that mergers frequently failed because of incompatible cultures. Considering that the number of corporate mergers around the world has been rising and the evidence that 7 out of 10 mergers and acquisitions failed to meet their financial promise, managers within merged companies would be well advised to consider the role of organizational culture in creating a new organization.[26]

These research results underscore the significance of organizational culture, as well as the need to learn more about the process of cultivating and changing an organization's culture. An organization's culture is not determined by fate. It is formed and shaped by the combination and integration of everyone who works in the organization.[27]

How Cultures Are Embedded in Organizations

An organization's initial culture is an outgrowth of the founder's philosophy. For example, an achievement culture is likely to develop if the founder is an achievement-oriented individual driven by success. Over time, the original culture is either embedded as is or modified to fit the current environmental situation. Edgar Schein, an OB scholar, notes that embedding a culture involves a teaching process in which organizational members instruct each other about the organization's preferred values, beliefs, expectations, and behaviors. This process is accomplished through various mechanisms:[28]

1. *Formal statements of organizational philosophy, mission, vision, values, and materials used for recruiting, selection, and socialization.* Sam Walton, the founder of Wal-Mart, established three basic beliefs or values that represent the core of the organization's culture: (1) respect for the individual, (2) service to our customer, and (3) striving for excellence.[29]

2. *The design of physical space, work environments, and buildings.*

3. *Slogans, language, acronyms, and sayings.* At the Ritz-Carlton hotel chain, the slogan "How may we be of assistance?" reinforces the idea that employees do not focus merely on providing a standardized service but on anticipating and fulfilling the needs of each guest. That guest-oriented emphasis has helped Ritz-Carlton maintain its reputation for exceptional quality.

4. *Deliberate role modeling, training programs, teaching, and coaching by managers and supervisors.* Boeing's CEO, Jim McNerney, leads by his example of "paying attention to the small things like remembering people's names, listening closely to their presentations, and not embarrassing underlings in public."[30]

5. *Explicit rewards, status symbols (such as titles), and promotion criteria.* Boeing has been revising its reward system in order to reform its culture. In the new system, Boeing links managers' bonuses to how well they adhere to a set of "leadership attributes," including the promotion of integrity and the avoidance of abusive behavior.[31]

6. *Stories, legends, and myths about key people and events.* Southwest Airlines does an excellent job of telling stories to reinforce the company's commitment to customer service. One example involves a mechanic in Buffalo who used a snowmobile during a blizzard to drive seven miles in 20 feet of snow to get to the airport to free up a plane for takeoff.[32] To find stories with impact, managers should daily observe and listen to others, looking for examples of people who are successful, take risks, lead others, go beyond what is required, embody the organization's values, help others succeed, and are "heroic" in that they are daring in service of the company's goals.[33]

7. *The organizational activities, processes, or outcomes that leaders pay attention to, measure, and control.* Jamie Dimon, CEO of JPMorgan Chase, has boosted the performance of that financial services company by ruthlessly monitoring data linked to sales and costs. For example, points are awarded to salespeople for selling credit cards, mortgages, and other financial products, with bonuses directly tied to the number of points earned. Division heads monitor overhead costs such as the number of human resource staff members per employee and the cost per computer transaction. Dimon's wide-ranging concern for measurement has everyone focused on cutting costs, which not only makes the company more efficient but also frees up money for JPMorgan to grow.[34]

8. *Leader reactions to critical incidents and organizational crises.* At Textron, a conglomerate that makes Bell helicopters, Cessna jets, armored security vehicles, and other products, the crisis was tumbling sales and profits during the economic downturn at the beginning of this decade. The company's CEO, Lewis B Campbell, responded by insisting that the company abandon its decentralized vision, in which each division operated independently. Campbell required the divisions to begin thinking of themselves as part of a larger whole, figuring out how they could share resources and get the best return on each dollar invested. The turnaround took several years, but Campbell remained steadfast throughout that time.[35]

Organizational socialization
Process by which employees learn an organization's values, norms, and required behaviors.

9. *The workflow and organizational structure.* Hierarchical structures are more likely to embed an orientation in control and authority than a flatter organization.

10. *Organizational systems and procedures.* Sales contests, for example, can promote achievement and competition.[36]

11. *Organizational goals and the associated criteria used for recruitment, selection, development, promotion, layoffs, and retirement of people.* PepsiCo reinforces a high-performance culture by setting challenging goals.

THE ORGANIZATIONAL SOCIALIZATION PROCESS

A key mechanism used by organizations to embed their organizational cultures is **organizational socialization,** which is "the process by which a person learns the values, norms, and required behaviors which permit him to participate as a member of the organization."[37]

In short, organizational socialization turns outsiders into fully functioning insiders by promoting and reinforcing the organization's core values and beliefs.

Phases of Organizational Socialization

An employee's first year in a complex organization can be confusing. The workplace seems to be a constant swirl of new faces, strange jargon, conflicting expectations, and apparently unrelated events. Some organizations treat new members in a haphazard, sink-or-swim manner. More typically, though, socialization takes place in a sequence of identifiable steps.[38]

Organizational behavior researcher Daniel Feldman has proposed a three-phase model of organizational socialization that promotes deeper understanding of this important process. As illustrated in Figure 12–2, the three phases are anticipatory socialization, encounter, and

FIGURE 12–2   **A Model of Organizational Socialization**

Source: Adapted from material in D C Feldman, "The Multiple Socialization of Organization Members," *Academy of Management Review*, April 1981, pp 309–18.

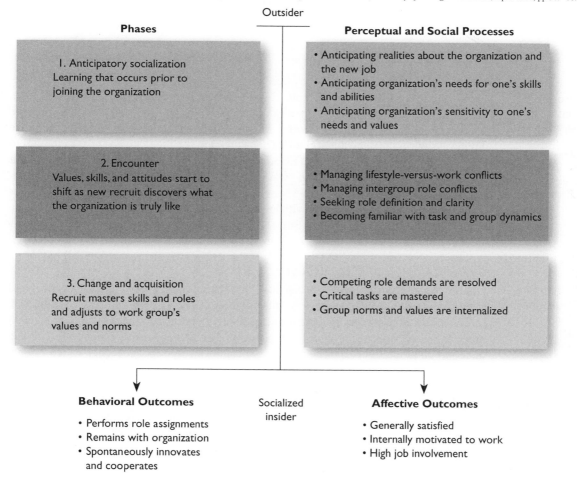

change and acquisition. At each phase, certain perceptual and social processes occur. Feldman's model also specifies behavioral and affective outcomes that indicate how well an individual has been socialized. The entire three-phase sequence may take from a few weeks to a year to complete, depending on individual differences and the complexity of the situation.

Phase 1: Anticipatory Socialization

Anticipatory socialization

Occurs before an individual joins an organization, and involves the information people learn about different careers, occupations, professions, and organizations.

Even before an individual actually joins an organization, **anticipatory socialization** occurs. It involves learning about different careers, occupations, professions, and organizations. For example, anticipatory socialization partially explains the different perceptions you might have about working for the U.S. government versus a high-technology company like Google or Microsoft.

The information for anticipatory socialization comes from many sources, including the organization's current employees. Sedona Center, which includes a resort, two shopping plazas, and three restaurants in Sedona, Arizona, has employees who are eager to tell others about the company's employee-focused organizational culture. As a result, job openings are filled with loyal employees who fit well with Sedona Center's culture.[39] All of the information received by a potential employee—whether formal or informal, accurate or inaccurate—helps the individual anticipate organizational realities. Unrealistic expectations about the nature of the work, pay, and promotions are often formulated during phase 1.

Phase 2: Encounter

Encounter phase

Employees learn what the organization is really like and reconcile unmet expectations.

When the employment contract has been signed, the employee enters the second phase. During this **encounter phase,** employees come to learn what the organization is really like. It is a time for reconciling unmet expectations and making sense of a new work environment.

Many companies use a combination of orientation and training programs to socialize employees during the encounter phase. One technique is called *onboarding,* a program to help employees integrate, assimilate, and transition to new jobs by making them familiar with corporate policies, procedures, and culture and by clarifying expectations for work roles and responsibilities.[40] Bristol-Myers Squibb has an onboarding program that focuses on executives, including meetings with important colleagues and follow-up over the course of a year to resolve any problems. Since using the onboarding program, the pharmaceutical company has seen an improvement in the retention rate for managers.[41]

Phase 3: Change and Acquisition

Change and acquisition

Requires employees to master tasks and roles and to adjust to work group values and norms.

Finally, in the **change and acquisition** phase, employees master important tasks and roles and adjust to their work group's values and norms. Table 12–2 describes socialization processes or tactics used by organizations to help employees through this adjustment process. Trilogy uses a variety of these tactics in its renowned socialization program. The three-month program takes place at the organization's corporate university, called Trilogy University (TU). In the first month, groups of 20 employees tackle assignments designed to mimic actual work assignments, presented in order of increasing difficulty. During the second month, teams of three to five employees create a product idea, develop a business model, make the product, and craft a marketing plan. Finally, employees who are not continuing to develop product ideas are assigned to "graduation projects," typically assignments to work within a business unit of Trilogy. The new employees leave TU individually when an established employee agrees to sponsor them. This change and acquisition phase

TABLE 12–2 Socialization Tactics

Source: Descriptions taken from B E Ashforth, *Role Transitions in Organizational Life: An Identity-Based Perspective* (Mahwah, NJ: Lawrence Erlbaum Associates, 2001), pp 149–83.

Tactic	Description
Collective vs. individual	Collective socialization consists of grouping newcomers and exposing them to a common set of experiences rather than treating each newcomer individually and exposing him or her to more or less unique experiences.
Formal vs. informal	Formal socialization is the practice of segregating a newcomer from regular organization members during a defined socialization period versus not clearly distinguishing a newcomer from more experienced members. Army recruits must attend boot camp before they are allowed to work alongside established soldiers.
Sequential vs. random	Sequential socialization refers to a fixed progression of steps that culminate in the new role, compared with an ambiguous or dynamic progression. The socialization of doctors involves a lock-step sequence from medical school, to internship, to residency before they are allowed to practice on their own.
Fixed vs. variable	Fixed socialization provides a timetable for the assumption of the role, whereas a variable process does not. American university students typically spend one year apiece as freshmen, sophomores, juniors, and seniors.
Serial vs. disjunctive	A serial process is one in which the newcomer is socialized by an experienced member, whereas a disjunctive process does not use a role model.
Investiture vs. divestiture	Investiture refers to the affirmation of a newcomer's incoming global and specific role identities and attributes. Divestiture is the denial and stripping away of the newcomer's existing sense of self and the reconstruction of self in the organization's image. During police training, cadets are required to wear uniforms and maintain an immaculate appearance, are addressed as "officer," and are told they are no longer ordinary citizens but are representatives of the police force.

is stressful, exhilarating, and critical for finding a place within Trilogy.[42] Returning to Table 12–2, can you identify the socialization tactics Trilogy uses?

Practical Application of Socialization Research

Research results suggest four practical guidelines for managing organizational socialization: First, managers should avoid a haphazard approach to organizational socialization because formalized socialization tactics positively affect new hires. Formalized orientation programs are more effective.[43]

Managers play a key role during the encounter phase. Studies of newly hired accountants demonstrated that the frequency and type of information obtained during their first six months of employment significantly affected their job performance, their role clarity, and the extent to which they were socially integrated.[44] Managers need to help new hires integrate within the organizational culture. Consider the approach used by John Chambers, CEO of Cisco Systems, who meets with new hires to welcome them. Those meetings are a good introduction to Cisco's culture and Chambers's leadership style; he also holds monthly meetings at which employees are encouraged to ask him any question, however difficult.[45]

The organization can benefit by training new employees to use proactive socialization behaviors. A study of 154 entry-level professionals showed that effectively using proactive socialization behaviors influenced the newcomers' general anxiety and stress during the first month of employment and their motivation and anxiety six months later.[46]

Finally, managers should pay attention to the socialization of diverse employees. Research demonstrated that diverse employees, particularly those with disabilities, experienced different socialization activities than other newcomers. In turn, these different experiences affected their long-term success and job satisfaction.[47]

EMBEDDING ORGANIZATIONAL CULTURE THROUGH MENTORING

Mentoring
Process of forming and maintaining developmental relationships between a mentor and a junior person.

The modern word *mentor* derives from Mentor, the name of a wise and trusted counselor in Greek mythology. Terms typically used in connection with mentoring are *teacher, coach, sponsor,* and *peer*. **Mentoring** is the process of forming and maintaining intensive and lasting developmental relationships between a variety of developers (people who provide career and psychosocial support) and a junior person (the protégé, if male, or protégée, if female).[48] Mentoring can serve to embed an organization's culture when developers and the protégé/protégée work in the same organization. One reason is that mentoring contributes to creating a sense of oneness by promoting the acceptance of the organization's core values throughout the organization. In addition, the socialization aspect of mentoring also promotes a sense of membership.

Not only is mentoring important as a tactic for embedding organizational culture, but research suggests it can also significantly influence the protégé/protégée's future career. For example, mentored employees performed better on the job and experienced more rapid career advancement than employees without mentors. Mentored employees also reported having higher job and career satisfaction, had lower turnover, and worked on more challenging job assignments.[49]

Functions of Mentoring

Kathy Kram, a Boston University researcher, conducted in-depth interviews with both members of 18 pairs of senior and junior managers. As a by-product of this study, Kram identified two general functions—career and psychosocial—of the mentoring process. Five *career functions* that enhanced career development were sponsorship, exposure and visibility, coaching, protection, and challenging assignments. Four *psychosocial functions* were role modeling, acceptance and confirmation, counseling, and friendship. The psychosocial functions clarified the participants' identities and enhanced their feelings of competence.[50]

Developmental Networks That Underlie Mentoring

Historically, it was thought that mentoring was primarily provided by one person, the mentor. Today, however, the changing nature of technology, organizational structures, and marketplace dynamics requires that people seek career information and support from many sources. Mentoring is currently viewed as a process in which protégés and protégées seek developmental guidance from a network of people, known as developers. Lori McKee, a project manager with Chubb Group of Insurance Cos., used a network of people to advance her career. She started a book club at the company, and 19 Chubb Group women across the country meet via teleconference once a month to discuss career issues associated with books they have read. McKee says the increased visibility in the company helped her obtain "bigger assignments, including one to help upgrade the company's financial systems worldwide."[51]

This example implies that obtaining the type of career assistance needed to manage a career is related to the diversity and strength of a person's network of relationships.

MASTER YOUR KNOWLEDGE
Mentoring

Increase your knowledge of mentoring basics by completing the online quiz at
[www.mhhe.com/obcore].

- In light of the description of mentors in the text and the online exercise, can
  you think of people who have acted as mentors for you? Have you ever mentored someone?
- How has mentoring helped your career so far, and what role would you like it to
  play in the future?

Diversity of developmental relationships
The variety of people in a network used for developmental assistance.

A developmental network will have a different pattern of relationships depending on whether those relationships are diverse and strong. The typology in Figure 12–3 shows the possible developmental networks according to their diversity and strength.[52] The **diversity of developmental relationships** reflects the variety of people within the network an individual uses for developmental assistance. Network diversity has two components: (1) the number of different people the person is networked with and (2) the various social systems from which the networked relationships stem (e.g., employer, school, family, community, professional associations, and religious affiliations). As shown in Figure 12–3, developmental

FIGURE 12–3
Developmental Networks Associated with Mentoring

Source: From *Academy of Management Review* by M Higgins and K Kram, "Reconceptualizing Mentoring at Work: A Developmental Network Perspective," April 2001, p 270. Copyright 2001 by Academy of Management. Reproduced with permission of Academy of Management via Copyright Clearance Center.

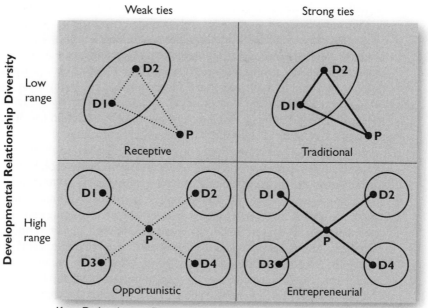

Developmental relationship strength
The quality of relationships among people in a network.

relationship diversity ranges from low (few people or social systems) to high (multiple people or social systems). **Developmental relationship strength** reflects the quality of relationships between the individual and each person involved in his or her developmental network. Strong ties reflect relationships based on frequent interactions, reciprocity, and positive affect. Weak ties indicate superficial relationships.

The four types of developmental networks that result from the diversity and strength of developmental relationships are receptive, traditional, entrepreneurial, and opportunistic. A *receptive* developmental network consists of a few weak ties from one social system such as an employer or a professional association. The single oval around D1 and D2 in Figure 12–3 represent two developers who come from one social system. In contrast, a *traditional* network contains a few strong ties between an employee and developers who come from one social system. An entrepreneurial network, which is the strongest type of developmental network, is made up of strong ties among several developers (D1–D4) who each come from a different social system. Finally, an opportunistic network involves weak ties with multiple developers from different social systems.

Personal and Organizational Implications

These principles of mentoring suggest two key personal implications. First, job and career satisfaction are likely to be influenced by the consistency between an individual's career goals and the type of developmental network at his or her disposal. For example, people with an entrepreneurial developmental network are more likely to experience change in their careers and to benefit from personal learning than people with receptive, traditional, and opportunistic networks. If change and learning sound attractive to you, you should try to increase the diversity and strength of your developmental relationships. Employees who desire to experience career advancement in multiple organizations experience lower levels of job satisfaction if they have receptive developmental networks. Receptive developmental networks, however, can be satisfying to someone who does not desire to be promoted up the career ladder.[53]

A second personal implication is that a developer's willingness to provide career and psychosocial assistance is a function of the protégé/protégée's ability and potential and the quality of the interpersonal relationship.[54] So, if you want to experience career advancement throughout your life, you must take ownership for enhancing your skills, abilities, and developmental networks.[55] Ways to do this include developing attractive qualities such as trust and respect, sharing information and helping others around you, investing time in identifying and building relationships with mentors, cultivating diverse formal and informal relationships, and accepting change in mentoring relationships.[56] In a recent study of 4,559 leaders and 944 human resource professionals from 42 countries, 91% of those who used a mentor found the experience moderately or greatly beneficial to their career success.[57]

Research also supports the view that mentoring delivers organizational benefits. In addition to the obvious benefit of employee development, mentoring enhances the effectiveness of organizational communication by increasing the amount of vertical communication in both directions. It also provides a mechanism for modifying or reinforcing organizational culture. Blue Cross and Blue Shield of North Carolina set up an effective mentoring program pairing "high-potential" employees with trained company leaders for a year at a time. The program dramatically reduced employee turnover and increased productivity.[58]

Chapter **Thirteen**

Organizational Design: How a Structure Connects Employees and Tasks

---

Learning Objectives

After reading the material in this chapter, you should be able to:

- Define *organizations* and their basic dimensions.
- Explain commonly used metaphors for organizations as closed or open systems, military/mechanical bureaucracies, and biological and cognitive systems.
- Describe basic criteria for organizational effectiveness.
- Summarize what is involved in the contingency approach to organization design.
- Discuss new-style and old-style organizations, including virtual organizations.

Virtually every aspect of life is affected at least indirectly by some type of organization.[1] Large and small organizations such as Kroger, Target, Pulte Homes, Arizona State University, and Microsoft feed, clothe, house, educate, and employ us. Netflix attends to our needs for entertainment, the Philadelphia police and fire departments protect us, Aetna offers insurance to help us prepare for disasters and unexpected illness, the local Curves franchise helps keep us healthy, American Airlines transports us where we need to go, the *Chicago Tribune* and ABC News keep us informed of today's events, AARP provides information on legal issues, and Beth Israel Deaconess Medical Center offers health care. All of these entities are organizations. Many of them seek a profit; others do not. Together, they all are the primary context for organizational behavior.

This chapter explores the effectiveness, design, and future of today's organizations. We begin by defining the term *organization,* discussing important dimensions of organizations, and examining metaphors for describing them. Our attention then turns to criteria for assessing organizational effectiveness. Next, we discuss the contingency approach to designing organizations. We conclude with a profile of new-style organizations, with special attention to virtual organizations.

ORGANIZATIONS: DEFINITION AND DIMENSIONS

As a necessary springboard for this chapter, we need to formally define what organizations are. We also identify the dimensions of organizational structures in terms of how they are represented on organizational charts.

What Is an Organization?

Organization
System of consciously coordinated activities of two or more people.

According to Chester I Barnard's classic definition, an **organization** is "a system of consciously coordinated activities or forces of two or more persons."[2] Embodied in the *conscious coordination* aspect of this definition are four common denominators of all organizations: coordination of effort, a common goal, division of labor, and a hierarchy of authority.[3] Organization theorists refer to these factors as the organization's *structure*.

When operating in concert, the four definitional factors—coordination of effort, common goal, division of labor, and hierarchy of authority—enable an organization to exist. Coordination of effort is achieved through formulation and enforcement of policies, rules, and regulations. Division of labor occurs when the common goal is pursued by individuals performing different but related tasks. The hierarchy of authority, also called the *chain of command,* is a control mechanism dedicated to making sure the right people do the right things at the right time.

Unity of command principle
Each employee should report to a single manager.

Historically, managers have maintained the integrity of the hierarchy of authority by adhering to a principle called *unity of command*. The **unity of command principle** specifies that each employee should report to only one manager. Otherwise, the argument goes, inefficiency would prevail because of conflicting orders and lack of personal accountability. (In fact, these are problems in today's more fluid and flexible organizations based on innovations such as cross-functional and self-managed teams.) Managers in the hierarchy of authority also administer rewards and punishments.

Organization Charts: Dimensions of an Organization's Structure

Organization chart
Boxes-and-lines illustration showing chain of formal authority and division of labor.

An **organization chart** is a graphic representation of formal authority and division of labor relationships. To the casual observer, the term *organization chart* means the family tree–like pattern of boxes and lines posted on workplace walls. Within each box you usually find the names and titles of current position holders. To organization theorists, however, organization charts reveal much more. The partial organization chart in Figure 13–1 reveals four basic dimensions of organizational structure: hierarchy of authority (who reports to whom), division of labor, spans of control, and line and staff positions.

Hierarchy of Authority

In the example in Figure 13–1, we can see an unmistakable hierarchy of authority.[4] Working from bottom to top, the 10 directors report to the two executive directors, who report to the president, who reports to the chief executive officer. Ultimately, the chief executive officer answers to the hospital's board of directors. The chart in Figure 13–1 shows strict unity of command up and down the line. A formal hierarchy of authority also delineates the official communication network.

FIGURE 13–1   **Sample Organization Chart for a Hospital (executive and director levels only)**

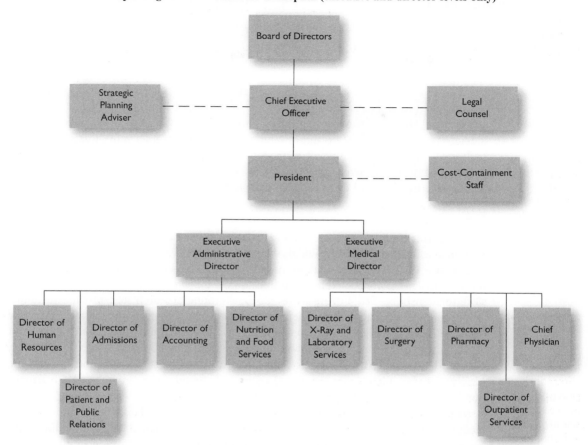

Division of Labor

In addition to showing the chain of command, the sample organization chart indicates extensive division of labor. Immediately below the hospital's president, one executive director is responsible for general administration, while another is responsible for medical affairs. Each of these two specialties is further subdivided as indicated by the next layer of positions. At each successively lower level in the organization, jobs become more specialized.

Spans of Control

Span of control
The number of people reporting directly to a given manager.

The **span of control** refers to the number of people reporting directly to a given manager.[5] Spans of control can range from narrow to wide. For example, the president in Figure 13–1 has a narrow span of control of two. (Staff assistants usually are not included in a manager's span of control.) The executive administrative director has a wider span of control of five. Spans of control exceeding 30 can be found in assembly-line operations where machine-paced and repetitive work substitutes for close supervision. Historically, spans of five to six were considered best. Despite years of debate, organization theorists have not arrived at a consensus regarding the ideal span of control.

Generally, the narrower the span of control, the closer the supervision and the higher the administrative costs as a result of a higher manager-to-worker ratio. Recent emphasis on leanness and administrative efficiency dictates spans of control as wide as possible but guarding against inadequate supervision and lack of coordination. Wider spans also complement the trend toward greater worker autonomy and empowerment.[6]

Line and Staff Positions

The organization chart in Figure 13–1 also distinguishes between line and staff positions. Line managers such as the president, the two executive directors, and the various directors occupy formal decision-making positions within the chain of command. Line positions generally are connected by solid lines on organization charts. Dotted lines indicate staff relationships. **Staff personnel** do background research and provide technical advice and recommendations to their **line managers,** who have the authority to make decisions. For example, the cost-containment specialists in the sample organization chart merely advise the president on relevant matters. Apart from supervising the work of their own staff assistants, they have no line authority over other organizational members. Modern trends such as cross-functional teams and reengineering are blurring the distinction between line and staff.

In a study of 207 police officers in Israel, line personnel exhibited greater job commitment than did their staff counterparts.[7] This result was anticipated because the line managers' decision-making authority empowered them and gave them comparatively more control over their work situations.

Staff personnel
Provide research, advice, and recommendations to line managers.

Line managers
Have authority to make organizational decisions.

ORGANIZATIONAL METAPHORS

The complexity of modern organizations makes them somewhat difficult to describe. Consequently, organization theorists have resorted to the use of metaphors.[8] A metaphor is a figure of speech that characterizes one object in terms of another object. Good metaphors help us comprehend complicated things by describing them in everyday terms. For example, organizations are often likened to an orchestra. Organizational behavior scholar Kim Cameron sums up the value of organizational metaphors as follows: "Each time a new metaphor is used, certain aspects of organizational phenomena are uncovered that were not evident with other metaphors. In fact, the usefulness of metaphors lies in their possession of some degree of falsehood so that new images and associations emerge."[9] The orchestra metaphor, for instance, could present an exaggerated picture of harmony in large and complex organizations, but it realistically encourages us to view managers as facilitators rather than absolute dictators.

Early managers and management theorists used military units and machines as metaphors for organizations. These rigid models gave way to more dynamic and realistic metaphors.

Needed: Open-System Thinking

Closed system
A relatively self-sufficient entity.

Open system
Organism that must constantly interact with its environment to survive.

Today's organizational metaphors require *open-system* thinking. A **closed system** is said to be a self-sufficient entity, "closed" to the surrounding environment. In contrast, an **open system** depends on constant interaction with the environment for survival. The distinction between closed and open systems is a matter of degree. Because every worldly system is partly closed and partly open, the key question is, How great a role does the environment play in the functioning of the system? For instance, a battery-powered clock is a relatively closed system. Once the battery is inserted, the clock performs its time-keeping function hour after hour until the battery goes dead. The human body, in contrast, is a highly open system because it requires a constant supply of life-sustaining oxygen from the environment, along with a frequent supply of nutrients from the environment. Open systems are capable of self-correction, adaptation, and growth, thanks to characteristics such as homeostasis and feedback control.

Newer metaphors are more likely to represent open systems. The traditional military/mechanical metaphor, discussed next, is a closed system model because it largely ignores environmental influences. It gives the impression that organizations are self-sufficient entities. The more recent biological and cognitive metaphors emphasize interaction between organizations and their environments. These models, based on open-system assumptions, offer instructive insights about organizations and how they work. In fact, each of the three metaphorical perspectives offers something useful.

Organizations as Military/Mechanical Bureaucracies

A major by-product of the Industrial Revolution was the factory system of production. People left their farms and cottage industries to operate steam-powered machines in centralized factories. The social unit of production evolved from the family to formally managed organizations encompassing hundreds or even thousands of people. To maximize the economic efficiency of large factories and offices, managers structured them according to military principles. At the turn of the 20th century, a German sociologist, Max Weber, formulated what he termed the most rationally efficient form of organization.[10] He patterned his ideal organization after the vaunted Prussian army and called it **bureaucracy.**

Bureaucracy
Max Weber's idea of the most rationally efficient form of organization.

According to Weber's theory, the following four factors should make bureaucracies the epitome of efficiency:

1. *Division of labor.* People become proficient when they perform standardized tasks over and over again.
2. *A hierarchy of authority.* A formal chain of command ensures coordination and accountability.
3. *A framework of rules.* Carefully formulated and strictly enforced rules ensure predictable behavior.
4. *Administrative impersonality.* Personnel decisions such as hiring and promoting should be based on competence, not favoritism.[11]

All organizations possess these characteristics but to varying degrees. Thus, every organization is a bureaucracy to some extent. In terms of the ideal metaphor, a bureaucracy should run the way a well-oiled machine does, and its members should perform with the precision of a polished military unit. But practical and ethical problems arise when bureaucratic characteristics become extreme or dysfunctional. For example, extreme expressions of specialization, rule following, and impersonality can cause a bureaucrat to treat a client as a number rather than as a person.[12]

Weber probably would be surprised and dismayed that his model of rational efficiency has become a synonym for inefficiency.[13] Today, bureaucracy stands for being put on hold, waiting in long lines, and getting shuffled from one office to the next. This irony can be explained largely by the fact that organizations with excessive or dysfunctional bureaucratic tendencies become rigid, inflexible, and resistant to environmental demands and influences.[14]

Organizations as Biological Systems

Drawing on the field of general systems theory that emerged during the 1950s,[15] organization theorists suggested a more dynamic model for modern organizations. This metaphor likens organizations to the human body, so it has been labeled the *biological model*.[16] In his often-cited organization theory text, *Organizations in Action,* James D Thompson explained that according to the biological model, "The complex organization is a set of interdependent parts which together make up a whole because each contributes something and receives something from the whole, which in turn is interdependent with some larger environment."[17] Through some form of evolutionary process, organizations develop parts and relationships aimed at the organization's survival. In addition, the organization copes with environmental threats through a process of "homeostasis, or self-stabilization, which spontaneously, or naturally, governs the necessary relationships among parts and activities and thereby keeps the system viable."[18]

Unlike the traditional military/mechanical theorists, who downplayed the environment, advocates of the biological model stress organization–environment interaction. As Figure 13–2 illustrates, the organization transforms inputs from the environment into various outputs to the environment. Thus, the outer boundary of the organization is permeable. People, information, capital, and goods and services move back and forth across this boundary. Moreover, each of the five organizational subsystems—goals and values, technical, psychosocial, structural, and managerial—depends on the others. The organization uses feedback about sales, customer satisfaction or dissatisfaction, and other matters to self-adjust and survive despite uncertainty and change.[19] In effect, the organization is alive.

Organizations as Cognitive Systems

A more recent metaphor characterizes organizations in terms of mental functions. According to respected organization theorists Richard Daft and Karl Weick, "Organizations are more than transformation processes or control systems." Instead, they "have mechanisms to interpret ambiguous events and to provide meaning and direction for participants. Organizations are meaning systems, and this distinguishes them from lower-level systems."[20] As meaning systems, organizations have decision makers who interpret problems and opportunities in the environment, so they can develop a response. This interpretation process, as it migrates throughout the organization, leads to organizational *learning* and adaptation.[21]

FIGURE 13–2   **The Organization as an Open System: The Biological Model**

Source: This model is a combination of Figures 5–2 and 5–3 in F E Kast and J E Rosenzweig, *Organization and Management: A Systems and Contingency Approach,* 4th ed (New York: McGraw-Hill, 1986), pp 112, 114. Copyright © 1986 by the McGraw-Hill Companies. Reprinted with permission.

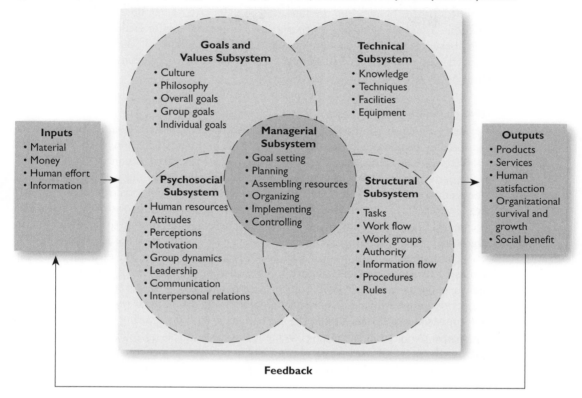

In fact, the concept of the *learning organization,*[22] discussed in the next chapter, is popular in management circles these days. Great Harvest Bread Co., based in Dillon, Montana, is an inspiring case in point. Unlike a traditional franchise operation, where the franchisor dictates operational details for every franchisee so that all customers will have essentially the same experience, Great Harvest gives franchise owners a one-year apprenticeship and then lets them make the day-to-day decisions, including the bread recipes to use. However, every franchise owner is encouraged to be part of Great Harvest's "learning community," which shares experiences, results, and ideas, promising not to keep secrets from one another.[23] As in this example, operating an organization as a cognitive system (or learning organization) requires a cooperative culture, mutual trust, and extensive communication.

STRIVING FOR ORGANIZATIONAL EFFECTIVENESS

An important reason why managers, stockholders, government agencies, and OB specialists are interested in the structure of organizations is to be able to make organizations more effective in meeting their goals. This section introduces a widely applicable and useful model of organizational effectiveness.

Generic Effectiveness Criteria

Four types of criteria are useful for assessing an organization's effectiveness. These effectiveness criteria apply whether organizations are large or small, operating for profit or not for profit. In addition, the four effectiveness criteria can be used in various combinations. However, none of the criteria alone is appropriate for evaluating the effectiveness of every type of organization in every situation.[24] As a result, different combinations of criteria might be needed to evaluate Coca-Cola, France Télécom, and the Food and Drug Administration.

Goal Accomplishment

The most widely used effectiveness criterion for organizations is goal accomplishment, measured by comparing key organizational results or outputs with previously stated goals or objectives. Deviations, either plus or minus, require corrective action to adjust the goals or the performance. This is simply an organizational variation of the personal goal-setting process discussed in Chapter 5.[25] Effectiveness, relative to the criterion of goal accomplishment, is gauged by how well the organization meets its goals. A well-known example of a goal-oriented company is General Electric, where managers are responsible for meeting specific targets such as challenging goals for growth. Managers who fall short are asked to leave.[26]

A common organization-level goal is productivity improvement, involving the relationship between inputs and outputs.[27] Goals also may be set for organizational efforts such as minority recruiting, pollution prevention, and quality improvement. Given today's competitive pressures and e-commerce revolution, *innovation* and *speed* are very important organizational goals worthy of measurement and monitoring.[28] During the past few years, many companies have dramatically slashed the time they need to develop and launch a new product. Motorola and Nokia now can launch a new cell phone in 6 to 9 months, down from 12 to 18 months; Nissan Motor Co. cut the time to launch a new car from 21 months to just $10^1/_2$ months.[29] Their competitors have to move faster simply to keep up with the pace.

Resource Acquisition

A second criterion, resource acquisition, relates to inputs rather than outputs. An organization is deemed effective in this regard if it acquires necessary factors of production such as raw materials, labor, capital, and managerial and technical expertise. Charitable organizations such as the Salvation Army also judge their effectiveness in terms of how much money they raise from private and corporate donations.

Internal Processes

Some refer to internal processes, the third effectiveness criterion, as the "healthy systems" approach. An organization is said to be a healthy system if information flows smoothly and if employee loyalty, commitment, job satisfaction, and trust prevail.[30] Goals may be set for any of these internal processes. Healthy systems, from a behavioral standpoint, tend to have a minimum of dysfunctional conflict and destructive political maneuvering. M Scott Peck, the physician who wrote *The Road Less Traveled,* characterizes healthy organizations in ethical terms as having "a genuine sense of community," where people listen, share feelings and ideas frankly, empathize with one another, and persevere in difficult times.[31] Healthy internal processes are associated with other markers of effectiveness, such as innovation.[32]

Strategic Constituencies Satisfaction

Strategic constituency
Any group of people with a stake in the organization's operation or success.

Organizations depend on people and affect the lives of people. Consequently, many consider the satisfaction of key interested parties to be an important criterion of organizational effectiveness. These key parties have been called **strategic constituencies,** defined as "any group of individuals who have some stake in the organization—for example, resource providers, users of the organization's products or services, producers of the organization's output, groups whose cooperation is essential for the organization's survival, or those whose lives are significantly affected by the organization."[33]

Strategic constituencies (or *stakeholders*) generally have competing or conflicting interests.[34] Consequently, executives have to do some strategic juggling to achieve workable balances. In a *BusinessWeek* interview following Microsoft's defense of a major antitrust lawsuit, the company's CEO, Steve Ballmer, offered this perspective: "The expectation bar, be it from government, be it from customers, be it from industry partners, is different, and the bar is higher. How do you hit the balance between being forceful and aggressive and still [having the] right level of cooperation [with our industry and] with government? We have worked hard on that theme of responsible leadership."[35]

Mixing Effectiveness Criteria: Practical Guidelines

Experts on the subject recommend a multidimensional approach to assessing the effectiveness of modern organizations. No single criterion is appropriate for all stages of the organization's life cycle, nor will a single criterion satisfy competing stakeholders. Well-managed organizations mix and match effectiveness criteria to fit the unique requirements of the situation.[36] Managers need to identify and seek input from strategic constituencies. This information, when merged with the organization's stated mission and philosophy, enables management to derive an appropriate combination of effectiveness criteria. The following guidelines are helpful in this regard:

- The *goal accomplishment approach* is appropriate when "goals are clear, consensual, time-bounded, measurable."[37]
- The *resource acquisition approach* is appropriate when inputs have a traceable effect on results or output. For example, the amount of money the American Red Cross receives through donations dictates the level of services it can provide.
- The *internal processes approach* is appropriate when organizational performance is strongly influenced by specific processes, such as the use of cross-functional teamwork.
- The *strategic constituencies approach* is appropriate when powerful stakeholders can significantly benefit or harm the organization.[38]

Federal Express's formula for long-term organizational effectiveness includes rewarding people for initiating positive changes, developing a clear strategy linked to rewards (and communicating that strategy to all employees), and insisting that managers treat each employee with dignity by listening to employees and ensuring they understand what is expected of them.[39]

THE CONTINGENCY APPROACH TO DESIGNING ORGANIZATIONS

Contingency approach to organization design
Creating an effective organization—environment fit.

According to the **contingency approach to organization design,** organizations tend to be more effective when they are structured to fit the demands of the situation.[40] Alternatives include mechanistic, organic, lean, and virtual organizations.

Mechanistic versus Organic Organizations

Mechanistic organizations
Rigid, command-and-control bureaucracies.

In their landmark contingency design study, British behavioral scientists Tom Burns and G M Stalker drew an instructive distinction between what they called mechanistic and organic organizations. **Mechanistic organizations** are rigid bureaucracies with strict rules, narrowly defined tasks, and top-down communication. An example is Home Depot under CEO Robert Nardelli, who has created a military-style structure and a culture that values discipline.[41] Ironically, this seemingly out-of-date approach also has found a home at the cutting edge of technology. In the highly competitive business of Web hosting—running clients' Web sites in high-security facilities humming with Internet servers—speed and reliability are everything. Enter military-style managers who require strict discipline, faithful adherence to thick rule books, and flawless execution. But as *BusinessWeek* observed, "The regimented atmosphere and military themes . . . may be tough to stomach for skilled workers used to a more free-spirited atmosphere."[42]

Organic organizations
Fluid and flexible network of multitalented people.

At the opposite extreme, **organic organizations** are flexible networks of multitalented individuals who perform a variety of tasks.[43] W L Gore & Associates, the Newark, Delaware, maker of waterproof Gore-Tex fabric, is a highly organic organization because it lacks job descriptions and a formalized hierarchy and deemphasizes titles and status.[44]

Importantly, each of the mechanistic-organic characteristics is a matter of degree. Organizations tend to be *relatively* mechanistic or *relatively* organic. Pure types are rare because divisions, departments, or units in the same organization may be more or less mechanistic or organic.

Approaches to Decision Making

Centralized decision making
Top managers make all key decisions.

Decentralized decision making
Lower-level managers are empowered to make important decisions.

Decision making tends to be centralized in mechanistic organizations and decentralized in organic organizations. **Centralized decision making** occurs when key decisions are made by top management. **Decentralized decision making** occurs when important decisions are made by middle- and lower-level managers. Generally, centralized organizations are more tightly controlled, while decentralized organizations are more adaptive to changing situations.[45] Each has its appropriate use. For example, home builders Lennar Corp and D R Horton are both successful but have sharply contrasting structures. Lennar's structure is more centralized, with a central division in charge of acquiring land at a pace the company can sustain. Horton is decentralized; in each of its 77 markets, a manager is responsible for decisions about when and where to build homes.[46]

Experts on the subject warn against extremes of centralization or decentralization. The challenge is to achieve a workable balance between the two extremes. A management consultant put it this way: "The modern organization in transition will recognize the pull of two polarities: a need for greater centralization to create low-cost shared resources and a need to improve market responsiveness with greater decentralization. Today's winning organizations are the ones that can handle the paradox and tensions of both pulls."[47] In other words, centralization and decentralization are not an either-or proposition; they are an *and-also* balancing act.

MASTER YOUR KNOWLEDGE
Mechanistic versus Organic Organizational Structures

Increase your knowledge of the distinction between mechanistic and organic structures by completing the online quiz at [www.mhhe.com/obcore].

- Which type of structure, mechanistic or organic, would you expect to be best suited to an organization that provides disaster relief? Why?
- Which type of structure would you expect to be best suited to an organization that processes credit card payments? Why?

Practical Research Insights

When Burns and Stalker classified a sample of actual companies as either mechanistic or organic, they discovered one type was not superior to the other. Each type had its appropriate place, depending on the environment. When the environment was relatively stable and certain, the successful organizations tended to be mechanistic. Organic organizations tended to be most successful when the environment was unstable and uncertain.[48]

In a more recent study of 103 department managers from eight manufacturing firms and two aerospace companies, managerial skill had a greater impact on a global measure of department effectiveness in organic departments than in mechanistic departments. Applying these results, the researchers recommended that companies assign their most experienced and talented managers to units with organic structures. Also, training is most important for managers being developed to lead organically structured departments.[49]

Another interesting finding comes from a study of 42 voluntary church organizations. As the organizations became more mechanistic (more bureaucratic), the intrinsic motivation of their members decreased. Mechanistic organizations apparently undermined the volunteers' sense of freedom and self-determination. Additionally, the researchers believe their findings help explain why bureaucracy tends to feed on itself: "A mechanistic organizational structure may breed the need for a more extremely mechanistic system because of the reduction in intrinsically motivated behavior."[50] Thus, bureaucracy begets greater bureaucracy.

Most recently, field research in two factories, one mechanistic and the other organic, found expected communication patterns. Command-and-control (downward) communication characterized the mechanistic factory. Consultative or participative (two-way) communication prevailed in the organic factory.[51]

Need for Mechanistic and Organic Structures

Although achievement-oriented students of OB typically express a distaste for mechanistic organizations, not all organizations or subunits can or should be organic. For example, McDonald's could not achieve its admired quality and service standards without extremely mechanistic restaurant operations. Imagine the food and service you would get if McDonald's employees used their own favorite ways of operating and worked at their own pace! On the other hand, mechanistic structure alienates some employees because it erodes their sense of self-control.

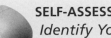

New-Style versus Old-Style Organizations

Organization theorists Jay R Galbraith and Edward E Lawler III have called for a "new logic of organizing."[52] They recommend organizations characterized by a whole new set of adjectives (see Table 13–1). Traditional pyramid-shaped organizations, conforming to the old-style pattern, tend to be too slow and inflexible today. Leaner, more organic organizations increasingly are needed to accommodate today's strategic balancing act among cost, quality, and speed. These new-style organizations embrace the total quality management (TQM) principles discussed in Chapter 1. This means they are customer focused, dedicated to continuous improvement and learning, and structured around teams. The hope is that these qualities, along with computerized information technology, will enable big organizations to mimic the speed and flexibility of small organizations.

Virtual Organizations

As with virtual teams, discussed in Chapter 6, modern information technology allows people in virtual organizations to get something accomplished despite being geographically dispersed.[53] Instead of relying heavily on face-to-face meetings, members of virtual organizations send e-mail and voice-mail messages, exchange project information over the

TABLE 13–1 New-Style versus Old-Style Organizations

Source: From J R Galbraith and E E Lawler III, "Effective Organizations: Using the New Logic of Organizing," p 298 in *Organizing for the Future: The New Logic for Managing Complex Organizations,* eds J R Galbraith, E E Lawler III, and Associates, 1993. Copyright © 1993 John Wiley & Sons, Inc. Reprinted with permission of John Wiley & Sons, Inc.

New	Old
Dynamic, learning	Stable
Information rich	Information is scarce
Global	Local
Small and large	Large
Product/customer oriented	Functional
Skills oriented	Job oriented
Team oriented	Individual oriented
Involvement oriented	Command/control oriented
Lateral/networked	Hierarchical
Customer oriented	Job requirements oriented

Internet, and convene videoconferences among far-flung participants. In addition, cellular phones and the wireless Internet have made the dream of doing business from the beach a reality. This disconnection between work and location is causing managers to question traditional assumptions about centralized offices and factories.

Various configurations have emerged. For example, JetBlue Airways Corp.'s Salt Lake City reservations "center" consists largely of sales agents working from their homes, using an online system that processes requests that come in via telephone or Internet links.[54] A more controversial form of virtual organization involves "offshoring" jobs to lower-wage countries. Half the employees of Sapient, a consulting firm based in Cambridge, Massachusetts, work in India, staying in touch over the Internet.[55] Yet another form of virtual organization is not a single organization, but rather a *network* of several organizations linked together contractually and electronically. Why own a computer factory when contract-manufacturer Solectron will do the job for you? Why own warehouses and fleets of delivery trucks when UPS and FedEx can provide a complete supply chain?

These different types of virtual organization—and the e-leadership challenges listed in Chapter 1—require new thinking about how to manage people who are out of sight but not out of mind.[56] These organizations need to select employees who can work independently and communicate well online. Communication by managers and employees alike requires special attention to build effective working relationships. Managers need to visit remote locations and provide face-to-face coaching and reinforcement. Processes such as routine audits and training keep performance up to standard. Finally, in using technology to monitor performance, managers must be careful to respect their employees' privacy.[57]

Gazing into the Crystal Ball

Here is how we envision life in the emerging virtual organizations and organizational networks. Work will be very interesting and profitable for the elite core of entrepreneurs and engineers who hit on the right business formula. Turnover among the financial and information "have nots"—data entry, customer service, and production employees—will be high because of glaring inequities and limited opportunities for personal fulfillment and growth. Telecommuters who work from home will feel liberated and empowered (and sometimes lonely). Commitment, trust, and loyalty could erode badly if managers do not heed this caution by Charles Handy, a British management expert: "A shared commitment still requires personal contact to make the commitment feel real. *Paradoxically, the more virtual an organization becomes the more its people need to meet in person.*"[58] Independent contractors, both individuals and organizations, will participate in many different organizational networks and thus feel diluted loyalty to any single one. Substandard working conditions and low pay at some smaller contractors will make them little more than Internet-age sweat shops.[59] Companies surviving from one contract to another will offer little in the way of job security and benefits. Offshoring of jobs in both the manufacturing and service sectors, despite being a politically charged issue, will continue as long as consumers demand low-cost (and often foreign-sourced) goods and services.[60] Opportunities to start new businesses will be numerous, but prolonged success could prove elusive at Internet speed.[61]

Needed: Self-Starting Team Players

The only certainty about tomorrow's organizations is that they will produce a lot of surprises. Only flexible, adaptable people who see problems as opportunities, are self-starters capable of teamwork, and are committed to lifelong learning will be able to handle whatever comes their way.

Chapter Fourteen

Change and Learning Organizations: How to Thrive in a Turbulent World

Learning Objectives

After reading the material in this chapter, you should be able to:

- Identify the forces that create a need for organizational change.
- Describe the change process in terms of two models of change.
- Summarize steps for leading organizational change.
- List reasons why employees resist change.
- Offer strategies for overcoming resistance to change.
- Discuss the process by which organizations build their learning capabilities.

If today's organizations can count on anything, it is that tomorrow will bring change. SBC Communications acquires AT&T and then calls its combined company AT&T. Burger King taps someone new for its CEO position—again. Microsoft reorganizes to better compete in the Internet computing environment. IBM sells its personal computer division to Chinese firm Lenovo and concentrates instead on consulting services. Embroiled in financial wrongdoing, WorldCom reforms and decides to revert to its old name: MCI. Increased global competition, startling breakthroughs in information technology, shifts in consumer preferences, and calls for stricter corporate ethics are forcing companies to change the way they operate in order to satisfy their customers, employees, and shareholders. The rate of organizational and societal change is clearly accelerating.

Change is most likely to succeed when it is planned, not merely reactive. To help managers navigate the journey of change, this chapter discusses the forces that create a need for organizational change, models of planned change, resistance to change, and creation of a learning organization.

FORCES OF CHANGE

How do organizations know when they should change? What cues should managers look for? No clear-cut answers exist, but managers can find cues signaling a need for change when they monitor the forces driving change. Organizations encounter many different forces for change. These forces come from sources outside the organization and from internal sources.

External Forces

External forces for change
Originate outside the organization.

When pressure for change comes from outside the organization, it is one of the **external forces for change.** Because these forces have global effects, they may cause an organization to question the essence of what business it is in and the process by which it produces goods and services. External forces for change most often involve demographic characteristics, technological advancements, market changes, and social and political pressures.

Demographic Characteristics

Chapter 2 detailed the demographic changes occurring in the U.S. workforce. Organizations need to manage the resulting diversity if they are to receive maximum contribution and commitment from employees. One recent change has been the entry into the workforce of people who grew up with widespread access to personal computers and the Internet. Workers born between 1977 and 1997 represent the first generation of workers offering skills with this powerful information technology.[1] The organizational challenge associated with this force for change involves fully motivating and utilizing this talented pool of employees.

Technological Advancements

Probably one of the biggest forces for change is the development and use of information technologies. Manufacturing and service organizations are increasingly using technology to improve productivity, competitiveness, and customer service. Microsoft, which became a dominant player by selling software for personal computers, recently hired software expert Ray Ozzie to lead the integration of its products with the Internet, a transformation that Ozzie says will require "staggering" costs.[2] Experts predict that e-business will continue to create evolutionary change in organizations around the world.

Other technological change is unrelated to the Internet. ExxonMobil tries to hold a position as technology leader with advanced equipment. For example, its Fast Drill Press drills oil wells much faster than standard technology; using it has helped the company save hundreds of millions of dollars a year.[3]

Customer and Market Changes

Increasing customer sophistication is requiring organizations to deliver higher value in their products and services. Customers are demanding more now than they did in the past. Also, the cost to switch sellers has been falling, so customers are more likely to shop elsewhere if they do not get what they want. Wal-Mart stays abreast of customer preferences by conducting surveys and focus groups. This effort has enabled Wal-Mart to customize the product mix in its stores to match local tastes.[4]

With respect to market changes, service companies are experiencing increased pressure to obtain more productivity because competition is fierce and prices have remained relatively

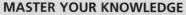

MASTER YOUR KNOWLEDGE
Macroenvironmental Forces

Increase your knowledge of forces for change by completing the online quiz at [www.mhhe.com/obcore].

- Which forces for change are affecting your university?
- Which forces for changes do you predict will have the largest impact on your future career?

stable.[5] In addition, the emergence of a global economy is forcing companies to change the way they do business. American companies have been forging new partnerships and alliances with their suppliers and potential competitors to gain advantages in the global marketplace.[6]

Social and Political Pressures

Events in the social and political spheres also generate pressure for change. The collapse of Enron and major accounting scandals at WorldCom, American International Group, and Fannie Mae have focused attention on the process by which organizations conduct financial reporting. Boards of directors have had to pay more attention to what CEOs are doing and exert more control over the manner in which organizations are being operated.[7]

In general, social and political pressure in the United States is exerted through legislative bodies that represent American citizens. Political events also can provoke substantial change. The war in Iraq, for instance, created tremendous opportunities for defense contractors and organizations like Halliburton that are involved in rebuilding the country. Although predicting changes in political forces is difficult, many organizations hire lobbyists and consultants to help them detect and respond to social and political changes.

Internal Forces

Internal forces for change
Originate inside the organization.

Changes that come from inside the organization, categorized as **internal forces for change,** can be as subtle as low job satisfaction or as obvious as low productivity and high turnover. Internal forces for change come from both human resource conflicts and managerial behavior, including decisions. Exelon, America's largest operator of nuclear power plants, undertook large-scale organizational change because its plants were running at only 47% capacity and safety problems landed the company on the Nuclear Regulatory Commission's watch list.[8] Unusual or high levels of absenteeism and turnover also represent forces for change, such as job redesign. Positive forces for change include employee participation and suggestions.

MODELS OF PLANNED CHANGE

American managers are criticized for emphasizing short-term, quick-fix solutions to organizational problems. When applied to organizational change, this approach is doomed. Quick fixes do not really solve underlying causes of problems, and they have little staying

HOT SEAT VIDEO
Change: More Pain than Gain

power. As a result, researchers and managers have tried to identify effective ways to manage the change process.

Lewin's Change Model

Most theories of organizational change originated from the landmark work of social psychologist Kurt Lewin. Lewin developed a three-stage model of planned change that explains how to initiate, manage, and stabilize the change process.[9] The three stages are unfreezing, changing, and refreezing.

Unfreezing

The focus of the first stage, unfreezing, is to create the motivation to change. Individuals are encouraged to replace old behaviors and attitudes with those desired by management. Managers can begin the unfreezing process by disconfirming the usefulness or appropriateness of employees' present behaviors or attitudes. In other words, employees need to become dissatisfied with the old way of doing things. Managers also create the motivation for change by presenting data regarding effectiveness, efficiency, or customer satisfaction. Mark Hurd, CEO of Hewlett-Packard (HP), unfroze the organization by communicating information from corporate customers and HP employees. Customers told Hurd they were so confused by HP's organizational structure that they didn't know whom to call for help. HP's salespeople complained that excessive paperwork was keeping them away from customers.[10]

Benchmarking
Process by which a company compares its performance with that of high-performing organizations.

A technique that can help unfreeze an organization is **benchmarking,** "the overall process by which a company compares its performance with that of other companies, then learns how the strongest-performing companies achieve their results."[11] One company for which we consulted discovered through benchmarking that its costs to develop software were twice as high as at the best companies in the industry, and the time the company took to get a new product to market was four times longer than at the benchmarked organizations. These data were used to unfreeze employees' attitudes and motivate them to change the organization's internal process so that it could remain competitive.

During this stage, managers also need to devise ways to reduce the barriers to change. That topic is addressed in the next section of this chapter.

Changing

Because change involves learning, the second stage entails providing employees with new information, new behavioral models, or new ways of looking at a situation. The purpose is to help employees learn new concepts or points of view. Consider, for example, the organizational changes implemented by KPMG Consulting as it transformed itself from an organization run by a partnership to one that is publicly held and focuses on meeting financial goals. Fancy offices were abandoned in favor of less-impressive but more economical work spaces. Employees were laid off, and those who remain are expected to focus on financial performance measures and on practical measures to win and satisfy clients.[12] During a change process like that at KPMG, organizations use role models, mentors, consultants, benchmarking results, and training to facilitate change. Experts recommend that the organization convey the idea that change is a continuous learning process, rather than a one-time event.

Refreezing

During refreezing, the organization stabilizes change by helping employees integrate the changed behavior or attitude into their normal way of working. This process is accomplished by first giving employees the chance to exhibit the new behaviors or attitudes. Once they are exhibited, positive reinforcement is used to reward the desired change. Additional coaching and modeling also reinforce the stability of the change. United Airlines used a new incentive system to refreeze employee behavior regarding productivity and customer service. United paid out $26 million under the bonus plan in the first quarter of a recent year after the company exceeded its goals. As in this example, monetary incentives can be a powerful way to reinforce behavioral changes.

A Systems Model of Change

A big-picture perspective on organizational change is the systems approach, which is based on the notion that any change, no matter what its size, has a cascading effect throughout an organization.[13] For example, promoting an individual to a new work group affects the group dynamics in both the old and new groups. Similarly, creating project or work teams may necessitate changes in compensation practices. As these examples illustrate, change creates additional change; today's solutions are tomorrow's problems. A systems model of change offers a framework for understanding the broad complexities of organizational change.[14] This model has three main components, shown in Figure 14–1:

Mission statement
Summarizes "why" an organization exists.

1. *Inputs.* All organizational changes should be consistent with the organization's mission, vision, and resulting strategic plan. A **mission statement** represents the "reason" an organization exists, and an organization's *vision* is a long-term goal that describes "what" an organization wants to become. For example, your university probably has a mission to educate people. This mission does not necessarily imply anything about change but instead simply defines the university's overall purpose. A vision for the university might be to be the "best" in the country by some measure. This vision requires the university to benchmark itself against other world-class universities and create plans that contain the details for achieving the vision. A **strategic plan** outlines the organization's long-term direction and actions necessary to achieve planned results, based on considering the organization's strengths and weaknesses relative to the opportunities and threats in its environment. By ensuring that organizational changes are consistent with its strategic plan, the organization avoids committing resources to counterproductive or conflicting activities.

Strategic plan
A long-term plan outlining actions needed to achieve planned results.

Target elements of change
Components of an organization that may be changed.

2. *Target elements of change.* The **target elements of change** are the components of an organization that may be changed. The target elements may include organizing arrangements, social factors, methods, goals, and people.[15] The choice of target elements depends on the strategy being pursued or the organizational problem at hand. Southwest Airlines is targeting technological changes to improve productivity and customer service while cutting costs. For example, the company cut the cost of its maintenance program by using software that tracks maintenance schedules and eliminates the need to enter data from stacks of paper forms.[16]

FIGURE 14–1 A Systems Model of Change

Sources: Adapted from D R Fuqua and D J Kurpius, "Conceptual Models in Organizational Consultation," *Journal of Counseling and Development,* July/August 1993, pp 602–18; and D A Nadler and M L Tushman, "Organizational Frame Bending: Principles for Managing Reorientation," *Academy of Management Executive,* August 1989, pp 194–203.

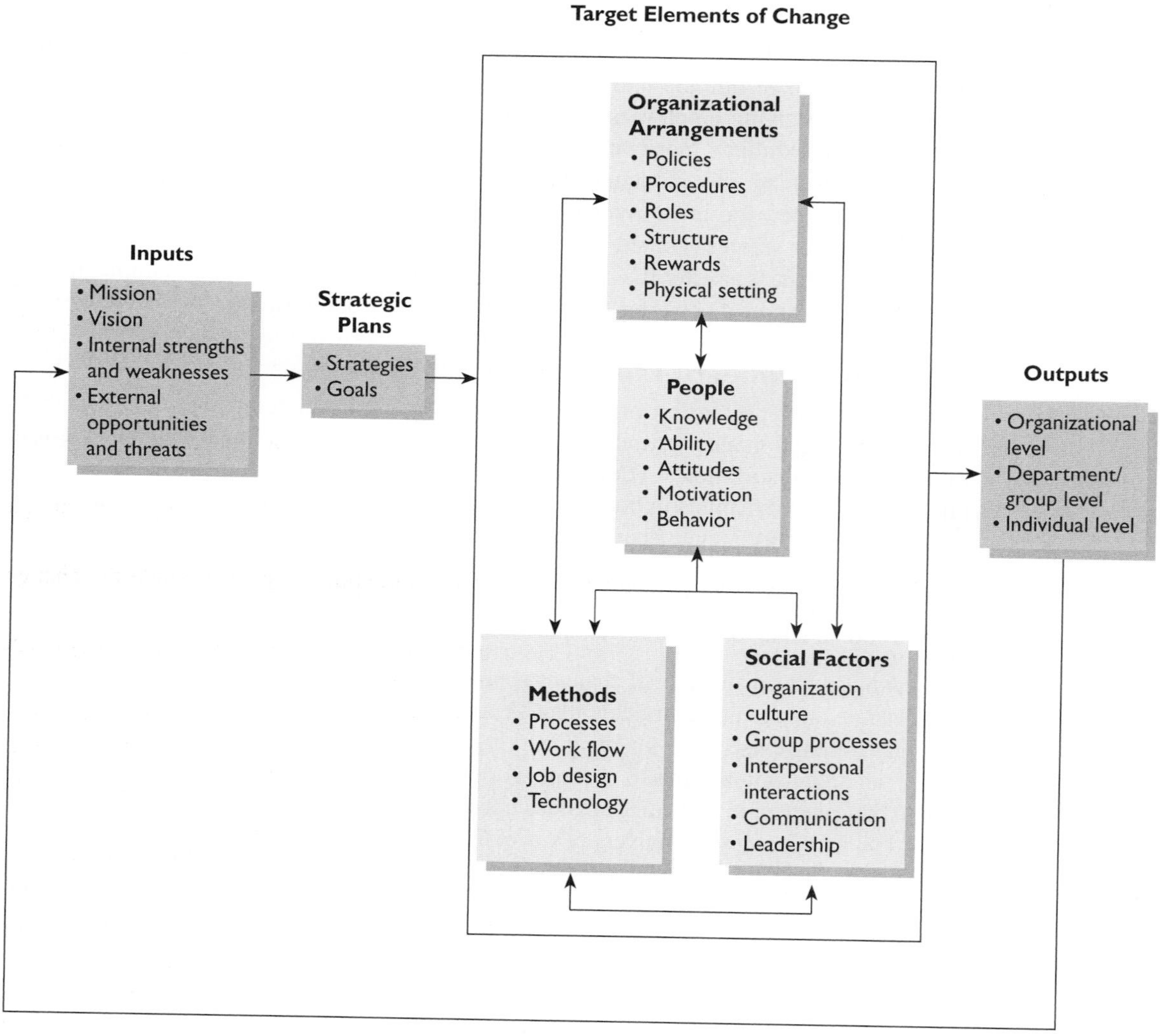

Target Elements of Change

Organizational Arrangements
- Policies
- Procedures
- Roles
- Structure
- Rewards
- Physical setting

Inputs
- Mission
- Vision
- Internal strengths and weaknesses
- External opportunities and threats

Strategic Plans
- Strategies
- Goals

People
- Knowledge
- Ability
- Attitudes
- Motivation
- Behavior

Outputs
- Organizational level
- Department/group level
- Individual level

Methods
- Processes
- Work flow
- Job design
- Technology

Social Factors
- Organization culture
- Group processes
- Interpersonal interactions
- Communication
- Leadership

3. *Outputs.* The desired end results of a change are the outputs of this model. The outputs should be consistent with the organization's strategic plan. Change may be directed at the level of the entire organization, the department or group, or the individual employee. Change efforts are most complicated at the organizational level, because changes at this level tend to affect several target elements of change.

To apply the systems model, managers may use it as an aid during strategic planning or as a framework for diagnosing the causes of an organizational problem and identifying solutions.[17] The management team at JP Morgan Chase & Co. used the first approach. They established goals for increasing revenue and decreasing costs. Changes included cutting jobs (a people factor), eliminating some executive perks (an organizational arrangements factor), and investing in information technology to use in a redesigned work flow (a method factor).[18] In a consulting project, we used the model as a diagnostic aid. The CEO of a software company wanted to understand why the presidents of three divisions were not collaborating with one another. Two of the presidents had submitted competing proposals to the same client, who was appalled and gave the job to another company. To investigate, we asked employees a set of questions related to each of the target elements of change. From their responses, we determined that the failure to collaborate resulted from the reward system (an organizational arrangement), a competitive culture and poor communications (social factors), and poor work flow (a methods factor).

Steps for Leading Organizational Change

John Kotter, an expert in leadership and change management, believes organizational change typically fails because senior management makes a host of implementation errors.[19] To avoid these implementation problems, Kotter advises, organizations should follow eight steps:

1. *Establish a sense of urgency.* Unfreeze the organization by creating a compelling reason why change is needed.
2. *Create the guiding coalition.* Create a cross-functional, cross-level group with enough power to lead the change.
3. *Develop a vision and strategy.* Create a vision and strategic plan to guide the change process.
4. *Communicate the change vision.* Create and implement a communication strategy that consistently conveys the new vision and strategic plan.
5. *Empower broad-based action.* Eliminate barriers to change, and use target elements of change to transform the organization. Encourage risk taking and creative problem solving.
6. *Generate short-term wins.* Plan for and create short-term improvements. Recognize and reward people who contribute to the wins.
7. *Consolidate gains and produce more change.* The guiding coalition uses credibility from short-term wins to create more change. More people are brought into the change process as change cascades throughout the organization. The change process is reinvigorated.
8. *Anchor new approaches in the culture.* Reinforce the changes by highlighting areas where new behaviors and processes are connected to organizational success. Develop methods to ensure leadership development and succession.[20]

Organization development (OD)
A set of techniques or tools that are used to implement organizational change.

These steps subsume Lewin's model of change. The first four steps represent Lewin's unfreezing stage. Steps 5, 6, and 7 represent changing, and step 8 corresponds to refreezing. The value of Kotter's steps is that they recommend specific behaviors that managers need to exhibit to lead organizational change. According to Kotter's research, skipping steps is ineffective, and the success of organizational change depends primarily on leadership.[21]

Organization Development

Further guidance on leading change comes from the applied field of **organization development (OD),** which is "concerned with helping managers plan change in organizing and managing people that will develop requisite commitment, coordination, and competence" in order to "enhance both the effectiveness of organizations and the well-being of their members through planned interventions in the organization's human processes, structures, and systems."[22] To accomplish this, OD applies the theory and practices of behavioral science.[23]

Stated more simply, OD constitutes a set of techniques or interventions used to implement organizational change. These techniques can be targeted to change individual attitudes and behavior, group dynamics, and organizations as a whole (at this level, often called *organizational transformation*). Also, these techniques or interventions apply to each of the change models discussed in this section. In Lewin's model, OD is used during the second stage (changing). In the systems model, OD is used to identify and implement targeted elements of change. In Kotter's model, OD may be used during steps 1, 3, 5, 6, and 7.

Identifying Characteristics

Organizational development has four identifying characteristics. First, OD involves change that is profound and delivers long-lasting improvement. Warner Burke, an OD consultant who strives for fundamental change in culture, described this fundamental change as not merely bringing about a correction to a problem or an improved process but instilling the notion that "some significant aspect of an organization's culture will never be the same."[24]

In addition, OD is value-loaded. Because this field is rooted partially in humanistic psychology, many OD consultants carry certain values or biases into the client organization. They prefer cooperation over conflict, self-control over institutional control, and democratic and participative management over autocratic management. Organization development practitioners now believe that change not only should be driven by their own values but also should reflect a customer-focused "value perspective" that OD should help the organization achieve its own vision and strategic goals. This approach implies that organizational interventions should aim to help satisfy customers' needs and thereby add to the value of the organization's products and services.

A third characteristic of OD is that it involves a cycle of diagnosis and prescription. This cycle invokes a medical model of organizations. Like medical doctors, internal and external OD consultants approach the "sick" organization, "diagnose" its ills, "prescribe" and implement an intervention, and monitor progress. Table 14–1 lists several OD interventions that can be used to change individual, group, or organizational behavior.[25]

Finally, OD is process-oriented. Ideally, OD consultants focus on the form, not the content of behavioral and administrative dealings. So, a consultant might coach product design engineers and marketing researchers on how to communicate more effectively with one another, even though the consultant does not know the technical details of their conversations. Along with communication, OD specialists focus on other processes, including problem solving, decision making, conflict handling, trust, power sharing, and career development.

Organization Development Research and Practical Implications

Organization development interventions apply many of the topics discussed in this book. Team building, for example, is often used to improve how work groups function. Thus, OD

TABLE 14–1 **Some OD Interventions for Implementing Change**

Source: A Kinicki and B Williams, *Management: A Practical Introduction,* 2nd ed (Burr Ridge, IL: McGraw-Hill/Irwin, 2006), p 329.

- **Survey feedback:** A questionnaire is distributed to employees to ascertain their perceptions and attitudes. The results are then shared with them. The questionnaire may ask about such matters as group cohesion, job satisfaction, and managerial leadership. Once the survey is done, meaningful results can be communicated with employees so that they can then engage in problem solving and constructive changes.
- **Process consultation:** An OD consultant observes the communication process—interpersonal-relations, decision-making, and conflict-handling patterns—occurring in work groups and provides feedback to the members involved. In consulting with employees (particularly managers) about these processes, the change agent hopes to give them the skills to identify and improve group dynamics on their own.
- **Team building:** Work groups are made to become more effective by helping members learn to function as a team. For example, members of a group might be interviewed independently by the OD change agent to establish how they feel about the group, then a meeting may be held away from their usual workplace to discuss the issues. To enhance team cohesiveness, the OD consultant may have members work together on a project such as rock climbing, with the consultant helping with communication and conflict resolution. The objective is for members to see how they can individually contribute to the group's goals and efforts.
- **Intergroup development:** Intergroup development resembles team building in many of its efforts. However, intergroup development attempts to achieve better cohesiveness among several work groups, not just one. During the process, the change agent tries to elicit misperceptions and stereotypes that the groups have for each other so that they can be discussed, leading to better coordination among them.
- **Technostructural activities:** Technostructural activities are interventions concerned with improving the work technology or organizational design with people on the job. An intervention involving a work-technology change might be the introduction of e-mail to improve employee communication. An intervention involving an organizational-design change might be making a company less centralized in its decision making.

research has practical implications for many aspects of organizational behavior. The following examples describe some insights that have resulted from OD-related interventions:

- A meta-analysis of 18 studies indicated that employee satisfaction with change was greater when top management was highly committed to the change effort.[26]
- A meta-analysis of 52 studies provided support for the systems model of organizational change. Specifically, varying one target element of change created changes in other target elements. Also, there was a positive relationship between individual behavior change and organizational-level change.[27]
- A meta-analysis of 126 studies demonstrated that multifaceted interventions using more than one OD technique were more effective in changing job attitudes and work attitudes than interventions that relied on only one approach.[28]
- According to a survey of 1,700 firms in China, Japan, the United States, and Europe, U.S. and European firms used OD interventions more often than the Asian firms. In addition, some OD interventions were found to be culture-free; others were not.[29]

This research suggests some practical implications. First, planned organizational change works. However, management and change agents should rely on multifaceted interventions. As we have discussed in other chapters, goal setting, feedback, recognition and rewards, training, participation, and challenging job design have good track records for improving performance and satisfaction. Another implication is that change programs are more successful when geared to meeting both short-term and long-term results. Managers should engage in organizational change not for the sake of change but to produce improvements. Third, organizational change is more likely to succeed when top management is truly committed to the change process and the goals of the change program, especially when organizations pursue large-scale transformation. Finally, the effectiveness of OD interventions is affected by cultural considerations. Managers and OD consultants should be aware of cultural characteristics when considering an OD intervention; its success in one culture does not guarantee its success in another.

RESISTANCE TO CHANGE

People are creatures of habit. Trying new ways of behaving is generally difficult. Precisely because of this basic human characteristic, most employees lack enthusiasm for change in the workplace. Rare is the manager who does not have several stories about carefully cultivated changes that died on the vine because of resistance to change. Managers need to learn to manage resistance because failed change efforts are costly—reducing employee loyalty, lowering the probability of achieving goals, and wasting money and resources.

Why Employees Resist Change

Resistance to change
Emotional/behavioral response to real or imagined work changes.

No matter how technically or administratively perfect a proposed change, its success ultimately depends on people. Individual and group reactions to an organizational change can take many forms, from enthusiastic acceptance to active resistance. **Resistance to change** is an emotional and behavioral response to real or imagined threats to an established work routine. Resistance can be as subtle as passive resignation or as overt as deliberate sabotage. Typical responses include the following eleven:[30]

1. *Individual predisposition to change.* This predisposition is highly personal and deeply ingrained. It is an outgrowth of how an individual learns to handle change and ambiguity as a child. Some people are suspicious of change, and others see it as a situation requiring flexibility, patience, and understanding.[31]

2. *Surprise and fear of the unknown.* When innovative or radically different changes are introduced without warning, affected employees fear the implications. Rumors fill the void created by lack of official announcements. When General Motors announced a plan to reduce costs by shrinking its workforce through an attrition program, employees began spreading rumors related to their fears about being out of work. One employee, 33-year GM veteran Larry Walker, told a reporter, "I talked about it with my buddies all day long. We're all trying to figure out what we should do."[32]

3. *Climate of mistrust.* Trust involves a reciprocal faith in others' intentions and behavior (see Chapter 6). Mutual mistrust can doom an otherwise well-conceived change. Mistrust encourages secrecy, which begets deeper mistrust. Managers who trust their employees make the change process open, honest, and participative. Employees who, in turn, trust management are more willing to expend effort and take chances with something different.

4. *Fear of failure.* Intimidating changes on the job can cause employees to doubt their capabilities. Self-doubt erodes self-confidence and cripples personal development.

5. *Loss of status and/or job security.* Administrative and technological changes that threaten to alter power bases or eliminate jobs generally trigger strong resistance. For example,

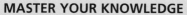

MASTER YOUR KNOWLEDGE
Technological Change

Increase your knowledge of change management by completing the online quiz at [www.mhhe.com/obcore].

- Do you think employees are more likely to resist technological change than other kinds of change? Explain.
- Suggest a way to overcome the resistance described in each question of the online exercise.

most corporate restructuring involves eliminating managerial jobs. Not surprisingly, middle managers often resist restructuring and participative-management programs that reduce their authority and status.

6. *Peer pressure.* Someone who is not directly affected by a change may actively resist it to protect the interest of his or her friends and co-workers.

7. *Disruption of cultural traditions and/or group relationships.* Whenever individuals are transferred, promoted, or reassigned, cultural and group dynamics are thrown out of balance.

8. *Personality conflicts.* Just as a friend can get away with telling us something we would resent hearing from an enemy, the personalities of change agents can breed resistance.

9. *Lack of tact and/or poor timing.* Undue resistance can occur because changes are introduced in an insensitive manner or at an awkward time.

10. *Nonreinforcing reward systems.* Individuals resist when they do not foresee desired rewards for changing. So, an employee is unlikely to support a change effort perceived as requiring longer work hours and more intense pressure.

11. *Past success.* Success can breed complacency, as well as reluctance to change, because people come to believe that what worked in the past will work in the future. This source of resistance undermined efforts to change Coca-Cola's strategy. The company became a worldwide leader by focusing on its highly profitable soft drinks, so when consumers started switching to bottled water, the company at first snubbed what it considered a "low-margin road to nowhere." The company also was slow to launch products in what would become other important categories, such as sports drinks and energy drinks.[33]

The Master Your Knowledge exercise addresses employees' resistance to changes brought about by advances in technology.

Strategies for Overcoming Resistance to Change

Any effort to overcome resistance to change must take into account several principles of change management:

- An organization must be ready for change. Just as a table must be set before you can eat, so must an organization be ready for change before it can be effective.[34]

SELF-ASSESSMENT
Assessing Your Flexibility

Go online at [www.mhhe.com/obcore] to discover how flexible you are.

- Does your score suggest you are flexible enough to succeed in today's fast-changing environment?
- Give an example of a work situation where you were or were not flexible, and describe whether more flexibility would have helped you. (If you cannot think of a work situation, use an example from school or volunteer work.)

GROUP EXERCISE
Overcoming Resistance to Change

**Commitment
to change**
A mind-set of
doing whatever
it takes to
effectively
implement
change.

- People are more likely to resist change when they do not agree about the causes of current problems and the need for change. To overcome this cognitive hurdle, managers must increase employees' commitment to change.[35] **Commitment to change** is a mind-set that "binds an individual to a course of action deemed necessary for the successful implementation of a change initiative."[36]
- Organizational change is less successful when top management fails to keep employees informed about the process of change.
- People do not necessarily resist change consciously. Rather than assuming everyone is resisting a change, managers should use a systems model of change to identify the obstacles affecting the implementation process.
- Employees' perceptions or interpretations of a change significantly affect resistance. Employees are less likely to resist when they perceive that the benefits of a change overshadow the personal costs.

At a minimum then, managers should give employees as much information as possible about the change, inform them about the reasons for the change, conduct meetings to address any questions about the change, and give employees a chance to discuss how the proposed change might affect them.[37] These recommendations underscore the importance of communicating with employees throughout the process of change.

Another way to reduce resistance is to invite employee participation in the change process. That said, participation is not a cure-all for resistance. Organizational change experts prefer a contingency approach, because resistance can take many forms and situation factors also vary. Table 14–2 lists strategies appropriate for several situations. Combining participation and involvement can be effective, but it tends to be time-consuming. Likewise, each of the other five strategies has its situational niches, advantages, and drawbacks. In short, no universal strategy overcomes all resistance to change. Managers need a complete repertoire of change strategies. At the same time, successful employees in today's dynamic

TABLE 14–2 **Six Strategies for Overcoming Resistance to Change**

Source: Reprinted by permission of the *Harvard Business Review*. An exhibit from "Choosing Strategies for Change" by J P Kotter and L A Schlesinger (March/April 1979). Copyright © 1979 by the Harvard Business School Publishing Corporation; all rights reserved.

Approach	Commonly Used in Situations	Advantages	Drawbacks
Education + Communication	Where there is a lack of information or inaccurate information and analysis.	Once persuaded, people will often help with the implementation of the change.	Can be very time consuming if lots of people are involved.
Participation + Involvement	Where the initiators do not have all the information they need to design the change and where others have considerable power to resist.	People who participate will be committed to implementing change, and any relevant information they have will be integrated into the change plan.	Can be very time consuming if participators design an inappropriate change.
Facilitation + Support	Where people are resisting because of adjustment problems.	No other approach works as well with adjustment problems.	Can be time consuming, expensive, and still fail.
Negotiation + Agreement	Where someone or some group will clearly lose out in a change and where that group has considerable power to resist.	Sometimes it is a relatively easy way to avoid major resistance.	Can be too expensive in many cases if it alerts others to negotiate for compliance.
Manipulation + Co-optation	Where other tactics will not work or are too expensive.	It can be a relatively quick and inexpensive solution to resistance problems.	Can lead to future problems if people feel manipulated.
Explicit + Implicit coercion	Where speed is essential and where the change initiators possess considerable power.	It is speedy and can overcome any kind of resistance.	Can be risky if it leaves people angry at the initiators.

environment will have the qualities, such as flexibility, that help them accept and cope with frequent changes.

CREATING A LEARNING ORGANIZATION

Organizations are finding that yesterday's competitive advantage is becoming the minimum entrance requirement for staying in business. As a result, organizations must learn how best to improve and stay ahead of competitors. In fact, researchers and practicing managers agree than an organization's capability to learn is a key strategic weapon. Organizations therefore should enhance and nurture their capability to learn.[38]

Organizational Learning and Learning Organizations

Susan Fisher and Margaret White, experts on organizational change and learning, define *organizational learning* as "a reflective process, played out by members at all levels of the organization, that involves the collection of information from both the external and internal environments," followed by filtering of the information "through a collective sensemaking process, which results in shared interpretations that can be used to instigate actions resulting in enduring changes to the organization's behavior and theories in use."[39] This definition highlights that organizational learning represents the gathering and interpretation of information through a cognitive, social process. The accumulated information from this interpretive process represents an organization's knowledge base. The knowledge is stored in organizational "memory," consisting of files, records, procedures, policies, and organizational culture.

Organizational knowledge is used by learning organizations to foster innovation and organizational effectiveness. The term *learning organization* gained popularity from the best-selling book *The Fifth Discipline* by Peter Senge, a professor at the Massachusetts Institute of Technology. Senge described a learning organization as "a group of people working together to collectively enhance their capacities to create results that they truly care about."[40] Applying these ideas, we define a **learning organization** as one that creates, acquires, and transfers knowledge and that changes its behavior on the basis of new knowledge and insights.

Learning organization
Proactively creates, acquires, and transfers knowledge throughout the organization.

The three components of this definition highlight the characteristics of a learning organization. First, new ideas are a prerequisite for learning. Learning organizations actively try to incorporate new ideas and information. They do this by constantly scanning their external environments, hiring new talent and expertise when needed, and devoting significant resources to train and develop their employees. Second, new knowledge must be transferred throughout the organization. Learning organizations strive to reduce structural, process, and interpersonal barriers to the sharing of information, ideas, and knowledge among organizational members. Finally, the new knowledge must produce changes in behavior. Learning organizations are results-oriented, fostering an environment in which employees are encouraged to use new behaviors and operational process to achieve corporate goals.[41]

Building an Organization's Learning Capability

Learning capabilities
The set of core competencies and internal processes that enable an organization to adapt to its environment.

Organizations can build and enhance their learning capability according to the model in Figure 14–2. **Learning capabilities** represent the set of core competencies (the special knowledge, skills, and technological know-how that differentiate an organization from its competitors) and process that enable an organization to adapt to its environment.[42] To use an analogy, learning capabilities are the fuel for organizational success. Just as gasoline enables a car's engine to perform, learning capabilities equip an organization to foresee and respond to internal and external changes. This capability, in turn, increases the chances of satisfying customers and boosting sales and profitability.[43] The two major contributors to an organization's learning capability are its facilitating factors and learning mode.

Facilitating factors represent "the internal structure and processes that affect how easy or hard it is for learning to occur and the amount of effective learning that takes place."[44] They include the following key facilitating factors:

- *Scanning imperative.* Interest in external happenings and in the nature of your environment; valuing the process of awareness and data generation; and curiosity about what is "out there."

FIGURE 14–2
Building an Organization's Learning Capability

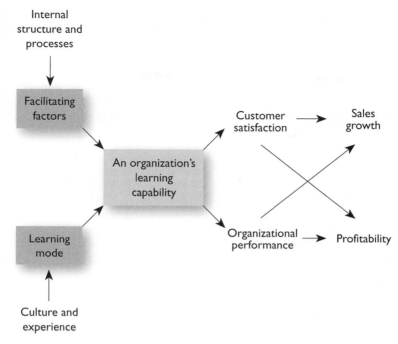

- *Performance gap.* Shared perception of a gap between actual and desired states of performance. Disconfirming feedback interrupts a string of success, and performance shortfalls are seen as opportunities to learn.
- *Concern for measurement.* Considerable effort spent defining and measuring key factors when venturing into new areas; striving for specific, quantifiable measures. Discourse over metrics is seen as a learning activity.
- *Experimental mind-set.* Support for trying new things; curiosity about how things work; ability to "play" with things. Small failures are encouraged, not punished. Changes in work process, policies, and structures are seen as a continuous series of graded tryouts.
- *Climate of openness.* Accessibility of information; relatively open boundaries; opportunities to observe others. Problems and errors are shared, not hidden. Debate and conflict are accepted.
- *Continuous education.* Ongoing commitment to education at all levels; support for growth and development of members.
- *Operational variety.* Variety in response modes, procedures, systems; significant diversity in personnel; pluralistic definition of valued internal capabilities.
- *Multiple advocates.* Acceptance of top-down and bottom-up initiatives. Multiple advocates and gatekeepers exist.
- *Involved leadership.* High-level leadership that articulates vision and is actively engaged in its actualization; ongoing steps taken to implement vision; hands-on involvement in educational and other implementation steps.

- *Systems perspective.* Strong focus on how parts of the organization are interdependent; optimization of organizational goals sought at the highest levels. Problems and solutions are seen in terms of systemic relationships.[45]

These factors can either enable or impede an organization's ability to respond to its environment. Consider, for example, the scanning imperative and concern for measurement. High-performance organizations are much more likely than low-performing organizations to have a conscientious and explicit process for making decisions based on the best available evidence. To follow such a process, organizations must be scanning their environment for information and measuring the effectiveness of their operations and decisions.[46] In this way, an organization's learning capabilities are a key component of making the analytic decisions that can help the organization create a competitive advantage.

Learning modes

The various ways in which organizations attempt to create and maximize their learning.

Learning modes represent the various ways in which organizations try to create and maximize learning. As shown in Figure 14–2, learning modes are directly influenced by an organization's culture and experience or history.[47] The Men's Wearhouse, for example, is highly committed to organizational learning. The company sends every employee to training averaging 40 hours a year. In a crowded retailing industry, says Eric Anderson, the director of training, Men's Wearhouse distinguishes itself by emphasizing that "we are in the people business, not the men's clothing business." In other words, its most important factor is its people, so the company uses training to "nurture creativity, empowerment, responsibility, trust, and excitement."[48]

Based on a review of the literature on organizational learning, Danny Miller identified six dominant modes of learning.[49] *Analytic learning* occurs through systematic gathering of internal and external information, which tends to be quantitative, so the analysis emphasizes deductive logic and objective data. *Synthetic learning* is more intuitive and generic, emphasizing the use of systems thinking to synthesize large amounts of complex information, looking for relationships among issues, problems, and opportunities. *Experimental learning* uses a rational methodology to conduct small experiments and monitor the results. *Interactive learning* involves a mainly inductive and intuitive exchange of information that results from learning by doing. *Structural learning* applies organizational routines for carrying out tasks and roles; by following the routines, employees learn standards, vocabularies, and the priorities to which they must direct their attention. *Institutional learning* is an inductive process by which organizations share and model values, beliefs, and practices from their senior executives or external environments; employees learn by observing the models, including mentors.

Leadership: Foundation of a Learning Organization

Fostering organizational learning and creating a learning organization require leadership. Effective leaders use both transactional and transformational leadership (see Chapter 11) to facilitate organizational learning.[50] To do so, leaders must adopt new roles and associated actions.[51]

Building a Commitment to Learning

Leaders need to instill an intellectual and emotional commitment to learning. Thomas Tierney, CEO of Bain & Company, proposes that leaders foster this commitment by building a culture that promotes the concept of "teacher-learners." His concept is based on the idea that organizational learning and innovation are enhanced when employees behave like teachers *and* learners: actively engaged in both activities, seeking out sources of information, making connections among ideas from different sources, and reflecting on what and how they learn.[52] Of course, leaders also must invest the financial resources needed to create a learning infrastructure.

Generating Ideas with Impact

Ideas have impact if they add value to one or more of an organization's three key stakeholders: employees, customers, and shareholders. To generate ideas with impact, say experts, organizations should implement continuous-improvement programs; increase employee competence through training or buy talent by hiring employees; experiment with new ideas, processes, and structural arrangements; look outside the organization for world-class ideas and processes; and instill systems thinking throughout the organization.

Generalizing Ideas with Impact

Leaders must make a concerted effort to reduce interpersonal, group, and organizational barriers to learning. Doing this involves creating a learning infrastructure.[53] That large-scale effort includes measuring and rewarding learning; increasing open and honest dialogue among organizational members; reducing conflict; increasing horizontal and vertical communication; promoting teamwork; rewarding risk taking and innovation; reducing the fear of failure; increasing the sharing of successes, failures, and best practices among organizational members; reducing stressors and frustration; reducing internal competition; increasing cooperation and collaboration; and creating a psychologically safe and comforting environment.[54]

Unlearning the Organization

At the same time they implement the ideas discussed earlier, organizations must unlearn organizational practices and paradigms that made them successful. Quite simply, traditional organizations and the associated organizational behaviors they created have outlived their usefulness. To create a learning organization, managers must seriously challenge the ways of thinking that worked in the past.[55] For example, the old management paradigm of planning, organizing, and control might be replaced with one of vision, values, and empowerment. Management and employees now must think as owners, not as "us" and "them" adversaries.

End Notes

Chapter 1

[1] J Pfeffer and J F Veiga, "Putting People First for Organizational Success," *Academy of Management Executive,* May 1999, p 37. See also J K Harter, F L Schmidt, and T L Hayes, "Business-Unit-Level Relationship between Employee Satisfaction, Employee Engagement, and Business Outcomes: A Meta-Analysis," *Journal of Applied Psychology,* April 2002, pp 268–79.

[2] See B Morris, "The Best Place to Work Now," *Fortune,* January 23, 2006, pp 78–84.

[3] See I S Fulmer, B Gerhart, and K S Scott, "Are the 100 Best Better? An Empirical Investigation of the Relationship Between Being a 'Great Place to Work' and Firm Performance," *Personnel Psychology,* Winter 2003, pp 965–93.

[4] H Mintzberg, "The Manager's Job: Folklore and Fact," *Harvard Business Review,* July/August 1975, p 61.

[5] See, for example, H Mintzberg, "Managerial Work: Analysis from Observation," *Management Science,* October 1971, pp B97–B110; and F Luthans, "Successful vs. Effective Real Managers," *Academy of Management Executive,* May 1988, pp 127–32. For an instructive critique of the structured observation method, see M J Martinko and W L Gardner, "Beyond Structured Observation: Methodological Issues and New Directions," *Academy of Management Review,* October 1985, pp 676–95. See also N Fondas, "A Behavioral Job Description for Managers," *Organizational Dynamics,* Summer 1992, pp 47–58.

[6] See L B Kurke and H E Aldrich, "Mintzberg Was Right! A Replication and Extension of *The Nature of Managerial Work,*" *Management Science,* August 1983, pp 975–84.

[7] For example, see N H Woodward, "The Coming of the X Managers," *HR Magazine,* March 1999, pp 74–80; J Gosling and H Mintzberg, "The Five Minds of a Manager," *Harvard Business Review,* November 2003, pp 54–63; A I Kraut, P R Pedigo, D D McKenna, and M D Dunnette, "The Role of the Manager: What's Really Important in Different Management Jobs," *Academy of Management Executive,* November 2005, pp 122–29; "Secrets of Greatness: How I Work," *Fortune,* March 20, 2006, pp 66–85; and J Jenkins, "Getting Up to Full Speed," *HR Magazine,* April 2006, pp 117–20.

[8] Validation studies can be found in E Van Velsor and J B Leslie, *Feedback to Managers,* vol 2: *A Review and Comparison of Sixteen Multi-Rater Feedback Instruments* (Greensboro, NC: Center for Creative Leadership, 1991); F Shipper, "A Study of the Psychometric Properties of the Managerial Skill Scales of the Survey of Management Practices," *Educational and Psychological Measurement,* June 1995, pp 468–79; and C L Wilson, *How and Why Effective Managers Balance Their Skills: Technical, Teambuilding, Drive* (Columbia, MD: Rockatech Multimedia, 2003).

[9] Shipper, "A Study of the Psychometric Properties"; and Wilson, *How and Why Effective Managers Balance Their Skills.*

[10] A J Daboub, A M A Rasheed, R L Priem, and D A Gray, "Top Management Team Characteristics and Corporate Illegal Activity," *Academy of Management Review,* January 1995, pp 138–70.

[11] L Simpson, "Taking the High Road," *Training,* January 2002, p 38.

[12] T Jackson, "Cultural Values and Management Ethics: A 10-Nation Study," *Human Relations,* October 2001, pp 1267–1302.

[13] C E Bagley, "The Ethical Leader's Decision Tree," *Harvard Business Review,* February 2003, pp 18–19.

[14] K Hodgson, *A Rock and a Hard Place: How to Make Ethical Business Decisions When the Choices Are Tough* (New York: AMACOM, 1992), pp 66–77.

[15] See Y Kashima, "Conceptions of Culture and Person for Psychology," *Journal of Cross-Cultural Psychology,* January 2000, pp 14–32; and the cultural dimensions in Table 1 of G T Chao and H Moon, "The Cultural Mosaic: A Metatheory for

Understanding the Complexity of Culture," *Journal of Applied Psychology,* November 2005, pp 1128–40.

[16] G Hofstede, *Culture's Consequences: International Differences in Work-Related Values,* abridged ed (Newbury Park, CA: Sage, 1984); G Hofstede, "The Interaction between National and Organizational Value Systems," *Journal of Management Studies,* July 1985, pp 347–57; and G Hofstede, "Management Scientists Are Human," *Management Science,* January 1994, pp 4–13.

[17] M Javidan and R J House, "Cultural Acumen for the Global Manager: Lessons from Project GLOBE," *Organizational Dynamics,* Spring 2001, pp 289–305; R House, M Javidan, P Hanges, and P Dorfman, "Understanding Cultures and Implicit Leadership Theories across the Globe: An Introduction to Project GLOBE," *Journal of World Business,* Spring 2002, p 4; the entire Spring 2002 issue of *Journal of World Business;* and R J House, P J Hanges, M Javidan, P W Dorfman, and V Gupta, eds, *Culture, Leadership, and Organizations: The GLOBE Study of 62 Societies* (Thousand Oaks, CA: Sage, 2004).

[18] Adapted from the list in House, Javidan, Hanges, and Dorfman, "Understanding Cultures," pp 5–6.

[19] See T W Malone, *The Future of Work: How the New Order of Business Will Shape Your Organization, Your Management Style, and Your Life* (Boston: Harvard Business School Press, 2004); and P Aburdene, *Megatrends 2010: The Rise of Conscious Capitalism* (Charlottesville, VA: Hampton Roads Publishing, 2005).

[20] Essential sources on reengineering are M Hammer and J Champy, *Reengineering the Corporation: A Manifesto for Business Revolution* (New York: HarperCollins, 1993); and J Champy, *Reengineering Management: The Mandate for New Leadership* (New York: HarperCollins, 1995).

[21] See J Weber, "'Mosh Pits' of Creativity," *BusinessWeek,* November 7, 2005, pp 98–100; R D Hof, "Collaboration: Teamwork, Supercharged," *BusinessWeek,* November 21, 2005, pp 90–94; P Kaihla, "Google: Office Graffiti," *Business 2.0,* April 2006, p 90; and M A Prospero, "Top Scalpel," *Fast Company,* April 2006, p 31.

[22] See S Ghoshal and H Bruch, "Going Beyond Motivation to the Power of Volition," *MIT Sloan Management Review,* Spring 2003, pp 51–57;

C L Pearce and C C Manz, "The New Silver Bullets of Leadership: The Importance of Self- and Shared Leadership in Knowledge Work," *Organizational Dynamics,* no. 2 (2005): 130–40; F Vogelstein, "Star Power: Greg Brown, Motorola," *Fortune,* February 6, 2006, p 57; and R E Boyatzis, M L Smith, and N Blaize, "Developing Sustainable Leaders through Coaching and Compassion," *Academy of Management Learning and Education,* March 2006, pp 8–24.

[23] See K Carnes, D Cottrell, and M C Layton, *Management Insights: Discovering the Truths to Management Success* (Dallas: CornerStone Leadership Institute, 2004).

[24] J B Miner, "The Rated Importance, Scientific Validity, and Practical Usefulness of Organizational Behavior Theories: A Quantitative Review," *Academy of Management Learning and Education,* September 2003, pp 250–68.

[25] Evidence indicating that the original conclusions of the famous Hawthorne studies were unjustified may be found in R G Greenwood, A A Bolton, and R A Greenwood, "Hawthorne a Half Century Later: Relay Assembly Participants Remember," *Journal of Management,* Fall-Winter 1983, pp 217–31; and R H Franke and J D Kaul, "The Hawthorne Experiments: First Statistical Interpretation," *American Sociological Review,* October 1978, pp 623–43. For a positive interpretation of the Hawthorne studies, see J A Sonnenfeld, "Shedding Light on the Hawthorne Studies," *Journal of Occupational Behaviour,* April 1985, pp 111–30.

[26] See M Parker Follett, *Freedom and Coordination* (London: Management Publications Trust, 1949).

[27] D McGregor, *The Human Side of Enterprise* (New York: McGraw-Hill, 1960). See also D Jacobs, "Book Review Essay: Douglas McGregor—The Human Side of Enterprise in Peril," *Academy of Management Review,* April 2004, pp 293–96.

[28] J Hall, "Americans Know How to Be Productive if Managers Will Let Them," *Organizational Dynamics,* Winter 1994, p 38.

[29] L Wah, "The Almighty Customer," *Management Review,* February 1999, p 17.

[30] "AMA Global Survey on Key Business Issues," *Management Review,* December 1998, p 30. See also

"1999 Annual Survey: Corporate Concerns," *Management Review,* March 1999, pp 55–56.

[31] Instructive background articles on TQM are R Zemke, "A Bluffer's Guide to TQM," *Training,* April 1993, pp 48–55; R R Gehani, "Quality Value-Chain: A Meta-Synthesis of Frontiers of Quality Movement," *Academy of Management Executive,* May 1993, pp 29–42; P Mears, "How to Stop Talking about, and Begin Progress toward, Total Quality Management," *Business Horizons,* May–June 1993, pp 11–14; and the Total Quality Special Issue of *Academy of Management Review,* July 1994.

[32] M Sashkin and K J Kiser, *Putting Total Quality Management to Work* (San Francisco: Berrett-Koehler, 1993), p 39.

[33] R J Schonberger, "Total Quality Management Cuts a Broad Swath—through Manufacturing and Beyond," *Organizational Dynamics,* Spring 1992, p 18. Other quality-related articles include H Liao and A Chuang, "A Multilevel Investigation of Factors Influencing Employee Service Performance and Customer Outcomes," *Academy of Management Journal,* February 2004, pp 41–58; L Heuring, "Six Sigma in Sight," *HR Magazine,* March 2004, pp 76–80; N Brodsky, "You're Fired!" *Inc.,* May 2004, pp 51–52; and D McDonald, "Roll Out the Blue Carpet," *Business 2.0,* May 2004, pp 53–54.

[34] Deming's landmark work is W E Deming, *Out of the Crisis* (Cambridge, MA: MIT, 1986).

[35] See M Trumbull, "What Is Total Quality Management?" *The Christian Science Monitor,* May 3, 1993, p 12; and J Hillkirk, "World-Famous Quality Expert Dead at 93," *USA Today,* December 21, 1993, pp 1B–2B.

[36] Based on M Walton, *Deming Management at Work* (New York: Putnam/Perigee, 1990).

[37] Ibid., p 20.

[38] Adapted from D E Bowen and E E Lawler III, "Total Quality-Oriented Human Resources Management," *Organizational Dynamics,* Spring 1992, pp 29–41. Also see P B Seybold, "Get Inside the Lives of Your Customers," *Harvard Business Review,* May 2001, pp 80–89.

[39] See, for example, P LaBarre, "The Industrialized Revolution," *Fast Company,* November 2003, pp 116, 118.

[40] B E Becker, M A Huselid, and D Ulrich, *The HR Scorecard: Linking People, Strategy, and Performance* (Boston: Harvard Business School Press, 2001), p 4.

[41] See L Bassi and D McMurrer, "How's Your Return on People?" *Harvard Business Review* (March 2004): 18; B Hall, "Here Comes Human Capital Management," *Training,* March 2004, pp 16–17; "Employers Say Measuring Is Vital but Still Don't Do It," *HR Magazine,* April 2004, p 18; R J Grossman, "Developing Talent," *HR Magazine,* January 2006, pp 40–46; and M Bolch, "Bearing Fruit," *HR Magazine,* March 2006, pp 56–60.

[42] Intel Corporation, "Intel Innovation in Education," *About Intel* page, www.intel.com.

[43] "The 100 Best Companies to Work For," *Fortune,* February 4, 2002, p 84.

[44] Inspired by P S Adler and S Kwon, "Social Capital: Prospects for a New Concept," *Academy of Management Review,* January 2002, pp 17–40. Also see "Social Capitalists: The Top 20 Groups That Are Changing the World," *Fast Company,* January 2004, pp 45–57; and J Allik and Anu Realo, "Individualism-Collectivism and Social Capital," *Journal of Cross-Cultural Psychology,* January 2004, pp 29–49.

[45] "What Makes a Job OK," *USA Today,* May 15, 2002, p 1B.

[46] See R Levering and M Moskowitz, "The 100 Best Companies to Work For," *Fortune,* January 23, 2006, pp 89–108.

[47] L Bassi and D McMurrer, "Developing Measurement Systems for Managing in the Knowledge Era," *Organizational Dynamics* no. 2 (2005): 185–96.

[48] L D Tyson, "Good Works—with a Business Plan," *BusinessWeek,* May 3, 2004, p 32.

[49] M E P Seligman and M Csikszentmihalyi, "Positive Psychology: An Introduction," *American Psychologist,* January 2000, p 5. See also the other 15 articles in the January 2000 issue of *American Psychologist;* and M Elias, "What Makes People Happy; Psychologists Now Know," *USA Today,* December 9, 2002, pp 1A–2A.

[50] See F Luthans, K W Luthans, and B C Luthans, "Positive Psychological Capital: Beyond Human and

Social Capital," *Business Horizons,* January/February 2004, pp 45–50.

[51] F Luthans, "The Need for and Meaning of Positive Organizational Behavior," *Journal of Organizational Behavior,* September 2002, pp 698. See also T A Wright, "Positive Organizational Behavior: An Idea Whose Time Has Truly Come," *Journal of Organizational Behavior,* June 2003, pp 437–42; and S Fineman, "On Being Positive: Concerns and Counterpoints," *Academy of Management Review,* April 2006, pp 270–91.

[52] F Luthans, *The Academy of Management Executive: The Thinking Manager's Source* (2002).

[53] "The 100 Best Companies to Work For: And the Winners Are," *Fortune,* January 23, 2006, pp 90, 96.

[54] See M Athitakis, "How to Make Money on the Net," *Business 2.0,* May 2003, pp 83–90; L W Lam and L J Harrison-Walker, "Toward an Objective-Based Typology of E-Business Models," *Business Horizons,* November/December 2003, pp 17–26; B Stone, "The New Wisdom of the Web," *Newsweek,* April 3, 2006, pp 46–35; and A Lashinsky, "The Boom Is Back," *Fortune,* May 1, 2006, pp 70–87.

[55] M J Mandel and R D Hof, "Rethinking the Internet," *BusinessWeek,* March 26, 2001, p 118.

[56] Six implications excerpted from B J Avolio and S S Kahai, "Adding the 'E' to E-Leadership: How It May Impact Your Leadership," *Organizational Dynamics* 4 (2003): 333.

[57] W Echikson, "Nestlé: An Elephant Dances," *BusinessWeek E.Biz,* December 11, 2000, pp EB47–EB48. See also B Sosnin, "Digital Newsletters 'E-volutionize' Employee Communications," *HR Magazine,* May 2001, pp 99–107.

[58] See G Meyer, "eWorkbench: Real-Time Tracking of Synchronized Goals," *HR Magazine,* April 2001, pp 115–18.

[59] See A Majchrzak, A Malhotra, J Stamps, and J Lipnack, "Can Absence Make a Team Grow Stronger?" *Harvard Business Review,* May 2004, pp 131–37.

[60] R Moss Kanter, *Evolve! Succeeding in the Digital Culture of Tomorrow* (Boston: Harvard Business School Press, 2001), p 206. Also see R Moss Kanter, "You Are Here," *Inc.,* February 2001, pp 84–90.

[61] "Hurry Up and Decide!" *BusinessWeek,* May 14, 2001.

[62] See M A Tucker, "E-Learning Evolves," *HR Magazine,* October 2005, pp 74–78; S Boehle, "Putting the 'Learning' Back in E-Learning," *Training,* January 2006, pp 30–34; B West, "Online, It's All about Design," *Training,* March 2006, p 76; and J Gordon, "Seven Revelations about E-Learning," *Training,* April 2006, pp 28–31.

[63] G Johnson, "Uncharted Territory," *Training,* September 2003, p 24.

[64] S Overman, "Dow, Hewlett-Packard Put E-Learning to Work to Save Time and Money," *HR Magazine,* February 2004, p 32.

[65] B Hall, "The Time Is Now," *Training,* February 2004, p 16.

[66] See B Lessard and S Baldwin, *Net Slaves: True Tales of Working the Web* (New York: McGraw-Hill, 2000); P Babcock, "America's Newest Export: White-Collar Jobs," *HR Magazine,* April 2004, pp 50–57; B W Hornaday, "Conseco Shows Outsourcing Is Not Always Best Call," *USA Today,* April 26, 2004, p 10B; and D Altman, "A More Productive Outsourcing Debate," *Business 2.0,* May 2004, p 39.

Chapter 2

[1] C Palmeri, "I Survived Enron," *BusinessWeek,* February 6, 2006, p 53.

[2] The negativity bias was examined by Y Ganzach, "Negativity (and Positivity) in Performance Evaluation: Three Field Studies," *Journal of Applied Psychology,* August 1995, pp 491–99; and N K Smith, J T Larsen, T L Chartrand, and J T Cacioppo, "Being Bad Isn't Always Good: Affective Context Moderates the Attention Bias toward Negative Information," *Journal of Personality and Social Psychology,* February 2006, pp 210–20.

[3] E Rosch, C B Mervis, W D Gray, D M Johnson, and P Boyes-Braem, "Basic Objects in Natural Categories," *Cognitive Psychology,* July 1976, p 383.

[4] For a thorough discussion of the role of schemata during encoding, see S T Fiske and S E Taylor, *Social Cognition,* 2nd ed (Reading, MA: Addison-Wesley, 1991).

[5] The use of stereotypes is discussed by Z Kunda and S J Spencer, "When Do Stereotypes Come to Mind

and When Do They Color Judgment? A Goal-Based Theoretical Framework for Stereotype Activation and Application," *Psychological Bulletin,* June 2003, pp 522–44; and D C Molden and C S Dweck, "Finding 'Meaning' in Psychology," *American Psychologist,* April 2006, pp 192–203.

[6] C M Judd and B Park, "Definition and Assessment of Accuracy in Social Stereotypes," *Psychological Review,* January 1993, p 110.

[7] "Accounting and Race: A Long Way to Go," *Training,* April 2006, p 15.

[8] C Daniels, "Young, Gifted, Black—and Out of Here," *Fortune,* May 3, 2004, p 48.

[9] J L Berdahl and C Moore, "Workplace Harassment: Double Jeopardy for Minority Women," *Journal of Applied Psychology,* March 2006, pp 426–36.

[10] M Biernat, "Toward a Broader View of Social Stereotyping," *American Psychologist,* December 2003, pp 1019–27.

[11] G V Bodenhausen, C N Macrae, and J W Sherman, "On the Dialectics of Discrimination," in *Dual-Process Theories in Social Psychology,* ed S Chaiken and Y Trope (New York: Guilford Press, 1999), pp 271–90.

[12] For a thorough discussion of the structure and organization of memory, see L R Squire, B Knowlton, and G Musen, "The Structure and Organization of Memory," in *Annual Review of Psychology* 44, ed L W Porter and M R Rosenzweig (Palo Alto, CA: Annual Reviews, 1993), pp 453–95.

[13] Event memory is discussed by D Zohar and G Luria, "Organizational MetaScripts as a Source of High Reliability: The Case of an Army Armored Brigade," *Journal of Organizational Behavior,* November 2003, pp 837–59.

[14] A thorough discussion of the reasoning process used to make judgments and decisions is provided by S A Sloman, "The Empirical Case for Two Systems of Reasoning," *Psychological Bulletin,* January 1996, pp 3–22.

[15] See C Saunders, C Van Slyke, and D R Vogel, "My Time or Yours? Managing Time Visions in Global Virtual Teams," *Academy of Management Executive,* February 2004, pp 19–31.

[16] A good discussion of doing business in Mexico is G K Stephens and C R Greer, "Doing Business in Mexico: Understanding Cultural Differences," *Organizational Dynamics,* Summer 1995, pp 39–55.

[17] See A C Bluedorn, C F Kaufman, and P M Lane, "How Many Things Do You Like to Do at Once? An Introduction to Monochronic and Polychronic Time," *Academy of Management Executive,* November 1992, pp 17–26.

[18] See M Archer, "Too Busy to Read This Book? Then You Really Need To," *USA Today,* April 17, 2006, p 10B.

[19] C M Marlowe, S L Schneider, and C E Nelson, "Gender and Attractiveness Biases in Hiring Decisions: Are More Experienced Managers Less Biased?" *Journal of Applied Psychology,* February 1996, pp 11–21.

[20] C K Stevens, "Antecedents of Interview Interactions, Interviewers' Ratings, and Applicants' Reactions," *Personnel Psychology,* Spring 1998, pp 55–85.

[21] The effectiveness of rater training was supported by D V Day and L M Sulsky, "Effects of Frame-of-Reference Training and Information Configuration on Memory Organization and Rating Accuracy," *Journal of Applied Psychology,* February 1995, pp 158–67.

[22] J S Phillips and R G Lord, "Schematic Information Processing and Perceptions of Leadership in Problem-Solving Groups," *Journal of Applied Psychology,* August 1982, pp 486–92.

[23] K D Elsbach, "How to Pitch a Brilliant Idea," *Harvard Business Review,* September 2003, p 119.

[24] H H Kelley, "The Processes of Causal Attribution," *American Psychologist,* February 1973, pp 107–28.

[25] For examples, see J Susskind, K Maurer, V Thakkar, D L Hamilton, and J W Sherman, "Perceiving Individuals and Groups: Expectancies, Dispositional Inferences, and Causal Attributions," *Journal of Personality and Social Psychology,* February 1999, pp 181–91; and K White, D R Lehman, K J Hemphill, and D R Mandel, "Causal Attributions, Perceived Control, and Psychological Adjustment: A Study of Chronic Fatigue Syndrome," *Journal of Applied Social Psychology* (2006), pp 75–99.

[26] D A Hofmann and A Stetzer, "The Role of Safety Climate and Communication in Accident Interpretation: Implications for Learning from Negative Events," *Academy of Management Journal,*

December 1998, pp 644–57; and I Choi, R E Nisbett, and A Norenzayan, "Causal Attribution across Cultures: Variation and Universality," *Psychological Bulletin,* January 1999, pp 47–63.

[27] L Woellert, "The-Reporter-Did-It Defense," *BusinessWeek,* May 8, 2006, p 34.

[28] S E Moss and M J Martinko, "The Effects of Performance Attributions and Outcome Dependence on Leader Feedback Behavior Following Poor Subordinate Performance," *Journal of Organizational Behavior,* May 1998, pp 259–74; and E C Pence, W C Pendelton, G H Dobbins, and J A Sgro, "Effects of Causal Explanations and Sex Variables on Recommendations for Corrective Actions Following Employee Failure," *Organizational Behavior and Human Performance,* April 1982, pp 227–40.

[29] See D Konst, R Vonk, and R V D Vlist, "Inferences about Causes and Consequences of Behavior of Leaders and Subordinates," *Journal of Organizational Behavior,* March 1999, pp 261–71.

[30] See J Silvester, F Patterson, and E Ferguson, "Comparing Two Attributional Models of Job Performance in Retail Sales: A Field Study," *Journal of Occupational and Organizational Psychology,* March 2003, pp 115–32.

[31] K Somers, "A Proven Record of Success," *Arizona Republic,* January 10, 2004, p C1.

[32] Definitions of diversity are discussed by A Wellner, "How Do You Spell Diversity?" *Training,* April 2000, pp 34–38; and R R Thomas Jr, *Redefining Diversity* (New York: AMACOM, 1996), pp 4–9.

[33] L Gardenswartz and A Rowe, *Diverse Teams at Work* (New York: McGraw-Hill, 1994), pp 31–57.

[34] This distinction is made by M Loden, *Implementing Diversity* (Chicago: Irwin, 1996).

[35] E Garsten, "Ford Muslim Workers Organize 'Islam,'" *Arizona Republic,* December 13, 2001, p D2.

[36] F J Crosby, A Iyer, S Clayton, and R A Downing, "Affirmative Action: Psychological Data and the Policy Debates," *American Psychologist,* February 2003, p 94.

[37] See M Frase-Blunt, "Thwarting the Diversity Backlash," *HR Magazine,* June 2003, pp 137–44.

[38] See D A Kravitz and S L Klinberg, "Reactions to Two Versions of Affirmative Action among Whites,

Blacks, and Hispanics," *Journal of Applied Psychology,* August 2000, pp 597–611; and C L Renfro, A Duran, W G Stephan, and D L Clason, "The Role of Threat in Attitudes toward Affirmative Action and Its Beneficiaries," *Journal of Applied Social Psychology,* 2006, pp 41–74.

[39] See Crosby, Iyer, Clayton, and Downing, "Affirmative Action," pp 93–115.

[40] A M Morrison, *The New Leaders: Guidelines on Leadership Diversity in America* (San Francisco: Jossey-Bass, 1992), p 78.

[41] H Fullerton Jr and M Toossi, "Labor Force Projections to 2010: Steady Growth and Changing Composition," *Monthly Labor Review,* November 2001, Table 9, p 35, Bureau of Labor Statistics Web site, www.bls.gov/opub/mlr/2001/11/art2abs.htm.

[42] "Women CEOs for *Fortune* 500 Companies," *Fortune,* http://money.cnn.com/magazines/fortune/fortune500/womenceos/, accessed November 13, 2006.

[43] Bureau of Labor Statistics, *Women in the Labor Force: A Databook,* BLS Web site, www.bls.gov/cps/wlf-databook2005.htm, Table 16, accessed December 15, 2005.

[44] K S Lyness and D E Thompson, "Above the Glass Ceiling: A Comparison of Matched Samples of Female and Male Executives," *Journal of Applied Psychology,* June 1997, pp 359–75.

[45] K S Lyness and M K Judiesch, "Are Women More Likely to Be Hired or Promoted into Management Positions?" *Journal of Vocational Behavior,* February 1999, pp 158–73.

[46] B R Ragins, B Townsend, and M Mattis, "Gender Gap in the Executive Suite: CEOs and Female Executives Report on Breaking the Glass Ceiling," *Academy of Management Executive,* February 1998, pp 28–42.

[47] Fullerton and Toossi, "Labor Force Projections to 2010.

[48] See G C Armas, "Almost Half of U.S. Likely to Be Minorities by 2050," *Arizona Republic,* March 18, 2004, p A5.

[49] Equal Employment Opportunity Commission, "Race-Based Charges: FY 1992–FY 2005," EEOC Web site, http://www.eeoc.gov/stats/race.html, modified January 27, 2006.

[50] US Census Bureau, "Income of Households by Race and Hispanic Origin Using 2- and 3-Year Averages: 2000–2002," http://www.census.gov, last revised May 13, 2004.

[51] For a review of this research, see L Roberson and C J Block, "Racioethnicity and Job Performance: A Review and Critique of Theoretical Perspectives on the Causes of Group Differences," in *Research in Organizational Behavior* 23, ed B M Staw and R I Sutton (New York: JAI Press, 2001), pp 247–326.

[52] U.S. Census Bureau, "USA Statistics in Brief—Law, Education, Communications, Transportation, Housing," http://www.census.gov, revised March 16, 2004.

[53] D Dooley and J Prause, "Underemployment and Alcohol Misuse in the National Longitudinal Survey of Youth," *Journal of Studies on Alcohol,* November 1998, pp 669–80; and D C Feldman, "The Nature, Antecedents and Consequences of Under-employment," *Journal of Management,* 1966, pp 385–407.

[54] Bureau of Labor Statistics, "Education Pays . . . ," *BLS Employment Projections,* http://www.bls.gov/emp, modified December 7, 2005.

[55] U.S. Census Bureau, "Summary Measures of Educational Attainment of the U.S. Population: March 2002," http://www/census.gov/Press-Release/www/2003/cb03-51.html, revised March 21, 2003.

[56] H London, "The Workforce, Education, and the Nation's Future," *American Outlook,* Summer 1998, Hudson Institute, www.hudson.org/american_outlook/.

[57] S Armour, "Welcome Mat Rolls Out for Hispanic Workers: Corporate America Cultivates Talent as Ethnic Population Booms," *USA Today,* April 12, 2001, pp 1B–2B.

[58] K Tyler, "I Say Potato, You Say Patata," *HR Magazine,* January 2004, pp 85–86.

[59] Approaches for handling elder care are discussed by T F Shea, "Help with Elder Care," *HR Magazine,* September 2003, pp 113–14, 116, 118.

[60] Managerial issues and solutions for an aging work-force are discussed by J W Hedge, W C Borman, and S E Lammelein, *The Aging Workforce: Realities, Myths, and Implications for Organizations* (Washington, DC: American Psychological Association, 2006).

[61] These barriers were taken from discussions in Loden, *Implementing Diversity;* E E Spragins, "Benchmark: The Diverse Work Force," *Inc.,* January 1993, p 33; and Morrison, *The New Leaders.*

[62] See the related discussion in A Fisher, "The Sky's the Limit," *Fortune,* May 1, 2006, pp 124B–124H.

[63] Morrison, *The New Leaders.*

[64] "The Diversity Factor," *Fortune,* October 13, 2003, p S4.

[65] R Koonce, "Redefining Diversity," *Training & Development,* December 2001, pp 24, 26.

Chapter 3

[1] D Seligman, "The Trouble with Buyouts," *Fortune,* November 30, 1992, p 125.

[2] See G A Odums, "A New Year's Resolution: Optimize Older Workers," *Training and Development,* January 2006, pp 34–36; P Babcock, "Detecting Hidden Bias," *HR Magazine,* February 2006, pp 50–55; J A Segal, "Time Is on Their Side," *HR Magazine,* February 2006, pp 129–33; A Fisher, "The Sky's the Limit," *Fortune,* May 1, 2006, pp 124B–124H; S Kehrli and T Sopp, "Managing Generation Y," *HR Magazine,* May 2006, pp 113–19; and M Orey, "White Men Can't Help It," *BusinessWeek,* May 15, 2006, pp 54, 57.

[3] Quoted in A Deutschman, "What I Know Now," *Fast Company,* September 2005, p 96.

[4] V Gecas, "The Self-Concept," in *Annual Review of Sociology,* ed R H Turner and J F Short Jr. (Palo Alto, CA: Annual Reviews, 1982), vol. 8, p 3.

[5] L Festinger, *A Theory of Cognitive Dissonance* (Stanford, CA: Stanford University Press, 1957), p 3.

[6] A Canadian versus Japanese comparison of self-concept can be found in J D Campbell, P D Trapnell, S J Heine, I M Katz, L F Lavallee, and D R Lehman, "Self-Concept Clarity: Measurement, Personality Correlates, and Cultural Boundaries," *Journal of Personality and Social Psychology,* January 1996, pp 141–56. See also R W Tafarodi, C Lo, S Yamaguchi, W W S Lee, and H Katsura, "The Inner Self in Three Countries," *Journal of Cross-Cultural Psychology,* January 2004, pp 97–117.

[7] See D C Barnlund, "Public and Private Self in Communicating with Japan," *Business Horizons,*

March/April 1989, pp 32–40; and the section on "Doing Business with Japan" in P R Harris and R T Moran, *Managing Cultural Differences,* 4th ed (Houston: Gulf Publishing, 1996), pp 267–76.

[8] Based in part on a definition found in Gecas, "The Self-Concept." See also N Branden, *Self-Esteem at Work: How Confident People Make Powerful Companies* (San Francisco: Jossey-Bass, 1998).

[9] H W Marsh, "Positive and Negative Global Self-Esteem: A Substantively Meaningful Distinction or Artifacts?" *Journal of Personality and Social Psychology,* April 1996, p 819.

[10] For example, see P Borghesi, "I Was out of a Job—and an Identity," *Newsweek,* January 30, 2006, p 13.

[11] E Diener and M Diener, "Cross-Cultural Correlates of Life Satisfaction and Self-Esteem," *Journal of Personality and Social Psychology,* April 1995, p 662. For cross-cultural evidence of a similar psychological process for self-esteem, see T M Singelis, M H Bond, W F Sharkey, and C S Y Lai, "Unpackaging Culture's Influence on Self-Esteem and Embarrassability," *Journal of Cross-Cultural Psychology,* May 1999, pp 315–41.

[12] See C Kobayashi and J D Brown, "Self-Esteem and Self-Enhancement in Japan and America," *Journal of Cross-Cultural Psychology,* September 2003, pp 567–80.

[13] Nathaniel Branden, *Self-Esteem at Work: How Confident People Make Powerful Companies* (San Francisco: Jossey-Bass, 1998), pp 33–36.

[14] Based on data in F L Smoll, R E Smith, N P Barnett, and J J Everett, "Enhancement of Children's Self-Esteem through Social Support Training for Youth Sports Coaches," *Journal of Applied Psychology,* August 1993, pp 602–10.

[15] W J McGuire and C V McGuire, "Enhancing Self-Esteem by Directed-Thinking Tasks: Cognitive and Affective Positivity Asymmetries," *Journal of Personality and Social Psychology,* June 1996, p 1124.

[16] S Begley, "Real Self-Esteem Builds on Achievement, Not Praise for Slackers," *The Wall Street Journal,* April 18, 2003, p B1.

[17] M E Gist, "Self-Efficacy: Implications for Organizational Behavior and Human Resource Management," *Academy of Management Review,* July 1987, p 472. Also see A Bandura, "Self-Efficacy:

Toward a Unifying Theory of Behavioral Change," *Psychological Review,* March 1977, pp 191–215; M E Gist and T R Mitchell, "Self-Efficacy: A Theoretical Analysis of Its Determinants and Malleability," *Academy of Management Review,* April 1992, pp 183–211; and T J Maurer and K D Andrews, "Traditional, Likert, and Simplified Measures of Self-Efficacy," *Educational and Psychological Measurement,* December 2000, pp 965–73.

[18] C Brennan, "Tiger Loses Favorite Driver," *USA Today,* May 4, 2006, p 3C.

[19] Based on D H Lindsley, D A Brass, and J B Thomas, "Efficacy-Performance Spirals: A Multilevel Perspective," *Academy of Management Review,* July 1995, pp 645–78.

[20] See, for example, V Gecas, "The Social Psychology of Self-Efficacy," in *Annual Review of Sociology,* ed W R Scott and J Blake (Palo Alto, CA: Annual Reviews, 1989), vol. 15, pp 291–316; C K Stevens, A G Bavetta, and M E Gist, "Gender Differences in the Acquisition of Salary Negotiation Skills: The Role of Goals, Self-Efficacy, and Perceived Control," *Journal of Applied Psychology,* October 1993, pp 723–35; and D Eden and Y Zuk, "Seasickness as a Self-Fulfilling Prophecy: Raising Self-Efficacy to Boost Performance at Sea," *Journal of Applied Psychology,* October 1995, pp 628–35.

[21] For more on learned helplessness, see Gecas, "The Social Psychology of Self-Efficacy"; M J Martinko and W L Gardner, "Learned Helplessness: An Alternative Explanation for Performance Deficits," *Academy of Management Review,* April 1982, pp 195–204; and C R Campbell and M J Martinko, "An Integrative Attributional Perspective of Empowerment and Learned Helplessness: A Multimethod Field Study," *Journal of Management,* no. 2, 1998, pp 173–200. Also see A Dickerson and M A Taylor, "Self-Limiting Behavior in Women: Self-Esteem and Self-Efficacy as Predictors," *Group and Organization Management,* June 2000, pp 191–210.

[22] For an update on Bandura, see D Smith, "The Theory Heard 'Round the World," *Monitor on Psychology,* October 2002, pp 30–32.

[23] Research on this connection is reported in R B Rubin, M M Martin, S S Bruning, and D E Powers, "Test of a Self-Efficacy Model of Interpersonal Communication Competence," *Communication Quarterly,* Spring 1993, pp 210–20.

[24] Excerpted from T Petzinger Jr, "Bob Schmonsees Has a Tool for Better Sales, and It Ignores Excuses," *The Wall Street Journal,* March 26, 1999, p B1.

[25] A D Stajkovic and F Luthans, "Self-Efficacy and Work-Related Performance: A Meta-Analysis," *Psychological Bulletin,* September 1998, pp 240–61.

[26] Based in part on discussion in Gecas, "The Social Psychology of Self-Efficacy."

[27] See S K Parker, "Enhancing Role Breadth Self-Efficacy: The Roles of Job Enrichment and Other Organizational Interventions," *Journal of Applied Psychology,* December 1998, pp 835–52.

[28] The positive relationship between self-efficacy and readiness for retraining is documented in L A Hill and J Elias, "Retraining Midcareer Managers: Career History and Self-Efficacy Beliefs," *Human Resource Management,* Summer 1990, pp 197–217. Also see A M Saks, "Longitudinal Field Investigation of the Moderating and Mediating Effects of Self-Efficacy on the Relationship between Training and Newcomer Adjustment," *Journal of Applied Psychology,* April 1995, pp 211–25.

[29] See A D Stajkovic and F Luthans, "Social Cognitive Theory and Self-Efficacy: Going beyond Traditional Motivational and Behavioral Approaches," *Organizational Dynamics,* Spring 1998, pp 62–74.

[30] See P C Earley and T R Lituchy, "Delineating Goal and Efficacy Effects: A Test of Three Models," *Journal of Applied Psychology,* February 1991, pp 81–98.

[31] See P Tierney and S M Farmer, "Creative Self-Efficacy: Its Potential Antecedents and Relationship to Creative Performance," *Academy of Management Journal,* December 2002, pp 1137–48.

[32] See W S Silver, T R Mitchell, and M E Gist, "Response to Successful and Unsuccessful Performance: The Moderating Effect of Self-Efficacy on the Relationship between Performance and Attributions," *Organizational Behavior and Human Decision Processes,* June 1995, pp 286–99; R Zemke, "The Corporate Coach," *Training,* December 1996, pp 24–28; and J P Masciarelli, "Less Lonely at the Top," *Management Review,* April 1999, pp 58–61.

[33] For a comprehensive update, see S W Gangestad and M Snyder, "Self-Monitoring: Appraisal and Reappraisal," *Psychological Bulletin,* July 2000, pp 530–55.

[34] M Snyder and S Gangestad, "On the Nature of Self-Monitoring: Matters of Assessment, Matters of Validity," *Journal of Personality and Social Psychology,* July 1986, p 125.

[35] M Kilduff and D V Day, "Do Chameleons Get Ahead? The Effects of Self-Monitoring on Managerial Careers," *Academy of Management Journal,* August 1994, pp 1047–60.

[36] D B Turban and T W Dougherty, "Role of Protege Personality in Receipt of Mentoring and Career Success," *Academy of Management Journal,* June 1994, pp 688–702.

[37] See F Luthans, "Successful vs. Effective Managers," *Academy of Management Executive,* May 1988, pp 127–32.

[38] See A Bandura, *Social Learning Theory* (Englewood Cliffs, NJ: Prentice Hall, 1977). A further refinement is reported in A D Stajkovic and F Luthans, "Social Cognitive Theory and Self-Efficacy: Going beyond Traditional Motivational and Behavioral Approaches," *Organizational Dynamics,* Spring 1998, pp 62–74.

[39] Bandura, *Social Learning Theory,* p 13.

[40] For related research, see M Castaneda, T A Kolenko, and R J Aldag, "Self-Management Perceptions and Practices: A Structural Equations Analysis," *Journal of Organizational Behavior,* January 1999, pp 101–20. An alternative model is discussed in K M Sheldon, D B Turban, K G Brown, M R Barrick, and T M Judge, "Applying Self-Determination Theory to Organizational Research," in *Research in Personnel and Human Resources Management* 22, ed J J Martocchio and G R Ferris (New York: Elsevier, 2003), pp 357–93.

[41] See L Nash and H Stevenson, "Success That Lasts," *Harvard Business Review,* February 2004, pp 102–09.

[42] S R Covey, *The 7 Habits of Highly Effective People* (New York: Simon & Schuster, 1989); S R Covey, *The 8th Habit: From Effectiveness to Greatness* (New York: Free Press, 2004); and S Covey, "Power to the People," *Training,* April 2006, p 64.

[43] "Labor Letter: A Special News Report on People and Their Jobs in Offices, Fields, and Factories," *The Wall Street Journal,* October 15, 1985, p 1.

[44] J Chatzky, "The 4 Steps to Setting Goals & 6 Keys to Achieving Them," *Money,* November 2003, pp 111, 113.

[45] R McGarvey, "Rehearsing for Success," *Executive Female,* January/February 1990, p 36.

[46] See W P Anthony, R H Bennett, III, E N Maddox, and W J Wheatley, "Picturing the Future: Using Mental Imagery to Enrich Strategic Environmental Assessment," *Academy of Management Executive,* May 1993, pp 43–56.

[47] For excellent tips on self-management, see C P Neck, "Managing Your Mind," *Internal Auditor,* June 1996, pp 60–63.

[48] C Zastrow, *Talk to Yourself: Using the Power of Self-Talk* (Englewood Cliffs, NJ: Prentice Hall, 1979), p 60. Also see C C Manz and C P Neck, "Inner Leadership: Creating Productive Thought Patterns," *Academy of Management Executive,* August 1991, pp 87–95; C P Neck and R F Ashcraft, "Inner Leadership: Mental Strategies for Nonprofit Staff Members," *Nonprofit World,* May/June 2000, pp 27–30; and T C Brown, "The Effect of Verbal Self-Guidance Training on Collective Efficacy and Team Performance," *Personnel Psychology,* Winter 2003, pp 935–64.

[49] E Franz, "Private Pep Talk," *Selling Power,* May 1996, p 81.

[50] Drawn from A Bandura, "Self-Reinforcement: Theoretical and Methodological Considerations," *Behaviorism,* Fall 1976, pp 135–55.

[51] R Kreitner and F Luthans, "A Social Learning Approach to Behavioral Management: Radical Behaviorists 'Mellowing Out,'" *Organizational Dynamics,* Autumn 1984, p 63.

[52] See K Painter, "We Are Who We Are, or Are We?" *USA Today,* October 3, 2002, p 9; S Begley, "In the Brave Guppy and Hyper Octopus, Clues to Personality," *The Wall Street Journal,* October 10, 2003, p B1; and S Kuchinskas, "A Match Made in Hormones," *Business 2.0,* January/February 2006, p 24.

[53] The landmark report is J M Digman, "Personality Structure: Emergence of the Five-Factor Model," *Annual Review of Psychology* 41 (1990), pp 417–40. See also M K Mount, M R Barrick, S M Scullen, and J Rounds, "Higher-Order Dimensions of the Big Five Personality Traits and the Big Six Vocational Interest Types," *Personnel Psychology,* Summer 2005, pp 447–78; P Warr, D Bartram, and A Brown, "Big Five Validity: Aggregation Method Matters," *Journal of Occupational and Organizational Psychology,* September 2005, pp 377–86; and A B Bakker, K I Van Der Zee, K A Lewig, and M F Dollard, "The Relationship between the Big Five Personality Factors and Burnout: A Study among Volunteer Counselors," *Journal of Social Psychology,* February 2006, pp 31–50.

[54] For more on personality measurement and assessment, see P Barrett, "What if There Were No Psychometrics? Constructs, Complexity, and Measurement," *Journal of Personality Assessment,* October 2005, pp 134–40; S Stark, O S Chernyshenko, F Drasgow, and B A Williams, "Examining Assumptions about Item Responding in Personality Assessment: Should Ideal Point Methods Be Considered for Scale Development and Scoring?" *Journal of Applied Psychology,* January 2006, pp 25–39; and J R Matthews and L H Matthews, "Personality Assessment Training: View from a Licensing Board," *Journal of Personality Assessment,* February 2006, pp 46–50.

[55] S V Paunonen et al., "The Structure of Personality in Six Cultures," *Journal of Cross-Cultural Psychology,* May 1996, pp 339–53. Also see C Ward, C Leong, and M Low, "Personality and Sojourner Adjustment: An Exploration of the Big Five and the Cultural Fit Proposition," *Journal of Cross-Cultural Psychology,* March 2004, pp 137–51.

[56] J Allik and R R McCrae, "Toward a Geography of Personality Traits: Patterns of Profiles across 36 Cultures," *Journal of Cross-Cultural Psychology,* January 2004, p 13.

[57] See M R Barrick and M K Mount, "The Big Five Personality Dimensions and Job Performance: A Meta-Analysis," *Personnel Psychology,* Spring 1991, pp 1–26. See also J E Kurtz and S B Tiegreen, "Matters of Conscience and Conscientiousness: The Place of Ego Development in the Five-Factor Model," *Journal of Personality Assessment,* December 2005, pp 312–17; and N M Dudley, K A Orvis, J E Lebiecki, and J M Cortina, "A Meta-Analytic Investigation of Conscientiousness in the Prediction of Job Performance: Examining the Intercorrelations and the Incremental Validity of Narrow Traits," *Journal of Applied Psychology,* January 2006, pp 40–57.

[58] Barrick and Mount, "The Big Five Personality Dimensions," p 21.

[59] L A Witt and G R Ferris, "Social Skill as Moderator of the Conscientiousness-Performance Relationship: Convergent Results across Four Studies," *Journal of Applied Psychology,* October 2003, pp 809–20. See also H Liao and A Chuang, "A Multilevel Investigation of Factors Influencing Employee Service Performance and Customer Outcomes," *Academy of Management Journal,* February 2004, pp 41–58.

[60] Lead researcher William Fleeson, quoted in M Dittmann, "Acting Extraverted Spurs Positive Feelings, Study Finds," *Monitor on Psychology,* April 2003, p 17.

[61] J M Crant, "Proactive Behavior in Organizations," *Journal of Management,* no. 3, 2000, p 439.

[62] Ibid., pp 439–41.

[63] E Schonfeld, "Five Ways to Start a Company (without Quitting Your Day Job)," *Business 2.0,* May 2006, p 44.

[64] See S B Gustafson and M D Mumford, "Personal Style and Person-Environment Fit: A Pattern Approach," *Journal of Vocational Behavior,* April 1995, pp 163–88.

[65] For an instructive update, see J B Rotter, "Internal versus External Control of Reinforcement: A Case History of a Variable," *American Psychologist,* April 1990, pp 489–93. A critical review of locus of control and a call for a meta-analysis can be found in R W Renn and R J Vandenberg, "Differences in Employee Attitudes and Behaviors Based on Rotter's (1966) Internal-External Locus of Control: Are They All Valid?" *Human Relations,* November 1991, pp 1161–77.

[66] For an overall review of research on locus of control, see P E Spector, "Behavior in Organizations as a Function of Employee's Locus of Control," *Psychological Bulletin,* May 1982, pp 482–97. The relationship between locus of control and performance and satisfaction is examined in D R Norris and R E Niebuhr, "Attributional Influences on the Job Performance–Job Satisfaction Relationship," *Academy of Management Journal,* June 1984, pp 424–31. Salary differences between internals and externals were examined by P C Nystrom, "Managers' Salaries and Their Beliefs about Reinforcement Control," *Journal of Social Psychology,* August 1983, pp 291–92.

[67] S R Hawk, "Locus of Control and Computer Attitude: The Effect of User Involvement," *Computers in Human Behavior,* no. 3, 1989, pp 199–206. Also see A S Phillips and A G Bedeian, "Leader-Follower Exchange Quality: The Role of Personal and Interpersonal Attributes," *Academy of Management Journal,* August 1994, pp 990–1001.

[68] These recommendations are from Spector, "Behavior in Organizations as a Function."

[69] M Fishbein and I Ajzen, *Belief, Attitude, Intention and Behavior: An Introduction to Theory and Research* (Reading, MA: Addison-Wesley, 1975), p 6. For more, see D Andrich and I M Styles, "The Structural Relationship between Attitude and Behavior Statements from the Unfolding Perspective," *Psychological Methods,* December 1998, pp 454–69; A P Brief, *Attitudes in and around Organizations* (Thousand Oaks, CA: Sage Publications, 1998); and "Tips to Pick the Best Employee," *BusinessWeek,* March 1, 1999, p 24.

[70] B M Staw and J Ross, "Stability in the Midst of Change: A Dispositional Approach to Job Attitudes," *Journal of Applied Psychology,* August 1985, pp 469–80.

[71] P S Visser and J A Krosnick, "Development of Attitude Strength over the Life Cycle: Surge and Decline," *Journal of Personality and Social Psychology,* December 1998, pp 1389–1410.

[72] For interesting reading on intelligence, see J R Flynn, "Searching for Justice: The Discovery of IQ Gains over Time," *American Psychologist,* January 1999, pp 5–20; and E Benson, "Intelligent Intelligence Testing," *Monitor on Psychology,* February 2003, pp 48–54.

[73] For an excellent update on intelligence, including definitional distinctions and a historical perspective of the IQ controversy, see R A Weinberg, "Intelligence and IQ," *American Psychologist,* February 1989, pp 98–104. Genetics and intelligence are discussed in R Plomin and F M Spinath, "Intelligence: Genetics, Genes, and Genomics," *Journal of Personality and Social Psychology,* January 2004, pp 112–29.

[74] Ibid. See also M Elias, "Mom's IQ, Not Family Size, Key to Kids' Smarts," *USA Today,* June 12, 2000, p 1D; and R Sapolsky, "Score One for Nature—or Is It Nurture?" *USA Today,* June 21, 2000, p 17A.

[75] S L Wilk, L Burris Desmarais, and P R Sackett, "Gravitation to Jobs Commensurate with Ability: Longitudinal and Cross-Sectional Tests," *Journal of Applied Psychology,* February 1995, p 79.

[76] B Azar, "People Are Becoming Smarter—Why?" *APA Monitor,* June 1996, p 20. Also see "'Average' Intelligence Higher than It Used to Be," *USA Today,* February 18, 1997, p 6D.

[77] See F L Schmidt and J E Hunter, "Employment Testing: Old Theories and New Research Findings," *American Psychologist,* October 1981, p 1128; and N R Kuncel, S A Hezlett, and D S Ones, "Academic Performance, Career Potential, Creativity, and Job Performance: Can One Construct Predict Them All?" *Journal of Personality and Social Psychology,* January 2004, pp 148–61. A brief overview of the foregoing study can be found in M Greer, "General Cognition Also Makes the Difference on the Job, Study Finds," *Monitor on Psychology,* April 2004, p 12. See also F L Schmidt and J Hunter, "General Mental Ability in the World of Work: Occupational Attainment and Job Performance," *Journal of Personality and Social Psychology,* January 2004, pp 162–73; and R L Cardy and T T Selvarajan, "Competencies: Alternative Frameworks for Competitive Advantage," *Business Horizons,* May/June 2006, pp 235–45.

[78] A Reinhardt, "I've Left a Few Dead Bodies," *BusinessWeek,* January 31, 2000, p 69.

[79] D Lieberman, "Fear of Failing Drives Diller," *USA Today,* February 10, 1999, p 3B.

[80] R S Lazarus, *Emotion and Adaptation* (New York: Oxford University Press, 1991), p 6. Also see J A Russell and L F Barrett, "Core Affect, Prototypical Emotional Episodes, and Other Things Called *Emotion:* Dissecting the Elephant," *Journal of Personality and Social Psychology*, May 1999, pp 805–19; S Fineman, *Understanding Emotion at Work* (Thousand Oaks, CA: Sage, 2003); and D DeSteno, R E Petty, D D Rucker, D T Wegener, and J Braverman, "Discrete Emotions and Persuasion: The Role of Emotion-Induced Expectancies," *Journal of Personality and Social Psychology,* January 2004, pp 43–56.

[81] Based on discussion in R D Arvey, G L Renz, and T W Watson, "Emotionality and Job Performance: Implications for Personnel Selection," in *Research in Personnel and Human Resources Management* 16, ed G R Ferris (Stamford, CT: JAI Press, 1998), pp 103–47. Also see L A King, "Ambivalence over Emotional Expression and Reading Emotions," *Journal of Personality and Social Psychology,* March 1998, pp 753–62; and J L Tsai and Y Chentsova-Dutton, "Variation among European Americans in Emotional Facial Expression," *Journal of Cross-Cultural Psychology,* November 2003, pp 650–57.

[82] S D Pugh, "Service with a Smile: Emotional Contagion in the Service Encounter," *Academy of Management Journal,* October 2001, pp 1018–27.

[83] P Totterdell, S Kellett, K Teuchmann, and R B Briner, "Evidence of Mood Linkage in Work Groups," *Journal of Personality and Social Psychology,* June 1998, pp 1504–15. Also see C D Fisher, "Mood and Emotions while Working: Missing Pieces of Job Satisfaction," *Journal of Organizational Behavior,* March 2000, pp 185–202; K M Lewis, "When Leaders Display Emotion: How Followers Respond to Negative Emotional Expression of Male and Female Leaders," *Journal of Organizational Behavior,* March 2000, pp 221–34; and A Singh-Manoux and C Finkenauer, "Cultural Variations in Social Sharing of Emotions: An Intercultural Perspective," *Journal of Cross-Cultural Psychology,* November 2001, pp 647–61.

[84] Quoted in D Jones, "Music Director Works to Blend Strengths," *USA Today,* October 27, 2003, p 6B.

[85] N M Ashkanasy and C S Daus, "Emotion in the Workplace: The New Challenge for Managers," *Academy of Management Executive,* February 2002, p 79. See also A A Grandey, "When 'The Show Must Go On': Surface Acting and Deep Acting as Determinants of Emotional Exhaustion and Peer-Rated Service Delivery," *Academy of Management Journal,* February 2003, pp 86–96; C M Brotheridge and R T Lee, "Development and Validation of the Emotional Labour Scale," *Journal of Occupational and Organizational Psychology,* September 2003, pp 365–79; Y Guerrier and A Adib, "Work at Leisure and Leisure at Work: A Study of the Emotional Labour of Tour Reps," *Human Relations,* November 2003, pp 1399–1417; A A Grandey, G M Fisk, and D D Steiner, "Must 'Service with a Smile' Be Stressful? The Moderating Role of Personal Control for American and French Employees," *Journal of Applied Psychology,* September 2005, pp 893–904; R H Gosserand and J M Diefendorff, "Emotional Display Rules and Emotional Labor:

The Moderating Role of Commitment," *Journal of Applied Psychology,* November 2005, pp 1256–64; and P O'Connell, "Taking the Measure of Mood," *Harvard Business Review,* March 2006, pp 25–26.

[86] A M Kring and A H Gordon, "Sex Differences in Emotions: Expression, Experience, and Physiology," *Journal of Personality and Social Psychology,* March 1998, pp 686–703.

[87] D Goleman, *Emotional Intelligence* (New York: Bantam Books, 1995), p 34. For more, see M Dittmann, "How 'Emotional Intelligence' Emerged," *Monitor on Psychology,* October 2003, p 64; I Goldenberg, K Matheson, and J Mantler, "The Assessment of Emotional Intelligence: A Comparison of Performance-Based and Self-Report Methodologies," *Journal of Personality Assessment,* February 2006, pp 33–45; and J E Barbuto Jr. and M E Burbach, "The Emotional Intelligence of Transformational Leaders: A Field Study of Elected Officials," *Journal of Social Psychology,* February 2006, pp 51–64.

[88] See the box titled "Get Happy Carefully" on p 49 of D Goleman, R Boyatzis, and A McKee, "Primal Leadership: The Hidden Driver of Great Performance," *Harvard Business Review,* Special Issue: Breakthrough Leadership, December 2001, pp 43–51.

[89] M N Martinez, "The Smarts That Count," *HR Magazine,* November 1997, pp 72–78.

[90] "What's Your EQ at Work?" *Fortune,* October 26, 1998, p 298.

[91] M Davies, L Stankov, and R D Roberts, "Emotional Intelligence: In Search of an Elusive Construct," *Journal of Personality and Social Psychology,* October 1998, pp 989–1015; and K A Barchard, "Does Emotional Intelligence Assist in the Prediction of Academic Success?" *Educational and Psychological Measurement,* October 2003, pp 840–58. See also B P Chapman and B Hayslip Jr, "Incremental Validity of a Measure of Emotional Intelligence," *Journal of Personality Assessment,* October 2005, pp 154–69.

[92] A Fisher, "Success Secret: A High Emotional IQ," *Fortune,* October 26, 1998, p 294. See also D Goleman, "Never Stop Learning," *Harvard Business Review,* Special Issue: Inside the Mind of the Leader, January 2004, pp 28–29.

Chapter 4

[1] T R Mitchell, "Motivation: New Direction for Theory, Research, and Practice," *Academy of Management Review,* January 1982, p 81.

[2] A review of content and process theories of motivation is provided by R M Steers, R T Mowday, and D L Shapiro, "The Future of Work Motivation Theory," *Academy of Management Review,* July 2004, pp 379–87.

[3] For a complete description of Maslow's theory, see A H Maslow, "A Theory of Human Motivation," *Psychological Review,* July 1943, pp 370–96.

[4] P Babcock, "Find What Workers Want," *HR Magazine,* April 2005, pp 53–54.

[5] For a complete review of ERG theory, see C P Alderfer, *Existence, Relatedness, and Growth: Human Needs in Organizational Settings* (New York: Free Press, 1972).

[6] Ibid.; and J P Wanous and A Zwany, "A Cross-Sectional Test of Need Hierarchy Theory," *Organizational Behavior and Human Performance,* February 1977, pp 78–97.

[7] See S Glazer, "Past, Present and Future of Cross-Cultural Studies in Industrial and Organizational Psychology," in *International Review of Industrial and Organizational Psychology* 17, ed C L Cooper and I T Robertson (West Sussex, England: Wiley, 2002), pp 145–86.

[8] L Buchanan, "Managing One-to-One," *Inc.,* October 2001, p 87.

[9] H A Murray, *Exploration in Personality* (New York: Wiley, 1938), p 164.

[10] K G Shaver, "The Entrepreneurial Personality Myth," *Business and Economic Review,* April/June 1995, pp 20–23.

[11] See "Can't We All Just Get Along?" *HR Magazine,* April 2005, p 16.

[12] See D K McNeese-Smith, "The Relationship between Managerial Motivation, Leadership, Nurse Outcomes and Patient Satisfaction," *Journal of Organizational Behavior,* March 1999, pp 243–59; A M Harrell and M J Stahl, "A Behavioral Decision Theory Approach for Measuring McClelland's

Trichotomy of Needs," *Journal of Applied Psychology,* April 1981, pp 242–47; and M J Stahl, "Achievement, Power and Managerial Motivation: Selecting Managerial Talent with the Job Choice Exercise," *Personnel Psychology,* Winter 1983, pp 775–89.

[13] For a review of the foundation of achievement motivation training, see D C McClelland, "Toward a Theory of Motive Acquisition," *American Psychologist,* May 1965, pp 321–33. Evidence for the validity of motivation training can be found in H Heckhausen and S Krug, "Motive Modification," in *Motivation and Society,* ed A J Stewart (San Francisco: Jossey-Bass, 1982). See also S Hamm, "A Red Flag in the Brain Game," *BusinessWeek,* May 1, 2006, pp 32–35.

[14] D B Turban and T L Keon, "Organizational Attractiveness: An Interactionist Perspective," *Journal of Applied Psychology,* April 1993, pp 184–93.

[15] D Steele Johnson and R Perlow, "The Impact of Need for Achievement Components on Goal Commitment and Performance," *Journal of Applied Social Psychology,* November 1992, pp 1711–20; and R Eisenberger, J R Jones, F Stinglhamber, L Shanock, and A T Randall, "Flow Experiences at Work: For High Need Achievers Alone?" *Journal of Organizational Behavior,* November 2005, pp 755–75.

[16] F Herzberg, B Mausner, and B B Snyderman, *The Motivation to Work* (New York: Wiley, 1959).

[17] For an application, see D Lacy, "Recordkeeping, Social Security, Recognition," *HR Magazine,* March 2005, pp 43–44.

[18] M Conlin and A Bernstein, "Working . . . and Poor," *BusinessWeek,* May 31, 2004, p 60.

[19] F Herzberg, "One More Time: How Do You Motivate Employees?" *Harvard Business Review,* January/February 1968, p 56.

[20] See C C Pinder, *Work Motivation: Theory, Issues, and Applications* (Glenview, IL: Scott, Foresman, 1984).

[21] P Babcock, "Find What Workers Want," *HR Magazine,* April 2005, pp 51–56.

[22] L K Scheer, N A Kumar, J-B E M Steenkamp, "Reactions to Perceived Inequity in US and Dutch Interorganizational Relationships," *Academy of Management Journal,* June 2003, pp 303–16.

[23] E E Umphress, G Labianca, D J Brass, E Kass, and L Scholten, "The Role of Instrumental and Express Social Ties in Employees' Perceptions of Organizational Justice," *Organization Science,* November/December 2003, pp 738–53.

[24] M N Bing and S M Burroughs, "The Predictive and Interactive Effects of Equity Sensitivity in Teamwork-Oriented Organizations," *Journal of Organizational Behavior,* May 2001, p 271.

[25] Ibid., pp 271–90; and K S Sauley and A G Bedeian, "Equity Sensitivity: Construction of a Measure and Examination of Its Psychometric Properties," *Journal of Management,* 2000, pp 885–910.

[26] D Brady, "Executive Pay: No Hair Shirts, but Still . . . ," *BusinessWeek,* May 1, 2006, p 36.

[27] For a thorough review of organizational justice theory and research, see R Cropanzano, D E Rupp, C J Mohler, and M Schminke, "Three Roads to Organizational Justice," in *Research in Personnel and Human Resources Management* 20, ed G R Ferris (New York: JAI Press, 2001), pp 269–329.

[28] J A Colquitt, D E Conlon, M J Wesson, C O L H Porter, and K Y Ng, "Justice at the Millennium: A Meta-Analytic Review of 25 Years of Organizational Justice Research," *Journal of Applied Psychology,* June 2001, p 426.

[29] Y Cohen-Charash and P E Spector, "The Role of Justice in Organizations: A Meta-Analysis," *Organizational Behavior and Human Decision Processes,* November 2001, pp 278–321; and Colquitt et al., "Justice at the Millennium."

[30] For recent studies that support the impact of justice on employee attitudes and behaviors, see A G Tekleab, R Takeuchi, and M S Taylor, "Extending the Chain of Relationships among Organizational Justice, Social Exchange, and Employee Reactions: The Role of Contract Violations," *Academy of Management Journal,* February 2005, pp 146–57; D D Cremer, B van Knippenberg, D van Knippenberg, D Mullenders, and F Stinglhamber, "Rewarding Leadership and Fair Procedures as Determinants of Self-Esteem," *Journal of Applied Psychology,* January 2005, pp 3–12; P A Siegel, C Post, J Brockner, A Y Fishman, and C Garden, "The Moderating Influence of Procedural Fairness on the Relationship between Work-Life Conflict and Organizational

Commitment," *Journal of Applied Psychology,* January 2005, pp 13–24; and T A Judge and J A Colquitt, "Organizational Justice and Stress: The Mediating Role of Work/Family Conflict," *Journal of Applied Psychology,* June 2004, pp 395–404.

[31] R C Ford, "Darden Restaurants CEO Joe Lee on the Impact of Core Values: Integrity and Fairness," *Academy of Management Executive,* February 2002, p 35.

[32] The impact of groups on justice perceptions was investigated by D A Jones and D P Skarlicki, "The Effects of Overhearing Peers to Discuss an Authority's Fairness Reputation on Reactions to Subsequent Treatment," *Journal of Applied Psychology,* March 2005, pp 363–72; and J A Colquitt, "Does the Justice of the One Interact with the Justice of the Many? Reactions to Procedural Justice in Teams," *Journal of Applied Psychology,* August 2004, pp 633–46.

[33] K Mollica, "Perceptions of Fairness," *HR Magazine,* June 2004, pp 169–78.

[34] D R Avery and M A Quiñones, "Disentangling the Effects of Voice: The Incremental Roles of Opportunity, Behavior, and Instrumentality in Predicting Procedural Fairness," *Journal of Applied Psychology,* February 2002, pp 81–86.

[35] D P Skarlicki, R Folger, and P Tesluk, "Personality as a Moderator in the Relationship between Fairness and Retaliation," *Academy of Management Journal,* February 1999, pp 100–08.

[36] H Liao and D E Rupp, "The Impact of Justice Climate and Justice Orientation on Work Outcomes: A Cross-Level Multifoci Framework," *Journal of Applied Psychology,* March 2005, pp 242–56.

[37] D E Bowen, S W Gilliland, and R Folger, "HRM Service Fairness: How Being Fair with Employees Spills over to Customers," *Organizational Dynamics,* Winter 1999, pp 7–23.

[38] V H Vroom, *Work and Motivation* (New York: Wiley, 1964).

[39] See J Chowdhury, "The Motivational Impact of Sales Quotas on Effort," *Journal of Marketing Research,* February 1993, pp 28–41; and C C Pinder, *Work Motivation* (Glenview, IL: Scott, Foresman, 1984), Ch. 7.

[40] The measurement and importance of valence were investigated by N T Feather, "Values, Valences, and Choice: The Influence of Values on the Perceived Attractiveness and Choice of Alternatives," *Journal of Personality and Social Psychology,* June 1995, pp 1135–51; and A Pecotich and G A Churchill Jr, "An Examination of the Anticipated-Satisfaction Importance Valence Controversy," *Organizational Behavior and Human Performance,* April 1981, pp 213–26.

[41] "Federal Express's Fred Smith," *Inc.,* October 1986, p 38.

[42] W van Eerde and H Thierry, "Vroom's Expectancy Models and Work-Related Criteria: A Meta-Analysis," *Journal of Applied Psychology,* October 1996, pp 575–86.

[43] See J P Wanous, T L Keon, and J C Latack, "Expectancy Theory and Occupational/ Organizational Choices: A Review and Test," *Organizational Behavior and Human Performance,* August 1983, pp 66–86.

[44] T R Mitchell and D Daniels, "Motivation," in *Handbook of Psychology* 12, ed W C Borman, D R Ilgen, and R J Klimoski (Hoboken, NJ: Wiley, 2003), pp 225–54.

[45] E A Locke, K N Shaw, L M Saari, and G P Latham, "Goal Setting and Task Performance: 1969–1980," *Psychological Bulletin,* July 1981, p 126.

[46] A Barrett, "Cracking the Whip at Wyeth," *BusinessWeek,* February 6, 2006, pp 70–71.

[47] P M Wright, "Operationalization of Goal Difficulty as a Moderator of the Goal Difficulty–Performance Relationship," *Journal of Applied Psychology,* June 1990, pp 227–34. See also G Seijts and G P Latham, "Learning versus Performance Goals: When Should Each Be Used?" *Academy of Management Executive,* February 2005, pp 124–31.

[48] R E Wood, A J Mento, and E A Locke, "Task Complexity as a Moderator of Goal Effects: A Meta-Analysis," *Journal of Applied Psychology,* August 1987, pp 416–25.

[49] Supportive results can be found in K L Langeland, C M Johnson, and T C Mawhinney, "Improving Staff Performance in a Community Mental Health Setting: Job Analysis, Training, Goal Setting, Feedback, and

Years of Data," *Journal of Organizational Behavior Management,* 1998, pp 21–43.

[50] See E A Locke and G P Latham, *A Theory of Goal Setting and Task Performance* (Englewood Cliffs, NJ: Prentice Hall, 1990).

[51] J J Donovan and D J Radosevich, "The Moderating Role of Goal Commitment on the Goal Difficulty-Performance Relationship: A Meta-Analytic Review and Critical Reanalysis," *Journal of Applied Psychology,* April 1998, pp 308–15.

[52] G H Seijts and G P Latham, "The Effect of Distal Learning, Outcome, and Proximal Goals on a Moderately Complex Task," *Journal of Organizational Behavior,* May 2001, pp 291–307.

[53] J L Bowditch and A F Buono, *A Primer on Organizational Behavior* (New York: Wiley, 1985), p 210.

[54] M A Campion and P W Thayer, "Development and Field Evaluation of an Interdisciplinary Measure of Job Design," *Journal of Applied Psychology,* February 1985, pp 29–43.

[55] These outcomes are discussed by J R Edwards, J A Scully, and M D Brtek, "The Nature and Outcomes of Work: A Replication and Extension of Interdisciplinary Work-Design Research," *Journal of Applied Psychology,* December 2000, pp 860–68.

[56] G D Babcock, *The Taylor System in Franklin Management,* 2nd ed (New York: Engineering Magazine Co., 1917), p 31.

[57] See F B Copley, *Frederick W Taylor: The Principles of Scientific Management* (New York: Harper & Brothers, 1911).

[58] For supporting research, see B Melin, U Lundberg, J Söderlund, and M Granqvist, "Psychological and Physiological Stress Reactions of Male and Female Assembly Workers: A Comparison between Two Different Forms of Work Organization," *Journal of Organizational Behavior,* January 1999, pp 47–61.

[59] For an example, see M Workman and W Bommer, "Redesigning Computer Call Center Work: A Longitudinal Field Experiment," *Journal of Organizational Behavior,* May 2004, pp 317–37.

[60] This type of program was developed and tested by M A Campion and C L McClelland, "Follow-Up and Extension of the Interdisciplinary Costs and Benefits of Enlarged Jobs," *Journal of Applied Psychology,* June 1993, pp 339–51.

[61] R J Grossman, "Putting HR in Rotation," *HR Magazine,* March 2003, p 53. See also G Colvin, "What Makes GE Great?" *Fortune,* March 6, 2006, http://moneycnn.com/magazines/fortune.

[62] J R Hackman, G R Oldham, R Janson, and K Purdy, "A New Strategy for Job Enrichment," *California Management Review,* Summer 1975, p 58.

[63] For a review of this research, see M L Ambrose and C T Kulik, "Old Friends, New Faces: Motivation Research in the 1990s," *Journal of Management,* 1999, pp 231–92.

[64] R Levering and M Moskowitz, "The 100 Best Companies to Work For: And the Winners Are . . . ," *Fortune,* January 23, 2006, pp 100, 106.

[65] F P Morgeson, K Delaney-Klinger, and M A Hemingway, "The Importance of Job Autonomy, Cognitive Ability, and Job-Related Skill for Predicting Role Breadth and Job Performance," *Journal of Applied Psychology,* March 2005, pp 399–406; and C W Langfred and N A Moye, "Effects of Task Autonomy on Performance: An Extended Model Considering Motivational, Informational, and Structural Mechanisms," *Journal of Applied Psychology,* December 2004, pp 934–45.

[66] M R Kelley, "New Process Technology, Job Design, and Work Organization: A Contingency Model," *American Sociological Review,* April 1990, pp 191–208.

[67] See S Sonnentag and F R H Zijlstra, "Job Characteristics and Off-Job Activities as Predictors of Need for Recovery, Well-Being, and Fatigue," *Journal of Applied Psychology,* March 2006, pp 330–50; and D Moyer, "Best with Rest," *Harvard Business Review,* March 2006, p 152.

[68] R E Kopelman, *Managing Productivity in Organizations* (New York: McGraw-Hill, 1986).

[69] R W Griffeth, P W Hom, and S Gaertner, "A Meta-Analysis of Antecedents and Correlates of Employee Turnover: Update, Moderator Tests, and Research Implications for the Next Millennium," *Journal of Management,* 2000, pp 463–88; and Y Fried and G R Ferris, "The Validity of the Job Characteristics Model: A Review and Meta-Analysis," *Personnel Psychology,* Summer 1987, pp 287–322.

[70] K Dobbs, "Knowing How to Keep Your Best and Brightest," *Workforce,* April 2001, pp 557–60.

[71] This description is taken from Edwards, Scully, and Brtek, "The Nature and Outcomes of Work."

[72] S Armour, "Young Tech Workers Face Crippling Injuries," *USA Today,* February 9, 2001, p 2B.

[73] See R Malkin, S D Hudock, C Hayden, T J Lentz, J Topmiller, and R W Niemeier, "An Assessment of Occupational Safety and Health Hazards in Selected Small Businesses Manufacturing Wood Pallets— Part 1, Noise and Physical Hazards," *Journal of Occupational and Environmental Hygiene,* April 2005, pp D18–D21.

[74] Bureau of Labor Statistics, "Repetitive Motion Results in Longest Work Absences," *Monthly Labor Review: The Editor's Desk,* http://www.bls.gov/ opub/ted/2004/mar/wk5/art02.htm, last updated March 30, 2005; "NINDS Repetitive Motion Disorders Information Page," http://www.ninds.nih. gov/disorders/repetitive-motion.htm, last updated February 7, 2006.

[75] T R Mitchell, "Motivation: New Directions for Theory, Research, and Practice," *Academy of Management Review,* January 1982, p 81.

[76] See, for example, "Contented Employees Mean Satisfied Customers at Baptist Health Care," *Training,* January 2005, p 11.

[77] D Patrick, "Summitt Still Driven to Be Best," *USA Today,* March 15, 2005, p 2C.

Chapter 5

[1] L Buchanan, "For Knowing the Power of Respect," *Inc.,* April 2004, p 143.

[2] G P Latham, J Almost, S Mann, and C Moore, "New Developments in Performance Management," *Organizational Dynamics* 1 (2005), pp 77–87; G Johnson, "Room for Improvement," *Training,* December 2003, pp 18–19; P Falcone, "Watch What You Write," *HR Magazine,* November 2004, pp 125–28; and K Ellis, "Individual Development Plans: The Building Blocks of Development," *Training,* December 2004, pp 20–25. See also D Zielinski, "Best and Brightest," *Training,* January 2006, pp 11–16.

[3] See E E Lawler III, *Treat People Right: How Organizations and Individuals Can Propel Each Other into a Virtuous Spiral of Success* (San Francisco: Jossey-Bass, 2003); A Rossett and E Mohr, "Performance Support Tools: Where Learning, Work, and Results Converge," *Training & Development,* February 2004, pp 24–39; L A Weatherly, "Performance Management: Getting It Right from the Start," 2004 Research Quarterly, *HR Magazine,* October 2004, pp 86–94; and A Kleingeld, H Van Tuijl, and J A Algera, "Participation in the Design of Performance Management Systems: A Quasi-Experimental Field Study," *Journal of Organizational Behavior,* November 2004, pp 831–51.

[4] "Coming Up Short? Join the Club," *Training,* April 2006, p 14.

[5] G H Seijts and G P Latham, "Learning versus Performance Goals: When Should Each Be Used?" *Academy of Management Executive,* February 2005, pp 126–27.

[6] A thorough discussion of MBO appears in P F Drucker, *The Practice of Management* (New York: Harper, 1954); and P F Drucker, "What Results Should You Expect? A User's Guide to MBO," *Public Administration Review,* January/February 1976, pp 12–19.

[7] See R Rodgers and J E Hunter, "Impact of Management by Objectives on Organizational Productivity," *Journal of Applied Psychology,* April 1991, pp 322–36; and R Rodgers, J E Hunter, and D L Rogers, "Influence of Top Management Commitment on Management Program Success," *Journal of Applied Psychology,* February 1993, pp 151–55.

[8] C L Porath and T S Bateman, "Self-Regulation: From Goal Orientation to Job Performance," *Journal of Applied Psychology,* January 2006, pp 185–86.

[9] Ibid., pp 185–92; Y Gong and J Fan, "Longitudinal Examination of the Role of Goal Orientation in Cross-Cultural Adjustment," *Journal of Applied Psychology,* January 2006, pp 176–84; and R P Deshon and J Z Gillespie, "A Motivated Action Theory Account of Goal Orientation," *Journal of Applied Psychology,* November 2005, pp 1096–127.

[10] See S Kerr and S Landauer, "Using Stretch Goals to Promote Organizational Effectiveness and Personal Growth: General Electric and Goldman

Sachs," *Academy of Management Executive,* November 2004, pp 134–38.

[11] See E A Locke, "Linking Goals to Monetary Incentives," *Academy of Management Executive,* November 2004, pp 130–33.

[12] For more on goal setting, see G B Yeo and A Neal, "A Multilevel Analysis of Effort, Practice, and Performance: Effects of Ability, Conscientiousness, and Goal Orientation," *Journal of Applied Psychology,* April 2004, pp 231–47; E A Locke, "Guest Editor's Introduction: Goal-Setting Theory and Its Applications to the World of Business," *Academy of Management Executive,* November 2004, pp 124–25; G P Latham, "The Motivational Benefits of Goal-Setting," *Academy of Management Executive,* November 2004, pp 126–29; K N Shaw, "Changing the Goal-Setting Process at Microsoft," *Academy of Management Executive,* November 2004, pp 139–42; and D C Kayes, "The Destructive Pursuit of Idealized Goals," *Organizational Dynamics,* November 2005, pp 391–401.

[13] Cited in K Tyler, "One Bad Apple," *HR Magazine,* December 2004, p 85.

[14] C O Longenecker and D A Gioia, "The Executive Appraisal Paradox," *Academy of Management Executive,* May 1992, p 18.

[15] C Bell and R Zemke, "On-Target Feedback," *Training,* June 1992, p 36. See also R Zemke, "The Feather Factor: You Gotta Believe," *Training,* May 2002, p 10.

[16] A Rossett and G Marino, "If Coaching Is Good, Then E-Coaching Is . . . ," *Training and Development,* November 2005, pp 46–53.

[17] The definition of feedback and functions of feedback are based on discussion in D R Ilgen, C D Fisher, and M S Taylor, "Consequences of Individual Feedback on Behavior in Organizations," *Journal of Applied Psychology,* August 1979, pp 349–71; and R E Kopelman, *Managing Productivity in Organizations: A Practical People-Oriented Perspective* (New York: McGraw-Hill, 1986), p 175.

[18] See P C Earley, G B Northcraft, C Lee, and T R Lituchy, "Impact of Process and Outcome Feedback on the Relation of Goal Setting to Task Performance," *Academy of Management Journal,* March 1990, pp 87–105. See also D VandeWalle, W L

Cron, and J W Slocum Jr, "The Role of Goal Orientation following Performance Feedback," *Journal of Applied Psychology,* August 2001, pp 629–40; J S Goodman, R E Wood, and M Hendrickx, "Feedback Specificity, Exploration, and Learning," *Journal of Applied Psychology,* April 2004, pp 248–62; and J S Goodman and R E Wood, "Feedback Specificity, Learning Opportunities, and Learning," *Journal of Applied Psychology,* October 2004, pp 809–21.

[19] Data from A N Kluger and A DeNisi, "The Effects of Feedback Interventions on Performance: A Historical Review, a Meta-Analysis, and a Preliminary Feedback Intervention Theory," *Psychological Bulletin,* March 1996, pp 254–84. See also G Morse, "Feedback Backlash," *Harvard Business Review,* October 2004, p 28.

[20] K D Harber, "Feedback to Minorities: Evidence of a Positive Bias," *Journal of Personality and Social Psychology,* March 1998, pp 622–28.

[21] See D M Herold and D B Fedor, "Individuals' Interaction with Their Feedback Environment: The Roles of Domain-Specific Individual Differences," in *Research in Personnel and Human Resources Management* 16, ed G R Ferris (Stamford, CT: JAI Press, 1998), pp 215–54.

[22] See P E Levy, M D Albright, B D Cawley, and J R Williams, "Situational and Individual Determinants of Feedback Seeking: A Closer Look at the Process," *Organizational Behavior and Human Decision Processes,* April 1995, pp 23–37; M R Leary, E S Tambor, S K Terdal, and D L Downs, "Self-Esteem as an Interpersonal Monitor: The Sociometer Hypothesis," *Journal of Personality and Social Psychology,* June 1995, pp 518–30; and M A Quinones, "Pretraining Context Effects: Training Assignment as Feedback," *Journal of Applied Psychology,* April 1995, pp 226–38.

[23] See T Matsui, A Okkada, and T Kakuyama, "Influence of Achievement Need on Goal Setting, Performance, and Feedback Effectiveness," *Journal of Applied Psychology,* October 1982, pp 645–48.

[24] S J Ashford, "Feedback-Seeking in Individual Adaptation: A Resource Perspective," *Academy of Management Journal,* September 1986, pp 465–87. See also D B Fedor, R B Rensvold, and S M Adams, "An Investigation of Factors Expected to Affect

Feedback Seeking: A Longitudinal Field Study," *Personnel Psychology,* Winter 1992, pp 779–805; and M F Sully De Luque and S M Sommer, "The Impact of Culture on Feedback-Seeking Behavior: An Integrated Model and Propositions," *Academy of Management Review,* October 2000, pp 829–49.

[25] See D B Turban and T W Dougherty, "Role of Protégé Personality in Receipt of Mentoring and Career Success," *Academy of Management Journal,* June 1994, pp 688–702. See also M E Burkhardt, "Social Interaction Effects following a Technological Change: A Longitudinal Investigation," *Academy of Management Journal,* August 1994, pp 869–98.

[26] See B D Bannister, "Performance Outcome Feedback and Attributional Feedback: Interactive Effects on Recipient Responses," *Journal of Applied Psychology,* May 1986, pp 203–10; and J B Vancouver and E C Tischner, "The Effect of Feedback Sign on Task Performance Depends on Self-Concept Discrepancies," *Journal of Applied Psychology,* December 2004, pp 1092–98.

[27] R A Baron, "Countering the Effects of Destructive Criticism: The Relative Efficacy of Four Interventions," *Journal of Applied Psychology,* June 1990, pp 235–45. See also M L Smith, "Give Feedback, Not Criticism," *Supervisory Management,* February 1993, p 4.

[28] See P M Posakoff and J-L Farh, "Effects of Feedback Sign and Credibility on Goal Setting and Task Performance," *Organizational Behavior and Human Decision Processes,* August 1989, pp 45–67. See also S J Ashford and A S Tsui, "Self-Regulation for Managerial Effectiveness: The Role of Active Feedback Seeking," *Academy of Management Journal,* June 1991, pp 251–80.

[29] W S Silver, T R Mitchell, and M E Gist, "Responses to Successful and Unsuccessful Performance: The Moderating Effect of Self-Efficacy on the Relationship between Performance and Attributions," *Organizational Behavior and Human Decision Processes,* June 1995, p 297. See also T A Louie, "Decision Makers' Hindsight Bias after Receiving Favorable and Unfavorable Feedback," *Journal of Applied Psychology,* February 1999, pp 29–41.

[30] See M De Gregorio and C D Fisher, "Providing Performance Feedback: Reactions to Alternate

Methods," *Journal of Management,* December 1988, pp 605–16.

[31] See R B Jelley and R D Goffin, "Can Performance-Feedback Accuracy Be Improved? Effects of Rater Priming and Rating-Scale Format on Rating Accuracy," *Journal of Applied Psychology,* February 2001, pp 134–44; G L Graham, "If You Want Honesty, Break Some Rules," *Harvard Business Review,* April 2002, pp 42–47; and S Aryee, P S Budhwar, and Z X Chen, "Trust as a Mediator of the Relationship between Organizational Justice and Work Outcomes: Test of a Social Exchange Model," *Journal of Organizational Behavior,* May 2002, pp 267–85.

[32] Ilgen, Fisher, and Taylor, "Consequences of Individual Feedback on Behavior in Organizations," pp 367–68. See also A M O'Leary-Kelly, "The Influence of Group Feedback on Individual Group Member Response," in *Research in Personnel and Human Resources Management* 16, ed G R Ferris (Stamford, CT: JAI Press, 1998), pp 255–94.

[33] See S E Moss and M J Martinko, "The Effects of Performance Attributions and Outcome Dependence on Leader Feedback Behavior Following Poor Subordinate Performance," *Journal of Organizational Behavior,* May 1998, pp 259–74; and K Leung, S Su, and M W Morris, "When Is Criticism *Not* Constructive? The Roles of Fairness Perceptions and Dispositional Attributions in Employee Acceptance of Critical Supervisory Feedback," *Human Relations,* September 2001, pp 1123–54.

[34] C Bell and R Zemke, "On-Target Feedback," *Training,* June 1992, pp 36–44.

[35] A Serwer, "The Education of Michael Dell," *Fortune,* March 7, 2005, p 76.

[36] H J Bernardin, S A Dahmus, and G Redmon, "Attitudes of First-Line Supervisors toward Subordinate Appraisals," *Human Resource Management,* Summer/Fall 1993, p 315.

[37] See L Atwater, P Roush, and A Fischthal, "The Influence of Upward Feedback on Self- and Follower Ratings of Leadership," *Personnel Psychology,* Spring 1995, pp 35–59; and J W Smither, M London, N L Vasilopoulos, R R Reilly, R E Millsap, and N Salvemini, "An Examination of the Effects of an Upward Feedback Program over Time," *Personnel*

Psychology, Spring 1995, pp 1–34. For a discussion of problems with traditional performance appraisal systems, see M Weinstein, "Study: HR Execs Don't Trust Employee Evaluations," *Training,* April 2006, p 11.

[38] J J Salopek, "Rethinking Likert," *Training & Development,* September 2004, pp 26–29.

[39] J W Smither, M London, and R R Reilly, "Does Performance Improve following Multisource Feedback? A Theoretical Model, Meta-Analysis, and Review of Empirical Findings," *Personnel Psychology,* Spring 2005, p 33.

[40] "The Stat," *BusinessWeek,* October 4, 2004, p 16. See also J Kerr and J W Slocum, Jr, "Managing Corporate Culture through Reward Systems," *Academy of Management Executive,* November 2005, pp 130–38; and J Brockner, "Why It's So Hard to Be Fair," *Harvard Business Review,* March 2006, pp 122–29.

[41] L Cauley, "BellSouth Rings Up Wins in Big Easy," *USA Today,* November 9, 2005, p 3B.

[42] J L Pearce and R H Peters, "A Contradictory Norms View of Employer-Employee Exchange," *Journal of Management,* Spring 1985, pp 19–30. See also C Garvey, "Philosophizing Compensation," *HR Magazine,* January 2005, pp 73–76.

[43] "The 100 Best Companies to Work For," *Fortune,* February 4, 2002, p 90; and R Levering, "And the Winners Are: The 100 Best Companies to Work For," *Fortune,* January 11, 2006, http://money.cnn.com/magazines/fortune.

[44] See E L Deci, R Koestner, and R M Ryan, "A Meta-Analytic Review of Experiments Examining the Effects of Extrinsic Rewards on Intrinsic Motivation," *Psychological Bulletin,* November 1999, pp 627–68; and R Eisenberger, W D Pierce, and J Cameron, "Effects of Reward on Intrinsic Motivation—Negative, Neutral, and Positive: Comment on Deci, Koestner, and Ryan (1999)," *Psychological Bulletin,* November 1999, pp 677–91.

[45] See E L Deci and R M Ryan, "The 'What' and 'Why' of Goal Pursuits: Human Needs and Self-Determination of Behavior," *Psychological Inquiry,* December 2000, pp 227–68.

[46] K W Thomas, *Intrinsic Motivation at Work: Building Energy and Commitment* (San Francisco: Berrett-Koehler, 2000).

[47] M Littman, "Best Bosses Tell All," *Working Woman,* October 2000, p 55.

[48] D R Spitzer, "Power Rewards: Rewards That Really Motivate," *Management Review,* May 1996, p 47; and A Fox, "The Right Rewards?" *HR Magazine,* May 2002, p 8.

[49] "Performance-Based Pay Plans," *HR Magazine,* June 2004, p 22.

[50] For both sides of the debate over money's motivational power, see N Gupta and J D Shaw, "Let the Evidence Speak: Financial Incentives *Are* Effective!" *Compensation & Benefits Review,* March/April 1998, pp 26, 28–32; A Kohn, Challenging Behaviorist Dogma: Myths about Money and Motivation," *Compensation & Benefits Review,* March/April 1998, pp 27, 33–37; B Ettorre, "Is Salary a Motivator?" *Management Review,* January 1999, p 8; and W J Duncan, "Stock Ownership and Work Motivation," *Organizational Dynamics* (Summer 2001), pp 1–11.

[51] D Kiley, "Crafty Basket Makers Cut Downtime, Waste," *USA Today,* May 10, 2001, p 3B.

[52] See M V Copeland, "The Shrink Shrinker," *Business 2.0,* April 2006, p 86; P Kaihla, "The Antistar System," *Business 2.0,* April 2006, p 87; and "Coke Links Directors' Pay, Performance," *USA Today,* April 6, 2006, p 1B.

[53] M Bloom and G T Milkovich, "Relationships among Risk, Incentive Pay, and Organizational Performance," *Academy of Management Journal,* June 1998, pp 283–97.

[54] G D Jenkins Jr, N Gupta, A Mitra, and J D Shaw, "Are Financial Incentives Related to Performance? A Meta-Analytic Review of Empirical Research," *Journal of Applied Psychology,* October 1998, pp 777–87.

[55] M J Mandel, "Those Fat Bonuses Don't Seem to Boost Performance," *BusinessWeek,* January 8, 1990, p 26; J Pfeffer, "The Pay-for-Performance Fallacy," *Business 2.0,* July 2005, p 64; and L A Bebchuk and J M Fried, "Pay without Performance: Overview of the Issues," *Academy of Management Perspectives,* February 2006, pp 5–24.

[56] "Performance-Based Pay Plans," p 22.

[57] C Ginther, "Incentive Programs That Really Work," *HR Magazine,* August 2000, pp 117–20; and

E A Locke, "Linking Goals to Monetary Incentives," *Academy of Management Executive,* November 2004, pp 130–33.

[58] J S Dematteo, L T Eby, and E Sundstrom, "Team-Based Rewards: Current Empirical Evidence and Directions for Future Research," in *Research in Organizational Behavior* 20, ed B M Staw and L L Cummings (Greenwich, CT: JAI Press, 1998), p 152.

[59] Ranking based on research evidence in F Trompenaars, *Riding the Waves of Culture: Understanding Diversity in Global Business* (Chicago: Irwin, 1994), p 52.

[60] See J E Beatty, "Grades as Money and the Role of the Market Metaphor in Management Education," *Academy of Management Learning and Education,* June 2004, pp 187–96.

[61] P V LeBlanc and P W Mulvey, "Research Study: How American Workers See the Rewards of Work," *Compensation & Benefits Review,* January/February 1998, pp 24–28.

[62] For example, see R L Heneman and C von Hippel, "Balancing Group and Individual Rewards: Rewarding Individual Contributions to the Team," *Compensation & Benefits Review,* July/August 1995, pp 63–68; A Muoio, "At SEI, Teamwork Pays," *Fast Company,* April 1999, p 186; L N McClurg, "Team Rewards: How Far Have We Come?" *Human Resource Management,* Spring 2001, pp 73–86; C Garvey, "Steer Teams with the Right Pay," *HR Magazine,* May 2002, pp 71–78; and M D Johnson, J R Hollenbeck, S E Humphrey, D R Ilgen, D Jundt, and C J Meyer, "Cutthroat Cooperation: Asymmetrical Adaptation to Changes in Team Reward Structures," *Academy of Management Journal,* February 2006, pp 103–19.

[63] See E L Thorndike, *Educational Psychology: The Psychology of Learning* 2 (New York: Columbia University Teachers College, 1913).

[64] Recent discussions involving behaviorism include M R Ruiz, "B F Skinner's Radical Behaviorism: Historical Misconstructions and Grounds for Feminist Reconstructions," *Psychology of Women Quarterly,* June 1995, pp 161–79; J A Nevin, "Behavioral Economics and Behavioral Momentum," *Journal of the Experimental Analysis of Behavior,* November 1995, pp 385–95; H Rachlin, "Can We

Leave Cognition to Cognitive Psychologists? Comments on an Article by George Loewenstein," *Organizational Behavior and Human Decision Processes,* March 1996, pp 296–99; and J W Donahoe, "The Unconventional Wisdom of B F Skinner: The Analysis-Interpretation Distinction," *Journal of the Experimental Analysis of Behavior,* September 1993, pp 453–56.

[65] B F Skinner, *The Behavior of Organisms* (New York: Appleton-Century-Crofts, 1938).

[66] For modern approaches to respondent behavior, see B Azar, "Classical Conditioning Could Link Disorders and Brain Dysfunction, Researchers Suggest," *APA Monitor,* March 1999, p 17.

[67] For interesting discussions of Skinner and one of his students, see M B Gilbert and T F Gilbert, "What Skinner Gave Us," *Training,* September 1991, pp 42–48; and "HRD Pioneer Gilbert Leaves a Pervasive Legacy," *Training,* January 1996, p 14. See also F Luthans and R Kreitner, *Organizational Behavior Modification and Beyond: An Operant and Social Learning Approach* (Glenview, IL: Scott, Foresman, 1985).

[68] The effect of praise is explored in C M Mueller and C S Dweck, "Praise for Intelligence Can Undermine Children's Motivation and Performance," *Journal of Personality and Social Psychology,* July 1998, pp 33–52. Also see C Garvey, "Meaningful Tokens of Appreciation," *HR Magazine,* August 2004, pp 101–06; K Hannon, "Praise Cranks Up Productivity," *USA Today,* August 30, 2004, p 6B; and D Jones, "Coach Says Honey Gets Better Results than Vinegar," *USA Today,* February 21, 2005, p 4B.

[69] Research on punishment is presented in B P Niehoff, R J Paul, and J F S Bunch, "The Social Effects of Punishment Events: The Influence of Violator Past Performance Record and Severity of the Punishment on Observers' Justice Perceptions and Attitudes," *Journal of Organizational Behavior,* November 1998, pp 589–602; and L E Atwater, D A Waldman, J A Carey, and P Cartier, "Recipient and Observer Reactions to Discipline: Are Managers Experiencing Wishful Thinking?" *Journal of Organizational Behavior,* May 2001, pp 249–70.

[70] See C B Ferster and B F Skinner, *Schedules of Reinforcement* (New York: Appleton-Century-Crofts, 1957).

[71] L M Saari and G P Latham, "Employee Reactions to Continuous and Variable Ratio Reinforcement Schedules Involving a Monetary Incentive," *Journal of Applied Psychology,* August 1982, pp 506–08.

[72] For a circus lion tamer in action, see R Underwood, "A Day in the Life of Work," *Fast Company,* October 2004, p 124.

[73] K L Alexander, "Continental Airlines Soars to New Heights," *USA Today,* January 23, 1996, p 4B; and M Knez and D Simester, "Making Across-the-Board Incentives Work," *Harvard Business Review,* February 2002, pp 16–17.

[74] A T Hollingsworth and D Tanquay Hoyer, "How Supervisors Can Shape Behavior," *Personnel Journal,* May 1985, pp 86, 88.

Chapter 6

[1] E Van Velsor and J Brittain Leslie, "Why Executives Derail: Perspectives across Time and Cultures," *Academy of Management Executive,* November 1995, pp 62–63.

[2] See also F J Flynn, "Identity Orientations and Forms of Social Exchange in Organizations," *Academy of Management Review,* October 2005, pp 737–50; and J E Perry-Smith, "Social yet Creative: The Role of Social Relationships in Facilitating Individual Creativity," *Academy of Management Journal,* February 2006, pp 85–101.

[3] This definition is based in part on D Horton Smith, "A Parsimonious Definition of 'Group': Toward Conceptual Clarity and Scientific Utility," *Sociological Inquiry,* Spring 1967, pp 141–67. See also W B Swann Jr, J T Polzer, D C Seyle, and S J Ko, "Finding Value in Diversity: Verification of Personal and Social Self-Views in Diverse Groups," *Academy of Management Review,* January 2004, pp 9–27.

[4] E H Schein, *Organizational Psychology,* 3rd ed (Englewood Cliffs, NJ: Prentice Hall, 1980), p 145. For more, see L R Weingart, "How Did They Do That? The Ways and Means of Studying Group Process," in *Research in Organizational Behavior* 19, ed L L Cummings and B M Staw (Greenwich, CT: JAI Press, 1997), pp 189–239.

[5] See R Cross, N Nohria, and A Parker, "Six Myths about Informal Networks—and How to Overcome Them," *MIT Sloan Management Review,* Spring 2002, pp 67–75; C Shirky, "Watching the Patterns

Emerge," *Harvard Business Review,* February 2004, pp 34–35; P Chattopadhyay, M Tluchowska, and E George, "Identifying the Ingroup: A Closer Look at the Influence of Demographic Dissimilarity on Employee Social Identity," *Academy of Management Review,* April 2004, pp 180–202; and E Watters, "The Organization Woman," *Business 2.0,* April 2006, pp 106–10.

[6] "Co-workers Support Each Other," *USA Today,* May 28, 2003, p 1B.

[7] See Schein, *Organizational Psychology,* pp 149–53.

[8] J Castro, "Mazda U," *Time,* October 20, 1986, p 65.

[9] For an instructive overview of five different theories of group development, see J P Wanous, A E Reichers, and S D Malik, "Organizational Socialization and Group Development: Toward an Integrative Perspective," *Academy of Management Review,* October 1984, pp 670–83. See also L R Offermann and R K Spiros, "The Science and Practice of Team Development: Improving the Link," *Academy of Management Journal,* April 2001, pp 376–92; and A Chang, P Bordia, and J Duck, "Punctuated Equilibrium and Linear Progression: Toward a New Understanding of Group Development," *Academy of Management Journal,* February 2003, pp 106–17.

[10] B W Tuckman, "Developmental Sequence in Small Groups," *Psychological Bulletin,* June 1965, pp 384–99; and B W Tuckman and M A C Jensen, "Stages of Small-Group Development Revisited," *Group & Organization Studies,* December 1977, pp 419–27. For an instructive adaptation of the Tuckman model, see L Holpp, "If Empowerment Is So Good, Why Does It Hurt?" *Training,* March 1995, p 56.

[11] J McGregor, "Forget Going with Your Gut," *BusinessWeek,* March 20, 2006, p 112.

[12] A useful resource book is T Ursiny, *The Coward's Guide to Conflict: Empowering Solutions for Those Who Would Rather Run than Fight* (Naperville, IL: Sourcebooks, 2003). See also M D Johnson, J R Hollenbeck, S E Humphrey, D R Ilgen, D Jundt, and C J Meyer, "Cutthroat Cooperation: Asymmetrical Adaptation to Changes in Team Reward Structures," *Academy of Management Journal,* February 2006, pp 103–19.

[13] For related research, see M Van Vugt and C M Hart, "Social Identity as Social Glue: The Origins of

Group Loyalty," *Journal of Personality and Social Psychology,* April 2004, pp 585–98.

[14] See T Postmes, R Spears, A T Lee, and R J Novak, "Individuality and Social Influence in Groups: Inductive and Deductive Routes to Group Identity," *Journal of Personality and Social Psychology,* November 2005, pp 747–63.

[15] G Graen, "Role-Making Processes within Complex Organizations," in *Handbook of Industrial and Organizational Psychology,* ed M D Dunnette (Chicago: Rand McNally, 1976), p 1201. See also T Schellens, H Van Keer, and M Valcke, "The Impact of Role Assignment on Knowledge Construction in Asynchronous Discussion Groups: A Multilevel Analysis," *Small Group Research,* December 2005, pp 704–45.

[16] See K D Benne and P Sheats, "Functional Roles of Group Members," *Journal of Social Issues,* Spring 1948, pp 41–49.

[17] See H J Klein and P W Mulvey, "Two Investigations of the Relationships among Group Goals, Goal Commitment, Cohesion, and Performance," *Organizational Behavior and Human Decision Processes,* January 1995, pp 44–53; D F Crown and J G Rosse, "Yours, Mine, and Ours: Facilitating Group Productivity through the Integration of Individual and Group Goals," *Organizational Behavior and Human Decision Processes,* November 1995, pp 138–50; and D Knight, C C Durham, and E A Locke, "The Relationship of Team Goals, Incentives, and Efficacy to Strategic Risk, Tactical Implementation, and Performance," *Academy of Management Journal,* April 2001, pp 326–38.

[18] A Zander, "The Value of Belonging to a Group in Japan," *Small Group Behavior,* February 1983, pp 7–8. See also E Gundling, *Working GlobeSmart: 12 People Skills for Doing Business across Borders* (Palo Alto, CA: Davies-Black, 2003).

[19] R R Blake and J Srygley Mouton, "Don't Let Group Norms Stifle Creativity," *Personnel,* August 1985, p 28.

[20] See D Kahneman, "Reference Points, Anchors, Norms, and Mixed Feelings," *Organizational Behavior and Human Decision Processes,* March 1992, pp 296–312; and J M Marques, D Abrams, D Paez, and C Martinez-Taboada, "The Role of Categorization and In-Group Norms in Judgments of Groups and Their Members," *Journal of Personality and Social Psychology,* October 1998, pp 976–88.

[21] See J Pfeffer, "Bring Back Shame," *Business 2.0,* September 2003, p 80.

[22] P Sellers, "Gap's New Guy Upstairs," *Fortune,* April 14, 2003, p 112.

[23] D C Feldman, "The Development and Enforcement of Group Norms," *Academy of Management Review,* January 1984, pp 50–52.

[24] Ibid.

[25] "Top 10 Leadership Tips from Jeff Immelt," *Fast Company,* April 2004, p 96.

[26] J Pfeffer and J F Veiga, "Putting People First for Organizational Success," *Academy of Management Executive,* May 1999, p 41.

[27] See N Enbar, "What Do Women Want? Ask 'Em," *BusinessWeek,* March 29, 1999, p 8; and M Hickins, "Duh! Gen Xers Are Cool with Teamwork," *Management Review,* March 1999, p 7. For related reading, see L Gerdes, "Why Put Real Work Off Till Tomorrow?" *BusinessWeek,* May 8, 2006, p 92.

[28] D Jones, "Optimism Puts Rose-Colored Tint in Glasses of Top Execs," *USA Today,* December 16, 2005, p 2B.

[29] J R Katzenbach and D K Smith, *The Wisdom of Teams: Creating the High-Performance Organization* (New York: HarperBusiness, 1999), p 45.

[30] Ibid., p 214. See also B Beersma, J R Hollenbeck, S E Humphrey, H Moon, D Conlon, and D R Ilgen, "Cooperation, Competition, and Team Performance: Toward a Contingency Approach," *Academy of Management Journal,* October 2003, pp 572–90; R D Hof, "Teamwork Supercharged," *BusinessWeek,* November 21, 2005, pp 90–94; J M Howell and C M Shea, "Effects of Champion Behavior, Team Potency, and External Communication Activities on Predicting Team Performance," *Group and Organization Management,* April 2006, pp 180–211.

[31] See A Levin, "In the Cockpit, Safety Isn't Someone Else's Job," *USA Today,* March 2, 2004, p 4A; and R J Trent, "Becoming an Effective Teaming Organization," *Business Horizons,* March/April 2004, pp 33–40.

[32] J R Katzenbach and D K Smith, "The Discipline of Teams," *Harvard Business Review,* March/April 1993, p 112.

[33] "A Team's-Eye View of Teams," *Training,* November 1995, p 16.

[34] G Chen, L M Donahue, and R I Klimoski, "Training Undergraduates to Work in Organizational Teams," *Academy of Management Learning and Education,* March 2004, Appendix A, p 40.

[35] C Hymowitz, "In the Lead: Rewarding Competitors over Collaborators No Longer Makes Sense," *The Wall Street Journal,* February 13, 2006, p B1.

[36] S Zuboff, "From Subject to Citizen," *Fast Company,* May 2004, p 104. See also "Minorities Distrust Companies," *USA Today,* January 14, 2004, p 1B; and "Little Faith in Top Executives," *USA Today,* April 5, 2004, p 1B.

[37] See D M Rousseau, S B Sitkin, R S Burt, and C Camerer, "Not So Different After All: A Cross-Discipline View of Trust," *Academy of Management Review,* July 1998, pp 393–404; and A C Wicks, S L Berman, and T M Jones, "The Structure of Optimal Trust: Moral and Strategic Implications," *Academy of Management Review,* January 1999, pp 99–116.

[38] J D Lewis and A Weigert, "Trust as a Social Reality," *Social Forces,* June 1985, p 971.

[39] Adapted from C Johnson-George and W C Swap, "Measurement of Specific Interpersonal Trust: Construction and Validation of a Scale to Assess Trust in a Specific Other," *Journal of Personality and Social Psychology,* December 1982, pp 1306–17; and D J McAllister, "Affect- and Cognition-Based Trust as Foundations for Interpersonal Cooperation in Organizations," *Academy of Management Journal,* February 1995, pp 24–59.

[40] L Prusak and D Cohen, "How to Invest in Social Capital," *Harvard Business Review,* June 2001, p 90. See also V U Druskat and S B Wolff, "Building the Emotional Intelligence of Groups," *Harvard Business Review,* March 2001, pp 80–90.

[41] Adapted from F Bartolomé, "Nobody Trusts the Boss Completely—Now What?" *Harvard Business Review,* March/April 1989, pp 135–42. For more on building trust, see R Galford and A S Drapeau, "The Enemies of Trust," *Harvard Business Review,*

February 2003, pp 88–95; L C Abrams, R Cross, E Lesser, and D Z Levin, "Nurturing Interpersonal Trust in Knowledge-Sharing Networks," *Academy of Management Executive,* November 2003, pp 64–77; S A Joni, "The Geography of Trust," *Harvard Business Review,* March 2004, pp 82–88; and R Goffee and G Jones, "Managing Authenticity: The Paradox of Great Leadership," *Harvard Business Review,* December 2005, pp 86–94.

[42] See R Zemke, "Little Lies," *Training,* February 2004, p 8.

[43] For support, see G M Spreitzer and A K Mishra, "Giving Up Control without Losing Control: Trust and Its Substitutes' Effects on Managers' Involving Employees in Decision Making," *Group & Organization Management,* June 1999, pp 155–87. See also G Johnson, "11 Keys to Leadership," *Training,* January 2004, p 18.

[44] C Joinson, "Teams at Work," *HR Magazine,* May 1999, pp 30–36.

[45] B Dumaine, "Who Needs a Boss?" *Fortune,* May 7, 1990, p 52. See also D Vredenburgh and I Y He, "Leadership Lessons from a Conductorless Orchestra," *Business Horizons,* September/October 2003, pp 19–24; and C A O'Reilly III and M L Tushman, "The Ambidextrous Organization," *Harvard Business Review,* April 2004, pp 74–81.

[46] Adapted from Table 1 in V U Druskat and J V Wheeler, "Managing from the Boundary: The Effective Leadership of Self-Managing Work Teams," *Academy of Management Journal,* August 2003, pp 435–57.

[47] "1996 Industry Report: What Self-Managing Teams Manage," *Training,* October 1996, p 69.

[48] See L L Thompson, *Making the Team: A Guide for Managers* (Upper Saddle River, NJ: Prentice Hall, 2000).

[49] See A E Randal and K S Jaussi, "Functional Background Identity, Diversity, and Individual Performance in Cross-Functional Teams," *Academy of Management Journal,* December 2003, pp 763–74; and G S Van Der Vegt and J S Bunderson, "Learning Performance in Multidisciplinary Teams: The Importance of Collective Team Identification," *Academy of Management Journal,* June 2005, pp 532–47.

50 "Fast Talk," *Fast Company,* February 2004, p 50. For cross-functional teams in action, see B Nussbaum, "How to Build Innovative Companies: Get Creative!" *BusinessWeek,* August 1, 2005, pp 61–68; C Edwards, "Inside Intel," *BusinessWeek,* January 9, 2006, pp 46–54; "How to Break Out of Commodity Hell," *BusinessWeek,* March 27, 2006, p 76; and B Finn, "Outside-In R&D," *Business 2.0,* April 2006, p 85.

51 J Merritt, "How to Rebuild a B-School," *BusinessWeek,* March 29, 2004, pp 90–91.

52 P S Goodman, R Devadas, and T L Griffith Hughson, "Groups and Productivity: Analyzing the Effectiveness of Self-Managing Teams," in *Productivity in Organizations,* ed J P Campbell, R J Campbell, et al. (San Francisco: Jossey-Bass, 1988), pp 295–327. See also E F Rogers, W Metlay, I T Kaplan, and T Shapiro, "Self-Managing Work Teams: Do They Really Work?" *Human Resource Planning,* no. 2, 1995, pp 53–57; R Batt, "Who Benefits from Teams? Comparing Workers, Supervisors, and Managers," *Industrial Relations,* January 2004, pp 183–209; and S Kauffeld, "Self-Directed Work Groups and Team Competence," *Journal of Occupational and Organizational Psychology,* March 2006, pp 1–21.

53 For more, see W F Cascio, "Managing a Virtual Workplace," *Academy of Management Executive,* August 2000, pp 81–90; and the collection of articles on E-leadership and virtual teams in *Organizational Dynamics,* no 4, 2003.

54 M Conlin, "The Easiest Commute of All," *BusinessWeek,* December 12, 2005, pp 78–79. See also J T Arnold, "Making the Leap," *HR Magazine,* May 2006, pp 80–86.

55 See A M Townsend, S M DeMarie, and A R Hendrickson, "Virtual Teams: Technology and the Workplace of the Future," *Academy of Management Executive,* August 1998, pp 17–29.

56 See C Saunders, C Van Slyke, and D R Vogel, "My Time or Yours? Managing Time Visions in Global Virtual Teams," *Academy of Management Executive,* February 2004, pp 19–31.

57 K Naughton, "Styling with Digital Clay," *Newsweek,* April 28, 2003, pp 46–47. For a large-scale example, see S E Ante, "Collaboration: IBM," *BusinessWeek,* November 24, 2003, p 84.

58 P Bordia, N DiFonzo, and A Chang, "Rumor as Group Problem Solving: Development Patterns in Informal Computer-Mediated Groups," *Small Group Research,* February 1999, pp 8–28.

59 K A Graetz, E S Boyle, C E Kimble, P Thompson, and J L Garloch, "Information Sharing in Face-to-Face, Teleconferencing, and Electronic Chat Groups," *Small Group Research,* December 1998, pp 714–43.

60 F Niederman and R J Volkema, "The Effects of Facilitator Characteristics on Meeting Preparation, Set Up, and Implementation," *Small Group Research,* June 1999, pp 330–60.

61 J J Sosik, B J Avolio, and S S Kahai, "Inspiring Group Creativity: Comparing Anonymous and Identified Electronic Brainstorming," *Small Group Research,* February 1998, pp 3–31. See also A M Hardin, M A Fuller, and J S Valacich, "Measuring Group Efficacy in Virtual Teams: New Questions in an Old Debate," *Small Group Research,* February 2006, pp 65–85.

62 See B L Kirkman, B Rosen, C B Gibson, P E Tesluk, and S O McPherson, "Five Challenges to Virtual Team Success: Lessons from Sabre, Inc.," *Academy of Management Executive,* August 2002, pp 67–79; P J Hinds and D E Bailey, "Out of Sight, Out of Sync: Understanding Conflict in Distributed Teams," *Organization Science,* November/December 2003, pp 615–32; and Y Shin, "Conflict Resolution in Virtual Teams," *Organizational Dynamics,* November 2005, pp 331–45.

63 E Kelley, "Keys to Effective Virtual Global Teams," *Academy of Management Executive,* May 2001, pp 132–33.

64 Practical perspectives are offered in "Virtual Teams that Work," *HR Magazine,* July 2003, p 121; D D Davis, "The Tao of Leadership in Virtual Teams," *Organizational Dynamics,* no 1, 2004, pp 47–62; A Majchrzak, A Malhotra, J Stamps, and J Lipnack, "Can Absence Make a Team Grow Stronger?" *Harvard Business Review,* May 2004, pp 131–37; and J Gordon, "Do Your Virtual Teams Deliver Only Virtual Performance?" *Training,* June 2005, pp 20–26.

65 For a comprehensive update on groupthink, see the entire February/March 1998 issue of *Organizational Behavior and Human Decision Processes* (12 articles).

[66] I L Janis, *Groupthink,* 2nd ed (Boston: Houghton Mifflin, 1982), p 9. Alternative models are discussed in K Granstrom and D Stiwne, "A Bipolar Model of Groupthink: An Expansion of Janis's Concept," *Small Group Research,* February 1998, pp 32–56; A R Flippen, "Understanding Groupthink from a Self-Regulatory Perspective," *Small Group Research,* April 1999, pp 139–65; and M Harvey, M M Novicevic, M R Buckley, and J R B Halbesleben, "The Abilene Paradox after Thirty Years: A Global Perspective," *Organizational Dynamics,* no 2, 2004, pp 215–26.

[67] Ibid. For an alternative model, see R J Aldag and S Riggs Fuller, "Beyond Fiasco: A Reappraisal of the Groupthink Phenomenon and a New Model of Group Decision Processes," *Psychological Bulletin,* May 1993, pp 533–52. Also see A A Mohamed and F A Wiebe, "Toward a Process Theory of Groupthink," *Small Group Research,* August 1996, pp 416–30.

[68] Adapted from Janis, *Groupthink,* pp 174–75. See also J M Wellen and M Neale, "Deviance, Self-Typicality, and Group Cohesion: The Corrosive Effects of the Bad Apples on the Barrel," *Small Group Research,* April 2006, pp 165–86.

[69] L Baum, "The Job Nobody Wants," *BusinessWeek,* September 8, 1986, p 60. See also L Perlow and S Williams, "Is Silence Killing Your Company?" *Harvard Business Review,* May 2003, pp 52–58; W F Cascio, "Board Governance: A Social Systems Perspective," *Academy of Management Executive,* February 2004, pp 97–100; W Schiano and J W Weiss, "Y2K All Over Again: How Groupthink Permeates IS and Compromises Security," *Business Horizons,* March/April 2006, pp 115–25; and N Fick, "General Dissent: When Less Isn't More," *USA Today,* April 25, 2006, p 13A.

[70] For an ethical perspective, see R R Sims, "Linking Groupthink to Unethical Behavior in Organizations," *Journal of Business Ethics,* September 1992, pp 651–62.

[71] Adapted from Janis, *Groupthink,* Ch 11.

[72] Based on discussion in B Latane, K Williams, and S Harkins, "Many Hands Make Light the Work: The Causes and Consequences of Social Loafing," *Journal of Personality and Social Psychology,* June 1979, pp 822–32; and D A Kravitz and B Martin, "Ringelmann Rediscovered: The Original Article," *Journal of Personality and Social Psychology,* May 1986, pp 936–41.

[73] See S J Karau and K D Williams, "Social Loafing: Meta-Analytic Review and Theoretical Integration," *Journal of Personality and Social Psychology,* October 1993, pp 681–706; and L Thompson, "Improving the Creativity of Organizational Work Groups," *Academy of Management Executive,* February 2003, pp 96–109.

[74] See S J Zaccaro, "Social Loafing: The Role of Task Attractiveness," *Personality and Social Psychology Bulletin,* March 1984, pp 99–106; J M Jackson and K D Williams, "Social Loafing on Difficult Tasks: Working Collectively Can Improve Performance," *Journal of Personality and Social Psychology,* October 1985, pp 937–42; and J M George, "Extrinsic and Intrinsic Origins of Perceived Social Loafing in Organizations," *Academy of Management Journal,* March 1992, pp 191–202.

[75] For complete details, see K Williams, S Harkins, and B Latane, "Identifiability as a Deterrent to Social Loafing: Two Cheering Experiments," *Journal of Personality and Social Psychology,* February 1981, pp 303–11.

[76] See J M Jackson and S G Harkins, "Equity in Effort: An Explanation of the Social Loafing Effect," *Journal of Personality and Social Psychology,* November 1985, pp 1199–1206.

[77] Both studies are reported in S G Harkins and K Szymanski, "Social Loafing and Group Evaluation," *Journal of Personality and Social Psychology,* June 1989, pp 934–41.

[78] J A Wagner III, "Studies of Individualism-Collectivism: Effects on Cooperation in Groups," *Academy of Management Journal,* February 1995, pp 152–72. See also P W Mulvey and H J Klein, "The Impact of Perceived Loafing and Collective Efficacy on Group Goal Processes and Group Performance," *Organizational Behavior and Human Decision Processes,* April 1998, pp 62–87; P W Mulvey, L Bowes-Sperry, and H J Klein, "The Effects of Perceived Loafing and Defensive Impression Management on Group Effectiveness," *Small Group Research,* June 1998, pp 394–415; and H Goren, R Kurzban, and A Rapoport, "Social Loafing vs. Social Enhancement: Public Goods Provisioning in Real-Time with Irrevocable Commitments," *Organizational Behavior and Human Decision Processes,* March 2003, pp 277–90.

[79] See S G Scott and W O Einstein, "Strategic Performance Appraisal in Team-Based Organizations: One Size Does Not Fit All," *Academy of Management Executive*, May 2001, pp 107–16.

Chapter 7

[1] R C Morias, "Mind the Gap," *Forbes*, August 11, 2003, p 58.

[2] For a thorough discussion of the rational model, see M H Bazerman, *Judgment in Managerial Decision Making* (Hoboken, NJ: Wiley, 2006).

[3] H A Simon, "Rational Decision Making in Business Organizations," *American Economic Review*, September 1979, p 510.

[4] P C Nutt, "Expanding the Search for Alternatives during Strategic Decision Making," *Academy of Management Executive*, November 2004, pp 13–28.

[5] For a complete discussion of bounded rationality, see H A Simon, *Administrative Behavior*, 2nd ed (New York: Free Press, 1957). See also M H Bazerman and D Chugh, "Decisions without Blinders," *Harvard Business Review*, January 2006, pp 88–97.

[6] Biases associated with using shortcuts in decision making are discussed by A Tversky and D Kahneman, "Judgment under Uncertainty: Heuristics and Biases," *Science*, September 1974, pp 1124–31; and E Hölzl and E Kirchler, "Causal Attribution and Hindsight Bias for Economic Developments," *Journal of Applied Psychology*, January 2005, pp 167–74.

[7] See T DeAngelis, "Too Many Choices?" *Monitor on Psychology*, June 2004, pp 56–57. See also J S Hammond, R L Keeney, and H Raiffa, "The Hidden Traps in Decision Making," *Harvard Business Review*, January 2006, pp 118–26.

[8] L Kopeikina, "The Elements of a Clear Decision," *MIT Sloan Management Review*, Winter 2006, p 19.

[9] D W De Long and P Seemann, "Confronting Conceptual Confusion and Conflict in Knowledge Management," *Organizational Dynamics*, Summer 2000, p 33.

[10] Melanie Trottman, "Bad Weather, Tough Choices," *The Wall Street Journal*, February 14, 2006, http://online.wsj.com. See also C Stoll, "Writing the Book on Knowledge Management," *American Society of Association Executives*, April 2004, pp 47–50; and A C Inkpen and E W K Tsang, "Social Capital, Networks, and Knowledge Transfer," *Academy of Management Review*, January 2005, pp 145–65.

[11] P Babcock, "Shedding Light on Knowledge Management," *HR Magazine*, May 2004, pp 47–50.

[12] R Lubit, "Tacit Knowledge and Knowledge Management: The Keys to Sustainable Competitive Advantage," *Organizational Dynamics*, 2001, p 166.

[13] The role of intuition in decision making is discussed by C C Miller and R D Ireland, "Intuition in Strategic Decision Making: Friend or Foe in the Fast-Paced 21st Century," *Academy of Management Executive*, February 2005, pp 19–30.

[14] A M Hayashi, "When to Trust Your Gut," *Harvard Business Review*, February 2001, p 61.

[15] See Lubit, "Tacit Knowledge and Knowledge Management."

[16] R D Hof, "The Power of Us," *BusinessWeek*, June 20, 2005, pp 74–81. See also M Overfelt, "Wireless Grapes," *Fortune*, March 6, 2006, pp 158B–D.

[17] R Cross, A Parker, L Prusak, and S P Borgatti, "Knowing What We Know: Supporting Knowledge Creation and Sharing in Social Networks," *Organizational Dynamics*, Fall 2001, p 109.

[18] Ibid.

[19] This definition was derived from A J Rowe and R O Mason, *Managing with Style: A Guide to Understanding, Assessing and Improving Decision Making* (San Francisco: Jossey-Bass, 1987).

[20] Ibid.

[21] See ibid.; M J Dollinger and W Danis, "Preferred Decision-Making Styles: A Cross-Cultural Comparison," *Psychological Reports*, 1998, pp 755–61; and Z Stambor, "Older Consumers Factor More Positives, Specifics into Product Choices," *Monitor on Psychology*, April 2005, p 10.

[22] A thorough discussion of escalation situations can be found in B M Staw and J Ross, "Behavior in Escalation Situations: Antecedents, Prototypes, and Solutions," in *Research in Organizational Behavior* 9, ed L L Cummings and B M Staw (Greenwich, CT: JAI Press, 1987), pp 39–78.

[23] J Ross and B M Staw, "Organizational Escalation and Exit: Lessons from the Shoreham Nuclear Power Plant," *Academy of Management Journal*, August 1993, pp 701–32.

[24] Ibid.

[25] Supportive results can be found in H Moon, "Looking Forward and Looking Back: Integrating Completion and Sunk-Cost Effects within an Escalation-of-Commitment Progress Decision," *Journal of Applied Psychology*, February 2001, pp 104–13.

[26] D A Hantula and J L D Bragger, "The Effects of Feedback Equivocality on Escalation of Commitment: An Empirical Investigation of Decision Dilemma Theory," *Journal of Applied Social Psychology*, February 1999, pp 424–44.

[27] C R Greer and G K Stephens, "Escalation of Commitment: A Comparison of Differences between Mexican and U.S. Decision Makers," *Journal of Management*, 2001, pp 51–78.

[28] Ross and Staw, "Organizational Escalation and Exit."

[29] See S Hamm, "Innovation: The View from the Top," *BusinessWeek*, April 3, 2006, pp 52–54; M Weinstein, "Innovate or Die Trying," *Training*, May 2006, pp 40–44; and F Vogelstein, "Mastering the Art of Disruption," *Fortune*, February 6, 2006, pp 23–24.

[30] This definition was based on R J Sternberg, "What Is the Common Thread of Creativity?" *American Psychologist*, April 2001, pp 360–62.

[31] R Langreth and Z Moukheiber, "Medical Merlins," *Forbes*, June 2003, p 115.

[32] See O Janssen, E V De Vliert, and M West, "The Bright and Dark Sides of Individual and Group Innovation: A Special Issue Introduction," *Journal of Organizational Behavior*, March 2004, pp 129–45.

[33] S Holmes, "Just Plain Genius," *BusinessWeek*, April 17, 2006, p 20.

[34] E Tahmincioglu, "Gifts that Gall," *Workforce Management*, April 2004, p 45.

[35] M Basadur, "Managing Creativity: A Japanese Model," *Academy of Management Executive*, May 1992, pp 29–42.

[36] See P Loewe and J Dominiquini, "Overcoming the Barriers to Effective Innovation," *Strategy & Leadership*, 2006, pp 24–31; and J S Lublin, "Nurturing Innovation," *The Wall Street Journal*, March 20, 2006, pp B1, B3.

[37] Loewe and Dominiquini, "Overcoming the Barriers to Effective Innovation."

[38] M Mangalindan, "The Grown-Up at Google," *The Wall Street Journal*, March 29, 2004, p B1.

[39] C K W De Dreu and M A West, "Minority Dissent and Team Innovation: The Importance of Participation in Decision Making," *Journal of Applied Psychology*, December 2001, pp 1191–201.

[40] These recommendations were derived from R Y Hirokawa, "Group Communication and Decision-Making Performance: A Continued Test of the Functional Perspective," *Human Communication Research*, October 1988, pp 487–515.

[41] See the related discussion in B B Baltes, M W Dickson, M P Sherman, C C Bauer, and J S LaGanke, "Computer-Mediated Communication and Group Decision Making: A Meta-Analysis," *Organizational Behavior and Human Decision Processes*, January 2002, pp 156–79. See also P Rogers and M Blenko, "What Has the D?" *Harvard Business Review*, January 2006, pp 53–61.

[42] These guidelines were derived from G P Huber, *Managerial Decision Making* (Glenview, IL: Scott, Foresman, 1980), p 149.

[43] G W Hill, "Group versus Individual Performance: Are $N + 1$ Heads Better than One?" *Psychological Bulletin*, May 1982, p 535.

[44] See T Connolly and L Ordóñez, "Judgment and Decision Making," in *Handbook of Psychology* 12, ed W C Borman, D R Ilgen, and R J Klimoski (Hoboken, NJ: Wiley, 2003), pp 493–518. See also S Dingfelder, "Groups May Find More Elegant Solutions than Individuals," *Monitor on Psychology*, May 2006, p 15.

[45] J T Delaney, "Workplace Cooperation: Current Problems, New Approaches," *Journal of Labor Research*, Winter 1996, pp 45–61.

[46] For an extended discussion of this model, see M Sashkin, "Participative Management Is an Ethical

Imperative," *Organizational Dynamics,* Spring 1984, pp 4–22.

[47] S Carey, "The Thrifty Get Thriftier," *The Wall Street Journal,* May 10, 2004, p R7.

[48] For a review of this research, see M J Handel and D I Levine, "Editors' Introduction: The Effects of New Work Practices on Workers," *Industrial Relations,* January 2004, pp 1–43.

[49] B D Cawley, L M Keeping, and P E Levy, "Participation in the Performance Appraisal Process and Employee Reactions: A Meta-Analytic Review of Field Investigations," *Journal of Applied Psychology,* August 1998, pp 615–33.

[50] J A Wagner III, C R Leana, E A Locke, and D M Schweiger, "Cognitive and Motivational Frameworks in US Research on Participation: A Meta-Analysis of Primary Effects," *Journal of Organizational Behavior,* 1997, pp 49–65.

[51] J Barbian, "Decision Making: The Tyranny of Managers," *Training,* January 2002, p 19.

[52] S A Mohrman, E E Lawler III, and G E Ledford Jr, "Organizational Effectiveness and the Impact of Employee Involvement and TQM Programs: Do Employee Involvement and TQM Programs Work?" *Journal for Quality and Participation,* January/February 1996, pp 6–10.

[53] See R Rodgers, J E Hunter, and D L Rogers, "Influence of Top Management Commitment on Management Program Success," *Journal of Applied Psychology,* February 1993, pp 151–55.

[54] G M Parker, *Team Players and Teamwork: The New Competitive Business Strategy* (San Francisco: Jossey-Bass, 1990).

[55] The effect of group dynamics on brainstorming is discussed by P B Paulus and H-C Yang, "Idea Generation in Groups: A Basis for Creativity in Organizations," *Organizational Behavior and Human Decision Processes,* May 2000, pp 76–87.

[56] These recommendations were obtained from Parker, *Team Players and Teamwork.*

[57] See A F Osborn, *Applied Imagination: Principles and Procedures of Creative Thinking,* 3rd ed (New York: Scribners, 1979).

[58] See W H Cooper, R Brent Gallupe, S Pollard, and J Cadsby, "Some Liberating Effects of Anonymous Electronic Brainstorming," *Small Group Research,* April 1998, pp 147–78.

[59] These recommendations and descriptions were derived from B Nussbaum, "The Power of Design," *BusinessWeek,* May 17, 2004, pp 88, 90–92, 94.

[60] The NGT procedure is discussed by L Thompson, "Improving the Creativity of Organizational Work Groups," *Academy of Management Executive,* February 2003, pp 96–109. For an application of NGT, see C Y Yiu, H K Ho, S M Lo, and B Q Hu, "Performance Evaluation for Cost Estimators by Reliability Interval Method," *Journal of Construction Engineering and Management,* January 2005, pp 108–16.

[61] See Thompson, "Improving the Creativity."

[62] See N C Dalkey, D L Rourke, R Lewis, and D Snyder, *Studies in the Quality of Life: Delphi and Decision Making* (Lexington, MA: Lexington Books, 1972).

[63] For applications of the Delphi technique, see A Alahlafi and S Burge, "What Should Undergraduate Medical Students Know about Psoriasis? Involving Patients in Curriculum Development: Modified Delphi Technique," *British Medical Journal,* March 19, 2005, pp 633–36; and A M Deshpande, R N Shiffman, and P M Nadkarni, "Metadata-Driven Delphi Rating on the Internet," *Computer Methods and Programs in Biomedicine,* January 2005, pp 49–56.

[64] For a thorough description of computer-aided decision-making systems, see M C Er and A C Ng, "The Anonymity and Proximity Factors in Group Decision Support Systems," *Decision Support Systems,* May 1995, pp 75–83.

[65] M Weinstein, "So Happy Together," *Training,* May 2006, pp 34–39.

[66] S S Lam and J Schaubroeck, "Improving Group Decisions by Better Polling Information: A Comparative Advantage of Group Decision Support Systems," *Journal of Applied Psychology,* August 2000, pp 565–73; and I Benbasat and J Lim, "Information Technology Support for Debiasing Group Judgments: An Empirical Evaluation," *Organizational Behavior and Human Decision Processes,* September 2000, pp 167–83.

[67] Baltes et al., "Computer-Mediated Communication and Group Decision Making."

Chapter 8

[1] D Tjosvold, *Learning to Manage Conflict: Getting People to Work Together Productively* (New York: Lexington Books, 1993), pp xi–xii.

[2] For recent examples, see R Grover, "Steve Burke: Payback Time for an Ex-Boy Wonder?" *Business-Week*, February 23, 2004, p 42; and S Hamm, "A Probe—and a Bitter Feud," *BusinessWeek*, April 12, 2004, pp 78–82.

[3] J A Wall, Jr, and R Robert Callister, "Conflict and Its Management," *Journal of Management*, no. 3 (1995), p 517.

[4] Ibid., p 544.

[5] See O Jones, "Scientific Management, Culture and Control: A First-Hand Account of Taylorism in Practice," *Human Relations*, May 2000, pp 631–53.

[6] See S Alper, D Tjosvold, and K S Law, "Interdependence and Controversy in Group Decision Making: Antecedents to Effective Self-Managing Teams," *Organizational Behavior and Human Decision Processes*, April 1998, pp 33–52.

[7] See "Dying from Work-Related Incidents," *USA Today*, August 10, 2004, p 1A; T Maxon, "Violence in Workplace," *Arizona Republic*, November 13, 2004, p D3; A Fisher, "How to Prevent Violence at Work," *Fortune*, February 21, 2005, p 42; H Mohr, "Lockheed Sued after Slayings at Plant," *Arizona Republic*, March 20, 2005, pp D1, D3; and A M O'Leary-Kelly, R W Griffin, and D J Glew, "Organization-Motivated Aggression: A Research Framework," *Academy of Management Review*, January 1996, pp 225–53.

[8] S P Robbins, "'Conflict Management' and 'Conflict Resolution' Are Not Synonymous Terms," *California Management Review*, Winter 1978, p 70.

[9] Cooperative conflict is discussed in Tjosvold, *Learning to Manage Conflict*. See also A C Amason, "Distinguishing the Effects of Functional and Dysfunctional Conflict on Strategic Decision Making: Resolving a Paradox for Top Management Teams," *Academy of Management Journal*, February 1996, pp 123–48; D E Warren, "Constructive and Destructive Deviance in Organizations," *Academy of Management Review*, October 2003, pp 622–32; A Hanft, "The Joy of Conflict," *Inc.*, August 2005, p 112; and J Pfeffer,

"The Courage to Rise Above," *Business 2.0*, May 2006, p 86.

[10] K Brooker, "Can Anyone Replace Herb?" *Fortune*, April 17, 2000, p 190.

[11] K Brooker, "I Built This Company, I Can Save It," *Fortune*, April 30, 2001, p 102. See also L Stack, "Employees Behaving Badly," *HR Magazine*, October 2003, pp 111–16.

[12] Adapted in part from discussion in A C Filley, *Interpersonal Conflict Resolution* (Glenview, IL: Scott, Foresman, 1975), pp 9–12; and B Fortado, "The Accumulation of Grievance Conflict," *Journal of Management Inquiry*, December 1992, pp 288–303. See also D Tjosvold and M Poon, "Dealing with Scarce Resources: Open-Minded Interaction for Resolving Budget Conflicts," *Group and Organization Management*, September 1998, pp 237–55.

[13] T Ursiny, *The Coward's Guide to Conflict: Empowering Solutions for Those Who Would Rather Run than Fight* (Naperville, IL: Sourcebooks, 2003), p 27.

[14] Adapted from Tjosvold, *Learning to Manage Conflict*, pp 12–13.

[15] L Gardenswartz and A Rowe, *Diverse Teams at Work: Capitalizing on the Power of Diversity* (New York: McGraw-Hill, 1994), p 32.

[16] "Do I Have It?" *BusinessWeek*, July 7, 2003, p 14.

[17] F Keenan, "EMC: Turmoil at the Top?" *Business-Week*, March 11, 2002, pp 58–60; and "Joseph Tucci, EMC," *BusinessWeek*, January 10, 2005, p 60.

[18] See O Barker, "Whatever Happened to Thank-You Notes?" *USA Today*, December 27, 2005, pp 1A–2A; S Armour, "Music Hath Charms for Some Workers—Others It Really Annoys," *USA Today*, March 24, 2006, p 1B; and S Jayson, "Are Social Norms Steadily Unraveling?" *USA Today*, April 13, 2006, p 4D.

[19] M Weinstein, "Racism, Sexism, Ageism: Workplace Not Getting Any Friendlier," *Training*, May 2006, p 11.

[20] C M Pearson and C L Porath, "On the Nature, Consequences and Remedies of Workplace Incivility: No Time for 'Nice'? Think Again," *Academy of Management Executive*, February 2005, p 7. See also K Montgomery, K Kane, and C M Vance, "Accounting

for Differences in Norms of Respect: A Study of Assessments of Incivility through the Lenses of Race and Gender," *Group and Organization Management,* April 2004, pp 248–68; S Jayson, "On or off the Field, It's a 'Civility' War out There," *USA Today,* November 30, 2004, p 9D; L W Andrews, "Hard-Core Offenders," *HR Magazine,* December 2004, pp 42–48; "When Bosses Attack," *Training,* May 2005, p 10; and K Gurchiek, "Bullying: It's Not Just on the Playground," *HR Magazine,* June 2005, p 40.

21 See D L Coutu, "In Praise of Boundaries: A Conversation with Miss Manners," *Harvard Business Review,* December 2003, pp 41–45; R Kurtz, "Is Etiquette a Core Value?" *Inc.,* May 2004, p 22; D Weinstein, "Grace in Small Space: Cubicles Encourage New Era of Etiquette," *Arizona Republic,* March 12, 2005, p D3; and K Gurchiek, "Office Etiquette Breaches: Dial It Down," *HR Magazine,* May 2006, p 36.

22 D Stamps, "Yes, Your Boss Is Crazy," *Training,* July 1998, pp 35–39. See also K Robinson, "Stigma Prevents Depressed Workers from Seeking Treatment, Study Shows," *HR Magazine,* June 2004, p 50; G Morse, "Executive Psychopaths," *Harvard Business Review,* October 2004, pp 20, 22; "Weirdos in the Workplace," *Training,* January 2005, p 14; M Elias, "On the Couch: Mental Health," *USA Today,* April 27, 2005, p 6D; and M Elias, "Mental Illness: Surprising, Disturbing Findings," *USA Today,* June 7, 2005, p 8D.

23 See L W Andrews, "Hiring People with Intellectual Disabilities," *HR Magazine,* July 2005, pp 74–77; L M Franze and M B Burns, "Risky Business," *HR Magazine,* November 2005, pp 119–25; F Jossi, "High-Tech Enables Employee," *HR Magazine,* February 2006, pp 109–15; and A Smith, "ADA Accommodation Is Not One-Stop Shopping," *HR Magazine,* May 2006, p 34.

24 See N W Janove, "Sexual Harassment and the Three Big Surprises," *HR Magazine,* November 2001, pp 123–30; and M M Clark, "Failure to Cure Harassment Can Be 'Continuing Violation,'" *HR Magazine,* February 2003, p 106.

25 See D Smith, "Hostility Associated with Immune Function," *Monitor on Psychology,* March 2003, p 47; "The Walking Time Bomb," *Inc.,* December 2003, p 52; D L Coutu, "Losing It," *Harvard Business Review,*

April 2004, pp 37–42; and K Gurchiek, "Domestic Abuse: Serious Hidden Workplace Problem," *HR Magazine,* March 2006, p 38.

26 For practical advice, see N Nicholson, "How to Motivate Your Problem People," *Harvard Business Review,* Special Issue: Motivating People, January 2003, pp 56–65; and M Archer, "How to Work with Annoying People," *USA Today,* March 20, 2006, p 4B.

27 J C McCune, "The Change Makers," *Management Review,* May 1999, pp 16–22.

28 Based on G Labianca, D J Brass, and B Gray, "Social Networks and Perceptions of Intergroup Conflict: The Role of Negative Relationships and Third Parties," *Academy of Management Journal,* February 1998, pp 55–67. See also C Gómez, B L Kirkman, and D L Shapiro, "The Impact of Collectivism and In-Group/Out-Group Membership on the Evaluation Generosity of Team Members," *Academy of Management Journal,* December 2000, pp 1097–106; and K A Jehn and E A Mannix, "The Dynamic Nature of Conflict: A Longitudinal Study of Intragroup Conflict and Group Performance," *Academy of Management Journal,* April 2001, pp 238–51.

29 See R J Eidelson and J I Eidelson, "Dangerous Ideas: Five Beliefs That Propel Groups toward Conflict," *American Psychologist,* March 2003, pp 182–92; D A Rabuzzi, "The Duh Factor: Understanding Intergenerational Differences in Association Life," *Association Management,* July 2004, pp 24–27, 83; L A Rudman and S A Goodwin, "Gender Differences in Automatic In-Group Bias: Why Do Women Like Women More than Men Like Men?" *Journal of Personality and Social Psychology,* October 2004, pp 494–509; G Cowan, "Interracial Interactions at Racially Diverse University Campuses," *Journal of Social Psychology,* February 2005, pp 49–63; and S Kehrli and T Sopp, "Managing Generation Y," *HR Magazine,* May 2006, pp 113–19.

30 Labianca, Brass, and Gray, "Social Networks and Perceptions of Intergroup Conflict," p 63 (emphasis added).

31 For example, see S C Wright, A Aron, T McLaughlin-Volpe, and S A Ropp, "The Extended Contact Effect: Knowledge of Cross-Group Friendships and Prejudice," *Journal of Personality and Social Psychology,* July 1997, pp 73–90.

[32] Labianca, Brass, and Gray, "Social Networks and Perceptions of Intergroup Conflict"; C D Batson et al., "Empathy and Attitudes: Can Feeling for a Member of a Stigmatized Group Improve Feelings toward the Group?" *Journal of Personality and Social Psychology,* January 1997, pp 105–18; and S C Wright et al., "The Extended Contact Effect: Knowledge of Cross-Group Friendships and Prejudice," *Journal of Personality and Social Psychology,* July 1997, pp 73–90. See also C D Batson, M P Polycarpou, E Harmon-Jones, H J Imhoff, E C Mitchener, L L Bednar, T R Klein, and L Highberger, "Empathy and Attitudes: Can Feeling for a Member of a Stigmatized Group Improve Feelings toward the Group?" *Journal of Personality and Social Psychology,* January 1997, pp 105–18.

[33] For more, see N J Adler, *International Dimensions of Organizational Behavior,* 4th ed (Cincinnati: South-Western, 2002); P Engardio, "The Future of Outsourcing," *BusinessWeek,* January 30, 2006, pp 50–58; F Balfour, "One Foot in China," *Business-Week,* May 1, 2006, pp 44–45; L Buchanan, "The Thinking Man's Outsourcing," *Inc.,* May 2006, pp 31–33; B Einhorn, "The Hunt for Chinese Talent," *BusinessWeek,* May 22, 2006, p 104; and R Buderi, "The Talent Magnet," *Fast Company,* June 2006, pp 80–84.

[34] For an interesting case study, see W Kuemmerle, "Go Global—or No?" *Harvard Business Review,* June 2001, pp 37–49.

[35] "Negotiating South of the Border," *Harvard Management Communication Letter,* August 1999, p 12.

[36] A Rosenbaum, "Testing Cultural Waters," *Management Review,* July/August 1999, p 43.

[37] See R L Tung, "American Expatriates Abroad: From Neophytes to Cosmopolitans," *Journal of World Business,* Summer 1998, pp 125–44.

[38] See H M Guttman, "Conflict Management as a Core Leadership Competency," *Training,* November 2005, pp 34–39.

[39] See J Weiss and J Hughes, "What Collaboration? Accept—and Actively Manage—Conflict," *Harvard Business Review,* March 2005, pp 92–101; and G Colvin, "The Wisdom of Dumb Questions," *Fortune,* June 27, 2005, p 157.

[40] R A Cosier and C R Schwenk, "Agreement and Thinking Alike: Ingredients for Poor Decisions," *Academy of Management Executive,* February 1990, p 71. See also J P Kotter, "Kill Complacency," *Fortune,* August 5, 1996, pp 168–70; and S Caudron, "Keeping Team Conflict Alive," *Training & Development,* September 1998, pp 48–52.

[41] For example, see "Facilitators as Devil's Advocates," *Training,* September 1993, p 10. See also K L Woodward, "Sainthood for a Pope?" *Newsweek,* June 21, 1999, p 65.

[42] Good background reading on devil's advocacy can be found in C R Schwenk, "Devil's Advocacy in Managerial Decision Making," *Journal of Management Studies,* April 1984, pp 153–68. See also the critique of devil's advocacy in T Kelley and J Littman, *The Ten Faces of Innovation* (New York: Currency Doubleday, 2005), pp 2–3.

[43] See G Katzenstein, "The Debate on Structured Debate: Toward a Unified Theory," *Organizational Behavior and Human Decision Processes,* June 1996, pp 316–32.

[44] W Kiechel III, "How to Escape the Echo Chamber," *Fortune,* June 18, 1990, p 130.

[45] D M Schweiger, W R Sandberg, and P L Rechner, "Experiential Effects of Dialectical Inquiry, Devil's Advocacy, and Consensus Approaches to Strategic Decision Making," *Academy of Management Journal,* December 1989, pp 745–72.

[46] J S Valacich and C Schwenk, "Devil's Advocacy and Dialectical Inquiry Effects on Face-to-Face and Computer-Mediated Group Decision Making," *Organizational Behavior and Human Decision Processes,* August 1995, pp 158–73.

[47] Quoted in D Jones, "CEOs Need X-Ray Vision in Transition," *USA Today,* April 23, 2001, p 4B.

[48] C K W De Dreu and M A West, "Minority Dissent and Team Innovation: The Importance of Parti-cipation in Decision Making," *Journal of Applied Psychology,* December 2001, pp 1191–201.

[49] For a statistical validation for this model, see M A Rahim and N R Magner, "Confirmatory Factor Analysis of the Styles of Handling Interpersonal Conflict: First-Order Factor Model and Its Invariance across Groups," *Journal of Applied Psychology,* February 1995, pp 122–32.

[50] M A Rahim, "A Strategy for Managing Conflict in Complex Organizations," *Human Relations,* January 1985, p 84.

[51] See R Rubin, "Study: Bullies and Their Victims Tend to Be More Violent," *USA Today,* April 15, 2003, p 9D; and D Salin, "Ways of Explaining Workplace Bullying: A Review of Enabling, Motivating and Precipitating Structures and Processes in the Work Environment," *Human Relations,* October 2003, pp 1213–232.

[52] For more on managing conflict, see Y Shin, "Conflict Resolution in Virtual Teams," *Organizational Dynamics,* no. 4 (2005), pp 331–45; and M DuPraw, "Cut the Conflict with Consensus Building," *Training,* May 2006, p 8.

[53] See J Rasley, "The Revolution You Won't See on TV," *Newsweek,* November 25, 2002, p 13; and C Bendersky, "Organizational Dispute Resolution Systems: A Complementarities Model," *Academy of Management Review,* October 2003, pp 643–56.

[54] M Bordwin, "Do-It-Yourself Justice," *Management Review,* January 1999, pp 56–58.

[55] B Morrow and L M Bernardi, "Resolving Workplace Disputes," *Canadian Manager,* Spring 1999, p 17.

[56] Adapted from K O Wilburn, "Employment Disputes: Solving Them Out of Court," *Management Review,* March 1998, pp 17–21; and Morrow and Bernardi, "Resolving Workplace Disputes," pp 17–19, 27. See also L Ioannou, "Can't We Get Along?" *Fortune,* December 7, 1998, p 244[E]; and D Weimer and S A Forest, "Forced into Arbitration? Not Any More," *BusinessWeek,* March 16, 1998, pp 66–68.

[57] For more, see M M Clark, "A Jury of Their Peers," *HR Magazine,* January 2004, pp 54–59.

[58] Wilburn, "Employment Disputes," p 19.

[59] For more, see S Armour, "Arbitration's Rise Raises Fairness Issue," *USA Today,* June 12, 2001, pp 1B–2B; G Weiss and D Serchuk, "Walled Off from Justice?" *BusinessWeek,* March 22, 2004, pp 90–92; and J Janove, "In Defense of Litigation," *HR Magazine,* May 2006, pp 125–29.

[60] Based on a definition in M A Neale and M H Bazerman, "Negotiating Rationally: The Power and Impact of the Negotiator's Frame," *Academy of Management Executive,* August 1992, pp 42–51.

[61] See, for example, A Fisher, "How to Ask for—and Get—a Raise Now," *Fortune,* December 27, 2004, p 47; B Rosenstein, "Successful Negotiating Depends on Respect for Others, Yourself," *USA Today,* October 10, 2005, p 6B; and R Grover, "The Prime (Time) of Nancy Tellem," *BusinessWeek,* May 29, 2006, pp 50–51.

[62] M H Bazerman and M A Neale, *Negotiating Rationally* (New York: The Free Press, 1992), p 16. See also G Cullinan, J Le Roux, and R Weddigen, "When to Walk Away from a Deal," *Harvard Business Review,* April 2004, pp 96–104; and P H Kim, R L Pinkley, and A R Fragale, "Power Dynamics in Negotiations," *Academy of Management Review,* October 2005, pp 799–822.

[63] Good win-win negotiation strategies can be found in R R Reck and B G Long, *The Win-Win Negotiator: How to Negotiate Favorable Agreements That Last* (New York: Pocket Books, 1987); R Fisher and W Ury, *Getting to Yes: Negotiating Agreement without Giving In* (Boston: Houghton Mifflin, 1981); and R Fisher and D Ertel, *Getting Ready to Negotiate: The Getting to Yes Workbook* (New York: Penguin Books, 1995). See also B Booth and M McCredie, "Taking Steps toward 'Getting to Yes' at Blue Cross and Blue Shield of Florida," *Academy of Management Executive,* August 2004, pp 109–12; and L Thompson and G J Leonardelli, "The Big Bang: The Evolution of Negotiation Research," *Academy of Management Executive,* August 2004, pp 113–17.

[64] Adapted from K Albrecht and S Albrecht, "Added Value Negotiating," *Training,* April 1993, pp 26–29. For an interesting look at Donald Trump's negotiating style, see "The Trophy Life," *Fortune,* April 19, 2004, pp 70–83.

[65] L Babcock, S Laschever, M Gelfand, and D Small, "Nice Girls Don't Ask," *Harvard Business Review,* October 2003, p 14. See also L A Barron, "Ask and You Shall Receive? Gender Differences in Negotiators' Beliefs about Requests for a Higher Salary," *Human Relations,* June 2003, pp 635–62; L D Tyson, "New Clues to the Pay and Leadership Gap," *BusinessWeek,* October 27, 2003, p 36; D Kersten, "Women Need to Learn the Art of the Deal," *USA Today,* November 17, 2003, p 7B; A Fels, "Do Women Lack Ambition?" *Harvard Business Review,* April

2004, pp 50–60; B Brophy, "Bargaining for Bigger Bucks: A Step-by-Step Guide to Negotiating Your Salary," *Business 2.0,* May 2004, p 107; and H R Bowles, L Babcock, and K L McGinn, "Constraints and Triggers: Situational Mechanics of Gender in Negotiation," *Journal of Personality and Social Psychology,* December 2005, pp 951–65.

[66] Based on Brophy, "Bargaining for Bigger Bucks."

Chapter 9

[1] J L Bowditch and A F Buono, *A Primer on Organizational Behavior,* 4th ed (New York: Wiley, 1997), p 120.

[2] For a detailed discussion about selecting an appropriate medium, see B Barry and I Smithey-Fulmer, "The Medium and the Message: The Adaptive Use of Communication Media in Dyadic Influence," *Academy of Management Review,* April 2004, pp 272–92.

[3] M Orey, "Lawyer's Firing Signals Turmoil in Legal Circles," *The Wall Street Journal,* May 21, 2001, p B1.

[4] C Hymowitz, "Diebold's New Chief Shows How to Lead after a Sudden Rise," *The Wall Street Journal,* May 8, 2006, p B1.

[5] See A Fisher, "Offshoring Could Boost Your Career," *Fortune,* January 24, 2005, p 36; and M L Smith, G W Cottrell, F Gosselin, and P G Schyns, "Transmitting and Decoding Facial Expressions," *Psychological Science,* no 3, 2005, pp 184–89.

[6] S Greenhouse and M Barbaro, "Wal-Mart's Leader Shows Sides Online," *Arizona Republic,* February 19, 2006, p D4.

[7] Noise associated with conference calls is discussed in J Sandberg, "Funny Things Happen as Conference Callers Attempt to Multitask," *The Wall Street Journal,* January 26, 2005, p B1.

[8] For a thorough discussion of communication distortion, see E W Larson and J B King, "The Systematic Distortion of Information: An Ongoing Challenge to Management," *Organizational Dynamics,* Winter 1996, pp 49–61.

[9] J Fulk and S Mani, "Distortion of Communication in Hierarchical Relationships," in *Communication Yearbook* 9, ed M L McLaughlin (Beverly Hills, CA: Sage, 1986), p 483.

[10] For a review of this research, see ibid., pp 483–510.

[11] M Frase-Blunt, "Boss: Understanding and Improve Communications," *HR Magazine,* June 2003, p 96.

[12] J D Johnson, W A Donohue, C K Atkin, and S Johnson, "Communication, Involvement, and Perceived Innovativeness," *Group & Organization Management,* March 2001, pp 24–52; and B Davenport Sypher and T E Zorn Jr, "Communication-Related Abilities and Upward Mobility: A Longitudinal Investigation," *Human Communication Research,* Spring 1986, pp 420–31.

[13] Communication competence is discussed in J S Hinton and M W Kramer, "The Impact of Self-Directed Videotape Feedback on Students' Self-Reported Levels of Communication Competence and Apprehension," *Communication Education,* April 1998, pp 151–61; and L J Carrell and S C Willmington, "The Relationship between Self-Report Measures of Communication Apprehension and Trained Observers' Ratings of Communication Competence," *Communication Reports,* Winter 1998, pp 87–95.

[14] See E Raudsepp, "Are You Properly Assertive?" *Supervision,* June 1992, pp 17–18; and D A Infante and F Timmins and C McCabe, "How Assertive Are Nurses in the Workplace? A Preliminary Pilot Study," *Journal of Nursing Management,* January 2005, pp 61–67.

[15] J A Waters, "Managerial Assertiveness," *Business Horizons,* September/October 1982, p 25.

[16] Ibid., p 27.

[17] This statistic was provided by A Fisher, "How Can I Survive a Phone Interview?" *Fortune,* April 19, 2004, p 54.

[18] For a study of decoding nonverbal cues, see E L Cooley, "Attachment Style and Decoding of Nonverbal Cues," *North American Journal of Psychology,* 2005, pp 25–33.

[19] Problems with analyzing body language are discussed in A Pihulyk, "Communicate with Clarity: The Key to Understanding and Influencing Others," *Canadian Manager,* Summer 2003, pp 12–13.

[20] For related research, see J A Hall, "Male and Female Nonverbal Behavior," in *Multichannel Integrations of Nonverbal Behavior,* ed A W Siegman and S Feldstein (Hillsdale, NJ: Lawrence Erlbaum, 1985), pp 195–226.

[21] See R E Axtell, *Gestures: The Do's and Taboos of Body Language around the World* (New York: Wiley, 1991).

[22] See J A Russell, "Facial Expressions of Emotion: What Lies Beyond Minimal Universality?" *Psychological Bulletin*, November 1995, pp 379–91; and Z Stambor, "Women's Facial Expressions Interpreted as Angrier, Less Happy than Men's," *Monitor on Psychology*, January 2005, p 21.

[23] Norms for cross-cultural eye contact are discussed in C Engholm, *When Business East Meets Business West: The Guide to Practice and Protocol in the Pacific Rim* (New York: Wiley, 1991).

[24] These recommendations are based on P Preston, "Nonverbal Communication: Do You Really Say What You Mean?" *Journal of Healthcare Management*, March/April 2005, pp 83–86.

[25] D Knight, "Perks Keeping Workers out of Revolving Door," *The Wall Street Journal*, April 30, 2005, p D3; and G Roper, "Managing Employee Relations," *HR Magazine*, May 2005, pp 101–04.

[26] The discussion of listening styles is based on CrossRoads Institute, "5 Listening Styles," http://www.crossroadsinstitute.org/listyle.html, accessed February 17, 2006; and Pediatric Services, "Listening and Thinking: What's Your Style?" http://www.pediatricservices.com/prof/prof-10.htm, last modified August 10, 2002.

[27] Additional advice for improving listening skills is provided by S D Boyd, "The Human Side of Business: Effective Listening," *Agency Sales*, February 2004, pp 35–37; and B Brooks, "The Power of Active Listening," *Agency Sales*, December 2003, p 47.

[28] S R Covey, *The 7 Habits of Highly Effective People* (New York: Simon & Schuster, 1989).

[29] J Jay, "On Communicating Well," *HR Magazine*, January 2005, pp 87–88.

[30] D Tannen, "The Power of Talk: Who Gets Heard and Why," *Harvard Business Review*, September/October 1995, p 139.

[31] For a thorough review of the evolutionary explanation of sex differences in communication, see A H Eagly and W Wood, "The Origins of Sex Differences in Human Behavior," *American Psychologist*, June 1999, pp 408–23. For a recent critique of evolutionary psychology, see S Begley, "Evolutionary Psych May

Not Help Explain Our Behavior after All," *The Wall Street Journal*, April 29, 2005, p B1.

[32] See D Tannen, "The Power of Talk: Who Gets Heard and Why," in *Negotiation: Readings, Exercises, and Cases*, 3rd ed, ed R J Lewicki and D M Saunders (Boston: Irwin/McGraw-Hill, 1999), pp 160–73; and D Tannen, *You Just Don't Understand: Women and Men in Conversation* (New York: Ballantine Books, 1990).

[33] See M Dainton and E D Zelley, *Applying Communication Theory for Professional Life: A Practical Introduction* (Thousand Oaks, CA: Sage, 2005).

[34] Tannen, "The Power of Talk," pp 147–48.

[35] D Caterinicchia, "University HR's Self-Service Solution," *HR Magazine*, February 2005, pp 105–09.

[36] H Green, S Rosenbush, R O Crockett, and S Holmes, "Wi-Fi Means Business," *BusinessWeek*, April 28, 2003, pp 86–92.

[37] See L Bealko, "Running Effective Online Training," *Techsoup*, January 12, 2006, http://www.techsoup. org/howto/articles/training/page4245.cfm.

[38] M E Medland, "Time Squeeze," *HR Magazine*, November 2004, pp 66–70.

[39] See D Buss, "Spies Like Us," *Training*, December 2001, pp 44–48.

[40] B Meador, "2006 Email Usage Survey Overview," ClearContext Corporate Weblog, July 17, 2006, http://blog.clearcontext.com/2006/07/2006_email_usa g.html; and B Meador, "On the Bright Side, We're Getting Less Spam," ClearContext Corporate Weblog, July 18, 2006, http://blog.clearcontext.com/ 2006/07/the_importance_.html.

[41] J Yaukey, "E-Mail Out of Control for Many: Take Steps to Ease Load," *The Wall Street Journal*, May 8, 2001, p F1.

[42] E Chambers, "Web Watch: The Lid on Spam Is Still Loose," *BusinessWeek*, February 7, 2005, p 10.

[43] L Winerman, "E-Mails and Egos," *Monitor on Psychology*, February 2006, pp 16–17; and J Kruger, N Epley, J Parker, and Z-W Ng, "Egocentrism over E-Mail: Can We Communicate as Well as We Think?" *Journal of Applied Psychology*, December 2005, pp 925–36.

44 M S Thompson and M S Feldman, "Electronic Mail and Organizational Communication: Does Saying 'Hi' Really Matter?" *Organization Science,* November/December 1998, pp 685–98.

45 S Prasso, "Workers, Surf at Your Own Risk," *BusinessWeek,* June 11, 2001, p 14. See also A Pomeroy, "Business 'Fast and Loose' with E-Mail, IMs—Study," *HR Magazine,* November 2004, pp 32, 34.

46 Based on C Cavanagh, *Managing Your E-Mail: Thinking Outside the Inbox* (Hoboken, NJ: Wiley, 2003).

47 J M Alterio, "IBM Taps into Blogosphere," *Arizona Republic,* January 21, 2006, p D3.

48 Alterio, "IBM Taps into Blogosphere."

49 D Kirkpatrick, "Sun Microsystems: It's Hard to Manage if You Don't Blog," *Fortune,* October 4, 2004, p 46; and A Lashinsky, "Is This the Right Man for Intel?" *Fortune,* April 18, 2005, pp 110–20.

50 "Firms Taking Action against Worker Blogs," *MSNBC News,* March 7, 2005, www.msnbc.msn.com/id/7116338.

51 J Gordon, "Straight Talk: Wasting Time on the Company Dime," *Training,* May 2006, p 6.

52 E Krell, "Videoconferencing Gets the Call," *Training*, December 2001, p 38.

53 S A Rains, "Leveling the Organizational Playing Field—Virtually: A Meta-Analysis of Experimental Research Assessing the Impact of Group Support System Use on Member Influence Behaviors," *Communication Research,* April 2005, pp 193–234.

54 See S O'Mahony and S R Barley, "Do Digital Telecommunications Affect Work and Organization? The State of Our Knowledge," in *Research in Organizational Behavior* 21, ed R I Sutton and B M Staw (Stamford, CT: JAI Press, 1999), pp 125–61.

55 M Naylor, "There's No Workforce Like Home," *BusinessWeek Online,* May 2, 2006, www.businessweek.com; and S Shellenbarger, "Outsourcing Jobs to the Den: Call Centers Tap People Who Want to Work at Home," *The Wall Street Journal,* January 12, 2006, p D1.

56 A Donoghue, "2010: The Year of the Techie," *ZDNet UK News,* May 13, 2006, http://news.zdnet.co.uk/business/o,39020645,39269493,00.htm.

57 B Hemphill, "Telecommuting Productively," *Occupational Health & Safety,* March 2004, pp 16, 18; R Konrad, "Sun's 'iWork' Shuns Desks for Flexibility," *Arizona Republic,* May 28, 2003, p D4; and C Hymowitz, "Remote Managers Find Ways to Narrow the Distance Gap," *The Wall Street Journal,* April 6, 1999, p B1.

58 See M Tan-Solano and B Kleiner, "Virtual Workers: Are They Worth the Risk?" *Nonprofit World,* November/December 2003, pp 20–22.

59 The barriers identified in this paragraph are discussed in J P Scully, "People: The Imperfect Communicators," *Quality Progress,* April 1995, pp 37–39.

60 For a thorough discussion of these barriers, see C R Rogers and F J Roethlisberger, "Barriers and Gateways to Communication," *Harvard Business Review,* July/August 1952, pp 46–52.

61 Ibid., p 47.

62 See M Munter, "Cross-Cultural Communication for Managers," *Business Horizons,* May/June 1993, pp 69–78.

63 I Adler, "Between the Lines," *Business Mexico,* October 2000, p 24.

64 R Drew, "Working with Foreigners," *Management Review,* September 1999, p 6.

65 S Srivastava, "Why India Worries about Outsourcing," *San Francisco Chronicle,* March 21, 2004, p E3.

66 J Sandberg, "In the Workplace, Every Bleeping Word Can Show Your Rank," *The Wall Street Journal,* March 21, 2006, p B1.

67 See C Hymowitz, "Mind Your Language: To Do Business Today, Consider Delayering," *The Wall Street Journal,* March 27, 2006, p B1.

Chapter 10

1 See A Hanft, "Every Business Needs a Nanny," *Inc.,* March 2006, p 128.

2 See D Kipnis, S M Schmidt, and J Wilkinson, "Intraorganizational Influence Tactics: Explorations in Getting One's Way," *Journal of Applied Psychology,* August 1980, pp 440–52. See also

C A Schriesheim and T R Hinkin, "Influence Tactics Used by Subordinates: A Theoretical and Empirical Analysis and Refinement of the Kipnis, Schmidt, and Wilkinson Subscales," *Journal of Applied Psychology,* June 1990, pp 246–57; and G Yukl and C M Falbe, "Influence Tactics and Objectives in Upward, Downward, and Lateral Influence Attempts," *Journal of Applied Psychology,* April 1990, pp 132–40.

3 See C D Cooper, "Just Joking Around? Employee Humor Expression as an Ingratiatory Behavior," *Academy of Management Review,* October 2005, pp 765–76.

4 Based on Table 1 in G Yukl, C M Falbe, and J Y Youn, "Patterns of Influence Behavior for Managers," *Group and Organization Management,* March 1993, pp 5–28. An additional influence tactic is presented in B P Davis and E S Knowles, "A Disrupt-then-Reframe Technique of Social Influence," *Journal of Personality and Social Psychology,* February 1999, pp 192–99. See also Table 1 in P P Fu, T K Peng, J C Kennedy, and G Yukl, "Examining the Preferences of Influence Tactics in Chinese Societies: A Comparison of Chinese Managers in Hong Kong, Taiwan and Mainland China," *Organizational Dynamics,* no. 1, 2004, pp 32–46.

5 For related reading, see K D Elsbach, "How to Pitch a Brilliant Idea," *Harvard Business Review,* September 2003, pp 117–23; "Daddy Dearest," *Inc.,* January 2004, p 46; K Hannon, "Working for the I-Boss," *USA Today,* March 1, 2004, p 5B; J Battelle, "The Net of Influence," *Business 2.0,* March 2004, p 70; B Barry and I S Fulmer, "The Medium and the Message: The Adaptive Use of Communication Media in Dyadic Influence," *Academy of Management Review,* April 2004, pp 272–92; and C Bartz, "If You Think You Can't, You're Right," *Business 2.0,* December 2005, p 118.

6 Based on discussion in G Yukl, H Kim, and C M Falbe, "Antecedents of Influence Outcomes," *Journal of Applied Psychology,* June 1996, pp 309–17.

7 See R E Boyatzis, M L Smith, and N Blaize, "Developing Sustainable Leaders through Coaching and Compassion," *Academy of Management Learning and Education,* March 2006, pp 8–24.

8 C Tkaczyk, "Follow These Leaders," *Fortune,* December 12, 2005, p 125.

9 Yukl, Kim, and Falbe, "Antecedents of Influence Outcomes."

10 G Yukl and J B Tracey, "Consequences of Influence Tactics Used with Subordinates, Peers, and the Boss," *Journal of Applied Psychology,* August 1992, pp 525–35. See also C M Falbe and G Yukl, "Consequences for Managers of Using Single Influence Tactics and Combinations of Tactics," *Academy of Management Journal,* August 1992, pp 638–52.

11 R A Gordon, "Impact of Ingratiation on Judgments and Evaluations: A Meta-Analytic Investigation," *Journal of Personality and Social Psychology,* July 1996, pp 54–70. See also S J Wayne, R C Liden, and R T Sparrowe, "Developing Leader-Member Exchanges," *American Behavioral Scientist,* March 1994, pp 697–714; A Oldenburg, "These Days, Hostile Is Fitting for Takeovers Only," *USA Today,* July 22, 1996, pp 8B, 10B; and J H Dulebohn and G R Ferris, "The Role of Influence Tactics in Perceptions of Performance Evaluations' Fairness," *Academy of Management Journal,* June 1999, pp 288–303.

12 Yukl, Kim, and Falbe, "Antecedents of Influence Outcomes."

13 C Pornpitakpan, "The Persuasiveness of Source Credibility: A Critical Review of Five Decades' Evidence," *Journal of Applied Social Psychology,* February 2004, pp 243–81.

14 B J Tepper, R J Eisenbach, S L Kirby, and P W Potter, "Test of a Justice-Based Model of Subordinates' Resistance to Downward Influence Attempts," *Group and Organization Management,* June 1998, pp 144–60. See also H G Enns and D B McFarlin, "When Executives Influence Peers: Does Function Matter?" *Human Resource Management,* Summer 2003, pp 125–42.

15 J E Driskell, B Olmstead, and E Salas, "Task Cues, Dominance Cues, and Influence in Task Groups," *Journal of Applied Psychology,* February 1993, p 51. See also H Aginis and S K R Adams, "Social-Role versus Structural Models of Gender and Influence Use in Organizations: A Strong Inference Approach," *Group and Organization Management,* December 1998, pp 414–46; and R J Green, J C Sandall, and C Phelps, "Effect of Experimenter Attire and Sex on Participant Productivity," *Social Behavior and Personality,* no. 2, 2005, pp 125–32.

[16] See P P Fu et al., "The Impact of Societal Cultural Values and Individual Social Beliefs on the Perceived Effectiveness of Managerial Influence Strategies: A Meso Approach," *Journal of International Business Studies,* July 2004, pp 284–305.

[17] B Moses, "You Can't Make Change; You Have to Sell It," *Fast Company,* April 1999, p 101. See also D Jones, "Debating Skills Come in Handy in Business," *USA Today,* September 30, 2004, p 3B; and J Reingold, "Suck Up and Move Up," *Fast Company,* January 2005, p 34.

[18] A R Cohen and D L Bradford, *Influence without Authority* (New York: Wiley, 1990), pp 23–24.

[19] Ibid., pp 23–24.

[20] Ibid., p 28. See also R B Cialdini, *Influence* (New York: William Morrow, 1984); R B Cialdini, "Harnessing the Science of Persuasion," *Harvard Business Review,* October 2001, pp 72–79; and G A Williams and R B Miller, "Change the Way You Persuade," *Harvard Business Review,* May 2002, pp 64–73.

[21] See, for example, H Ma, R Karri, and K Chittipeddi, "The Paradox of Managerial Tyranny," *Business Horizons,* July/August 2004, pp 33–40; A Pomeroy, "The Ethics Squeeze," *HR Magazine,* March 2006, pp 48–55; R A Caro, "Lessons in Power: Lyndon Johnson Revealed," *Harvard Business Review,* April 2006, pp 47–52; and M Hosenball and E Thomas, "Hold the Phone: Big Brother Knows Whom You Call," *Newsweek,* May 22, 2006, pp 22–32.

[22] D Tjosvold, "The Dynamics of Positive Power," *Training and Development Journal,* June 1984, p 72. See also T A Stewart, "Get with the New Power Game," *Fortune,* January 13, 1997, pp 58–62.

[23] See, for example, L Lavelle, "How to Groom the Next Boss," *BusinessWeek,* May 10, 2004, pp 93–94; J Welch and S Welch, "Tough Guys Finish First," *BusinessWeek,* April 24, 2006, p 112; and W B Werther, "From Manager to Executive," *Organizational Dynamics,* no. 2 (2006): 196–204.

[24] M W McCall Jr, *Power, Influence, and Authority: The Hazards of Carrying a Sword,* Technical Report No. 10 (Greensboro, NC: Center for Creative Leadership, 1978), p 5. For an excellent overview of power, see E P Hollander and L R Offermann, "Power and Leadership in Organizations," *American Psychologist,* February 1990, pp 179–89.

[25] D Weimer, "Daughter Knows Best," *BusinessWeek,* April 19, 1999, pp 132, 134. For an update, see C L Bernick, "When Your Culture Needs a Makeover," *Harvard Business Review,* June 2001, pp 53–61. See also "How to Stage a Coup," *Inc.,* March 2005, p 52.

[26] J R P French and B Raven, "The Bases of Social Power," in *Studies in Social Power,* ed D Cartwright (Ann Arbor: University of Michigan Press, 1959), pp 150–67. See also C M Fiol, E J O'Connor, and H Aguinis, "All for One and One for All? The Development and Transfer of Power across Organizational Levels," *Academy of Management Review,* April 2001, pp 224–42.

[27] For examples, see "Greenberg and Sons," *Fortune,* February 21, 2005, pp 104–14; and C Dickey, "The Demise of the Don," *Newsweek,* April 24, 2006, p 40.

[28] See M Goldsmith, "It's Not a Fair Fight if You're the CEO," *Fast Company,* December 2004, p 99; E Thornton, "Maybe Low-Key Is the Answer," *BusinessWeek,* February 7, 2005, pp 70–71; and S M Farmer and H Aguinis, "Accounting for Subordinate Perceptions of Supervisor Power: An Identity-Dependence Model," *Journal of Applied Psychology,* November 2005, pp 1069–83.

[29] J R Larson Jr, C Christensen, A S Abbott, and T M Franz, "Diagnosing Groups: Charting the Flow of Information in Medical Decision-Making Teams," *Journal of Personality and Social Psychology,* August 1996, pp 315–30.

[30] Research involving expert and referent power is reported in J S Bunderson, "Team Member Functional Background and Involvement in Management Teams: Direct Effects and the Moderating Role of Power Centralization," *Academy of Management Journal,* August 2003, pp 458–74. See also M Maccoby, "Why People Follow the Leader: The Power of Transference," *Harvard Business Review,* September 2004, pp 76–85; and D A Nadler, "Confessions of a Trusted Counselor," *Harvard Business Review,* September 2005, pp 68–77.

[31] P M Podsakoff and C A Schriesheim, "Field Studies of French and Raven's Bases of Power: Critique, Reanalysis, and Suggestions for Future Research," *Psychological Bulletin,* May 1985, p 388. See also M A Rahim and G F Buntzman, "Supervisory Power Bases, Styles of Handling Conflict with Subordinates, and Subordinate

Compliance and Satisfaction," *Journal of Psychology,* March 1989, pp 195–210; D Tjosvold, "Power and Social Context in Superior-Subordinate Interaction," *Organizational Behavior and Human Decision Processes,* June 1985, pp 281–93; and C A Schriesheim, T R Hinkin, and P M Podsakoff, "Can Ipsative and Single-Item Measures Produce Erroneous Results in Field Studies of French and Raven's (1950) Five Bases of Power? An Empirical Investigation," *Journal of Applied Psychology,* February 1991, pp 106–14.

[32] T R Hinkin and C A Schriesheim, "Relationships between Subordinate Perceptions and Supervisor Influence Tactics and Attributed Bases of Supervisory Power," *Human Relations,* March 1990, pp 221–37. See also D J Brass and M E Burkhardt, "Potential Power and Power Use: An Investigation of Structure and Behavior," *Academy of Management Journal,* June 1993, pp 441–70; and K W Mossholder, N Bennett, E R Kemery, and M A Wesolowski, "Relationships between Bases of Power and Work Reactions: The Mediational Role of Procedural Justice," *Journal of Management,* no. 4, 1998, pp 533–52.

[33] See H E Baker III, "'Wax On–Wax Off': French and Raven at the Movies," *Journal of Management Education,* November 1993, pp 517–19; and J A Clair, R DuFresne, N Jackson, and J Ladge, "Being the Bearer of Bad News: Challenges Facing Downsizing Agents in Organizations," *Organizational Dynamics,* no. 2 (2006), pp 131–44.

[34] See R Forrester, "Empowerment: Rejuvenating a Potent Idea," *Academy of Management Executive,* August 2000, pp 67–80; P J Sauer, "Open-Door Management," *Inc.,* June 2003, p 44; L Grensing-Pophal, "Involve Your Employees in Cost Cutting," *HR Magazine,* November 2003, pp 52–56; C L Pearce, and C C Manz, "The New Silver Bullets of Leadership: The Importance of Self- and Shared Leadership in Knowledge Work," *Organizational Dynamics,* no. 2 (2005): 130–40; R Adler, "Putting Sport into Organizations: The Role of the Accountant," *Business Horizons,* January/February 2006, pp 31–39; and H Dolezalek, "Working Smart," *Training,* April 2006, pp 40–44.

[35] J Macdonald, "The Dreaded 'E Word,'" *Training,* September 1998, p 19. See also R C Liden and S Arad, "A Power Perspective of Empowerment and

Work Groups: Implications for Human Resources Management Research," in *Research in Personnel and Human Resources Management* 14, ed G R Ferris (Greenwich, CT: JAI Press, 1996), pp 205–51.

[36] R M Hodgetts, "A Conversation with Steve Kerr," *Organizational Dynamics,* Spring 1996, p 71. See also S E Seibert, S R Silver, and W A Randolph, "Taking Empowerment to the Next Level: A Multiple-Level Model of Empowerment, Performance, and Satisfaction," *Academy of Management Journal,* June 2004, pp 332–49; B Roberts, "Empowerment or Imposition?" *HR Magazine,* June 2004, pp 157–66; H Mintzberg, "Enough Leadership," *Harvard Business Review,* November 2004, p 22; and K Ayers, "Creating a Responsible Workplace," *HR Magazine,* February 2005, pp 111–13.

[37] For related discussion, see R E Quinn and G M Spreitzer, "The Road to Empowerment: Seven Questions Every Leader Should Consider," *Organizational Dynamics,* Autumn 1997, pp 37–49; S Zuboff, "Ranking Ourselves to Death," *Fast Company,* November 2004, p 125; and "Managing a Micromanager," *Inc.,* April 2005, p 50.

[38] F Vogelstein, "Star Power: Greg Brown, Motorola," *Fortune,* February 6, 2006, p 57.

[39] For recent research, see S H Wagner, C P Parker, and N D Christiansen, "Employees That Think and Act Like Owners: Effects of Ownership Beliefs and Behaviors on Organizational Effectiveness," *Personnel Psychology,* Winter 2003, pp 847–71; D J Leach, T D Wall, and P R Jackson, "The Effect of Empowerment on Job Knowledge: An Empirical Test Involving Operators of Complex Technology," *Journal of Occupational and Organizational Psychology,* March 2003, pp 27–52; P T Coleman, "Implicit Theories of Organizational Power and Priming Effects on Managerial Power-Sharing Decisions: An Experimental Study," *Journal of Applied Social Psychology,* February 2004, pp 297–321; B L Kirkman, B Rosen, P E Tesluk, and C B Gibson, "The Impact of Team Empowerment on Virtual Team Performance: The Moderating Role of Face-to-Face Interaction," *Academy of Management Journal,* April 2004, pp 175–92; and M Ahearne, J Mathieu, and A Rapp, "To Empower or Not to Empower Your Sales Force? An Empirical Examination of the Influence of Leadership Empowerment Behavior on Customer Satisfaction and Performance," *Journal of Applied Psychology,* September 2005, pp 945–55.

[40] W A Randolph, "Navigating the Journey to Empowerment," *Organizational Dynamics,* Spring 1995, p 31.

[41] See K Naughton and Marc Peyser, "The World According to Trump," *Newsweek,* March 1, 2004, pp 48–57; D Jones, "It's Nothing Personal? On 'Apprentice,' It's All Personal," *USA Today,* March 26, 2004, p 6B; D Jones and B Keveney, "10 Lessons of 'The Apprentice,'" *USA Today,* April 15, 2004, pp 1A–5A; A Pomeroy, "Business Reality TV?" *HR Magazine,* January 2005, p 14; and R Underwood, "Fast Talk: What I Learned on *The Apprentice,*" *Fast Company,* May 2005, pp 45–50.

[42] C Pasternak, "Corporate Politics May Not Be a Waste of Time," *HR Magazine,* September 1994, p 18. See also D J Burrough, "Office Politics Mirror Popular TV Program," *Arizona Republic,* February 4, 2001, p EC1.

[43] See G Browning and J James, "Office Politics: The New Game," *Management Today,* May 2003, pp 54–59; P L Perrewé, K L Zellars, G R Ferris, A M Rossi, C J Kacmar, and D A Ralston, "Neutralizing Job Stressors: Political Skills as an Antidote to the Dysfunctional Consequences of Role Conflict," *Academy of Management Journal,* February 2004, pp 141–52; J Sandberg, "From the Front Lines: Bosses Muster Staffs for Border Skirmishes," *The Wall Street Journal,* February 18, 2004, p B1; K Hannon, "Change the Way You Play: Small Things You Can Do to Get Ahead," *USA Today,* March 15, 2004, p 6B; and G R Ferris, S L Davidson, and P L Perrewé, *Political Skill at Work* (Palo Alto, CA: Davies-Black, 2005).

[44] R W Allen, D L Madison, L W Porter, P A Renwick, and B T Mayes, "Organizational Politics: Tactics and Characteristics of Its Actors," *California Management Review,* Fall 1979, p 77. For a comprehensive overview, see K M Kacmar and R A Baron, "Organizational Politics: The State of the Field, Links to Related Processes, and an Agenda for Future Research," in *Research in Personnel and Human Resources Management* 17, ed G R Ferris (Stamford, CT: JAI Press, 1999), pp 1–39. See also K M Kacmar and G R Ferris, "Politics at Work: Sharpening the Focus of Political Behavior in Organizations," *Business Horizons,* July/August 1993, pp 70–74; G R Ferris, D C Treadway, R W Kolodinsky, W A Hochwarter, C J Kacmar, C Douglas, and D D Frink, "Development and Validation of the Political Skill

Inventory," *Journal of Management,* no. 1, 2005, pp 126–52; and T B Lawrence, M K Mauws, B Dyck, and R F Kleysen, "The Politics of Organizational Learning: Integrating Power into the 41 Framework," *Academy of Management Review,* January 2005, pp 180–91.

[45] See P M Fandt and G R Ferris, "The Management of Information and Impressions: When Employees Behave Opportunistically," *Organizational Behavior and Human Decision Processes,* February 1990, pp 140–58; L R Offermann, "When Followers Become Toxic," *Harvard Business Review,* Special Issue: Inside the Mind of the Leader, January 2004, pp 54–60; and K J Sulkowicz, "Worse than Enemies: The CEO's Destructive Confidant," *Harvard Business Review,* February 2004, pp 64–71.

[46] D R Beeman and T W Sharkey, "The Use and Abuse of Corporate Politics," *Business Horizons,* March/April 1987, pp 26–30; and A Raia, "Power, Politics, and the Human Resource Professional," *Human Resource Planning,* no. 4, 1985, p 203.

[47] "The Big Picture: Reasons for Raises," *Business-Week,* May 29, 2006, p 11.

[48] A J DuBrin, "Career Maturity, Organizational Rank, and Political Behavioral Tendencies: A Correlational Analysis of Organizational Politics and Career Experience," *Psychological Reports,* October 1988, p 535.

[49] This three-level distinction comes from A T Cobb, "Political Diagnosis: Applications in Organizational Development," *Academy of Management Review,* July 1986, pp 482–96.

[50] For an excellent historical and theoretical perspective of coalitions, see W B Stevenson, J L Pearce, and L W Porter, "The Concept of 'Coalition' in Organization Theory and Research," *Academy of Management Review,* April 1985, pp 256–68. See also A Kleiner, "Are You In with the In Crowd?" *Harvard Business Review,* July 2003, pp 86–92.

[51] See, for example, "How the HP Board KO'd Carly," *Fortune,* March 7, 2005, pp 99–102.

[52] See R Cross and S Colella, "Building Vibrant Employee Networks," *HR Magazine,* December 2004, pp 101–04; and B Uzzi and S Dunlap, "How to Build Your Network," *Harvard Business Review,* December 2005, pp 53–60.

[53] J Sandberg, "Better than Great—and Other Tall Tales of Self-Evaluations," *The Wall Street Journal,* March 12, 2003, p B1. See also see J Sandberg, "Sabotage 101: The Sinister Art of Back-Stabbing," *The Wall Street Journal,* February 11, 2004, p B1.

[54] Allen, Madison, Porter, Renwick, and Mayes, "Organizational Politics," p 77. See also D C Treadway, W A Hochwarter, C J Kacmar, and G R Ferris, "Political Will, Political Skill, and Political Behavior," *Journal of Organizational Behavior,* May 2005, pp 229–45.

[55] See W L Gardner III, "Lessons in Organizational Dramaturgy: The Art of Impression Management," *Organizational Dynamics,* Summer 1992, pp 33–46.

[56] A Rao, S M Schmidt, and L H Murray, "Upward Impression Management: Goals, Influence Strategies, and Consequences," *Human Relations,* February 1995, p 147. See also M C Andrews and K M Kacmar, "Impression Management by Association: Construction and Validation of a Scale," *Journal of Vocational Behavior,* February 2001, pp 142–61; P F Hewlin, "And the Award for Best Actor Goes to . . . : Facades of Conformity in Organizational Settings," *Academy of Management Review,* October 2003, pp 633–42; and D Rosato, "The 'Oh, S#&%!' Moment," *Money,* February 2006, pp 126–30.

[57] For related research, see M G Pratt and A Rafaeli, "Organizational Dress as a Symbol of Multilayered Social Identities," *Academy of Management Journal,* August 1997, pp 862–98. See also L M Roberts, "Changing Faces: Professional Image Construction in Diverse Organizational Settings," *Academy of Management Review,* October 2005, pp 685–711; L A McFarland, G Yun, C M Harold, L Viera Jr, and L G Moore, "An Examination of Impression Management Use and Effectiveness across Assessment Center Exercises: The Role of Competency Demands," *Personnel Psychology,* Winter 2005, pp 949–80; and D R Avery and P F McKay, "Target Practice: An Organizational Impression Management Approach to Attracting Minority and Female Job Applicants," *Personnel Psychology,* Spring 2006, pp 157–87.

[58] S Friedman, "What Do You Really Care About? What Are You Most Interested In?" *Fast Company,* March 1999, p 90. See also B M DePaulo and D A Kashy, "Everyday Lies in Close and Casual Relationships," *Journal of Personality and Social Psychology,* January 1998, pp 63–79; and J Alsever, "The Ethics Monitor," *Fast Company,* May 2005, p 33.

[59] S J Wayne and G R Ferris, "Influence Tactics, Affect, and Exchange Quality in Supervisor-Subordinate Interactions: A Laboratory Experiment and Field Study," *Journal of Applied Psychology,* October 1990, pp 487–99. For another version, see Table 1 (p 246) in S J Wayne and R C Liden, "Effects of Impression Management on Performance Ratings: A Longitudinal Study," *Academy of Management Journal,* February 1995, pp 232–60.

[60] See R Vonk, "The Slime Effect: Suspicion and Dislike of Likeable Behavior toward Superiors," *Journal of Personality and Social Psychology,* April 1998, pp 849–64; and M Wells, "How to Schmooze Like the Best of Them," *USA Today,* May 18, 1999, p 14E.

[61] See P Rosenfeld, R A Giacalone, and C A Riordan, "Impression Management Theory and Diversity: Lessons for Organizational Behavior," *American Behavioral Scientist,* March 1994, pp 601–04; R A Giacalone and J W Beard, "Impression Management, Diversity, and International Management," *American Behavioral Scientist,* March 1994, pp 621–36; and A Montagliani and R A Giacalone, "Impression Management and Cross-Cultural Adaptation," *Journal of Social Psychology,* October 1998, pp 598–608.

[62] M E Mendenhall and C Wiley, "Strangers in a Strange Land: The Relationship between Expatriate Adjustment and Impression Management," *American Behavioral Scientist,* March 1994, pp 605–20. See also J Kurman, "Why Is Self-Enhancement Low in Certain Collectivist Cultures? An Investigation of Two Competing Explanations," *Journal of Cross-Cultural Psychology,* September 2003, pp 496–510.

[63] For a humorous discussion of making a bad impression, see P Hellman, "Looking BAD," *Management Review,* January 2000, p 64.

[64] T E Becker and S L Martin, "Trying to Look Bad at Work: Methods and Motives for Managing Poor Impressions in Organizations," *Academy of Management Journal,* February 1995, p 191.

[65] Ibid., p 181.

[66] Ibid., pp 180–81.

[67] See ibid., pp 192–93.

[68] A Zaleznik, "Real Work," *Harvard Business Review,* January/February 1989, p 60.

[69] Adapted in part from L B MacGregor Serven, *The End of Office Politics as Usual* (New York: American Management Association, 2002), pp 184–99.

[70] B Morris, "The GE Mystique," *Fortune,* March 6, 2006, p 98. See also L A Witt, "Enhancing Organizational Goal Congruence: A Solution to Organizational Politics," *Journal of Applied Psychology,* August 1998, pp 666–74; and C C Rosen, P E Levy, and R J Hall, "Placing Perceptions of Politics in the Context of the Feedback Environment, Employee Attitudes, and Job Performance," *Journal of Applied Psychology,* January 2006, pp 211–20.

Chapter 11

[1] P G Northouse, *Leadership: Theory and Practice,* 3rd ed (Thousand Oaks, CA: Sage, 2004), p 3.

[2] The different levels of leadership are thoroughly discussed in F J Yammarino, F Dansereau, and C J Kennedy, "A Multiple-Level Multidimensional Approach to Leadership: Viewing Leadership through an Elephant's Eye," *Organizational Dynamics,* 2001, pp 149–62.

[3] B Kellerman, "Leadership Warts and All," *Harvard Business Review,* January 2004, p 45.

[4] See S Covey, "Why Is It Always about You?" *Training,* May 2006, p 64.

[5] See R Goffee and G Jones, "Followership: It's Personal, Too," *Harvard Business Review,* December 2001, p 148.

[6] S Lieberson and J F O'Connor, "Leadership and Organizational Performance: A Study of Large Corporations," *American Sociological Review,* April 1972, pp 117–30. The impact of leadership on financial performance is also supported by "How HR Can Affect the Bottom Line," *HR Magazine,* February 2005, pp 14, 16.

[7] K T Dirks, "Trust in Leadership and Team Performance: Evidence from NCAA Basketball," *Journal of Applied Psychology,* December 2000, pp 1004–12; and D Jacobs and L Singell, "Leadership and Organizational Performance: Isolating Links between Managers and Collective Success," *Social Science Research,* June 1993, pp 165–89.

[8] Leadership development programs are discussed in B J Avolio, *Leadership Development in Balance* (Mahway, NJ: Lawrence Erlbaum Associates, 2005); and B Hall, "The Top Training Priorities for 2005," *Training,* February 2005, pp 22–29.

[9] D A Kenny and S J Zaccaro, "An Estimate of Variance Due to Traits in Leadership," *Journal of Applied Psychology,* November 1983, pp 678–85.

[10] T A Judge, J E Bono, R Ilies, and M W Gerhardt, "Personality and Leadership: A Qualitative and Quantitative Review," *Journal of Applied Psychology,* August 2002, pp 765–80.

[11] T A Judge, A E Colbert, and R Ilies, "Intelligence and Leadership: A Quantitative Review and Test of Theoretical Propositions," *Journal of Applied Psychology,* June 2004, pp 542–52.

[12] See S Xavier, "Are You at the Top of Your Game? Checklist for Effective Leaders," *Journal of Business Strategy* (2005), pp 35–42.

[13] See R M Kramer, "The Great Intimidators," *Harvard Business Review,* February 2006, pp 88–96. For an example, see J Ball, "The New Act at Exxon," *The Wall Street Journal,* March 8, 2006, pp B1, B2.

[14] Kramer, "The Great Intimidators," pp 95–96.

[15] Gender and the emergence of leaders was examined in A H Eagly and S J Karau, "Gender and the Emergence of Leaders: A Meta-Analysis," *Journal of Personality and Social Psychology,* May 1991, pp 685–710; and R K Shelly and P T Munroe, "Do Women Engage in Less Task Behavior than Men?" *Sociological Perspectives,* Spring 1999, pp 49–67.

[16] A H Eagly, S J Karau, and B T Johnson, "Gender and Leadership Style among School Principals: A Meta-Analysis," *Educational Administration Quarterly,* February 1992, pp 76–102.

[17] Supportive findings are contained in J M Twenge, "Changes in Women's Assertiveness in Response to Status and Roles: A Cross-Temporal Meta-Analysis, 1931–1993," *Journal of Personality and Social Psychology,* July 2001, pp 133–45.

[18] For a summary of this research, see R Sharpe, "As Leaders, Women Rule," *BusinessWeek,* November 20, 2000, pp 74–84.

[19] The process of preparing a development plan is discussed in L Morgan, G Spreitzer, J Dutton, R Quinn, E Heaphy, and B Barker, "How to Play to Your Strengths," *Harvard Business Review,* January 2005, pp 75–80. Executive coaching is discussed in M F R Kets de Vries, "Leadership Group Coaching in Action: The Zen of Creating High-Performance Teams," *Academy of Management Executive,* February 2005, pp 61–76; and H Johnson, "The Ins and Outs of Executive Coaching," *Training,* May 2004, pp 36–41.

[20] A Pomeroy, "Head of the Class," *HR Magazine,* January 2005, pp 54–58.

[21] For corporate examples of leadership development, see J Sandberg, "Trying to Tease Out My Leadership Talent in One Easy Seminar," *The Wall Street Journal,* March 28, 2006, p B1; J Sandberg, "The Sensitive Me Won't Be Leading Corporate America," *The Wall Street Journal,* April 11, 2006, p B1; and S Max, "Seagate's Morale-athon," *BusinessWeek,* April 3, 2006, pp 110–12.

[22] B M Bass, *Bass & Stogdill's Handbook of Leadership: Theory, Research, and Managerial Applications,* 3rd ed (New York: Free Press, 1990), chs 20–25.

[23] The relationships between the frequency and mastery of leader behavior and various outcomes were investigated by F Shipper and C S White, "Mastery, Frequency, and Interaction of Managerial Behaviors Relative to Subunit Effectiveness," *Human Relations,* January 1999, pp 49–66.

[24] F E Fiedler, "Job Engineering for Effective Leadership: A New Approach," *Management Review,* September 1977, p 29.

[25] For more on this theory, see F E Fiedler, "A Contingency Model of Leadership Effectiveness," in *Advances in Experimental Social Psychology* 1, ed L Berkowitz (New York: Academic Press, 1964); and F E Fiedler, *A Theory of Leadership Effectiveness* (New York: McGraw-Hill, 1967).

[26] See L H Peters, D D Hartke, and J T Pohlmann, "Fiedler's Contingency Theory of Leadership: An Application of the Meta-Analyses Procedures of Schmidt and Hunter," *Psychological Bulletin,* March 1985, pp 274–85; and C A Schriesheim, B J Tepper, and L A Tetrault, "Least Preferred Co-Worker Score, Situational Control, and Leadership Effectiveness: A Meta-Analysis of Contingency Model Performance Predictions," *Journal of Applied Psychology,* August 1994, pp 561–73.

[27] D Kirkpatrick, "Inside Sam's $100 Billion Growth Machine," *Fortune,* June 14, 2004, pp 86, 88.

[28] For more detail on this theory, see R J House, "A Path–Goal Theory of Leader Effectiveness," *Administrative Science Quarterly,* September 1971, pp 321–38.

[29] This research is summarized in R J House, "Path–Goal Theory of Leadership: Lessons, Legacy, and a Reformulated Theory," *Leadership Quarterly,* Autumn 1996, pp 323–52.

[30] Ibid.

[31] Ibid.

[32] For examples, see K Brokker, "The Pepsi Machine," *Fortune,* February 6, 2006, pp 68–72; B Morris, "Star Power: Ursula Burns," *Fortune,* February 6, 2006, p 57; and P Burrows, HP's Ultimate Team Player," *BusinessWeek,* January 30, 2006, pp 76–78.

[33] For details, see S Tully, "The Contender in This Corner: Jamie Dimon," *Fortune,* April 3, 2006, pp 56, 58.

[34] P M Podsakoff, S B MacKenzie, M Ahearne, and W H Bommer, "Searching for a Needle in a Haystack: Trying to Identify the Illusive Moderators of Leadership Behaviors," *Journal of Management* (1995), pp 422–70.

[35] For a complete description of this theory, see B J Bass and B J Avolio, *Revised Manual for the Multi-Factor Leadership Questionnaire* (Palo Alto, CA: Mindgarden, 1997).

[36] For a definition and description of transactional leadership, see J Antonakis and R J House, "The Full-Range Leadership Theory: The Way Forward," in *Transformational and Charismatic Leadership: The Road Ahead,* ed B J Avolio and F J Yammarino (New York: JAI Press, 2002), pp 3–34.

[37] A Carter, "It's Norman Time," *BusinessWeek,* May 29, 2006, p 68.

[38] U R Dumdum, K B Lowe, and B J Avolio, "A Meta-Analysis of Transformational and Transactional Leadership Correlates of Effectiveness and

Satisfaction: An Update and Extension," in *Transformational and Charismatic Leadership: The Road Ahead,* ed B J Avolio and F J Yammarino (New York: JAI Press, 2002), p 38.

[39] Antonakis and House, "The Full-Range Leadership Theory."

[40] Carter, "It's Norman Time," pp 65, 67.

[41] T A Judge and J E Bono, "Five-Factor Model of Personality and Transformational Leadership," *Journal of Applied Psychology,* October 2000, pp 751–65; and R S Rubin, D C Munz, and W H Bommer, "Leading from Within: The Effects of Emotion Recognition and Personality on Transformational Leadership Behavior," *Academy of Management Journal,* October 2005, pp 845–58.

[42] See M Greer, "The Science of Savoir Faire," *Monitor on Psychology,* January 2005, pp 28–30; and T Divir, D Eden, B J Avolio, and B Shamir, "Impact of Transformational Leadership on Follower Development and Performance: A Field Experiment," *Academy of Management Journal,* August 2002, pp 735–44.

[43] These definitions are derived from R Kark, B Shamir, and C Chen, "The Two Faces of Transformational Leadership: Empowerment and Dependency," *Journal of Applied Psychology,* April 2003, pp 246–55.

[44] B Nanus, *Visionary Leadership* (San Francisco: Jossey-Bass, 1992), p 8.

[45] W H Bulkeley, "Back from the Brink: Mulcahy Leads a Renaissance at Xerox by Emphasizing Color, Customers, and Costs," *The Wall Street Journal,* April 24, 2006, pp B1, B3.

[46] Kark, Shamir, and Chen, "The Two Faces of Transformational Leadership."

[47] For supportive results, see Y Beson and B J Avolio, "Transformational Leadership and the Dissemination of Organizational Goals: A Case Study of a Telecommunication Firm," *Leadership Quarterly,* October 2004, pp 625–46; and B J Avolio, W Zhu, W Koh, and P Bhatia, "Transformational Leadership and Organizational Commitment: Mediating Role of Psychological Empowerment and Moderating Role of Structured Distance," *Journal of Organizational Behavior,* December 2004, pp 951–68; and W H

Bommer, G A Rich, and R S Rubin, "Changing Attitudes about Change: Longitudinal Effects of Transformational Leader Behavior on Employee Cynicism about Organizational Change," *Journal of Organizational Behavior,* November 2005, pp 733–53.

[48] Dumdum, Lowe, and Avolio, "A Meta-Analysis of Transformational and Transactional Leadership Correlates." See also R T Keller, "Transformational Leadership, Initiating Structure, and Substitutes for Leadership: A Longitudinal Study of Research and Development Project Team Performance," *Journal of Applied Psychology,* January 2006, pp 202–10.

[49] T A Judge and R F Piccolo, "Transformational and Transactional Leadership: A Meta-Analytic Test of Their Relative Validity," *Journal of Applied Psychology,* October 2004, pp 755–68.

[50] See A J Towler, "Effects of Charismatic Influence Training on Attitudes, Behavior, and Performance," *Personnel Psychology,* Summer 2003, pp 363–81; and L A DeChurch and M A Marks, "Leadership in Multiteam Systems," *Journal of Applied Psychology,* March 2006, pp 311–29.

[51] J Kornik, "Jack Welch: A Legacy of Leadership," *Training,* May 2006, pp 20–24; D Robb, "Succeeding with Succession," *HR Magazine,* January 2006, pp 89–94; and A Pomeroy, "Developing Leaders Is Key to Success," *HR Magazine,* June 2005, pp 20, 24.

[52] J M Howell and B J Avolio, "The Ethics of Charismatic Leadership: Submission or Liberation," *The Executive,* May 1992, pp 43–54.

[53] For background, see M Javidan and R J House, "Cultural Acumen for the Global Manager: Lessons from Project GLOBE," *Organizational* Dynamics, Spring 2001, pp 289–305; the entire Spring 2002 issue of *Journal of World Business;* and R J House, P J Hanges, P Dorfman, and V Gupta, eds, *Culture, Leadership, and Organizations: The GLOBE Study of 62 Societies* (Thousand Oaks, CA: Sage, 2004).

[54] R House, M Javidan, P Hanges, and P Dorfman, "Understanding Cultures and Implicit Leadership Theories across the Globe: An Introduction to Project GLOBE," *Journal of World Business,* Spring 2002, p 4.

[55] For example, see T Scandura and P Dorfman, "Leadership Research in an International and Cross-Cultural Context," *Leadership Quarterly,* April 2004, pp 277–307; M Javidan and N Lynton, "The

Changing Face of the Chinese Leadership," *Harvard Business Review,* December 2005, pp 28, 30; and M Javidan, P W Dorfman, M S de Luque, and R J House, "In the Eye of the Beholder: Cross-Cultural Lessons in Leadership from Project GLOBE," *Academy of Management Perspectives,* February 2006, pp 67–90.

[56] See F Dansereau, Jr, G Graen, and W Haga, "A Vertical Dyad Linkage Approach to Leadership within Formal Organizations," *Organizational Behavior and Human Performance,* February 1975, pp 46–78; and R M Dienesch and R C Liden, "Leader–Member Exchange Model of Leadership: A Critique and Further Development," *Academy of Management Review,* July 1986, pp 618–34.

[57] These descriptions were taken from D Duchon, S G Green, and T D Taber, "Vertical Dyad Linkage: A Longitudinal Assessment of Antecedents, Measures, and Consequences," *Journal of Applied Psychology,* February 1986, pp 56–60.

[58] For supportive results, see G B Graen, R C Liden, and W Hoel, "Role of Leadership in the Employee Withdrawal Process," *Journal of Applied Psychology,* December 1982, pp 868–72; M Wakabayashi and G B Graen, "The Japanese Career Progress Study: A 7-Year Follow-Up," *Journal of Applied Psychology,* November 1984, pp 603–14; C A Schriesheim, S L Castro, and F J Yammarino, "Investigating Contingencies: An Examination of the Impact of Span of Supervision and Upward Controllingness on Leader–Member Exchange Using Traditional and Multivariate within—and between—Entities Analysis," *Journal of Applied Psychology,* October 2000, pp 659–77; O Janssen and N W V Yperen, "Employees' Goal Orientations, the Quality of Leader–Member Exchange, and the Outcomes of Job Performance and Job Satisfaction," *Academy of Management Journal,* June 2004, pp 368–84; B Erdogan, M L Kraimer, and R C Liden, "Work Value Congruence and Intrinsic Career Success: The Compensatory Roles of Leader–Member Exchange and Perceived Organiz-ational Support," *Personnel Psychology,* Summer 2004, pp 305–32; and T N Bauer, B Erdogan, R C Liden, and S J Wayne, "A Longitudinal Study of the Moderating Role of Extraversion: Leader-Member Exchange, Performance, and Turnover during New Executive Development," *Journal of Applied Psychology,* March 2006, pp 298–310.

[59] For supportive results, see S J Wayne, L M Shore, and R C Liden, "Perceived Organizational Support and Leader–Member Exchange: A Social Exchange Perspective," *Academy of Management Journal,* February 1997, pp 82–111; K M Kacmar, L A Witt, S Zivnuska, and S M Gully, "The Interactive-Effect of Leader–Member Exchange and Communication Frequency on Performance Ratings," *Journal of Applied Psychology,* August 2003, pp 764–72; and B Erdogan, R C Liden, and M L Kraimer, "Justice and Leader-Member Exchange: The Moderating Role of Organizational Culture," *Academy of Management Journal,* April 2006, pp 395–406.

[60] "Fiorina Comments on Public Firing," *60 Minutes,* CBS News, October 8, 2006, www.cbsnews.com; P Burrows, "HP Says Goodbye to Drama," *Business-Week,* September 1, 2005, downloaded from Business & Company Resource Center, http://galenet. galegroup. com; and C J Loomis, "Why Carly's Big Bet Is Failing," *Fortune,* February 7, 2005, downloaded from Business & Company Resource Center, http://galenet. galegroup.com.

[61] G C Mage, "Leading Despite Your Boss," *HR Magazine,* September 2003, pp 139–44.

[62] R J House and R N Aditya, "The Social Scientific Study of Leadership: Quo Vadis?" *Journal of Management,* 1997, p 457.

[63] L L Berry, "The Collaborative Organization: Leadership Lessons from Mayo Clinic," *Organiza-tional Dynamics,* August 2004, pp 228–41.

[64] For a thorough discussion of shared leadership, see C L Pearce, "The Future of Leadership: Combining Vertical and Shared Leadership to Transform Know-ledge Work," *Academy of Management Executive,* February 2004, pp 47–57.

[65] M Levy, "Coaching Success Boils Down to Three Traits," *USA Today,* November 2, 2005, p 6C.

[66] B J Avolio, J J Soskik, D I Jung, and Y Berson, "Leadership Models, Methods, and Applications," in *Handbook of Psychology.*

[67] C L Pearce, "The Future of Leadership: Combining Vertical and Shared Leadership to Transform Know-ledge Work," *Academy of Management Executive,* February 2004, p 48.

[68] For an overall summary of servant-leadership, see L C Spears, ed, *Reflections on Leadership: How*

Robert K Greenleaf's Theory of Servant-Leadership Influenced Today's Top Management Thinkers (New York: Wiley, 1995).

[69] L C Spears, "Introduction: Servant-Leadership and the Greenleaf Legacy," in *Reflections on Leadership,* ed L C Spears, pp 1–14.

[70] H Kim and S Bannan, "The Best Business Leaders," *Arizona Republic,* March 16, 2006, p D3.

[71] J Stuart, *Fast Company,* September 1999, p 114.

[72] See J Collins, *Good to Great* (New York: Harper Business, 2001).

[73] J Collins, "Level 5 Leadership," *Harvard Business Review,* January 2001, p 68.

[74] A Serwer, "The Education of Michael Dell," *Fortune,* March 7, 2005, p 73.

[75] See Collins, *Good to Great.*

Chapter 12

[1] For details on Costco's effectiveness, see Stanley Holmes and Wendy Zellner, "The Costco Way," *BusinessWeek,* April 12, 2004, p 76.

[2] E H Schein, "Culture: The Missing Concept in Organization Studies," *Administrative Science Quarterly,* June 1996, p 236.

[3] This figure and related discussion are based on C Ostroff, A Kinicki, and M Tamkins, "Organizational Culture and Climate," in *Handbook of Psychology* 12, eds C Borman, D R Ilgen, and R J Klimoski (New York: Wiley, 2003), pp 565–93.

[4] This discussion is based on E H Schein, *Organizational Culture and Leadership,* 2nd ed (San Francisco: Jossey-Bass, 1992), pp 16–48.

[5] E Byron, "Call Me Mike!" *The Wall Street Journal,* March 27, 2006, p B1.

[6] S H Schwartz, "Universals in the Content and Structure of Values: Theoretical Advances and Empirical Tests in 20 Countries," in *Advances in Experimental Social Psychology,* ed M P Zanna (New York: Academic Press, 1992), p 4.

[7] For an example of identifying organizational values, see S Maitlis, "The Social Processes of Organizational Sensemaking," *Academy of Management Journal,* February 2005, pp 21–49.

[8] Julia Boorstin, "The 100 Best Companies to Work For," *Fortune,* January 12, 2004, p 58.

[9] P Babcock, "Is Your Company Two-Faced?" *HR Magazine,* January 2004, p 43.

[10] S Clarke, "Perceptions of Organizational Safety: Implications for the Development of Safety Culture," *Journal of Organizational Behavior,* March 1999, pp 185–98; and J R Detert, R G Schroeder, and J J Mauriel, "A Framework for Linking Culture and Improvement Initiatives in Organizations," *Academy of Management Review,* October 2000, pp 850–63.

[11] "Time to Take Action," *Training,* September 2004, p 18.

[12] For a description of Google's innovative culture, see J Larson, "Maintaining a Culture of Innovation," *Arizona Republic,* April 13, 2006, pp D1, D3.

[13] Adapted from L Smircich, "Concepts of Culture and Organizational Analysis," *Administrative Science Quarterly,* September 1983, pp 339–58.

[14] Statistics and data contained in the Southwest Airlines example can be found at Southwest Airlines, "Southwest Airlines Fact Sheet," *About SWA,* www.southwest.com, updated March 28, 2006.

[15] K D Godsey, "Slow Climb to New Heights," *Success,* October 1996, p 21.

[16] Southwest's mission statement can be found at Southwest Airlines, "Customer Service Commitment," *About SWA,* www.southwest.com, accessed April 4, 2006.

[17] See Ostroff, Kinicki, and Tamkins, "Organizational Culture and Climate."

[18] The validity of these cultural types was summarized and supported in R A Cooke and J L Szumal, "Using the Organizational Culture Inventory to Understand the Operating Cultures of Organizations," in *Handbook of Organizational Culture and Climate,* ed N M Ashkanasy, C P M Wilderom, and M F Peterson (Thousand Oaks, CA: Sage, 2000), pp 147–62.

[19] Brian Bremner and Gail Edmondson, "Japan: A Tale of Two Mergers," *BusinessWeek,* May 10, 2004, p 42.

[20] Vicki Lee Parker, "SciQuest Turns First Profit," *Raleigh (NC) News and Observer,* November 15, 2006, downloaded from Business & Company Resource Center, http://galenet.galegroup.com.

[21] For an examination of subcultures, see G Hofstede, "Identifying Organizational Subcultures: An Empirical Approach," *Journal of Management Studies,* January 1998, pp 1–12.

[22] R Cooke and J Szumal, "Measuring Normative Beliefs and Shared Behavioral Expectations in Organizations: The Reliability and Validity of the Organizational Culture Inventory," *Psychological Reports,* June 1993, pp 1299–330.

[23] See, for example, C Ostroff, Y Shin, and A Kinicki, "Multiple Perspectives of Congruence: Relationships between Value Congruence and Employee Attitudes," *Journal of Organizational Behavior,* September 2005, pp 591–623; and A L Kristof-Brown, R D Zimmerman, and E C Johnson, "Consequences of Individuals' Fit at Work: A Meta-analysis of Person-Job, Person-Organization, Person-Group, and Person-Supervision Fit," *Personnel Psychology,* Summer 2005, pp 281–342.

[24] See C Wilderom, U Glunk, and R Maslowski, "Organizational Culture as a Predictor of Organizational Performance," in *Handbook of Organizational Culture & Climate,* ed N Ashkanasy, C Wilderom, and M Peterson (Thousand Oaks, CA: Sage, 2000), pp 193–210.

[25] J P Kotter and J L Heskett, *Corporate Culture and Performance* (New York: Free Press, 1992).

[26] For a discussion of the success rate of mergers, see M J Epstein, "The Drivers of Success in Post-Merger Integration," *Organizational Dynamics,* May 2004, pp 174–89. For a practical application of culture change associated with a merger, see S Young, S Silver, and L Abboud, "Alcatel, Lucent Combine to Form Paris-Based Titan," *The Wall Street Journal,* April 3, 2006, pp A1, A12.

[27] For practical examples of culture change, see R Charan, "Home Depot's Blueprint for Culture Change," *Harvard Business Review,* April 2006, pp 60–70; M D Hovanesian, "Rewiring Chuck Prince," *BusinessWeek,* February 20, 2006, pp 75–78; and M Weinstein, "Out of the Blue," *Training,* April 2006, pp 22–27.

[28] See E H Schein, "The Role of the Founder in Creating Organizational Culture," *Organizational Dynamics,* Summer 1983, pp 13–28.

[29] Wal-Mart's values can be found at Wal-Mart Stores, "Our Company: Global Ethics Office," www.walmartstores.com, accessed April 4, 2006.

[30] S Holmes, "Cleaning Up Boeing," *BusinessWeek,* March 13, 2006, p 66.

[31] Ibid., p 68. See also J McGregor, "The Structure to Measure Performance," *BusinessWeek,* January 9, 2006, pp 26–28.

[32] This example appears in Barbara Kaufman, "Stories That Sell, Stories That Tell," *Journal of Business Strategy,* March/April 2003, p 15.

[33] Ibid., pp 11–15.

[34] S Tully, "In This Corner! The Contender—Jamie Dimon—the New CEO of JPMorgan Chase," *Fortune,* April 3, 2006, downloaded from Business & Company Resource Center, http://galenet.galegroup.com.

[35] B Hindo, "Making the Elephant Dance," *BusinessWeek,* May 1, 2006, pp 88–90.

[36] For practical examples, see P Dvorak, "A Firm's Culture Can Get Lost in Translation," *The Wall Street Journal,* April 3, 2006, pp B1, B3; and B E Litzky, K A Eddleston, and D L Kidder, "The Good, the Bad, and the Misguided: How Managers Inadvertently Encourage Deviant Behaviors," *Academy of Management Perspectives,* February 2006, pp 91–102.

[37] J Van Maanen, "Breaking In: Socialization to Work," in *Handbook of Work, Organization, and Society,* ed R Dubin (Chicago: Rand-McNally, 1976), p 67.

[38] For an instructive capsule summary of the five different organizational socialization models, see J P Wanous, A E Reichers, and S D Malik, "Organizational Socialization and Group Development: Toward an Integrative Perspective," *Academy of Management Review,* October 1984, pp 670–83, Table 1.

[39] J Stearns, "Sedona Company Wants Happy Employees," *Arizona Republic,* April 10, 2005, p D2.

[40] Onboarding programs are discussed in D Moscato, "Using Technology to Get Employees on Board," *HR Magazine,* March 2005, pp 107–09.

[41] S J Wells, "Diving In," *HR Magazine,* March 2005, p 56.

[42] N M Tichy, "No Ordinary Boot Camp," *Harvard Business Review,* April 2001, pp 63–70.

[43] See J Durett, "Training 101," *Training,* March 2006, pp 70–71; and K Gustafson, "A Better Welcome Mat," *Training,* June 2005, pp 34–41.

[44] See D Cable and C Parsons, "Socialization Tactics and Person-Organization Fit," *Personnel Psychology,* Spring 2001, pp 1–23.

[45] R Levering and M Moskowitz, "The 100 Best Companies to Work For: And the Winners Are . . . ," *Fortune,* January 23, 2006, p 94.

[46] See A M Saks and B E Ashforth, "Proactive Socialization and Behavioral Self-Management," *Journal of Vocational Behavior,* June 1996, pp 301–23.

[47] For a thorough review of research on the socialization of diverse employees with disabilities, see A Colella, "Organizational Socialization of Newcomers with Disabilities: A Framework for Future Research," in *Research in Personnel and Human Resources Management,* ed G R Ferris (Greenwich, CT: JAI Press, 1996), pp 351–417.

[48] This definition is based on the network perspective of mentoring proposed by M Higgins and K Kram, "Reconceptualizing Mentoring at Work: A Development Network Perspective," *Academy of Management Review,* April 2001, pp 264–88.

[49] For supportive results, see S C Payne and A H Huffman, "A Longitudinal Examination of the Influence of Mentoring on Organizational Commitment and Turnover," *Academy of Management Journal,* February 2005, pp 158–68; Monica L Forret and Thomas W Dougherty, "Networking Behaviors and Career Outcomes: Differences for Men and Women?" *Journal of Organizational Behavior,* May 2004, pp 419–37; and L Eby, M Butts, A Lockwood, and S A Simon, "Protégés' Negative Mentoring Experiences: Construct Development and Nomological Validation," *Personnel Psychology,* Summer 2004, pp 411–47.

[50] For a detailed discussion of career functions, see K Kram, *Mentoring of Work: Developmental Relationships in Organizational Life* (Glenview, IL: Scott, Foresman, 1985).

[51] Kris Maher, "The Jungle: Focus on Retirement, Pay and Getting Ahead," *The Wall Street Journal,* February 24, 2004, p B8.

[52] This discussion is based on M Higgins and K Kram, "Reconceptualizing Mentoring at Work: A Developmental Network Perspective," *Academy of Management Review,* April 2001, pp 264–88.

[53] This discussion is based on Higgins and Kram, "Reconceptualizing Mentoring at Work."

[54] See T D Allen, L T Eby, and E Lentz, "The Relationship between Formal Mentoring Program Characteristics and Perceived Program Effectiveness," *Personnel Psychology,* Spring 2006, pp 125–543; and J Ewing, "Making Those Connections Work," *BusinessWeek,* March 13, 2006, p 91.

[55] For recommendations on how to improve your networking skills, see A Fisher, "How to Network—and Enjoy It," *Fortune,* April 4, 2005, p 38; and J C Berkshire, "'Social Network' Recruiting," *HR Magazine,* April 2005, pp 95–98.

[56] S C de Janasz, S E Sullivan, and V Whiting, "Mentor Networks and Career Success: Lessons for Turbulent Times," *Academy of Management Executive,* November 2003, pp 78–91.

[57] "Leadership Needs Development," *Training,* February 2006, p 7.

[58] "Best Practice: Mentoring—Blue Cross and Blue Shield of North Carolina," *Training,* March 2004, p 62.

Chapter 13

[1] See K H Hammonds, "We, Incorporated," *Fast Company,* July 2004, pp 87–89.

[2] C I Barnard, *The Functions of the Executive* (Cambridge, MA: Harvard University Press, 1938), p 73.

[3] E H Schein, *Organizational Psychology,* 3rd ed (Englewood Cliffs, NJ: Prentice Hall, 1980), pp 12–15.

[4] For an interesting historical perspective of hierarchy, see P Miller and T O'Leary, "Hierarchies and American Ideals, 1900–1940," *Academy of Management Review,* April 1989, pp 250–65. See also H J Leavitt, "Why Hierarchies Thrive," *Harvard Business Review,* March 2003, pp 96–102.

[5] For an excellent overview of the span of control concept, see D D Van Fleet and A G Bedeian, "A History of the Span of Management," *Academy of Management Review,* July 1977, pp 356–72. See also E E Lawler III and J R Galbraith, "New Roles for the Staff: Strategic Support and Service," in *Organizing for the Future: The New Logic for Managing Complex Organizations,* eds J R Galbraith, E E Lawler III, et al. (San Francisco: Jossey-Bass, 1993), pp 65–83.

[6] For a contrary example involving Southwest Airlines, see J Pfeffer, "How Companies Get Smart," *Business 2.0,* January/February 2005, p 74.

[7] M Koslowsky, "Staff/Line Distinctions in Job and Organizational Commitment," *Journal of Occupational Psychology,* June 1990, pp 167–73.

[8] For an illustrative management-related metaphor, see J E Beatty, "Grades as Money and the Role of the Market Metaphor in Management Education," *Academy of Management Learning and Education,* June 2004, pp 187–96. See also C Oswick and P Jones, "Beyond Correspondence? Metaphor in Organization Theory," *Academy of Management Review,* April 2006, pp 483–85; and J Cornelissen, "Metaphor in Organization Theory: Progress and the Past," *Academy of Management Review,* April 2006, pp 485–88.

[9] K S Cameron, "Effectiveness as Paradox: Consensus and Conflict in Conceptions of Organizational Effectiveness," *Management Science,* May 1986, pp 540–41. See also S Sackmann, "The Role of Metaphors in Organization Transformation," *Human Relations,* June 1989, pp 463–84; and H Tsoukas, "The Missing Link: A Transformational View of Metaphors in Organizational Science," *Academy of Management Review,* July 1991, pp 566–85.

[10] See W R Scott, "The Mandate Is Still Being Honored: In Defense of Weber's Disciples," *Administrative Science Quarterly,* March 1996, pp 163–71. See also D Jones, "Military a Model for Execs," *USA Today,* June 9, 2004, p 4B.

[11] Based on M Weber, *The Theory of Social and Economic Organization,* trans A M Henderson and T Parsons (New York: Oxford University Press, 1947). For an instructive analysis of the mistranslation of Weber's work, see R M Weiss, "Weber on Bureaucracy: Management Consultant or Political Theorist?" *Academy of Management Review,* April 1983, pp 242–48.

[12] For a critical appraisal of bureaucracy, see R P Hummel, *The Bureaucratic Experience,* 3rd ed (New York: St. Martin's Press, 1987). The positive side of bureaucracy is presented in C T Goodsell, *The Case for Bureaucracy: A Public Administration Polemic* (Chatham, NJ: Chatham House, 1983).

[13] See G Pinchot and E Pinchot, "Beyond Bureaucracy," *Business Ethics,* March/April 1994, pp 26–29; and O Harari, "Let the Computers Be the Bureaucrats," *Management Review,* September 1996, pp 57–60.

[14] For examples of what managers are doing to counteract bureaucratic tendencies, see B Dumaine, "The Bureaucracy Busters, " *Fortune,* June 17, 1991, pp 36–50; and C J Cantoni, "Eliminating Bureaucracy—Roots and All," *Management Review,* December 1993, pp 30–33.

[15] For a management-oriented discussion of general systems theory (an interdisciplinary attempt to integrate the various fragmented sciences), see K E Boulding, "General Systems Theory—the Skeleton of Science," *Management Science,* April 1956, pp 197–208.

[16] See L Buchanan, "No More Metaphors," *Harvard Business Review,* March 2005, p 19; and L Prusak, "The Madness of Individuals," *Harvard Business Review,* June 2005, p 22.

[17] J D Thompson, *Organizations in Action* (New York: McGraw-Hill, 1967), pp 6–7. See also A C Bluedorn, "The Thompson Interdependence Demonstration," *Journal of Management Education,* November 1993, pp 505–09.

[18] Thompson, *Organizations in Action,* pp 6–7.

[19] For interesting updates on the biological systems metaphor, see A M Webber, "How Business Is a Lot Like Life," *Fast Company,* April 2001, pp 130–36; E Bonabeau and C Meyer, "Swarm Intelligence: A Whole New Way to Think about Business," *Harvard Business Review,* May 2001, pp 106–14; and R Adner, "Match Your Innovation Strategy to Your Innovation Ecosystem," *Harvard Business Review,* April 2006, pp 98–107.

[20] R L Daft and K E Weick, "Toward a Model of Organizations as Interpretation Systems," *Academy of Management Review,* April 1984, p 293.

[21] See M Crossan, "Altering Theories of Learning and Action: An Interview with Chris Argyris," *Academy*

of Management Executive, May 2003, pp 40–46; D Gray, "Wanted: Chief Ignorance Officer," *Harvard Business Review,* November 2003, pp 22, 24; and G T M Hult, D J Ketchen Jr, and S F Slater, "Information Processing, Knowledge Development, and Strategic Supply Chain Performance," *Academy of Management Journal,* April 2004, pp 241–53.

22 For good background reading and updates, see the entire Autumn 1998 issue of *Organizational Dynamics;* J J Salopek, "Targeting the Learning Organization," *Training and Development,* March 2004, pp 46–51; T B Lawrence, M K Mauws, B Dyck, and R F Kleysen, "The Politics of Organizational Learning: Integrating Power into the 4I Framework," *Academy of Management Review,* January 2005, pp 180–91; J Gordon, "CLO: A Strategic Player?" *Training,* April 2005, pp 15–19; D Lei, J W Slocum, and R A Pitts, "Designing Organizations for Competitive Advantage: The Power of Unlearning and Learning," *Organizational Dynamics,* Winter 1999, pp 24–38; "Leading-Edge Learning: Two Views," *Training & Development,* March 1999, pp 40–42; and A M Webber, "Learning for a Change," *Fast Company,* May 1999, pp 178–88.

23 M Hopkins, "Zen and the Art of the Self-Managing Company," *Inc.,* November 2000, pp 56, 58.

24 K Cameron, "Critical Questions in Assessing Organizational Effectiveness," *Organizational Dynamics,* Autumn 1980, p 70. See also T D Wall, J Michie, M Patterson, S J Wood, M Sheehan, C W Clegg, and M West, "On the Validity of Subjective Measures of Company Performance," *Personnel Psychology,* Spring 2004, pp 95–118.

25 See G H Seijts, G P Latham, K Tasa, and B W Latham, "Goal Setting and Goal Orientation: An Integration of Two Different yet Related Literatures," *Academy of Management Journal,* April 2004, pp 227–39.

26 See G Colvin, "What Makes GE Great?" *Fortune,* March 6, 2006, pp 90–96.

27 See, for example, R O Brinkerhoff and D E Dressler, *Productivity Measurement: A Guide for Managers and Evaluators* (Newbury Park, CA: Sage Publications, 1990); and D Jones and B Hansen, "Productivity Gains Roll at Their Fastest Clip in 31 Years," *USA Today,* June 14, 2004, pp 1B–2B.

28 See N Noiso-Kanttila, "Time, Attention, Authenticity and Consumer Benefits of the Web," *Business Horizons,* January/February 2005, pp 63–70; S Baker, "Wiser about the Web," *BusinessWeek,* March 27, 2006, pp 54–58; S Levy and B Stone, "The New Wisdom of the Web," *Newsweek,* April 3, 2006, pp 46–53; and A Lashinski, "The Boom Is Back," *Fortune,* May 1, 2006, pp 70–87.

29 S Hamm, "Speed Demons," *BusinessWeek,* March 27, 2006, www.businessweek.com.

30 See M G Wilson, D M DeJoy, R J Vandenberg, H A Richardson, and A L McGrath, "Work Characteristics and Employee Health and Well-Being: Test of a Model of Healthy Work Organization," *Journal of Occupational and Organizational Psychology,* December 2004, pp 565–88.

31 "Interview: M Scott Peck," *Business Ethics,* March/April 1994, p 17. See also C B Gibson and J Birkinshaw, "The Antecedents, Consequences, and Mediating Role of Organizational Ambidexterity," *Academy of Management Journal,* April 2004, pp 209–26.

32 See P Puranam, H Singh, and M Zollo, "Organizing for Innovation: Managing the Coordination–Autonomy Dilemma in Technology Acquisition," *Academy of Management Journal,* April 2006, pp 263–80; R E Herzlinger, "Why Innovation in Health Care Is So Hard," *Harvard Business Review,* May 2006, pp 58–66; and D L Laurie, Y L Doz, and C P Sheer, "Creating New Growth Platforms," *Harvard Business Review,* May 2006, pp 80–90.

33 Cameron, "Critical Questions in Assessing Organizational Effectiveness," p 67. See also W Buxton, "Growth from Top to Bottom," *Management Review,* July/August 1999, p 11.

34 See R K Mitchell, B R Agle, and D J Wood, "Toward a Theory of Stakeholder Identification and Salience: Defining the Principle of Who and What Really Counts," *Academy of Management Review,* October 1997, pp 853–96; T J Rowley and M Moldoveanu, "When Will Stakeholder Groups Act? An Interest- and Identity-Based Model of Stakeholder Group Mobilization," *Academy of Management Review,* April 2003, pp 204–19; G Kassinis and N Vafeas, "Stakeholder Pressures and Environmental Performance," *Academy of Management Journal,* February 2006, pp 145–59; and N A Gardberg and C J Fombrun, "Corporate

Citizenship: Creating Intangible Assets across Institutional Environments," *Academy of Management Review,* April 2006, pp 329–46.

[35] S B Shepard, "Steve Ballmer on Microsoft's Future," *BusinessWeek,* December 1, 2003, p 72.

[36] See C Ostroff and N Schmitt, "Configurations of Organizational Effectiveness and Efficiency," *Academy of Management Journal,* December 1993, pp 1345–61; and J Welch and S Welch, "How Healthy Is Your Company?" *BusinessWeek,* May 8, 2006, p 126.

[37] K S Cameron, "Effectiveness as Paradox: Consensus and Conflict in Conceptions of Organizational Effectiveness," *Management Science,* May 1986, p 542.

[38] Alternative effectiveness criteria are discussed in ibid.; A G Bedeian, "Organization Theory: Current Controversies, Issues, and Directions," in *International Review of Industrial and Organizational Psychology,* ed C L Cooper and I T Robertson (New York: Wiley, 1987), pp 1–33; and M Keeley, "Impartiality and Participant-Interest Theories of Organizational Effectiveness," *Administrative Science Quarterly,* March 1984, pp 1–25.

[39] "How To Keep Your Company's Edge," *Business 2.0,* December 2003, p 93.

[40] For updates, see J M Pennings, "Structural Contingency Theory: A Reappraisal," *Research in Organizational Behavior* 14 (Greenwich, CT: JAI Press, 1992), pp 267–309; A D Meyer, A S Tsui, and C R Hinings, "Configurational Approaches to Organizational Analysis," *Academy of Management Journal,* December 1993, pp 1175–95; and D H Doty, W H Glick, and G P Huber, "Fit, Equifinality, and Organizational Effectiveness: A Test of Two Configurational Theories," *Academy of Management Journal,* December 1993, pp 1196–250.

[41] See B Grow, "Renovating Home Depot," *Business-Week,* March 6, 2006, pp 50–58.

[42] B Elgin, "Running the Tightest Ships on the Net," *BusinessWeek,* January 29, 2001, p 126.

[43] See D A Morand, "The Role of Behavioral Formality and Informality in the Enactment of Bureaucratic versus Organic Organizations," *Academy of Management Review,* October 1995, pp 831–72.

[44] See J Huey, "The New Post-Heroic Leadership," *Fortune,* February 21, 1994, pp 42–50; and F Shipper and C C Manz, "Employee Self-Management without Formally Designated Teams: An Alternative Road to Empowerment," *Organizational Dynamics,* Winter 1992, pp 48–61.

[45] See G P Huber, C C Miller, and W H Glick, "Developing More Encompassing Theories about Organizations: The Centralization-Effectiveness Relationship as an Example," *Organization Science,* no. 1, 1990, pp 11–40; and C Handy, "Balancing Corporate Power: A New Federalist Paper," *Harvard Business Review,* November/December 1992, pp 59–72. For a case study of decentralization, see K Maney, "CEO Helps Microsoft Enter Its 30s Gracefully," *USA Today,* January 25, 2005, pp 1B–2B.

[46] P Coy, "More than One Way to Build a Home," *BusinessWeek,* April 3, 2006, p 74.

[47] P Kaestle, "A New Rationale for Organizational Structure," *Planning Review,* July/August 1990, p 22.

[48] For details of this study, see T Burns and G M Stalker, *The Management of Innovation* (London: Tavistock, 1961). See also W D Sine, H Mitsuhashi, and D A Kirsch, "Revisiting Burns and Stalker: Formal Structure and New Venture Performance in Emerging Economic Sectors," *Academy of Management Journal,* February 2006, pp 121–32.

[49] D J Gillen and S J Carroll, "Relationship of Managerial Ability to Unit Effectiveness in More Organic versus More Mechanistic Departments," *Journal of Management Studies,* November 1985, pp 674–75.

[50] J D Sherman and H L Smith, "The Influence of Organizational Structure on Intrinsic versus Extrinsic Motivation," *Academy of Management Journal,* December 1984, p 883.

[51] See J A Courtright, G T Fairhurst, and L E Rogers, "Interaction Patterns in Organic and Mechanistic Systems," *Academy of Management Journal,* December 1989, pp 773–802.

[52] See J R Galbraith and E E Lawler III, "Effective Organizations: Using the New Logic of Organizing," in *Organizing for the Future: The New Logic for Managing Complex Organizations,* eds J R Galbraith, E E Lawler III, et al. (San Francisco: Jossey-Bass, 1993), pp 285–99.

[53] See Y Shin, "A Person-Environment Fit Model for Virtual Organizations," *Journal of Management,* no. 5, 2004, pp 725–43; M V Copeland and A Tilin, "The New Instant Companies," *Business 2.0,* June 2005, pp 82–94; S Alsop, "I've Seen the Real Future of Tech—and It Is Virtual," *Fortune,* April 14, 2003, p 390; D Brady, "Geography Is So Twentieth Century," *BusinessWeek,* December 19, 2005, pp 74–75; and R D Hof, "It's Not All Fun and Games," *BusinessWeek,* May 1, 2006, pp 76–77.

[54] "David Neeleman, JetBlue," *BusinessWeek,* September 29, 2003, p 124.

[55] J Hopkins, "Other Nations Zip by USA in High-Speed Net Race," *USA Today,* January 19, 2004, p 2B. See also P Engardio, "The Future of Outsourcing," *BusinessWeek,* January 30, 2006, pp 50–58; and B Helm, "Life on the Web's Factory Floor," *Business-Week,* May 22, 2006, pp 70–71.

[56] See B J Avolio and S S Kahai, "Adding the 'E' to E-Leadership: How It May Impact Your Leadership," *Organizational Dynamics,* no 4, 2003, pp 325–38; and S Parise and A Casher, "Alliance Portfolios: Designing and Managing Your Network of Business-Partner Relationships," *Academy of Management Executive,* November 2003, pp 25–39. For a good update on trust, see R Zemke, "The Confidence Crisis," *Training,* June 2004, pp 22–30.

[57] These guidelines are based on J W Janove, "Management by Remote Control," *HR Magazine,* April 2004, pp 119–24.

[58] C Handy, *The Hungry Spirit: Beyond Capitalism: A Quest for Purpose in the Modern World* (New York: Broadway Books, 1998), p 186. (Emphasis added.)

[59] See B Lessard and S Baldwin, *NetSlaves: True Tales of Working the Web* (New York: McGraw-Hill, 2000).

[60] See M Arndt, "Trade Winds: Made in Wherever," *BusinessWeek,* May 31, 2004, p 14; J E Garten, "Offshoring: You Ain't Seen Nothin' Yet," *Business-Week,* June 21, 2004, p 28; and S Hamm, "Services," *BusinessWeek,* June 21, 2004, pp 82–83.

[61] See S Hamm, "Linux Inc.," *BusinessWeek,* January 31, 2005, pp 60–68; A R Winger, "Face-to-Face Communication: Is It Really Necessary in a Digitizing World?" *Business Horizons,* May/June 2005, pp 247–53; D Ernst and J Bamford, "Your Alliances Are Too Stable," *Harvard Business* Review, June 2005, pp 133–41; and the series of articles in "Special Report: E-Biz," *BusinessWeek,* May 10, 2004, pp 80–90.

Chapter 14

[1] M L Alch, "Get Ready for the Net Generation," *Training & Development,* February 2000, pp 32, 34.

[2] D Kirkpatrick, "Microsoft's New Brain," *Fortune,* May 1, 2006, p 59.

[3] N D Schwartz, ". . . Is Also a Big Target," *Fortune,* April 17, 2006, p 87.

[4] J Mero and M Boyle, "Star Power: Eduardo Castro-Wright," *Fortune,* February 6, 2006, p 58.

[5] See S Hamm, S E Ante, A Reinhardt, and M Kripalani, "Services," *BusinessWeek,* June 21, 2004, pp 82–83.

[6] The link between corporate strategy and market changes is discussed in D Lei and J W Slocum Jr, "Strategic and Organizational Requirements for Competitive Advantage," *Academy of Management Executive,* February 2005, pp 31–45.

[7] See D Henry, M France, and L Lavelle, "The Boss on the Sidelines," *BusinessWeek,* April 25, 2005, pp 86–96.

[8] C Daniels, "Meet Mr. Nuke," *Fortune,* May 15, 2006, pp 140–46.

[9] For a thorough discussion of the model, see K Lewin, *Field Theory in Social Science* (New York: Harper & Row, 1951).

[10] P-W Tan, "System Reboot: Hurd's Big Challenge at HP," *The Wall Street Journal,* April 3, 2006, pp A1, A3; and A Lashinsky, "The Hurd Way," *Fortune,* April 17, 2006, pp 92–102.

[11] C Goldwasser, "Benchmarking: People Make the Process," *Management Review,* June 1995, p 40.

[12] L Lavelle, "KPMG's Brave Leap into the Cold," *BusinessWeek,* May 21, 2001, pp 72, 73.

[13] See T A Stewart, "Architects of Change," *Harvard Business Review,* April 2006, p 10.

[14] For more on systems models of change, see D W Haines, "Letting 'The System' Do the Work,"

Journal of Applied Behavioral Science, September 1999, pp 306–24.

[15] For a thorough discussion of the target elements of change, see M Beer and B Spector, "Organizational Diagnosis: Its Role in Organizational Learning," *Journal of Counseling & Development,* July/August 1993, pp 642–50.

[16] E Torbenson and S Marta, "Southwest Goes High-Tech to Stay Profitable," *Arizona Republic,* July 7, 2003, p D5.

[17] Organizational diagnosis is discussed in S E Ante, "The Science of Desire," *BusinessWeek,* June 5, 2006, pp 98–106.

[18] M D Hovanesian, "Dimon's Grand Design," *BusinessWeek,* March 28, 2005, pp 96–99; and S Tully, "The Contender: In This Corner Jamie Dimon," *Fortune,* April 3, 2006, pp 54–66.

[19] These errors are discussed in J P Kotter, "Leading Change: The Eight Steps to Transformation," in *The Leader's Change Handbook,* ed J A Conger, G M Spreitzer, and E E Lawler III (San Francisco: Jossey-Bass, 1999), pp 87–99.

[20] The steps were developed by J P Kotter, *Leading Change* (Boston: Harvard Business School Press, 1996).

[21] For a discussion of the type of leadership needed during organizational change, see R L Englund, R J Graham, and P C Dinsmore, *Creating the Project Office: A Manager's Guide to Leading Organizational Change* (San Francisco: Jossey-Bass, 2003); and F Ostroff, "Change Management in Government," *Harvard Business Review,* May 2006, pp 141–47.

[22] M Beer and E Walton, "Developing the Competitive Organization: Interventions and Strategies," *American Psychologist,* February 1990, p 154.

[23] For a historical overview of the field of OD, see J R Austin and J M Bartunek, "Theories and Practices of Organizational Development," in *Handbook of Psychology* 12, ed W C Borman, D R Ilgen, and R J Klimoski (Hoboken, NJ: Wiley, 2003), pp 309–32.

[24] W W Burke, *Organization Development: A Normative View* (Reading, MA: Addison-Wesley, 1987), p 9.

[25] A variety of intervention techniques are summarized in J R Austin and J M Bartunek, "Theories and Practices of Organizational Development."

[26] R Rodgers, J E Hunter, and D L Rogers, "Influence of Top Management Commitment on Management Program Success," *Journal of Applied Psychology,* February 1993, pp 151–55.

[27] P J Robertson, D R Roberts, and J I Porras, "Dynamics of Planned Organizational Change: Assessing Empirical Support for a Theoretical Model," *Academy of Management Journal,* June 1993, pp 619–34. See also A Cusick, "Organizational Development Facilitates Effective Regulation Compliance," *Leadership and Organization Development Journal,* no. 2, 2005, pp 106–19.

[28] G A Neuman, J E Edwards, and N S Raju, "Organizational Development Interventions: A Meta-Analysis of Their Effects on Satisfaction and Other Attitudes," *Personnel Psychology,* Autumn 1989, pp 461–90.

[29] C-M Lau and H-Y Ngo, "Organization Development and Firm Performance: A Comparison of Multinational and Local Firms," *Journal of International Business Studies,* First Quarter 2001, pp 95–114.

[30] Adapted in part from B W Armentrout, "Have Your Plans for Change Had a Change of Plan?" *HR Focus,* January 1996, p 19; and A S Judson, *Changing Behavior in Organizations: Minimizing Resistance to Change* (Cambridge, MA: Blackwell, 1991).

[31] For an investigation of an individual's predisposition to change, see C R Wanberg and J T Banas, "Predictors and Outcomes of Openness to Changes in a Reorganizing Workplace," *Journal of Applied Psychology,* February 2000, pp 132–42.

[32] G Chon, K Mahler, and C Dade, "On Plant Assembly Lines and at Kitchen Tables, Worry about the Future," *The Wall Street Journal,* March 23, 2006, p A1.

[33] B Morris, "Coke Gets a Jolt," *Fortune,* May 15, 2006, pp 77–78.

[34] Readiness for change is discussed in S R Madsen, "Wellness in the Workplace: Preparing Employees for Change," *Organization Development Journal,* Spring 2003, pp 46–56.

[35] Cognitive hurdles are discussed in W C Kim and R Mauborgne, "Tipping Point Leadership," *Harvard*

Business Review, April 2003, pp 60–69. See also D B Fedor, S Caldwell, and D M Herold, "The Effects of Organizational Change on Employee Commitment: A Multilevel Investigation," *Personnel Psychology,* Spring 2006, pp 1–29.

36 L Herscovitch and J P Meyer, "Commitment to Organizational Change: Extension of a Three-Component Model," *Journal of Applied Psychology,* June 2003, p 475.

37 For a discussion of how managers can reduce resistance to change by providing different explanations for an organizational change, see D M Rousseau and S A Tijoriwala, "What's a Good Reason to Change? Motivated Reasoning and Social Accounts in Promoting Organizational Change," *Journal of Applied Psychology,* August 1999, pp 514–28.

38 See K L Turner and M V Makhija, "The Role of Organizational Controls in Managing Knowledge," *Academy of Management Review,* January 2006, pp 197–217.

39 S Reynolds Fisher and M A White, "Downsizing in a Learning Organization: Are There Hidden Costs?" *Academy of Management Review,* January 2000, p 245.

40 R M Fulmer and J B Keys, "A Conversation with Peter Senge: New Development in Organizational Learning," *Organizational Dynamics,* Autumn 1998, p 35.

41 For discussion of a results-oriented approach to learning, see M Crossan, "Alternating Theories of Learning and Action: An Interview with Chris Argyris," *Academy of Management Executive,* May 2003, pp 40–46.

42 For discussion of learning capabilities and core competencies, see R Lubit, "Tacit Knowledge and Knowledge Management," *Organizational Dynamics,* 2001, pp 164–78.

43 For discussion of the relationship between organizational learning and various effectiveness criteria, see S F Slater and J C Narver, "Market Orientation and the Learning Organization," *Journal of Marketing,* July 1995, pp 63–74.

44 A J DiBella, E C Nevis, and J M Gould, "Organizational Learning Style as a Core Capability," in *Organizational Learning and Competitive Advantage,* ed B Moingeon and A Edmondson (Thousand Oaks, CA: Sage, 1996), pp 41–42.

45 List adapted from B Moingeon and A Edmondson, *Organizational Learning and Competitive Advantage* (Thousand Oaks, CA: Sage, 1996), p 43.

46 P A Salz, "High Performance: Intelligent Use of Information Is a Powerful Corporate Tool," *The Wall Street Journal,* April 27, 2006, p A10; T H Davenport, "Competing on Analytics," *Harvard Business Review,* January 2006, pp 99–108; and J Pfeffer and R I Sutton, "Evidence-Based Management," *Harvard Business Review,* January 2006, pp 63–74.

47 For a demonstration of the impact of organizational culture on organizational learning, see A Jashapara, "Cognition, Culture and Competition: An Empirical Test of the Learning Organization," *The Learning Organization,* 2003, pp 31–50.

48 Anderson quoted in V D Infante, "Men's Wearhouse: Tailored for Any Change That Retail Brings," *Workforce,* March 2001, p 48.

49 D Miller, "A Preliminary Typology of Organizational Learning: Synthesizing the Literature," *Journal of Management,* 1996, pp 485–505.

50 The role of leadership in organizational learning is thoroughly discussed in D Vera and M Crossan, "Strategic Leadership and Organizational Learning," *Academy of Management Review,* April 2004, pp 222–40.

51 This discussion is based in part on D Ulrich, T Jick, and M Von Glinow, "High-Impact Learning: Building and Diffusing Learning Capability," *Organizational Dynamics,* Autumn 1993, pp 52–66.

52 J C Meister, "The CEO-Driven Learning Culture," *Training & Development,* June 2000, p 54.

53 The creation of learning infrastructure is discussed in C R James, "Designing Learning Organizations," *Organizational Dynamics,* 2003, pp 46–61.

54 See J B Quinn, "Leveraging Intellect," *Academy of Management Executive,* November 2005, pp 78–94; and M T Hansen, M L Mors, and B Lovås, "Knowledge Sharing in Organizations: Multiple Networks, Multiple Phases," *Academy of Management Journal,* October 2005, pp 776–93.

55 See the related discussion in D Lei, J W Slocum, and R A Pitts, "Designing Organizations for Competitive Advantage: The Power of Unlearning and Learning," *Organizational Dynamics,* Winter 1999, pp 24–38.

Glossary

A

accountability practices   Focus on treating diverse employees fairly.

added-value negotiation (AVN)   Cooperatively developing multiple-deal packages while building a long-term relationship.

affirmative action   Focuses on achieving equality of opportunity in an organization.

aggressive style   Expressive and self-enhancing, but takes unfair advantage of others.

alternative dispute resolution   Avoiding costly lawsuits by resolving conflicts informally or through mediation or arbitration.

anticipatory socialization   Occurs before an individual joins an organization, and involves the information people learn about different careers, occupations, professions, and organizations.

assertive style   Expressive and self-enhancing, but does not take advantage of others.

attention   Being consciously aware of something or someone.

attitude   Learned predisposition toward a given object.

availability heuristic   Tendency to base decisions on information readily available in memory.

B

benchmarking   Process by which a company compares its performance with that of high-performing organizations.

blog   Online journal in which people comment on any topic.

bounded rationality   Constraints that restrict decision making.

brainstorming   Process to generate a quantity of ideas.

bureaucracy   Max Weber's idea of the most rationally efficient form of organization.

C

causal attributions   Suspected or inferred causes of behavior.

centralized decision making   Top managers make all key decisions.

change and acquisition   Requires employees to master tasks and roles and to adjust to work group values and norms.

closed system   A relatively self-sufficient entity.

coalition   Temporary groupings of people who actively pursue a single issue.

coercive power   Obtaining compliance through threatened or actual punishment.

cognitions   A person's knowledge, opinions, or beliefs.

cognitive categories   Mental depositories for storing information.

commitment to change   A mind-set of doing whatever it takes to effectively implement change.

communication   Interpersonal exchange of information and understanding.

communication competence   Ability to effectively use communication behaviors in a given context.

communication distortion   Purposely modifying the content of a message.

conflict   One party perceives its interests are being opposed or set back by another party.

consensus   Presenting opinions and gaining agreement to support a decision.

consideration   Creating mutual respect and trust with followers.

content theories of motivation   Identify internal factors influencing motivation.

contingency approach   Using management tools and techniques in a situationally appropriate manner; avoiding the one-best-way mentality.

contingency approach to organization design   Creating an effective organization–environment fit.

contingency factors   Variables that influence the appropriateness of a leadership style.

continuous reinforcement   Reinforcing every instance of a behavior.

creativity   Process of developing something new or unique.

cross-functionalism   Team made up of technical specialists from different areas.

D

decentralized decision making Lower-level managers are empowered to make important decisions.

decision making Identifying and choosing solutions that lead to a desired end result.

decision-making style A combination of how individuals perceive and respond to information.

Delphi technique Process to generate ideas from physically dispersed experts.

development practices Focus on preparing diverse employees for greater responsibility and advancement.

developmental relationship strength The quality of relationships among people in a network.

devil's advocacy Assigning someone the role of critic.

dialectic method Fostering a debate of opposing viewpoints to better understand an issue.

distributive justice The perceived fairness of how resources and rewards are distributed.

diversity The host of individual differences that make people different from and similar to each other.

diversity of developmental relationships The variety of people in a network used for developmental assistance.

dysfunctional conflict Threatens organization's interests.

E

e-business Running the *entire* business via the Internet.

emotional intelligence Ability to manage oneself and interact with others in mature and constructive ways.

emotions Complex human reactions to personal achievements and setbacks that may be felt and displayed.

empowerment Sharing varying degrees of power with lower-level employees to better serve the customer.

enacted values The values and norms that are exhibited by employees.

encounter phase Employees learn what the organization is really like and reconcile unmet expectations.

equity sensitivity An individual's tolerance for negative and positive equity.

equity theory Holds that motivation is a function of fairness in social exchanges.

ERG theory Three basic needs—existence, relatedness, and growth—influence behavior.

escalation of commitment Sticking to an ineffective course of action too long.

espoused values The stated values and norms that are preferred by an organization.

ethics Study of moral issues and choices.

expectancy Belief that effort leads to a specific level of performance.

expectancy theory Holds that people are motivated to behave in ways that produce valued outcomes.

expert power Obtaining compliance through one's knowledge or information.

explicit knowledge Information that can be easily put into words and shared with others.

external factors Environmental characteristics that cause behavior.

external forces for change Originate outside the organization.

external locus of control Attributing outcomes to circumstances beyond one's control.

extinction Making behavior occur less often by ignoring or not reinforcing it.

extranet Connects internal employees with selected customers, suppliers, and strategic partners.

extrinsic rewards Financial, material, or social rewards from the environment.

F

feedback Objective information about performance.

formal group Formed by the organization.

functional conflict Serves organization's interests.

fundamental attribution bias Ignoring environmental factors that affect behavior.

G

glass ceiling Invisible barrier blocking women and minorities from top management positions.

goal What an individual is trying to accomplish.

goal commitment Amount of commitment to achieving a goal.

goal difficulty The amount of effort required to meet a goal.

goal specificity Quantifiability of a goal.

group Two or more freely interacting people with shared norms and goals and a common identity.

group cohesiveness A "we feeling" binding group members together.

group support systems (GSSs) Using computer software and hardware to help people work better together.

groupthink Janis's term for a cohesive in-group's unwillingness to realistically view alternatives.

H

high-context cultures Primary meaning derived from nonverbal situational cues.

human capital The productive potential of one's knowledge and actions.

hygiene factors Job characteristics associated with job dissatisfaction.

I

impression management Getting others to see us in a certain manner.

informal group Formed by friends.

in-group exchange A partnership characterized by mutual trust, respect, and liking.

initiating structure Organizing and defining what group members should be doing.

instrumentality A performance → outcome perception.

intelligence Capacity for constructive thinking, reasoning, problem solving.

interactional justice The perceived fairness of the decision maker's behavior in the process of decision making.

intermittent reinforcement Reinforcing some but not all instances of behavior.

internal factors Personal characteristics that cause behavior.

internal forces for change Originate inside the organization.

internal locus of control Attributing outcomes to one's own actions.

Internet The global system of networked computers.

intranet An organization's private Internet.

intrinsic motivation Motivation caused by positive internal feelings.

intrinsic rewards Self-granted, psychic rewards.

J

job design Changing the content and/or process of a specific job to increase job satisfaction and performance.

job enlargement Putting more variety into a job.

job rotation Moving employees from one specialized job to another.

judgmental heuristics Rules of thumb or shortcuts that people use to reduce information-processing demands.

K

knowledge management (KM) Implementing systems and practices that increase the sharing of knowledge and information throughout an organization.

L

law of effect Behavior with favorable consequences is repeated; behavior with unfavorable consequences disappears.

leadership Influencing employees to voluntarily pursue organizational goals.

leadership prototype Mental representation of the traits and behaviors possessed by leaders.

leader trait Personal characteristics that differentiate leaders from followers.

learned helplessness Debilitating lack of faith in one's ability to control the situation.

learning capabilities The set of core competencies and internal processes that enable an organization to adapt to its environment.

learning goal Encourages learning, creativity, and skill development.

learning modes The various ways in which organizations attempt to create and maximize their learning.

learning organization Proactively creates, acquires, and transfers knowledge throughout the organization.

legitimate power Obtaining compliance through formal authority.

line managers Have authority to make organizational decisions.

linguistic style A person's typical speaking pattern.

listening Actively decoding and interpreting verbal messages.

low-context cultures Primary meaning derived from written and spoken words.

M

maintenance roles Relationship-building group behavior.

management Process of working with and through others to achieve organizational objectives efficiently and ethically.

management by objectives   Management system incorporating participation in decision making, goal setting, and feedback.

managing diversity   Creating organizational changes that enable all people to perform up to their maximum potential.

mechanistic organizations   Rigid, command-and-control bureaucracies.

mentoring   Process of forming and maintaining developmental relationships between a mentor and a junior person.

mission statement   Summarizes "why" an organization exists.

monochronic time   Preference for doing one thing at a time because time is limited, precisely segmented, and schedule driven.

motivation   Psychological processes that arouse and direct goal-directed behavior.

motivators   Job characteristics associated with job satisfaction.

N

need for achievement   Desire to accomplish something difficult.

need for affiliation   Desire to spend time in social relationships and activities.

need for power   Desire to influence, coach, teach, or encourage others to achieve.

need hierarchy theory   Five basic needs—physiological, safety, love, esteem, and self-actualization and how they influence behavior.

needs   Physiological or psychological deficiencies that arouse behavior.

negative reinforcement   Making behavior occur more often by contingently withdrawing something negative.

negotiation   Give-and-take process between conflicting interdependent parties.

nominal group technique   Process to generate ideas and evaluate solutions.

nonassertive style   Timid and self-denying behavior.

nonverbal communication   Messages sent outside of the written or spoken word.

norm   Shared attitudes, opinions, feelings, or actions that guide social behavior.

normative beliefs   Thoughts and beliefs about expected behavior and modes of conduct.

O

open system   Organism that must constantly interact with its environment to survive.

operant behavior   Skinner's term for learned, consequence-shaped behavior.

optimizing   Choosing the best possible solution.

organic organizations   Fluid and flexible network of multitalented people.

organization   System of consciously coordinated activities of two or more people.

organizational behavior   Interdisciplinary field dedicated to better understanding and managing people at work.

organizational culture   Shared values and beliefs that underlie a company's identity.

organizational politics   Intentional enhancement of self-interest.

organizational socialization   Process by which employees learn an organization's values, norms, and required behaviors.

organization chart   Boxes-and-lines illustration showing chain of formal authority and division of labor.

organization development   A set of techniques or tools that are used to implement organizational change.

ostracism   Rejection by other group members.

out-group exchange   A partnership characterized by a lack of mutual trust, respect, and liking.

P

participative management   Involving employees in various forms of decision making.

pay for performance   Monetary incentives tied to one's results or accomplishments.

perception   Process of interpreting one's environment.

performance management   Continuous cycle of improving job performance with goal setting, feedback and coaching, and rewards and positive reinforcement.

performance outcome goal   Targets a specific end result.

personality   Stable physical and mental characteristics responsible for a person's identity.

personality conflict   Interpersonal opposition driven by personal dislike or disagreement.

polychronic time   Preference for doing more than one thing at a time because time is flexible and multidimensional.

positive organizational behavior (POB) The study and improvement of employees' positive attributes and capabilities.

positive reinforcement Making behavior occur more often by contingently presenting something positive.

proactive personality Action-oriented person who shows initiative and perseveres to change things.

problem Gap between an actual and desired situation.

procedural justice The perceived fairness of the process and procedures used to make allocation decisions.

process theories of motivation Identify the process by which internal factors and cognitions influence motivation.

programmed conflict Encourages different opinions without protecting management's personal feelings.

punishment Making behavior occur less often by contingently presenting something negative or withdrawing something positive.

R

rational model Logical four-step approach to decision making.

reciprocity The belief that both good and bad deeds should be repaid in kind.

recruitment practices Attempts to attract qualified, diverse employees at all levels.

referent power Obtaining compliance through charisma or personal attraction.

representativeness heuristic Tendency to assess the likelihood of an event occurring based on impressions about similar occurrences.

resistance to change Emotional/behavioral response to real or imagined work changes.

respondent behavior Skinner's term for unlearned stimulus-response reflexes.

reward power Obtaining compliance with promised or actual rewards.

roles Expected behaviors for a given position.

S

satisficing Choosing a solution that meets a minimum standard of acceptance.

schema Mental picture of an event or object.

scientific management Using research and experimentation to find the most efficient way to perform a job.

self-concept Person's self-perception as a physical, social, spiritual being.

self-efficacy Belief in one's ability to do a task.

self-esteem One's overall self-evaluation.

self-managed teams Groups of employees granted administrative oversight for their work.

self-monitoring Observing one's own behavior and adapting it to the situation.

self-serving bias Taking more personal responsibility for success than failure.

self-talk Evaluating thoughts about oneself.

servant-leadership Focuses on increased service to others rather than to oneself.

shared leadership Simultaneous, ongoing, mutual influence process in which people share responsibility for leading.

situational theories Propose that leader styles should match the situation at hand.

social capital The productive potential of strong, trusting, and cooperative relationships.

social loafing Decrease in individual effort as group size increases.

social power Ability to get things done with human, informational, and material resources.

societal culture Socially derived, taken-for-granted assumptions about how to think and act.

span of control The number of people reporting directly to a given manager.

staff personnel Provide research, advice, and recommendations to line managers.

stereotype Beliefs about the characteristics of a group.

strategic constituency Any group of people with a stake in the organization's operation or success.

strategic plan A long-term plan outlining actions needed to achieve planned results.

T

tacit knowledge Information gained through experience that is difficult to express and formalize.

target elements of change Components of an organization that may be changed.

task roles Task-oriented group behavior.

team Small group with complementary skills who hold themselves mutually accountable for common purpose, goals, and approach.

team-based pay Linking pay to teamwork behavior and/or team results.

telecommuting   Doing work that is generally performed in the office away from the office using different information technologies.

theory Y   McGregor's modern and positive assumptions about employees being responsible and creative.

360-degree feedback   Comparison of anonymous feedback from one's superior, subordinates, and peers with self-perceptions.

total quality management   An organizational culture dedicated to training, continuous improvement, and customer satisfaction.

transactional leadership   Focuses on interpersonal interactions between managers and employees.

transformational leadership   Transforms employees to pursue organizational goals over self-interests.

trust   Reciprocal faith in others' intentions and behavior.

U

underemployment   The result of taking a job that requires less education, training, or skills than possessed by a worker.

unity of command principle   Each employee should report to a single manager.

upward feedback   Employees evaluate their boss.

V

valence   The value of a reward or outcome.

values   Enduring belief in a mode of conduct or end-state.

virtual team   Information technology allows group members in different locations to conduct business.

Index